Astrology
for the
Soul

Also by Jan Spiller

Spiritual Astrology
(with Karen McCoy)

Astrology for Women: Roles and
Relationships (contributing author,
edited by Gloria Star)

Astrology
for the
Soul

Jan Spiller

BANTAM BOOKS
New York
Toronto
London
Sydney
Auckland

Astrology for the Soul
A Bantam Book / November 1997

BOOK DESIGN BY JAMES SINCLAIR

Cover art copyright © 1997 by PhotoDisc

The Glyphs of the Signs by Kerry Tinney

Library of Congress Cataloging-in-Publication Data

Spiller, Jan.
Astrology for the soul / by Jan Spiller.
p.   cm.
ISBN 0-553-37838-4
1. Astrology. 2. Moon—Miscellanea. I. Title.
BF1723.S65   1997
133.5—dc21   97-12068
CIP

Published simultaneously in the United States and Canada

Bantam Books are published by Bantam Books, a division of Bantam Doubleday Dell Publishing Group, Inc. Its trademark, consisting of the words "Bantam Books" and the portrayal of a rooster, is Registered in U.S. Patent and Trademark Office and in other countries. Marca Registrada. Bantam Books, 1540 Broadway, New York, New York 10036.

Printed in the United States of America
20 19 18 17 16 15 14 13

Acknowledgments

On a practical level, I would like to acknowledge my editor throughout the years, Judith Horton, whose work on this book was truly monumental. Thanks also go to my editor at Bantam: Stephanie Kip.

I would like to acknowledge all the teachers, those spiritually based and those astrologically based, who have helped me along the way. Spiritually: Ramana Maharshi, through Gangaji, Nome, and Bob Spiegel. Astrologically: Morningland, Martin Schulman (for his book on the Nodes), and Gina Ceaglio, my first astrology teacher. This work would not have been possible without the research and intuitive gifts of those who have gone before. I especially want to acknowledge the work of Martin Schulman and Zipporah Dobyns on the Nodes.

For his support, encouragement, and insights on this project, my father, Bill Nunn, together with the influence of his teacher, Bob Gibson. My clients and friends for their willingness to add insights and feedback on this and other projects, including but not limited to: Sheri Zucker, Helen Thomas-Williams, Sandy Ingoglia. Thanks to Philip Weiss for his ideas on integrating the music with the book. For his support and backing that gave me the conditions I needed to write this book, I would like to acknowledge my friend, Russell. Thank you.

Finally, I would like to acknowledge the presence of the Guides and Knowledge Banks available to all of us when we listen with an open heart and nonjudgmental mind to deeply understand the inner workings of others.

Jan Spiller

Contents

Contents   ix

The Location of Your North Node

LOCATE THE SPAN THAT INCLUDES YOUR BIRTH DATE IN THE CHART BELOW.
YOUR NORTH NODE POSITION IS LISTED TO THE RIGHT OF THESE DATES.

May 10, 1899—Jan. 21, 1901	Sagittarius
Jan. 22, 1901—July 21, 1902	Scorpio
July 22, 1902—Jan. 15, 1904	Libra
Jan. 16, 1904—Sept. 18, 1905	Virgo
Sept. 19, 1905—Mar. 30, 1907	Leo
Mar. 31, 1907—Sept. 27, 1908	Cancer
Sept. 28, 1908—Mar. 23, 1910	Gemini
Mar. 24, 1910—Dec. 8, 1911	Taurus
Dec. 9, 1911—June 6, 1913	Aries
June 7, 1913—Dec. 3, 1914	Pisces
Dec. 4, 1914—May 31, 1916	Aquarius
June 1, 1916—Feb. 13, 1918	Capricorn
Feb. 14, 1918—Aug. 15, 1919	Sagittarius
Aug. 16, 1919—Feb. 7, 1921	Scorpio
Feb. 8, 1921—Aug. 23, 1922	Libra
Aug. 24, 1922—Apr. 23, 1924	Virgo
Apr. 24, 1924—Oct. 26, 1925	Leo
Oct. 27, 1925—Apr. 16, 1927	Cancer
Apr. 17, 1927—Dec. 28, 1928	Gemini
Dec. 29, 1928—July 7, 1930	Taurus
July 8, 1930—Dec. 28, 1931	Aries
Dec. 29, 1931—June 24, 1933	Pisces
June 25, 1933—Mar. 8, 1935	Aquarius
Mar. 9, 1935—Sept. 14, 1936	Capricorn
Sept. 15, 1936—Mar. 3, 1938	Sagittarius
Mar. 4, 1938—Sept. 12, 1939	Scorpio
Sept. 13, 1939—May 24, 1941	Libra
May 25, 1941—Nov. 21, 1942	Virgo
Nov. 22, 1942—May 11, 1944	Leo
May 12, 1944—Dec. 13, 1945	Cancer
Dec. 14, 1945—Aug. 2, 1947	Gemini
Aug. 3, 1947—Jan. 26, 1949	Taurus
Jan. 27, 1949—July 26, 1950	Aries
July 27, 1950—Mar. 28, 1952	Pisces
Mar. 29, 1952—Oct. 9, 1953	Aquarius
Oct. 10, 1953—Apr. 2, 1955	Capricorn
Apr. 3, 1955—Oct. 4, 1956	Sagittarius
Oct. 5, 1956—June 16, 1958	Scorpio
June 17, 1958—Dec. 15, 1959	Libra
Dec. 16, 1959—June 10, 1961	Virgo
June 11, 1961—Dec. 23, 1962	Leo
Dec. 24, 1962—Aug. 25, 1964	Cancer
Aug. 26, 1964—Feb. 19, 1966	Gemini
Feb. 20, 1966—Aug. 19, 1967	Taurus
Aug. 20, 1967—Apr. 19, 1969	Aries

Date Range	Sign
Apr. 20, 1969—Nov. 2, 1970	Pisces
Nov. 3, 1970—Apr. 27, 1972	Aquarius
Apr. 28, 1972—Oct. 27, 1973	Capricorn
Oct. 28, 1973—July 10, 1975	Sagittarius
July 11, 1975—Jan. 7, 1977	Scorpio
Jan. 8, 1977—July 5, 1978	Libra
July 6, 1978—Jan. 12, 1980	Virgo
Jan. 13, 1980—Sept. 24, 1981	Leo
Sept. 25, 1981—Mar. 16, 1983	Cancer
Mar. 17, 1983—Sept. 11, 1984	Gemini
Sept. 12, 1984—Apr. 6, 1986	Taurus
Apr. 7, 1986—Dec. 2, 1987	Aries
Dec. 3, 1987—May 22, 1989	Pisces
May 23, 1989—Nov. 18, 1990	Aquarius
Nov. 19, 1990—Aug. 1, 1992	Capricorn
Aug. 2, 1992—Feb. 1, 1994	Sagittarius
Feb. 2, 1994—July 31, 1995	Scorpio
Aug. 1, 1995—Jan. 25, 1997	Libra
Jan. 26, 1997—Oct. 20, 1998	Virgo
Oct. 21, 1998—Apr. 9, 2000	Leo
Apr. 10, 2000—Oct. 12, 2001	Cancer
Oct. 13, 2001—Apr. 13, 2003	Gemini
Apr. 14, 2003—Dec. 25, 2004	Taurus
Dec. 26, 2004—June 21, 2006	Aries
June 22, 2006—Dec. 18, 2007	Pisces
Dec. 19, 2007—Aug. 21, 2009	Aquarius
Aug. 22, 2009—Mar. 3, 2011	Capricorn
Mar. 4, 2011—Aug. 29, 2012	Sagittarius
Aug. 30, 2012—Feb. 18, 2014	Scorpio
Feb. 19, 2014—Nov. 11, 2015	Libra
Nov. 12, 2015—May 9, 2017	Virgo
May 10, 2017—Nov. 6, 2018	Leo
Nov. 7, 2018—May 4, 2020	Cancer
May 5, 2020—Jan. 18, 2022	Gemini
Jan. 19, 2022—July 17, 2023	Taurus
July 18, 2023—Jan. 11, 2025	Aries
Jan. 12, 2025—July 26, 2026	Pisces
July 27, 2026—Mar. 26, 2028	Aquarius
Mar. 27, 2028—Sept. 23, 2029	Capricorn
Sept. 24, 2029—Mar. 20, 2031	Sagittarius
Mar. 21, 2031—Dec. 1, 2032	Scorpio
Dec. 2, 2032—June 3, 2034	Libra
June 4, 2034—Nov. 29, 2035	Virgo
Nov. 30, 2035—May 29, 2037	Leo
May 30, 2037—Feb. 9, 2039	Cancer
Feb. 10, 2039—Aug. 10, 2040	Gemini
Aug. 11, 2040—Feb. 3, 2042	Taurus
Feb. 4, 2042—Aug. 18, 2043	Aries
Aug. 19, 2043—Apr. 18, 2045	Pisces
Apr. 19, 2045—Oct. 18, 2046	Aquarius
Oct. 19, 2046—Apr. 11, 2048	Capricorn
Apr. 12, 2048—Dec. 14, 2049	Sagittarius
Dec. 15, 2049—June 28, 2051	Scorpio

Data courtesy of
The Astrology Center of America

On the Internet at:
http://www.astroamerica.com

Introduction

This book contains my professional secrets: the methods I have used to successfully read personal astrology charts for the past twenty years.

Many of my colleagues think I'm psychic. That may be true, but it's not the primary mindset I use when I look at an astrology chart. To interpret a chart with confidence and accuracy, astrologers must have a starting point—an area they focus on when they first look at an individual chart. It may be the Sun sign, or the position of the Moon, the Eclipses, the major aspects, the number of planets in Fire, Water, Earth, or Air signs—each astrologer has his or her own personal entry into accessing, "seeing," and interpreting the rest of the chart.

I use the Nodes. The Nodes have never failed to give me the information I need to correctly guide the individual in achieving success, self-confidence, and balance within the personality. The accuracy of my readings is not due to "psychic talents" but rather to my attention to the activity of the Nodes.

When I look at an individual astrology chart, I first notice the position of the North and South Nodes of the Moon, by sign and by house. Then I notice the geometric relationships (called "aspects" by astrologers) that the Nodes are making to other planets, and any unusual circumstances with the planets that rule the signs the Nodes are in.* Suddenly, the whole chart comes alive and I can understand the individual challenges this person has,

---

*The aspects are so important that they deserve a book of their own. This information will be covered thoroughly in a subsequent volume about the Nodes.

and the qualities of character that need to be developed for success and fulfillment in this lifetime.

ACCURACY

It is not necessary to have a belief in astrology in order for this book to be of value to you. Astrology, if explored from a psychological or scientific level, has nothing to do with belief. It's practical. It has to do with gaining knowledge and doing experiments. Are the psychological profiles offered by astrology useful tools of self-knowledge for you? Are the timing predictions astrology can make (when based on your *full* birth chart) helpful in using your time more effectively?

In evaluating the truth of the material presented in this book, it is important to listen to your own inner knowing and past experiences. Regardless of what others may think, only you know the nature of your own internal battles.

If you choose to do some of the experiments suggested for balancing your North Node personality type, look to your own energy for confirmation of whether or not you are on the right path. If, after running one of these experiments, your energy level soars and you feel happy and free, you're "on path"! Trust yourself. If not, try a different experiment. You will know if you are on track by whether or not you feel happy and/or free.

If some of the suggestions made in your North Node section do not "feel right" to you, then trust yourself there as well. It may be an area that you've already overcome or that, for some reason, is not fully applicable to you. It's like trying on a pair of shoes—only you know whether or not they fit. Again, trust yourself.

Some of these suggestions might be frightening at first because they're new for you. But if they feel right to you—if they seem accurate—take the risk and set them in motion. You'll find yourself emerging from your experiment with a sense of fearlessness and self-confidence that's permanent. You'll know changes are taking place because things that bothered you just a few weeks or months ago won't get to you anymore. Your friends may still be feeling those things, but you'll be feeling something else—a peacefulness that has eluded you in the past.

For each of us, our deepest core issues are shown in the sign and house positions of the North Node at the time of our birth. However, in the process of writing this book, I realized I had unresolved issues in signs other than my own nodal sign and house. The difference is in the depth of the dysfunction. If a person has North Node in Cancer or the 4th House, the issue of releasing control, trusting, and openly sharing feelings is *huge*—it's like chipping away at a block of granite! But someone whose North Node is in another sign may also have difficulty with sharing feelings openly. Reading the chapter on North Node in Cancer may help them heal their issues of vulnerability and suggest practical approaches to create balance and ease. The difference is that it won't be as difficult to apply the suggestions in these "alternate" areas as it will be in the area of your own nodal placement.

For example, I have the North Node neither in Aries nor in the 1st House, but when I was working on the Aries North Node chapter I realized that I had problems with self-assertion and some of the other issues that those folks are working out. In the creative process of writing that chapter, something in me was healed and I spontaneously began asserting myself more constructively and being more honest. And my life became a whole lot easier! Once I "got it," it was easy for me to adjust and change. However, in the sign and house containing my North Node, it's a lot tougher. I started "getting it" twenty years ago, and I'm *still* working through it.

COMPASSION THROUGH KNOWLEDGE

When astrology is approached from a level of true open-minded understanding, it leads directly to unconditional love. When you fully understand a person's inner mechanics and where their "glitches" are, how can you be angry with them? We are all doing the best we can with the light we have and seeking to overcome our imperfections. Why? Because it's practical. The glitches get in the way of getting what we want. We are all in this together.

Sun sign astrology, such as the horoscopes covered in daily newspapers and magazines, are predictions that take into account only the sign position of the Sun. Full natal astrology takes into account the sign positions of ten planets (the Sun and Moon are considered planets in this context, as the galaxy is seen from the point of view of its effect on the Earth), the axis that was active when the individual was born, and several other points: the

Nodes, Eclipses, and so on. In fact, each of us is entirely unique; a birth chart isn't duplicated for 25,000 years because all the planets are traveling at different speeds around the Sun. In the moment you took your first breath, all of humankind—all the people alive at that time—passed through that moment with you. Everyone did the best they could to make the moment joyful for themselves, but then the next moment came along and human-kind had to handle it—and the next moment and the next, on into the current moment. But the moment when you were born was stamped on the cellular level of your very being, and it remains a part of you.

With that connection, you took charge of purifying that moment for everyone else on the planet, and you alone have the power to perfect the moment of your own birth. It's as though you took that sliver of time, slowed it down, and stretched it out to last an entire incarnation. And as you begin to work with that moment, taking parts of your "wiring" that aren't working too well and adjusting them—thus creating happiness, laughter, and joy in your own life—the positive energy of these changes affects everyone else. Through your own personal life you are essentially altering a moment that occurred in the past, and when you change the past, it changes the present for everyone. I've heard many spiritual teachers say that the best we can do for others is to work on ourselves. We are all interconnected on the deepest level—we're One.

INTERNAL WIRING

The astrology chart itself is actually a schematic: a graph that shows people's "inner wiring." The wiring in each of us is different. It's not "good" or "bad," it's just wired the way it's wired. Your birth chart provides a picture of the inner wiring you were born with, but what you do with that wiring is up to you.

When you can objectively see the patterns of your own behavior, you can make adjustments for more efficient results and better performance. When any miswiring is corrected, the result is a more smoothly operating life (first internally, and then externally). By having a clear picture of your inner wiring, you can become aware of the built-in "glitches," and you can choose not to continue behaviors that aren't working for you.

For example, if a person knew objectively (from seeing the graph of their birth chart) that they had a tendency to assume they already know the answers to everything, and thus become impatient and display a self-righteous attitude that isolates them from others (as would be the case if they had the North Node in Gemini or in the 3rd House), knowing about this tendency would allow him or her to *consciously* take more time to respectfully receive the factual input of others before venturing his or her own opinion. That single adjustment would make a major difference in the person's social interactions.

We all have tendencies that lead to inappropriate behavior and feelings of isolation and unhappiness. The trick is to discover our own glitches and empower ourselves to avoid them. With this objective knowledge, we are no longer operating in the dark, not understanding why life keeps giving us feedback that makes us unhappy. Life is too short to walk around blindfolded. It is the intention of this book to clarify what works and what doesn't within the twelve personality types depicted by the North and South Nodes of the Moon.

This book is predicated on recognizing that you are not just the sum total of your chart. The chart is a picture of your personality structure, but *you* are the factor that lies behind the chart and have the power to use the personality (the energies depicted in your birth chart) in any manner you choose. Whether you allow the personality to operate unconsciously, or you take charge and purify the energy so that life flows to your advantage, is up to you.

HOW TO WIN/HOW TO LOSE

There are ten different kingdoms inside the personality, represented by the ten different planets used in astrology. We can look at the graph of your birth chart and see that some parts of yourself are constantly battling with other parts, creating all kinds of conflicting energy. Other parts of you are in total harmony; there will never be a struggle in those areas of your life. On an even deeper level, we can see the foundation from which everything else in your personality is emerging. The intention of this book is to delve into that foundation, describe it, and make some adjustments to it. These adjustments will allow the energies of the planets to coexist in a more harmonious manner.

Imagine that there is a natural General within you around which everything else is willing to unite at a moment's notice. All you have to do is sound the bugle call of that General, and right away the parts that are warring with each other will drop their weapons and line up behind the General. The parts of you that are at peace and perhaps getting a little lazy will hear the call, get off their duffs, and also line up behind the General. When this happens, you instantly feel united and centered, and the outer situations in your life begin to change. Most important, your relationship to those situations shifts. From this new vantage point you see clearly what to do, and the action you take will automatically succeed.

In your chart, the North Node of the Moon represents that General. Once you access the underlying formula for uniting and balancing your inner self, it's like a particle of magic. It will work 100 percent of the time in every situation in your life, if you just "remember to remember" the formula and are willing to try running the "experiments" that will allow the inner energy—and thus the outer situations—to shift to your advantage.

In the beginning, doing these experiments may not be easy. It may even be frightening. For example, if you are in the group whose North Node is in Cancer, you don't *know* that being vulnerable and revealing your feelings and fears is going to work out for you. You weren't used to being vulnerable in your past lives; as a matter of fact, you may feel as though you're going to die if you actually reveal your true feelings. Everything in you may resist it. And yet, if you do it anyway, a shift will happen for you. You'll find that something did die, but it wasn't you—it was a fear that had attached itself to you. When you ran the experiment, that fear dissipated and you emerged with a new sense of fearlessness and confidence. But it's up to you. Nothing happens unless you take the risk; positive action is the remedy for fear.

In examining the position of your North Node, you are looking at the basic lesson underlying this entire lifetime. Therefore, the changes may not happen all at once. Keep in mind that as you take steps in a new direction, you're going against habits that have become deeply ingrained over many incarnations. That's why you need to keep remembering to remember to do things in a new way and keep moving toward resolution of the past life imbalances you've inherited.

The purpose of this book is not to give you another tool to "make yourself wrong" and pick out past life habits you haven't given up. Its purpose is to show you how to experiment with doing things in a new way. You'll find that every time you remember to apply the formula, the situation shifts to your advantage and the world validates you. Yet even in the face of success, sometimes remembering to apply a new pattern takes time. It's a process, after all.

Simply reading the chapter on your North Node will make a difference and start a process of natural change. Practicing the suggestions will speed up the process, but ultimately consciousness alone can make the transformation. For example, if a person knew they would be hit by a truck prior to crossing a street against the light, would they do it? Of course not. We all want to experience pleasure and avoid pain. Being conscious of a negative repercussion is often enough to keep from putting the cause in motion.

ASTROLOGY, MATERIAL SUCCESS, AND SPIRITUALITY

Material fulfillment is never the key to permanent, unbroken bliss. It is always temporary, and dissatisfaction always follows on the heels of simple material satisfaction. The ultimate resolution to the search for happiness is spiritual. Yet sometimes there is a worldly desire deep within us that cannot be denied or forgotten—it must be materially realized to be released.

To illustrate this point, consider the story of a Buddhist Master who was getting on in years and noticed that one of his favorite disciples had still not reached full enlightenment and bliss. This disciple had been with him for three decades, had been totally devoted to his Master and strict with his practices, and yet he still had not reached that highest state. One day the Master said to his disciple: "Come, I am going on a pilgrimage and you may come with me."

They walked for miles into the outlying mountain range. The days became weeks, then a month passed, and still they continued on their journey. One day the Master stopped and, pointing to a hill in the distance, said to his disciple: "Do you see that mountaintop?" The mist was just clearing from the top of the mountain, revealing a large castle at its summit shimmering in the rays of the sun.

Disciple: "Yes, Master."

Master: "And do you see that home standing on the summit of the mountain?"

Disciple: "Yes, Master."

Master: "For many lifetimes, you have desired a home and that desire has remained unsatisfied. It is the final thread that binds you and blocks your enlightenment and unending joy. None of the practices I have given you have dissolved that deep desire. Therefore, it must be manifested. That is your home now; you own it."

At that instant, the disciple became fully enlightened.

Some worldly or material desires we can dismiss simply because they aren't that important to us. After a time, we can let them go. Others will not leave us until we have manifested them on some level. Once the personality has been successfully integrated, desires that are of lesser importance begin to fade away, and those that demand manifestation can be more easily obtained in the material world.

It is the purpose of this book to offer a formula that will facilitate a practical reintegration of the personality structure, so that the individual can more easily gain the material experiences sought. Once the mechanism of self, or personality, is working efficiently and producing happy results in our daily lives, our basic needs are met and we become open to a higher level of happiness and fulfillment, beyond identifying with personal ego and gaining strictly material rewards. As desires are met and outer goals are no longer so compelling, the personality relaxes. Within this calm, we are open to higher states of consciousness and the deeper happiness that is our natural state: what the Bible describes as "experiencing the Kingdom of Heaven on Earth."

How to Use This Book

WHAT THE NODES ARE

The Nodes of the Moon are not planetary bodies; they are points formed by the Moon's orbit around the Earth intersecting with the Earth's path around the Sun. The direction of the nodes is counterclockwise: The North Node is the ascending node (the point closest to our North Pole), and the South Node is the descending node (the point closest to our South Pole). They are always exactly 180 degrees apart. Some astrologers use the "True Node" calculation (which takes into account the actual wobbling of the Moon's orbit), and some astrologers use the "Mean Node" (which does not take the wobbling into account). I use the True Nodes. The True Node and Mean Node positions are never more than 1 degree 45 minutes apart from each other.

THE NODAL AXIS

All the planets have a North and South Node. The Nodes covered in this book are the North and South Nodes of the Moon, also known as the "Nodal Axis" of the chart. The information in the chapters is actually a description of the Northern/Southern Nodal Axis, although for the sake of simplicity, I have simply called it the "North Node" position. The South

Node position in the chart (located at the point exactly opposite of the North Node) depicts an aspect in our character that has been overemphasized in past lives, and thus tends to take over the personality in this lifetime and throw us off balance. When we are acting without awareness, we tend to "act out" the South Node position in response to our environment because we have been accustomed to that approach working to our advantage. However, in this lifetime, our experiences show us that approaching a situation from the stance shown by the position of the Southern Node in our chart is no longer working. Although the main emphasis in this book is on the North Node, the information in these chapters is actually an integration of both "ends" of the Nodal Axis.

When astrologers refer to "the Nodes," they are generally referring to the North and South Nodes of the Moon. In astrology, the Moon rules our feelings, our moods, dependency, insecurity, the feeling of belonging—it rules our emotional bodies. The Moon rules our self-image, that is, the way we instinctively see ourselves regardless of what we are expressing in the world. I consider the Moon to be the most important planet in the chart, from a karmic/past life perspective. It underlies the rest of the personality structure. In my first astrology book, writing the chapter on the Moon took more time than the other nine chapters combined. I found the depth of the signs of the Moon to be endless—my research kept going deeper and deeper—until one day I just had to close the lid and say "That's it!" In following the path of the Nodes of the Moon, and thus rebalancing our emotional bodies, we are going a long way toward easing internal stress and reclaiming confidence in our individual beings.

SIGNS AND HOUSES

For each of us, the North Node is located in a sign and in a house. The sign position can be obtained by consulting the table in the front of this book, and the chapter relating to your sign position will provide information and direction designed specifically to help you realize your full potential. For the most complete view, I recommend also consulting the chapter relating to your house position, which can be obtained from a local astrologer or a computerized birth chart.

The sign in which the North Node falls denotes the psychological shift that needs to occur within the personality. The house containing the North Node shows the experiences that allow the person to access this new psychological awareness.

In my experience, the house is at least of equal importance to the sign. The house position indicates the arena in which the life lessons of the North Node are learned. For example, if your North Node is in Cancer in the 11th House, you are learning to get in touch with and communicate your feelings (Cancer) through cultivating the energy of friendships and learning to "go with the flow" (11th House); if your North Node is in Aries in the 4th House, through getting in touch with your gut instincts (4th House) you can discover and communicate who you are (Aries).

DUPLICATE SIGN/HOUSE POSITIONS

If the sign of your North Node is in the same sign as the house containing your North Node (for example, North Node in Gemini located in the 3rd House, which is also Gemini; or North Node in Pisces in the 12th House, which is also Pisces), it simply means double the intensity of the same life lesson.

OPPOSING SIGN/HOUSE POSITIONS

(This includes North Node in Aries in the 7th House; North Node in Taurus in the 8th House; North Node in Gemini in the 9th House; North Node in Cancer in the 10th House; North Node in Leo in the 11th House; North Node in Virgo in the 12th House; North Node in Libra in the 1st House; North Node in Scorpio in the 2nd House; North Node in Sagittarius in the 3rd House; North Node in Capricorn in the 4th House; North Node in Aquarius in the 5th House; North Node in Pisces in the 6th House.)

If your North Node is in a house *opposing* the sign of your North Node (as noted above), it will be necessary for you to carefully and continuously check with yourself to find the right blending of behavior. Remember that generally, the house indicates where to learn the lessons of the sign. The house is like a shell—the environment you need to support the content of the sign.

For example, if your North Node is in Aries in the 7th House, you are learning to develop a new sense of self-identity (North Node in Aries) through becoming aware of the identity of others (North Node in the 7th House). Through working cooperatively with other people and supporting them in reaching their goals, you will discover your own true identity. However, when you turn that around and focus on yourself, you lose your identity in trying to please others and be the nice person they expect you to be. In this case, the key to self-identity would actually lie in helping *others* in their search for identity.

OVERVIEW

Each chapter in this book begins with an overview. The purpose of the overview is to offer a quick reference point and a way of remembering a practical formula for achieving your life purpose. In a stressful situation, which is when you have the opportunity to implement a new choice in behavior that can lighten your karmic load, it's useful to have a simplified way of remembering "how to win/how to lose" to hold on to and practice.

In working with the material presented in the overview, I recommend that you take one or two points that seem the most relevant to you, and then consciously practice to purify those qualities in yourself. Little by little, as you practice, the self-defeating tendency will dissipate and joy will begin to take over. Then, when you are ready, choose something else to let go of or consciously practice developing. It's a process; although it takes effort and may seem like a tremendous personal risk, once you move forward you will never be pulled back into the fears and limitations of the past.

Some qualities take more time than others to purify or to let go of. Even if you are working to release a tendency that you worked on a week ago or a year ago, you will be working on it at a higher level and it won't be nearly as painful or difficult. In this way, growth is more like a spiral than a circle. As you progress, you will find life a lot less threatening and the things you desire manifesting more easily and naturally. A magic begins to flow as you find yourself emerging fearless, light, and free . . . as the invisible chains from past incarnations begin to dissipate and fall away.

Each chapter's overview gives a quick reference to Attributes to Develop, Tendencies to Leave Behind, Achilles' Heel/Trap to Avoid/The Bottom

Line, What These People Really Want, Talents/Profession, and Healing Affirmations.

ATTRIBUTES TO DEVELOP

These are gifts—talents—that are at your disposal in this lifetime. Just as you spent so much time and energy developing one aspect of your character in past lives, there was another part of you—the polar opposite—that was totally neglected. Thus, when you came into this incarnation, you were out of balance. (We all were, but the imbalance was different for each of us.) Life wants you to be happy. But as long as the imbalance exists, every happiness is going to be followed by an unhappiness. So you must consciously develop the part of you that was neglected in past lives by experimenting with, and building on, the talents and gifts described in this section. It's like a muscle that hasn't been used. Once you start exercising it, pretty soon it's built up and balanced with the rest of you. Developing the tendencies in this category will enable you to win—every time!

TENDENCIES TO LEAVE BEHIND

These are tendencies that you, and members of your group, were born with. In past lives these behaviors served you well; when you acted from these motivations, you won. So you came into this incarnation with a subconscious memory of success, and you keep pursuing the same behaviors that enabled you to thrive in your past lives. However, in this incarnation these same patterns do not work (that is, they don't produce success, confidence, and ease). If you look back over this lifetime, you can see that these behavior patterns have never worked for you, although you keep enacting them over and over again.

These qualities in and of themselves are not negative, but they describe part of your character that was overdeveloped in past lives. Lifetime after lifetime you kept strengthening this one part of yourself from every possible direction until it grew out of proportion. So in this incarnation, it is set up in your astrology chart for these old patterns *not* to work. Basically, following the tendencies in this section will cause you to lose—every time!

ACHILLES' HEEL/TRAP TO AVOID/THE BOTTOM LINE

This is a description of the trap that you and the members of your group most easily fall into—the temptation that is so attractive that it's easy to falter and go back into negative past life tendencies. It's a part of you that is magnified in this incarnation—an appetite so exaggerated that it's like a bottomless pit that can never be satisfied. This is the "red flag" category; when you find yourself driven by these motives, your best bet is to walk away, because you're going to lose.

WHAT THESE PEOPLE REALLY WANT

This category represents an integration of past life motivations and present life gifts. It means having the experiences we were born wanting—manifesting the desires in our hearts—through using the new tools that we were given in this lifetime to balance the personality.

In the beginning, it can be useful to exaggerate: totally negate (in our own mind) the past life tendencies, and concentrate fully on the present life qualities to be developed. It's the pendulum principle: Swinging too far in the opposite direction can help us come back to the middle. Ultimately, it is through combining past life strengths and present life gifts that we gain true fulfillment. But the past life paradigms are strong, and initially the individual may have to "blow them up" or walk away from them altogether just to get the energy moving in the right direction.

TALENTS/PROFESSION

This is a description of talents, bequeathed by the nodal positions, that could easily be turned into professional success in this lifetime. For a total picture of the profession or vocation, I recommend that the full astrology chart be consulted.

HEALING AFFIRMATIONS

These sample affirmations are designed to defuse the obstructive energy of past life tendencies and release you into the vibrant freedom that is available in the current incarnation. The best way to use this section is to choose one affirmation that feels particularly strengthening for the qualities you want to develop. Then, throughout the day, experiment with saying that one affirmation to yourself in different situations until the quality within that you want to strengthen is reinforced and energized.

When that particular affirmation is no longer potent for you (which may be a matter of a month or several months), then choose another and experiment with that for a while. The affirmations are best used by choosing only one during any specific period, depending on what you resonate with at that point in your development.

PERSONALITY

In each chapter, this section deals with the idiosyncrasies of each group and how they differ from other groups (their special mannerisms, concerns, unique feelings, etc.). In our own experience, it feels as though we are working with this karma only on the personal, individual level. However, as we clear out the negative energy in our own lives, members of our nodal group (all those who have the North Node in the same sign) are also purified and advanced. The energy of our entire group will support us internally in learning and growing. We aren't in this alone.

NEEDS

Those factors discussed under the Needs category, specific to each group, are valid desires. We do not have to change our essential selves or invalidate our needs. However, for success, it is sometimes necessary for us to alter our approach—the way we go about getting our needs met. This section describes our basic needs for security, what they feel like internally, and the best ways to fulfill them without getting "off track."

RELATIONSHIPS

This section examines how those in our group view relationships, their patterns of relating, and the special tendencies, obstacles, and resolutions that emerge when they are in a relationship (especially a close relationship, such as marriage or partnership).

GOALS

This section deals with the group's orientation toward goals—their strengths and weaknesses in obtaining what they seek. The information can assist group members in seeing their "blocks," thus empowering them to overcome their inner obstacles and achieve their external goals.

HEALING THEME SONG

Music has a special way of making magic in our lives, as it has access to a part of our brain that isn't touched by the written word. The people in each nodal position face a different set of challenges, so I have written lyrics for "theme" songs uniquely suited to reaching and healing the underlying misunderstandings in each group. These songs are designed to shift the energy in a positive way that can come most effortlessly through music. To begin the healing process, partial lyrics from each of the songs follow each chapter. The full lyrics for all twelve songs have been set to music and are available on both CD and cassette tape (for more information, see page 530). Although the message of each song targets those in a specific nodal group, all of the songs are universally uplifting and have a healing effect on the listener—regardless of their nodal position.

SOME DEFINITIONS OF TERMS

Past lives: Previous lives lived in other bodies, prior to the incarnation in your present body.

Present life: This lifetime, as lived in the body you were born into in this incarnation.

Early environment: The patterns of behavior stimulated and enacted in childhood that you used to survive and cope in your childhood environment. These patterns duplicate past life tendencies; in fact, it is the unconscious, past life patterns that are activated during childhood. Clearly, the environment didn't create these patterns or cause us to be this way, or they couldn't be predicted by the natal birth chart. We were born with these patterns ready to be activated.

Achilles' heel: The weakest, most vulnerable point in the personality structure.

Karma: Cause and effect; the results we experience from actions we have taken.

Native: A traditional astrological term referring to the group of people ruled by the sign being discussed.

The Guides: Each of us is surrounded by our own invisible helpers who assist us in successfully navigating life's pathways. These positive helpers could be called "Guides," "Guardian Angels," or simply the voice of "intuition."

She/He: At times I've used "she" or "he" to refer to a single person, but this is not meant to be exclusive to one gender or the other.

North Node in Aries

and North Node in the 1st House

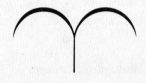

OVERVIEW

Attributes to Develop

Work in these areas can help uncover hidden gifts and talents

- Independence
- Self-awareness
- Trusting one's impulses
- Courage
- Constructive self-interest
- Moderation in giving
- Self-nurturance

Tendencies to Leave Behind

Working to reduce the influence of these tendencies can help make
life easier and more enjoyable

- Seeing oneself through others' eyes
- Debilitating selflessness
- Being Mr. or Ms. Nice
- Obsessive attachment to fairness and justice
- Co-dependence: attachment to external harmony
- "Tit for tat" mentality

ACHILLES' HEEL/TRAP TO AVOID/THE BOTTOM LINE

The Achilles' heel Aries North Node people need to be aware of is a preoccupation with justice ("My survival is dependent on everyone playing fair
with me"; this thought should signal that they are on shaky ground). These
folks are very giving by nature, yet their need for justice and absolute
fairness is a bottomless pit. They can start "playing fair" with themselves by
not giving beyond a point that feels comfortable, even if they know that
nothing will be reciprocated.

The trap that Aries North Node people need to avoid is an unending
search for an ideal, committed partnership ("If only I can find the perfect
partner, I'll feel complete within myself"). The feeling of completeness they
seek can only be achieved individually; it will not be the by-product of a
relationship, no matter how wonderful the partner. The bottom line is that
they'll never gain enough approval from others to have permission to be
themselves. At some point they must take the risk and pursue activities that
are meaningful to themselves. The irony is that once Aries North Nodes go
in their own direction, the appropriate people will be drawn into their life
to support them.

What These People Really Want

What Aries North Node people really want is to experience happiness, harmony, fairness, and support with one partner whom they love. To achieve this, they need to be their own partner first. By getting to know themselves, they begin to do the things that bring them joy and increase their level of self-nurturing so they feel strong, confident, and supported. As they treat themselves more fairly, they will feel the sense of balance and justice they seek. Only at this point can they establish a healthy partnership wherein two individuals share equally with each other without feeling debilitated.

Talents/Profession

These people need to be able to "do their thing" according to their own impulses, without being limited by the input of others. *They* are the leaders, the innovators, the pioneers. They need a profession that allows them the independence to follow their own instincts. They are successful in professions that require initiative and independent action: as surgeons, technicians, or entrepreneurs, for example.

From past lives, they have the gift of being able to see the other person's point of view and negotiate diplomatically to ensure fairness. They can use this innate ability to further their own success. However, in professions that emphasize mediating as a final goal, they are generally not as energized as when they use their negotiating talents to reach their own independent goals.

Healing Affirmations Specific to Aries North Node

- "When I trust myself and follow my impulses, everyone wins."
- "Before I can support others, I have to learn how to nurture myself."
- "I can help others best by truly being myself."
- "It's okay *not* to be nice all the time."

- "A sense of balance and strength comes from being fair with myself."

PERSONALITY

PAST LIVES

Aries North Node people have had many past lives of supporting others, and they have a natural talent for it. In past incarnations they were housewives, secretaries, counselors, and assistants. They were the people "behind the scenes" who gave others energy and support. This made the others bigger and stronger, because the natives infused all their own identity, power, and positive energy in supporting them. Aries North Node people also have had a lot of "householder" lifetimes and are accustomed to merging their energy with those in their immediate environment.

To support others successfully, they developed tremendous awareness and sensitivity. Their tools were love, reassurance, gentle words of encouragement, and confidence that the other person would emerge victorious in any situation. Their focus was the other person; whenever they saw their partner lacking confidence or needing support, they stepped right in to help—these folks never have to be asked. They are sensitive to others' needs and go out of their way to be accommodating. They have developed an incredibly loving and generous spirit. They are accustomed to giving, to being "a team player," and to supporting others without thoughts of self.

Although they were very giving in past lives, they also had an ulterior motive: They were part of a team, and if their partner did well, it also ensured their own survival. By keeping the partner's mood harmonious, Aries North Nodes ensured that the partner would be kindly disposed and generous toward them. So they gave up paying attention to their own needs in order to devote full attention to the partner—everything centered around keeping the partner strong and contented.

In past lives this system worked very well, but the present incarnation is not set up to work this way. In the process of supporting others, these folks extinguished their own identity. In this incarnation their destiny is now to get in touch with the strength and power of their *own* vibration. This is why every time they rely on a partner to come through for them without asking directly for help, they end up feeling disappointed. Actually, this is to their advantage, because depending on another prevents them from experiencing their ability to survive under their own power. So now when they sacrifice their own identity to make another strong, they lose—the rewards they expect don't come back. It's time to rediscover themselves.

LACK OF IDENTITY

Aries North Node people have spent so many incarnations supporting the identity of *others* that in this incarnation they have no sense of who they are. On an energetic level, they are missing the insulation of a sense of identity. When a baby is born, there's a band in its aura called "identity," and people in other nodal groups have this. It acts as a shield against the strong energy fields of others. Because of it, people can interact intensely without damaging one another.

For example, if Bill meets Sue on the street he may say: "*Hello,* Sue!" and have a tremendous amount of energy behind it. Sue responds in kind, they interact enthusiastically, and then they walk away without either having been changed. But if Bill meets an Aries North Node person and, with the same amount of energy, says: "*Hello,* Jim!" Jim is blown over! He feels overwhelmed by all that energy. Owing to the weakness of the "identity" band in Aries North Nodes' aura, these natives are very sensitive to others and are easily affected by others' moods and ideas, and they need to remember to do things to fortify their *self*-awareness.

These folks even tend to take on the identities of others. Generally, they pick up accents easily and unconsciously duplicate other people's mannerisms, even if they are only around them for a short time. Harmony is so important to them that they try to be all things to all people. One by-product of their receptivity to others is the tremendous love that is easily sparked within them. Since their own identity is weak, they readily feel a sense of oneness when they connect with others.

In this incarnation, Aries North Node people face the challenge of strengthening their sense of identity. Because they have no preconceived idea of "self," they are open to discovering what is real and natural within themselves. It's an innocent process. Their natural impulses validate their identity, and their identity is strengthened through their actions.

These folks need a lot of time alone to get to know themselves. They need a specific time each day when they can talk with themselves. Their first challenge is to find out who they are in their own right. *Then* they can learn how to maintain their boundaries with others. This process happens gradually. Self-discovery can't be rushed, but Aries North Node people make progress when they resolve to pay more attention to themselves.

A Loving Spirit

Aries North Node people have a tremendous amount of love stored up from past lives. They know about relationships, and they have received much appreciation and love in return for the help they have given others. Thus, they came into this incarnation feeling loved by others. All that love shines through them—and is passed on to almost everyone they meet.

They have an ability to see not just the rough edges in other people but the loving qualities too. They perceive who others really are, and then they celebrate that truth. In that state they feel totally high, because they are fully appreciating and celebrating the glory, strength, energy, light, and life in the other person—and it makes them feel incredibly loving! Their challenge in this life is to begin to see the same beauty in themselves.

Although these folks are open and loving, if others violate their space they become angry. Then, when their "not so loving" part begins to emerge, they feel guilty. Yet this dark side is part of the human experience. They are discovering themselves and learning to integrate both sides of their energy. Their loving energy becomes the backdrop for the personality and mood changes that happen to all of us. Their challenge is to remain centered in themselves.

Aries North Nodes' motive of wanting to give is correct, but if they are trying to give when they feel drained, at best, they are only creating a superficial harmony. Every time they become too outwardly focused, appreciating others and not valuing themselves, the "demons within" emerge to bring them back in touch with themselves. They don't want to be with people when their dark side is showing—it doesn't reflect the supportive, loving person they feel they should be—so they tend to feel guilty and go off by themselves.

Actually, when the dark within them arises, it's a good sign. It is the neglected part of themselves demanding attention. When they turn within and begin consciously loving themselves, noticing their own beauty and taking care of themselves, the demons melt away. Thus, Aries North Node people need to regularly take time to focus on themselves and see what they need to do to support themselves. Then they will be able to interact with others from a place of internal strength and harmony.

HYPERSENSITIVITY

HARMONY VERSUS SELF-SACRIFICE

Having spent many past incarnations being the support system for others, Aries North Node people developed a constant openness to others' identities. They intentionally remained aware of the other person and could sense the slightest unhappiness or disharmony in that person's mood. When they focused on keeping the partner's mood happy, they shared in that mood and remained happy themselves.

Although this worked well in past lives, in this incarnation another person's happiness is not enough to evoke true happiness in these folks. They don't have enough personal identity left in their "battery" to hold the "charge" from the other person. To be deeply happy in this lifetime, they must focus on developing their own identity and recharging their own battery.

These folks tend to pacify others, saying whatever is necessary to keep the peace. When they do this, they think they're being "nice" and serving others. But it's only a temporary solution; it postpones a more permanent resolution that would promote a solid relationship based on the identity and integrity of both individuals.

Aries North Node people are so sensitive to the atmosphere surrounding others that they tend to make "maintaining a harmonious atmosphere" their focus in relationships. They do need harmony in their lives to feel content and happy, but they get into trouble when they allow their personal sense of balance to depend on another person. Then they feel they must manipulate the other person into staying harmonious with them: "If you're happy, I'm happy." They think that if they balance the other person by filling in where he or she lacks strength, that person should happily reciprocate. They can't understand when others don't "do their part" to keep the harmony going, and they often feel as though they're the only ones doing their fair share. Maintaining harmony in the relationship can become a full-time job for them.

But it's not set up to work that way in this lifetime. In fact, this habit can enslave both partners: The other person loses autonomy and becomes dependent on Aries North Node to produce harmony, and Aries North Node becomes bound to the role of providing the harmony, regardless of the personal cost. Sadly, because of this, relationships can become burdensome for these folks.

What does work for them is to pay attention to their relationship with themselves. What activities promote their own feelings of inner harmony? If their balance is "off," what should they give to *themselves* in order to regain their inner harmony? These folks want to be Mr. or Ms. Nice, and nice people don't upset other people. This "peace at any price" syndrome may lead to self-negation, which is a form of dishonesty. Their motive is one of love, but love without honesty leads to resentment.

Aries North Node people have spent so many incarnations helping others obtain their desires that they often equate "supporting others" with "doing what the other person wants." So they sacrifice what *they* need to be happy in order to fill the other person's needs. In this incarnation, they are learning to re-evaluate what "support" actually is. It is not supportive to give more than one has to give. These natives love the energy of giving to others, but if they give beyond the point of feeling comfortable, they are not really supporting the other person. If they continue to call on their inner reserves of energy, they wear out their "battery" and nobody wins. These folks must trust themselves. When they feel an inner resistance to giving, it is a signal to pull back and begin taking care of themselves.

It does not work for them to be unaware of their separate identity. When they feed energy into the forcefield of the relationship (rather than to the other person as a separate entity), they create only temporary harmony at best. This is because they are feeding energy into something that's not really there. A relationship doesn't "exist" in physical reality—it's an energy connection between two people, and the energy constantly fluctuates as the two people have different experiences and changing moods.

When the relationship is harmonious, it is the result of both partners being strong and peaceful within themselves. Aries North Nodes lose when they try to constantly "prop the other person up" through manipulating the energy in the relationship. However, when they encourage independence and individuality in their relationships—dealing directly with the other person and supporting him or her in being strong and separate—they win, because the other person will give back in the same way, supporting Aries North Nodes' independence and individuality.

PARTICIPATING VERSUS HIDING

Aries North Node people have such a history of being the "support person" that they are instinctively open to others' moods. But in this incarnation, it's a habit that can be extremely draining. They may appear to have a boundary between themselves and the other person, but it's a very thin line. In actuality, they are merged with the other person's energy field in a very co-dependent way.

Sometimes, recognizing that they end up feeling drained, these folks avoid participation: They seem to be involved but, on an energy level, remain inside themselves. They are still saying "hello" and being polite, but they're really not connected with the energy. However, when they remain totally outside the dynamics of the interaction, afterwards they end up on the *other* extreme and become overly excited—bouncing off the walls with excess energy.

For these folks, being drained and being overly excited are two sides of the same coin: not dealing with what's actually happening in the moment. They have either given too much of themselves and feel drained, or given too little and absorbed others' energy, so that they feel overcharged. Both reactions are a by-product of not being present or grounded in their bodies and responding to the situation moment by moment as a separate person. The balance lies in being consciously aware of others' energy without being consumed by it. Aries North Nodes need to stay connected to their own power and be in touch with what they can comfortably contribute. The idea is to share their talents freely, to be of service, and to give from the heart without trying to be more—or less—than they actually are.

Aries North Node people often try to work within the dynamic of the merged energy field (theirs and the other person's)—they plug into the other's energy and add whatever ingredient is needed to keep things harmonious. And they feel good about doing this; it's an expression of their love. But another motive may be that they want to blend their energy with others' to avoid standing out as an individual. Then they can participate in the flow of things without being noticed. They have a fear of being acknowledged, which is in fact the fear of acknowledging themselves.

Because they are so sensitive and vulnerable, they fear that being acknowledged could be overwhelming. There would be joy in having their positive aspects reflected back to them, but they fear having the negative reflected back as well. They don't want to face their "demons" as a result of another's feedback. Maybe they won't be liked. Maybe the other person, in order to protect himself from dealing with his own demons, will lash out at them. They have a lot of concerns about the possible repercussions of being themselves, so they would rather just "go along" and not really be seen as an individual.

However, concerns about how others will see them are a factor *only* when Aries North Node people seek to see themselves through others' eyes. In past lives it was a positive thing to see themselves through their partner's eyes, as it showed them how to adjust their behavior to more effectively support the other person. However, through many lifetimes of overuse, their habit of "fitting in" has extinguished their own identity. In this incarnation it is *not* to their advantage to see themselves through others' eyes, as this inhibits their ability to build their own sense of self.

INDECISION

VACILLATION

When these folks make up their mind to go in a given direction, it's sometimes difficult for them to move in a straight line! Part of them may question whether or not it's what they really want, and then they consider all the other factors that might be involved. It may take them a long time to decide which direction they want to take.

The process goes something like this. They make a decision and tell all their friends about it, and then they have doubts. For example, they may decide: "I want to write adventure novels." Then they start thinking: "You know, I also like other kinds of books." They try to embrace one idea and are able to feel that "this is really right." But somewhere down the line they say: "No . . . I don't feel quite right about it," and then they are back in indecision!

When Aries North Node people do make a decision, they have no problem justifying it. They can find ways to make any decision right or wrong. However, this mechanism can actually deflect them from a true knowledge of where they stand. For example, when a decision arises they have an instinctive response, but then they think: "Well, I want to be fair about this, so I'll look at it from the opposite point of view." This causes them to become confused and lose sight of what they want.

In this lifetime, Aries North Node people are developing single-mindedness. Rather than weigh everything before making a choice, they are learning the value of following their initial impulse—just to see where it goes! It's fine for them to make a decision based on their spontaneous sense of inner excitement, and then put the full force of their intellect into implementing it. It's an experiment. Later on, if they lose a feeling of "rightness" about it and something else excites them, they can responsibly tie up the loose ends and go on to the next thing. This is a lifetime of new beginnings for them, so it's natural that many decisions they make will be subject to change.

Actually, this incarnation is not set up to be one of decision making—which usually implies considering two points of view and then finding a compromise. Rather than be the "referee," in this lifetime these natives are supposed to *be* one of the points of view! That is why it is in their best interest to form the habit of noticing their first impulses, which will guide them to correct decisions. Then the vitality, confidence, and joy will come back into their lives and it will be a blessing for everyone.

A major obstacle to this single-mindedness for Aries North Node people is that they can appreciate the beauty in all their choices. Owing to past incarnations of being deeply involved with others' lives, they are accustomed to appreciating the beauty in everything outside of themselves. They aren't in touch with having "favorites" of anything. Because they don't know what their own tastes and preferences are, they have a tough time picking out one thing and saying: "This is it!"

What they can do is make time to visualize different things "inside" themselves and learn to feel what their preferences are. For example, if asked what their favorite color is, they may waver. But if they go off by themselves, visualize the colors "inside" them, and tune in to how they resonate with each one, they will discover their preference.

When these folks have to make a decision, they often *feel* what the right choice is. But sometimes they are forced to decide before they've gotten in touch with that intuitive impulse. Again, visualization can help. They can take a few minutes and visualize themselves following one option, to see how they feel about it in their physical body. Then they can visualize following the other option, and see how they feel about that. If it's an important matter and they don't have an immediate impulsive response, it's fine to take as much time as they need to visualize so they can make the right choice.

RISKING OTHERS' JUDGMENT

If Aries North Node people allow others to be part of their decision-making process, they lose touch with themselves and are dissatisfied no matter how the situation turns out. In past lives their decisions involved "the team"— they had to consult the other person so the outcome would work for the partnership. But in this lifetime they want to develop their own identity, so it's better to ask themselves: "How do *I* feel about this decision?"

When they tell another person their decisions, they become vulnerable to that person's approval. And since they're so sensitive, if the other person doesn't agree, then they start thinking: "Maybe I didn't make the right decision." So it is better for them to keep decisions to themselves, knowing that their decisions will change as they themselves change and grow.

Because Aries North Node people are influenced by what they think other people think (especially if it's someone they respect), they have a tendency to trust others' judgment above their own instincts. But in this lifetime they are learning to take a stand for their own judgment, which has less to do with "being right" than with discovering more about themselves!

These folks fear others will judge them harshly if they make a decision that isn't based on sound logic. They see others making decisions based on logic, so if they make an impulsive decision, they think it is not as valid. However, for them it's correct to follow impulse, whereas a member of another nodal group may be better off following logic. For Aries North Nodes, decisions based on their first impulse generally work out best—then they can use logic to find the best way to implement the decisions.

If Aries North Node people are facing a decision and no initial impulse arises within them, it's okay *not* to make a decision. It may be a sign that it is not the time for them to make a decision, or that they really don't have a preference. Then it's fine to just say: "I don't know."

These natives always feel more comfortable responding to a situation when another point of view has already been put on the table. Then they can either agree or disagree with that opinion. It's scary for them to offer their opinion first. But it's their specialty in this incarnation to offer innovative ideas, seemingly out of nowhere! Aries North Node people are *great* at supporting another's decision, but in this lifetime they need to impulsively feel where *they* want to go, put *their* idea on the table, and support it 100 percent. In this lifetime, *they* are the trailblazers!

NEEDS

A SENSE OF IDENTITY

Owing to so many incarnations in which they sacrificed their own identity for the sake of supporting others, Aries North Node people enter this lifetime without an inborn sense of identity. Rediscovering and re-establishing a true sense of self is now a primary need. Especially in the early years, their entire sense of self is based on how others see them. They may go along with others' definition of who they are, or resist it completely. Regardless, it is not *their* identity—it's a reaction to *others'* construct of who they are. To begin the path to self-discovery, they need to ask themselves: "Who am I . . . apart from others' projections?" They will find an answer only by looking inside themselves.

SELF-AWARENESS

To answer their need for self-awareness, it would be helpful for these folks to begin "checking in" with themselves on a regular basis. When they're not in touch with themselves, they often end up acting in extremes. With others, they feel they have to be a lightbearer—loving, supportive, and self-sacrificing all the time. This represses the part of themselves that cannot possibly be that way all the time, which creates an intense polarity.

They're trying to always be loving and supportive because that's the role they played in past lives, but the extremity of this positive role will also evoke the depths of darkness. If they take a closer look at the darkness, they'll see that it's really just their more assertive side, which they haven't allowed themselves to express. It's part of their yang nature—their masculine side. It's polarized because it has been suppressed over so many past lives that it's not integrated with the rest of the personality. So it may come out in a very intense way, which causes Aries North Nodes to become embarrassed and think: "Where did *that* come from?"

The best resolution is to stay congruent with themselves: Stay inside their own energy field and stay in touch with what's going on within them. Then, when they are upset, just spontaneously communicate: "Gosh, for some reason I feel upset about this." Their job is to simply be themselves. When they first experiment with this, they may feel uncomfortable; but they need to trust that since their underlying motive is love, whatever comes out is going to be fundamentally correct.

Aries North Node people are learning to take charge, do what they need to do for themselves, and become self-sufficient by following their desires. When they feel an impulse to do something that they know would bring them a sense of satisfaction, they need to follow through with it. Owing to the self-purification accomplished in past lives, they can trust that their impulses are not harmful to others and, in fact, signal the direction in which they need to go. In every area of life, the idea is to operate freely on their first impulse of what action would be best in any situation. Any resistance from the ego should be disregarded. In this way, they maintain a balance with others that is based on authenticity and taking responsibility for themselves.

Since these folks are not innately aware of the value of self-sufficiency, they don't realize how much others value it. They may evoke a negative response when they start supporting someone who hasn't asked for their help. They enter the other person's force field and find out what he or she is feeling and thinking. It's fine for them to be aware of others' needs, but they are learning that others have boundaries and that they themselves have boundaries as well. As they learn to respect others' self-sufficiency, they begin to value self-sufficiency for themselves.

Aries North Node people tend to be reactionary when they see other people taking care of themselves. They become judgmental and think that others are self-involved, uncaring, and selfish. Yet becoming involved with themselves is the very thing these folks need to do! It bothers them when they see it in others, because they're not doing it themselves. When they notice "selfishness" in others, they could use it as a reminder to check in with their own needs. They must begin giving attention to themselves, even if at first they go a bit to extremes.

They might begin by allotting 30 to 40 minutes of solitude for themselves every day, no matter what. In a room by themselves with no interference from the outside world, they might have a cup of tea and plan their day, write in their journal, read an inspiring book, or just sit and reflect. The point is, it's *their* time; during that time, they come first. If they arrange that one thing for themselves, they will be able to give to others all day long without becoming resentful. Paying conscious attention to their breathing also helps: It keeps them in touch with their bodies. When they are with others, they could consciously take a deep breath from time to time to keep themselves inside their own boundaries.

Some nodal groups are here to learn about selflessness. But Aries North Nodes already know about selflessness—in this lifetime they need to learn about *selfishness*. When they stay in touch with themselves, it works for everyone. It's not logical, but it's practical. When they're being themselves they're afraid they may hurt others, whereas being themselves actually helps others on a deeper level than they could have anticipated. But Aries North Nodes have to experiment with being "selfish" (that is, acting on an idea solely because it gives them a sense of satisfaction) and see how it works out. It's time for them to be responsible for creating their own happiness.

GAINING RECOGNITION

From past lives, Aries North Node people are accustomed to helping others, supporting others' ideas, and carrying others' projects through to completion—so they understand "completion energy." However, in this incarnation their job is to *start* things. They need to initiate and then let others carry on. If others don't come along to help, then it's fine for them to take sole responsibility. But if others do show up, their job is to allow others to support them and complete things for them, so they can get the ball rolling on the next idea!

Sometimes these folks don't want to give their project to others because they fear someone else will get the recognition. They think that if someone else can do it, they are less valuable. They also worry that others will take over and leave them behind. They ask themselves: "What do *I* do then? What is *my* job? Where is *my* importance?"

These reactions are an outgrowth of painful misunderstandings that arise when Aries North Node people comingle their identity with others. To restore their equilibrium, they need to separate themselves so they can clearly see the role they are playing and the roles other people are playing. Then they can feel their worth in discovering the seed idea, and let other people bring the idea to fruition.

Sometimes their desire for taking credit and gaining recognition becomes so strong that they repel the creative energy of others who might have made the idea better and more profitable. If Aries North Nodes' idea is truly potent, other people will be drawn to support it, and each will bring his or her special talents. If Aries North Node people want their own ideas to become reality, they must acknowledge the individual talents of the people they have attracted. By recognizing others' special talents, they can learn to validate others without diminishing themselves.

Occasionally, Aries North Node people become so preoccupied with getting the credit that they try to diminish the importance of others' contributions. They want all the credit. Of course, if they want all the credit they have to take all the responsibility and do all the work, so a lot of their ideas never bear fruit. They need to realize that the most important thing is that their original idea gets recognition—that the seed idea is actualized and spread to the widest possible audience. For that to happen, they need to step out of the way and allow others to help. This is a role reversal for Aries North Nodes; they are the leaders but must allow others to support them and promote their ideas.

Since it's their destiny to develop a sense of identity in this lifetime, in a way their desire for recognition is an attempt to establish a sense of self. However, motive determines the result. If their motive is satisfaction and self-discovery, it is correct and they will win. If their motive is to win recognition from others, then they're still hooked on needing feedback for their sense of self-worth. They need to release the idea that others must recognize them in order for them to recognize themselves, and begin directly giving themselves credit. The irony is that when they let go of control and begin recognizing the special talents of those who are helping them, others will be inspired to contribute more and the entire project will be permeated with love. And no one else can do their job—they are discovering the seed ideas for everyone else to build on.

GROUNDING

Aries North Node people need a grounded, structured existence to enable them to share their message of love with the world. The key is in releasing preconceived images of the ways in which love can be expressed. If they limit the way they express themselves to fit their *ideas* of love (harmonious, gentle, sensitive, caring, giving, compassionate, etc.), they're going to miss the boat, because love extends beyond the boundaries of any definitions. If a child is crossing the street in the path of an oncoming car, love may involve grabbing the child's arm and roughly jerking him out of the way!

These folks already know that love is the only reality and all else is illusion. Thus, they are learning to trust that their impulses will be the correct expression of love in each situation. When these natives follow the feelings of love and appreciation within themselves, they are *being* themselves. However, they need to be grounded with the energy so that it's a solid place for them, rather than a state of being that allows them to be pushed around by others.

Aries North Node people have a need to experience this love with others. Their challenge is to maintain the integrity of their own inner being. The irony is that being just the way they are will teach others and evoke feelings of love. To do this, these folks must give up trying to manipulate the other person's view of them and focus instead on being themselves with as much authenticity and integrity as possible in each moment. It seems hard at first, and it takes discipline and gently reminding themselves to practice their new focus. But ultimately, they can only come from an honest, selfless place by staying true to themselves.

ROUTINES

One thing that helps these folks stay grounded is to be aware of their bodies—allowing their bodies to be a natural boundary that gives them a sense of self. They have a tendency to "get into" other people's consciousness and lose a sense of their own center. So it's healthy for them to exercise regularly in order to stay more grounded and experience the feeling of balance and harmony they need.

Having a routine is also good for them—it is a way to check in with themselves every day. It can be very mundane: making the bed first thing in the morning, brewing coffee, opening the blinds, following a daily exercise routine, meditating, preparing a healthy breakfast, walking the dog. Their tendency is to make the bed one day, the next day partially make the bed, the third day not make it at all, the fourth day—make it—maybe!

Inconsistency and lack of routine undermine their personal strength, so daily consistency in the routine is important. Additionally, they could have a weekly routine or ritual: Once a week they go to their place of worship, or meet the same group of friends for lunch. This will counter their tendency to feel victimized by the randomness of life; it will give them a sense of structure and discipline emanating from within. Rather than floating in and out of other people's energy and consciousness, a routine helps enhance their own identity.

However, Aries North Node people despise routine, and for good reason. In past lives, having a routine would make them less available to support others whenever they were needed. They didn't develop their own routines—their own life—so they could more easily adjust to others' needs. But in this incarnation, it is to their advantage to develop strong routines and allow others to adapt to *them*. Also, having their own routines keeps them from falling into other people's routines. The discipline this develops is strengthening for them: It evokes the warrior in them, and they feel great about it!

Exploring hobbies and talents is also a good way to develop a sense of self. As Aries North Node people spend time on their own interests, apart from their primary relationship, their identity blossoms. They need to develop these talents through consistent application: regularly taking the time to do the things that bring a sense of personal satisfaction. For example, if they have artistic talents, they might enroll in an art class. If their talent is music, they might take lessons. If they love dancing, they might take dance lessons and/or go dancing regularly with their partner or friends.

SELF-DISCIPLINE

Aries North Nodes' sense of being grounded involves self-discipline. Everything that will work to their advantage requires discipline: spending time alone on a daily basis, following a few self-chosen routines to make their lives strong, and remembering to appreciate themselves.

One experiment that will help these folks practice self-discipline and checking in with themselves is to become aware of their eating habits. The idea is to not eat unconsciously (out of boredom or to cope with feelings) but to notice when their bodies are hungry and then tune in to what their bodies would like to eat. They can use visualization in this. They can imagine having a bite of salad and notice how their bodies *feel* in response. If they imagine soup in their mouths, or a sandwich, or fruit, or mashed potatoes, they can tell how their bodies will respond.

Aries North Node people are so sensitive that when they visualize eating a particular food, their bodies will actually tell them whether that food will make them feel good, or sluggish, or energetic. Then they can eat depending on what they want to experience at the time. But they are so "out of touch" with themselves that even this process may be challenging at first. They may have to work on it; yet when they do it, it's very satisfying and will strengthen their connection with themselves.

Self-discipline is not a punishment, it's a practice. It involves strengthening the "take-charge" muscles and doing things on a habitual basis that promote strength, health, and well-being. These folks can use self-discipline as a tool to uncover their identity. Consciously practicing self-discipline will evoke the warrior within them in a balanced, harmonious way.

On a spiritual level, Aries North Node people are discovering who they really are—allowing a new, innate, and natural identity to emerge. However, sometimes they can use their lack of clear identity to their advantage in breaking troublesome habits. One easy way for these folks to practice self-discipline is through simply reinventing their identity. Since they have no preconceived, rigid perception of themselves, by changing their identity in their own minds they can make healthy changes in their lives. For example, I had a client with this nodal position who wasn't a smoker in his youth, but who began smoking heavily five years prior to my seeing him. One day he suddenly stopped smoking, with no side effects or withdrawal symptoms. He simply "remembered himself" as a nonsmoker!

ESTABLISHING ONE'S CENTER

RELATIONSHIP AS CENTER

Aries North Node people have had so many lifetimes of identifying with others that they have confused their "center"—their inner sense of self—with that of their partner. They are hypersensitive to the partner's moods because the other person actually rests at their "center." Thus, if the partner is unhappy or dissatisfied, Aries North Node will feel it. He can spend all his time and energy trying to make his partner happy so that his own sense of well-being and contentment remains undisturbed.

The problem is that nobody can take on the responsibility for making another person happy. The best one can do is "appease" the partner, adding an ingredient that will temporarily change her mood; but the partner must then constantly be appeased in order to stay happy. And it just isn't set up to work that way for Aries North Nodes in this lifetime.

Actually, the growth required of them is best achieved by de-emphasizing the idea that relationships are necessary for their survival. They are learning to stand alone and relate to others from a new perspective. However, despite their sensitivity, these folks are often blissfully ignorant about other people: what motivates them, what they are seeking, and what kind of success they would like to achieve. Sometimes they only see the other person (and themselves) on the superficial level of having immediate needs and desires that are, or are not, satisfied. They only see deeply enough into the other person's identity to manipulate him into keeping the mood harmonious. This is why people surprise or disappoint Aries North Nodes—they never saw who the other person really was.

In many ways, Aries North Node people are not relating to the other person at all—they are relating to the *relationship* between themselves and the other person. This does not lead to truly helping their partner—or themselves—to grow. The relationship is not an entity; it cannot grow unless the two individuals grow. Thus, no matter how much time and energy these folks devote to the relationship, it cannot give back to them. So they are better off examining the needs for autonomy and individual creative expression of both partners. By encouraging and inspiring the other person to achieve results on his or her own, they free both the partner and themselves to evolve as individuals.

Another drawback to Aries North Nodes' focusing on the relationship rather than on the other individual is that they can't really validate their partners' identity. When Aries North Node people believe in their partners' ability to be self-sufficient—rather than constantly appeasing them, reassuring them, or "picking up the slack"—they will begin to notice the other person's strengths and can encourage him or her to exercise those strengths. This sets the stage for also seeing *themselves* on a deeper level, noticing their own strengths and pursuing their own impulses for growth.

FAIRNESS AND SELF-ASSERTION

Aries North Node people are preoccupied with ideals of justice and fairness; when they think something is unjust, they fly off the handle. They want the world and other people to meet their rigid standards. They figure: "I'll play fair with others, and others should play fair with me." These folks sincerely wish the world were more just, but it's actually in their best interest that it doesn't work that way! Because their ideas of justice don't work, they are motivated to act directly from their instincts—their identity—as opposed to "being nice." For many incarnations they've been waiting for a time when it's okay to be themselves—and this is it!

In this lifetime their sense of fairness and justice is not an accurate barometer of whether these folks are on track or whether they have a right to be angry with another. In fact, whenever they "get on their high horse" about injustice or fairness, they are off path. First, their definition of "fair" has a lot to do with the fact that they sacrifice their needs and desires for others—they constantly violate the boundaries of how much they can give without loss to self. Then, in "fairness," they expect others to do the same. These natives are learning to stop violating their own natural limits and to not entice others to go beyond their boundaries.

Aries North Node people become resentful if they think something isn't fair. If they feel resentment, it's a signal to pull back and recharge. It also signals a need to express their emotions: "I seem to be feeling resentful, so I'm going to take some time by myself and work it out."

Honest expression validates and strengthens their sense of identity. It also gives the other person a chance to become aware of Aries North Node's needs and boundaries. From the other person's response, the native has a clearer idea of who he is dealing with. If the other person says: "Did I say something that offended you?" Aries North Node has the opportunity to work it out on the spot. He cannot expect others to be as sensitive as he is, since others have had different past life experiences. But once he openly expresses himself, he can tell from the other's response how much self-assertion will be necessary before the other person hears him and honors his needs.

Aries North Node people are learning to be assertive in a constructive way that promotes fairness through clear self-expression. For example, I had an Aries North Node client who was in the process of purchasing—through rather large monthly payments—some real estate from a friend of hers. One day the friend approached her with a need for money for an unexpected problem, and my client immediately gave her the money (the instinctive Aries North Node desire to help and share). She assumed the other person would either repay it or deduct the amount from her next payment. However, her friend never repaid or acknowledged that money in any way. My client felt hurt and resentful but never brought the matter up. Naturally, she emotionally distanced herself from her onetime friend.

This type of incident seems to occur frequently in Aries North Node peoples' lives; as a consequence, they feel let down by others. From a broader point of view, this is life's way of teaching these folks to assert themselves. They need to take responsibility for themselves in their interactions with others. In the example, when the friend approached her, my client could have said: "Sure—I'll just take the amount off my next payment, or I could take a third off on the next three payments, or, what will work for you?" In this way, she would have satisfied her need to share *and* taken care of herself in a direct, honest, fair way.

Aries North Node people truly do love to give—it's their nature. But their motive needs to be love, not creating co-dependence. Their giving must be pure, without an expectation of result, in order for them to be free of disappointment in their relationships. If they find they are giving in an imbalanced way, they can openly bargain with their partner so that both people's needs are equitably met. It's when they *expect* others to reciprocate, without letting them know exactly what they expect, that they go off track—they need to give their silent expectations a voice!

It's their job to be sure things are fair by asserting themselves and letting others know what they expect in return for their giving. If they do this they will feel happy because *they* were the ones who ensured that fairness came about. This builds their confidence. Rather than being displeased with others, they will be pleased with themselves.

Since they are the ones who know about fairness, they can teach others by openly stating their standards. Then they are not only giving to the other person but also sharing their knowledge of how to give and take in relationships.

These folks can access the fresh energy that is emerging in this lifetime through honest self-assertion—not by waiting and reacting to the expectations of others, but by getting in touch with (and expressing) the impulses of their own being. Even though their sensitivity to others is strong, they must continue to build a sense of their own identity. Through practicing self-sufficiency a new confidence will emerge, empowering them to relate to others in healthy, innovative ways.

RELATIONSHIPS

DEPENDENCE

Dependence on harmony with others (especially the marriage partner) is the primary issue for Aries North Node people in this lifetime. Actually, the problem goes beyond dependence—it may involve total identification with the partner, and sometimes with all significant others. Aries North Nodes often become so identified with their partners that they are overwhelmed by the other person's emotions. When the other person feels distraught, their first reaction is to rush to say whatever is necessary to restore harmony so that they (Aries North Nodes) can feel better. They handle the partner as an extension of themselves, and then they lose patience trying to get the other person to "straighten up" and be harmonious so that they can feel comfortable with themselves again. But their sense of urgency generally makes things worse.

These folks need to notice that when they try to regain their own inner harmony by manipulating their partner, it doesn't work. What does work when they feel a lack of harmony from their partner is to politely excuse themselves and spend some time alone. Aries North Nodes need to respect others enough to allow them to experience whatever they are feeling and to work through it on their own, unless they ask for help. This is how people reach a deeper level of self-awareness.

Additionally, these natives can gain a better understanding of what is happening with their partner when they get a little distance. This is why it is crucial for them to have their own space surrounded by their own personal possessions to reinforce their sense of identity. They need a private place to go when they become overidentified with the partner—a place where they can be alone.

BOUNDARIES

These folks can never experience inner tranquility as long as they refuse to acknowledge their own boundaries—and their partner's—and allow another person to be their "center." For example, I had an Aries North Node client who came to me hoping to resolve marriage difficulties. He had been married for twenty-three years, had a great deal of money, and his pattern had always been to appease his wife's moods by buying her things. They traveled extensively—anything to keep her happy—because when she was happy, he was happy. But it was all manipulation on his part so he could remain undisturbed and have a sense of solidity, because he had placed her at his center.

Over the years she became increasingly difficult to please, and eventually nothing could satisfy her. She became verbally abusive to other family members as a way of generating a sense of her own substance and individual personhood. The destructiveness accelerated until the negative energy even made her unhappy.

My client was beside himself; nothing he could do would keep his partner happy and his own center undisturbed. This is a lesson Aries North Node people are learning: Even under ideal conditions, it is impossible to remain peaceful when someone else rests in your center. None of us really knows what can keep another person happy, and we rob them of the challenge of discovering and fulfilling themselves if we take on that responsibility. If my client had not distracted his wife from her moments of unhappiness so that *he* could stay calm, she would have had the opportunity to learn to handle her own moods. This might have averted her need to become destructive as a means of finally being in charge of her own inner state of being.

Aries North Node people are not accustomed to declaring the boundaries of their own identity—immediately, as those boundaries arise within them. They still feel a need to support their partner, even if it goes against their own best interests. So if their partner disagrees with something they want to do, they may say: "Okay, I won't do it," but decide they are going to do it anyway. By not honestly standing up for themselves, they reinforce the unhealthy dependence within the relationship.

Some of these kinds of problems stem from the tremendous love and compassion that these folks are born with. They have spent so many past lifetimes developing sensitivity that now it is not unusual for them to feel more compassionate toward another person or situation than their partner does. Sometimes the partner may not want to deal with a certain problem and the Aries North Node says: "Okay, we won't," in order to avoid disharmony. Then he starts to feel resentful, yet helpless to correct the situation. His need to support others can lead him to go behind his partner's back and lend a helping hand; but then his partner feels a breach of trust, which damages the relationship, and the Aries North Node person feels unsupported in being who he really is.

Resolution for this problem can come through both parties expanding their idea of "we" to become more flexible: sometimes as a team, and sometimes as two separate individuals. In the above situation, Aries North Node should communicate what he is experiencing—which takes a lot of courage. For example: "Okay—I hear that you feel resistance to supporting this situation, and *I* want to put energy into it. So I will do this independently." When the recognition of a different preference arises, these folks need to risk saying: "I don't feel that way about it." The problem isn't in doing what they feel is correct; the problem is in lying about it.

CHOOSING A PARTNER

In seeking a mate or any other close connection, Aries North Node people are subconsciously seeking a relationship in which they can lose themselves. They wish to become so submerged in the other person that they are totally "safe." It's the old "1/2 + 1/2 = 1 whole" theory, but it doesn't work for these people. Rather, they are here to learn that "1 whole + 1 whole = a healthy team."

However, until they become aware, they will attempt to find someone with whom they can identify, and then they pour all their love and support into reinforcing that other person. But when they seek a partner from this position, it never works out. Often they are attracted to people who abuse them or let them down. In fact, just the opposite approach is scheduled to work for these folks. They need to stop focusing on others and concentrate on themselves instead. As they begin to focus on being themselves, allowing their own true, unique identity to emerge, and going in their own individual direction, their energy will attract the right person—someone who will appreciate and value them.

Aries North Node people are so accustomed to the joys of partnership from past lives that they subconsciously associate being happy with being in a relationship that is mutually, joyfully symbiotic. They came into this lifetime wanting to do everything with their partner, all the time. They are basically cheerful people, but an energy drain is taking place beneath the surface of the relationship that is based on feelings of dependence. Aries North Nodes' need for attention and to be included as part of the other person's identity are a bottomless pit.

Subconsciously, these folks believe they cannot survive without the energy of others. So they tend to cultivate a mutual dependence with stronger people around them. They take time and energy away from their own goals to help the partner reach hers. They give of their understanding, being more sensitive to others' needs than to their own. In this way they create a dependence, becoming an integral part of what the *other* person needs to survive.

Then Aries North Node people resent their partners for "interfering" with their independence and blame them when they don't reach their goals, even though the Aries North Nodes created the unhealthy dependence. They think it's love (indeed, these folks *are* very loving and cooperative), but a lot of their self-sacrifice is subconscious manipulation. Love never expects anything in return for giving, and resentment is a by-product of expecting something and not getting it. Aries North Node people must learn to be honest with themselves and others about how much they are willing to give and what they expect in return. Being part of a team means making sure *they* are also supported.

LEARNING INDEPENDENCE

Because these folks are learning the lesson of not depending on others, they subconsciously attract people who are undependable. Although this gives them the opportunity to learn to depend on themselves, the process can be quite painful.

Aries North Node people are often so intent on influencing the relationship in ways that result in the complete integration of two people that they don't fully notice the partner's identity. They see the other person only in terms of what it takes to please him or her. They don't generally stop to notice who the other person is on a deeper level, in terms of his or her true inner identity. Worse yet, because they are looking for someone to fill their center so they can feel complete, they assume that others also lack a sense of self and are looking for a partner in order to gain a sense of completion. Thus, they enter relationships with some very naïve and inaccurate premises.

Operating with flawed ideas of who the other person is and what he or she wants, Aries North Node people often become deeply emotionally invested and then end up confused when the other person leaves or lets them down. Many other people *do* have a sense of their own center, and many independent types will rebel against the stifling aspect of Aries North Node wanting to be connected at every moment, in consciousness if not physically.

Aries North Node people tend to gravitate to people who are selfish and require a great deal of personal attention. They attract types who expect total attention and accept their energy without giving back on an equal basis. Through indiscriminate giving, Aries North Nodes may also inadvertently cause an initially sensitive partner to become insensitive.

Generally, these folks are better off around people who show some sensitivity in return. They are more comfortable around people with whom they don't have to "clash energy." They have a tendency to allow the other person to completely submerge them, so they need to be with someone who encourages them to be themselves and who won't abuse their loving, giving nature. Of course, letting people know where they stand helps others to be sensitive in return.

INDIRECT APPROACHES

AVOIDING CONFLICTS

Aries North Node people sometimes are so attached to peace and harmony that they inadvertently damage their relationships by avoiding all conflict. They may start out saying: "Okay, I'm going to be a team player" and then foresee a conflict; rather than deal with it when it comes along, they postpone it until it becomes a major dispute.

Their challenge is to be vigilant in consistently standing their ground and verbalizing their impulses right away. For example, if an idea excites them, they need to say: "I want to do this" rather than lie about it or downplay it. What stops them is their fear that they are coming from a different point of view—or have a different objective—from that of their partner. They feel threatened because—when they don't deal with it instantly—they magnify the difference in their mind, telling themselves that it is so vast it can never be resolved. Actually, if Aries North Node people honestly reveal where they stand right from the start, these differences become opportunities to connect more deeply with their partner.

Often these folks postpone telling the truth for fear of widening an existing difference of opinion. If they want to do something and know their partner will object, they may try to do it without the other person knowing. Then, when the other person finds out, the difference of opinion remains, along with hurt and a breach of trust. By not discussing the situation, they have deprived their partner of the opportunity to be generous and support them in doing something for their own growth. Now a discussion may pacify the situation, but there will be a lot of work to do to repair the damage to the relationship.

For example, I had an Aries North Node client who was an airline pilot. As a side business, he delivered airplanes—which he greatly enjoyed. He wanted to deliver an airplane to Turkey, but his wife wanted him to keep other family commitments. He knew she didn't want him to go on this particular trip, but he felt he needed to do it—so he began making plans for the delivery without discussing it with her. Then, when the time came, he said: "Well, I'm going to go take this trip" and his wife said: "But we talked about this and you said you wouldn't go!" Then he was faced with the fact that he had lied to her. Now, in order to go, he would have to bring her into agreement *and* undo the hurt of the lie. By the time it reached this point, he gave up and didn't go.

This is how these folks often lose the opportunity to do what they want, because they know that solving the communication problem with their partner is more important than what they want to do. It brings the relationship back into sync, but they are left feeling resentful because once again they've sacrificed their own desires to keep the peace. This is why they must be willing to "come clean" from the beginning and let their partner see not only *what* they want to do but *why* it is important to them. They need to sit down with their partner and discuss their own desires and fears.

In the example, my client could have said to his wife: "There's something I want to share with you. It's something that's very important to me, and my concern is that you're not going to realize how important it is. I'm concerned that you won't support me, and then I won't do it." This may seem manipulative, but it's really an honest voicing of concerns. Once acknowledged, the fears dissolve. Then my client could have communicated his desired direction and motive: "I want to deliver an airplane to a buyer in Turkey. It's important to me because I want to build my own business and establish an independent income. It's something that will give me personal satisfaction and build my confidence."

Once the partner sees that the direction Aries North Node wants to take has a larger outcome, she has the opportunity to demonstrate love by supporting him. If the partner *still* doesn't support his independent direction, Aries North Node should re-evaluate whether the partnership is truly allowing for *both* people's individual growth.

POSTPONING DECISIONS

Aries North Node people habitually put the other person first and neglect feeding their own life force the energy it needs to grow stronger. When they give up the direction of their own life, they become weak on all levels—they need their partner's energy to survive. They are learning the necessity of participating in activities that excite them, as an individual.

Out of a desire to be fair, these folks often postpone making decisions for themselves until they have consulted their partner. Unfortunately, when they look at a situation from the other person's point of view, they may not be true to their own impulses for fear of hurting the other person.

When in doubt, they can ask themselves: "Are my actions making me feel good about myself?" If so, their best bet is first to verbalize what they want, and then ask the other person what he or she would like. It's a simple technique, yet one that supports them in being themselves in a way that is also fair to their partner.

For example, an Aries North Node person may be driving home from work and sees a marquee advertising the new release of *Gone With the Wind*. Instantly, her sense of excitement says: "*Yes!* I want to see that movie with Tom!" Normally, she would go home and say: "Hi, Tom! Do you have any plans for tonight?" And her husband might respond: "Gosh, I'm exhausted. I thought we'd just stay home, watch *Monday Night Football,* and take something out of the freezer for dinner." Being accustomed to diplomacy, tact, and manipulation, she would probably respond indirectly: "I'll bet it would make you feel a lot better to go to a movie tonight and just get out of the house." "I don't want to go out, and you know how much I like *Monday Night Football!*" "I know, Tom, but we haven't been out together in such a long time . . ." At that point her husband, feeling manipulated, would probably explode and insist on staying home. She would storm off, feeling resentful and thinking: "We never do what *I* want; we always have to do what *he* wants!" Yet the fact is, she never even mentioned the movie.

A better approach is for the Aries North Node person to mention *her* preference first, in a direct way, and then ask the other person what he had in mind. She could have said: "Hi, Tom! On the way home I noticed they're showing a new release of *Gone With the Wind* at the theater. I got so excited—I'd just love for us to go see it tonight! Did you have any plans?" He would have said: "Gosh, I'm exhausted. I was hoping we could stay home and watch *Monday Night Football*." Aries North Nodes are experts at compromise. Once *both* positions are on the table, they can see a solution that will be fair to both sides: "Well, I can see that you're tired and the only night for *Monday Night Football* is Monday night. So why don't we stay home tonight, and then tomorrow night we'll go out and see the movie."

FEAR OF COMMITMENT

Owing to past lives of feeling manipulated and abused in relationships, in this lifetime Aries North Node people are afraid of relationships and marriage—recognizing that they have a tendency to give too much and lose themselves. So although they are very attracted to relationships, part of them holds back, preferring the single life to taking the risk of once again losing independence. Although in many ways they are natural marriage partners, they may subconsciously sabotage close relationships before they reach the stage of making a commitment. Or they may convince themselves that as much as they long for a partner, they just haven't found the right person.

There are various modern-day solutions to their hesitancy: being in a monogamous relationship and maintaining separate residences, or living with their partner without a formal commitment. Marriage can work if they have first made a conscious decision to be faithful to themselves and their own integrity. Ultimately, it's the same challenge: first developing their own independent identity, and then learning how to relate with their partner in interdependent and cooperative ways.

INDEPENDENCE

Aries North Node people tend to think they need permission from their partner before it's "okay" for them to take independent action. They start "checking in" with the partner in a childlike way, indulging in extravagant manipulations and justifications to obtain approval and support. They give away their power to their partner and then feel they have to become adversarial to be themselves. Or they may simply give up on what they wanted to do.

In this lifetime it works better for them to approach other people on an adult level. This means letting their partner know their intentions and plans with the energy of leadership, courage, and excitement—without letting themselves *or* the other person know how inwardly fragile they feel. If their partner has reservations, they can explain that for their own self-discovery and personal growth they need to go ahead with their decision—at which point the partner will adapt and go along, or else they can begin negotiations for how both people can win.

For their primary relationship to be successful, Aries North Node people are learning the value of doing things by themselves and pursuing activities that bring a sense of personal satisfaction. Then they won't need to "share energy" with just one other person in order to be happy—they can expand and interact with many different people while developing and strengthening their own identity. Once they have developed their own sense of independence, they can really connect with—and enjoy—their primary partner, because each individual has something to offer. Because their battery has been charged *outside* the relationship, they have more energy to exchange *within* the relationship.

But Aries North Node people aren't always clear about what they want to do. It can be more difficult for them to make up their minds than for many of the other nodal groups. These folks are always trying to discern what others want, what they want, and what would be fair in any situation.

Naturally, weighing all these considerations takes time. If Aries North Nodes allow themselves to be pressured into making a hasty decision, they are generally unhappy with the results. These folks cannot allow themselves to get stampeded! When an emotional component is introduced into the situation, they lose clarity and become vulnerable to "going along" with something that may not be in their best interest. They are learning not to make any decisions or agree to anything under emotional pressure. When they feel this kind of energy in a situation, the best thing is to say: "I'm not going to make this decision under emotional pressure." That will give them time to regain balance and clarity. Or they could say: "It's going to take me some time to weigh what's been said. Everything sounds valid to me, but I need some time for it to settle in. I'd like to continue this at a later date."

Especially in personal relationships, they need to speak honestly and directly. "There's emotional pressure here. That's not the way I'm going to decide." Their feedback gives the other person the opportunity to become aware of what they are doing. It also validates one of the facets of the Aries North Node person's identity: sensitivity to others and awareness of what is going on in relationships. Being "up front" with their identity in this way helps Aries North Nodes to gain strength and self-confidence.

SELFISHNESS

In this culture, selfishness is considered a negative quality. However, Aries North Node people have overdone the quality of selflessness in past lives, so now they must consciously practice selfishness just to get back to center! The irony is that when they take action that they consider "selfish"— trusting themselves and acting on their initial impulse to do what makes them feel happy and strong—later they find that it was actually the best decision for everyone involved.

It can be tough for these folks to put themselves first. For example, if they are at a party and not feeling well, it takes a lot of courage for them to say: "I need to leave" or "Can you take me home?" They're thinking: "If I leave, what will others think? Do they need me to be here to make it easier for them?" They become so fixated on others that sometimes their bodies have to *really* overreact to force them to pay attention to themselves.

When Aries North Node people acknowledge their feelings and express their impulses, without having to be rational, it works for everyone. After all, no one can see the bigger picture. In the example, it could be that their need to go home will take the other person out of a situation that, had they stayed, would have resulted in a serious problem that no one could have foreseen.

Aries North Node people's honest, impulsive responses automatically bring justice to the circumstances around them. For example, they may feel uncomfortable in a situation and say: "For some reason I feel upset; I don't know what it is." Then the other person may say: "Gosh—I bet when I mentioned _____, it triggered that upset. That really wasn't fair." When Aries North Nodes communicate in a nonconfrontational way, it gives others a chance to recognize what they're doing and alter their behavior.

GOALS

Self-Discovery

The joy of self-discovery is one of the greatest highs for Aries North Node people in this lifetime. Their best technique for self-discovery is the courage to follow their impulses. It may seem illogical, but this approach will manifest vitality in their lives. Their style may resemble that of the Aries Ram (sometimes butting their heads, taking chances, and getting hurt), but that's how they find out who they are. The path of self-discovery involves taking risks and experiencing the different facets of themselves, rather than results. If self-discovery is their conscious, underlying motive behind any action, they will never lose—because whatever happens will reveal more about who they are.

Self-Reflection

When these folks see themselves through the eyes of others, they can see who others think they are or who others want them to be—but it isn't really *them*. They have to be themselves, no matter how others perceive them. And they aren't going to find out who they are until they begin expressing their inner impulses and letting people know what's really going on with them.

Seeing themselves through others' eyes equals "how to lose" for Aries North Nodes. It dilutes their confidence in making decisions based on their own nature. As they begin seeing themselves through their *own* eyes, they can start doing the things that please them, increase their energy, and bolster themselves so that they feel confident and nourished. They are learning that their behavior doesn't always have to be "logical" and that they don't have to justify themselves and their decisions.

They are also learning to shift focus from being sensitive to the ebbs and flows of *others'* needs and emotions, to being sensitive to the ebbs and flows within *themselves*. As they develop this skill and begin to live in a way that is fair to self, they find the sense of justice they have been seeking. Only by respecting and honoring themselves can they expect others to treat them fairly. They respect themselves when they let others know their needs and expectations in relationships. When they are honest about who they are and what they expect, they will attract people who resonate with their values and can give back to them what they need.

SELF-LOVE

Aries North Node people are learning to turn their well-developed capacity for love to loving themselves. One of the reasons they postpone letting others see where they stand is that they are insecure. Thus, one of their challenges is to validate and give approval to self. They need to support their sense of self by allowing themselves to be seen. Once they begin to reveal themselves to others, they build trust by seeing that self-revelation actually works.

To motivate themselves to take this risk, these folks can review their past experiences and see that the other ways they have tried to balance relationships (compromise or evasion) have not worked. To change the outcome, they need to change their methods for dealing with others in close relationships.

In loving self, they are supporting themselves in actualizing their own dreams. When they get to a place of loving themselves enough to really want their ideas to work out, they will realize that honesty is the only way to do it. "How am I going to make this idea work? The only way I can do it is by taking out the barrier of dishonesty." Then, the energy of the relationship supports them rather than opposes them. In the beginning, their fears make them think they will face opposition, but they have to be willing to walk through that fear for the sake of their idea. Then, because they are not hiding anything, they can focus all their energy in the direction they want to go, and even enlist the support of others in putting their plans into action.

When Aries North Node people put themselves first, in a natural way, everyone wins. What actions make them feel stronger, happier, more complete, and satisfied? Self-love involves making choices that support themselves. They can make a start by asking some basic questions: "What is going to help me survive? What will help me further my goals? Which road is best in terms of reducing stress and benefiting my health?"

ASSERTIVENESS

In realizing the goal of constructive assertiveness, Aries North Node people must let go of a subconscious attachment to being a "Nice Person," which was their identity in past lives. In order for their new, authentic identity to emerge, they need to express themselves with no preconceived notions of what they "ought" to do. The idea is to be impulsive and say what first comes to mind. Honest assertiveness will teach them who they are and validate their true identity, apart from others' projections.

Rather than wait for others, these folks need to allow their own inner impulses to motivate them to take immediate action. As they validate their impulses by acting on them, their impulses will become stronger and more energizing.

Aries North Node people are learning another aspect of assertiveness, which is to let others know the boundaries of their identity, to stand up for themselves, and to not allow others to abuse them. They assume that others will be sensitive to them out of love, but this is not always the case. Their job is to learn to be sensitive to themselves and have enough self-love to not allow themselves to be hurt.

There is a story of an Enlightened Master who was traveling through India. He came to a village and noticed there were no children playing. "Where are all the children?" the Master asked. "Master, there is a huge serpent in the woods who comes at night and eats the children," replied one of the villagers. "Please help us!" So the Master went into the woods: "Serpent, show yourself before me!" And because all beings are subject to an Enlightened Master, the serpent slid out of his hiding place. "Serpent, it is wrong of you to eat the children of this village. You must *never* eat another child!" admonished the Master. The serpent was ashamed and replied: "Yes, Master!"

The Enlightened Master continued his travels, and ten years later he came to the same village and saw children of all ages. But in one corner he noticed a group of children involved in some intense activity. The Master approached and in the center of their circle found the serpent, wounded and nearly dead from their torture. The Master chased the children away and said to the serpent: "My friend, how is it that you have let this happen to you?" The serpent replied: "But Master, you said I was not to eat the children." The Master answered: "Oh foolish serpent, I told you not to bite; I didn't tell you not to hiss!"

This is what Aries North Node people are learning: to "hiss" at the very beginning of abuse in relationships. They need to let others know when their sensitivity has been wounded, or when they feel inequity in giving, or when they need more support. The idea is to let others know *before* they feel taken advantage of and withdraw from the relationship, either physically or psychologically. If they allow others to abuse them, everyone loses.

TRUST

TRUSTING SELF

A major goal for Aries North Node people is learning to trust themselves and be themselves—to find a healthy way of relating that doesn't trap them into being a support system for other people. In their relationships, the end result won't be love and fairness unless they risk the honesty and integrity of being exactly who they are. It means trusting their intuitive wisdom—that it's coming from such a strong base of love that if they *really* express that inner spark, it will work out for everyone involved.

This takes courage and a willingness to experiment, but when these folks trust enough to risk it, they'll find that it works. Because they're not used to being a leader, they tend to fall back if others initially resist their direction. They think it's an indication that they're off track. Actually, their ideas are unique and innovative, so often the first response from others *is* resistance. (People nearly always resist a new idea because it means change. It's a natural response, and part of being a leader is understanding that.) As Aries North Nodes continue to "make a show of confidence" and follow their inner impulses, they'll find that others will often adapt and go along with their decisions.

They are learning to experience the joy of self-discovery. Life is an adventure, and as they view it that way and begin following up their spontaneous impulses and ideas with action, a sense of fullness and happiness begins to grow within them. But they have to make that decision to trust their own instinctive impulses.

For example, I had an Aries North Node client who had paid into an Oscar pool at work—she had her own intuition about who was going to win. But then she started talking to other people about their opinions, lost confidence in her choices, and went with someone else's decision. When she lost in the pool, she felt very defeated and wished she had trusted her own instincts instead.

These folks need to stop doubting themselves and simply start *being* themselves. Their challenge is to act on their spontaneous impulses. When they take responsibility for creating their own happiness by actively pursuing a direction that could help them reach their goal, they are led to activities and/or people that answer their needs. After taking one step, the right idea about what action to take next always seems to come to them.

For example, I had an Aries North Node client who had been yearning for an appropriate romantic partner for years. However, scarcity of *any* potential partners was interspersed with a few disastrous relationships. Unhappiness and depression plagued her until she had to turn to antidepressants for relief. Finally she let go of her fantasy of finding Prince Charming and began pursuing activities that gave her a feeling of confidence and made her happy.

She started feeling better as she became more actively involved in things. Jogging was a source of enjoyment for her, but she didn't want to begin a routine all by herself in the dark, early morning hours that were best for her schedule. Rather than postpone jogging until she met someone who had a similar schedule, she took the initiative and placed an ad for a morning jogging partner in the local paper. Four people responded, she began running with them, and one turned out to be Prince Charming! But this only came about when she ceased looking to others for fulfillment and began filling her needs in a direct and logical way.

TRUSTING NEGATIVE EMOTIONS

Aries North Node people always want to pretend that everything is fine. They feel guilty about having so-called negative emotions. Owing to lack of past life experience being in touch with their individuality, they aren't always aware of their emotional responses at the time they are happening. Sometimes they experience an emotion and do not recognize it until a few weeks later when they think back and realize: "I was really angry." A friend may say: "How was the month of January for you?" And they'll say: "Now that you mention it, I felt really lonely and depressed." But during January, if someone had asked how they felt, they would have responded: "Just fine!"

So it is to their advantage to give themselves "time out" on a regular basis to get in touch with what's going on inside. When they're not aware of their emotions, they often react to things in an irrational way that surprises them. When this happens, their tendency is to go off by themselves, re-experience the emotion, and think about it so they can be more rational. This works well, especially if they can let the other person know: "For some reason I feel upset, but I'm not sure why." In this way they are honestly acknowledging their feelings without taking it out on the other person. Even if they do explode, afterwards they can say: "For some reason I got upset. I'm not sure why, but I'll think about it and get back to you." Even after the fact, it's a helpful process.

Sometimes these folks are cruel and hurtful, and they feel good doing it. They are angry—there have been too many past incarnations when they were "nice" at their own expense. So now, out of the blue, they lash out at someone who's close to them—someone whose love they can count on anyway. They unleash their anger and then apologize. Subconsciously, they want to see if these people will love them no matter what (as they have so often accepted others), so they can better accept themselves.

In this lifetime, Aries North Node people are learning to integrate negative emotions: anger, resentment, and the like. This energy is healthy for them to express. It's their power that they suppressed in past lives to get along with others, and now these feelings demand attention. These so-called negative emotions are their strength, but in a coarse, unrefined form.

Rage, anger, and the like are all part of the yang energy (the potent, assertive, leadership energy—the masculine part of themselves) that has been so heavily repressed. Now Aries North Node people must tap into this energy and integrate it with the gentle, sensitive energy they have developed so well in past incarnations; this will facilitate the healthy expression of their warrior nature.

An excellent technique to help them with this process is a regular program of physical exercise. Taking a martial arts class would be perfect for releasing and integrating this intense energy. And if that energy is being released consistently and constructively, it won't come out inappropriately. These folks need hard physical exercise: aerobics, boxing, raquetball, tennis—activities that give expression to their warrior nature—and they'll feel great about doing it!

Aries North Node people have an aversion to competition, but actually competition is very good for them. They get nervous watching others compete, but when they themselves compete it brings out the best in them and they handle it beautifully. It strengthens and validates what has been suppressed in past lives. They may fear losing, but if they review their past experience, they are always able to shake it off—and then they are glad that the other person won. If they do win they feel good, and they handle winning in a way that's "nice." So they "win" either way, as long as they go in *wanting* to win.

For these folks to enjoy competition, they must feel that there is something worth competing for. They also can build strength by competing against themselves. Instead of giving up after five miles, they should try to go farther. They need to do things that reveal how strong and capable they are. Also, they may see other people doing things, and that gives them the impetus to try something new. In this sense, they are comparing themselves to others in a positive way that encourages their own growth.

CLAIMING ONE'S POWER

Aries North Node people are learning to claim their own power and to stand in their power when relating to others. They are coming into their own. Sometimes they get scared when they see how powerful they can be when they're present in their own bodies and fully grounded in their own identity. These natives still feel shy and have a fear of expressing themselves.

When they don't stand in their own power, often it is because their minds are making them afraid of being wrong.

"Being wrong" is not the problem for these folks. They're afraid that if they're wrong, their power is at risk of being invalidated. But if they look back on experiences when they've put themselves on the line and been wrong, they've still felt validated because they took a stand and discovered something new about themselves. Being present in their power and taking a stand are more important for them than the outcome.

They must follow their impulses and take action—*that* is what makes the difference in feeling good about themselves. Then they are owning their power, and they feel good about their life because they are in charge. When these folks verbalize their needs and follow through on their own ideas, they feel exhilarated.

LEADERSHIP

Aries North Node people have had many past lives supporting others and being followers. In this incarnation they are to lead: first themselves, and then others—so it is healthy for the warrior within them to emerge.

From a very early age, these folks tend to find gratification working in unusual areas, doing jobs that others usually don't do. This can lead to a position where they're doing harder work; but in the process of becoming really good at it, they gain a lot in terms of personal growth and development. They hesitate to enter jobs in which they are just "another number," regardless of material benefits, because it's so important to them to be an individual. When they analyze things, they have a slightly different point of view than most people and enjoy being "different" in every regard.

One of the primary "perks" of leadership for Aries North Node people is that they enjoy using their individuality to benefit others. If they are the leader, they can control the work atmosphere and set a positive mood for those around them.

Owing to so many past incarnations being the support person for others, these folks are born knowing how to be supportive: They're sensitive and know what other people need to be happy. Since we all subconsciously project that everyone else is like us, these folks assume that others also know about support. So when they begin to lead, they don't understand why others don't support them properly. After all, they are providing the leadership, the idea, the environment—even the good mood!

The reason others don't respond with support is that they don't have a clue about how to be good support people. Therefore, when they are acting as leaders, Aries North Node people must consciously focus on what they need from others to feel supported. Rather than silently expect that others will be sensitive to their needs, they need to communicate directly and objectively what they want. Rather than tell others what they are doing wrong or how they are a disappointment, Aries North Nodes must positively point the way, which gives others the energy to rise to the occasion. In this way, they allow others to grow and learn how to be supportive.

One of Aries North Nodes' jobs in this lifetime is to teach other people (primarily their partners) how to love and how to be sensitive to the identity of another person. They are learning to creatively teach others how to be supportive, rather than resenting them for not knowing how. A support person has to be conscious of the other person all the time. It takes effort, but that's what makes people feel supported. This is some of the knowledge that Aries North Node people are uniquely equipped to impart. By being themselves, they teach others how to be supportive through love and compassion.

INTERDEPENDENCE

Aries North Node people tend to be classic "co-dependent" types. They have a history of depending on others to fill their needs and then feeling that people have let them down. In this incarnation they want to develop their independent self, without closing themselves off to the benefits of a primary relationship. To gain success, they need to view their relationships in terms of *interdependence*—whereby two people assist each other in developing their own independent strengths, encouraging each other in their capacity to fend for themselves. Then, complete within themselves, they can have separate adventures appropriate to each one's unique identity—and two different worlds of experience to share with each other.

A healthy relationship is one in which two people bolster each other's identities as separate individuals while working toward a common goal.

Rather than being caught up in the energy of the relationship dynamic, the idea is for each to consciously remain in his or her own power while participating with the partner.

These folks have had many past incarnations supporting others with no thought for themselves. So they tend to discount their instinct that tells them when they are giving beyond the point of balance, which drains their life force. They don't usually notice the energy loss as long as the other person is there; but when they're alone, they feel drained. In this lifetime they are learning to reattune themselves and allow their internal sense of moderation to regulate their giving. The process of sharing energy needs to be mutually regenerative.

After all, the supply of golden eggs one has to give others depends on the goose being alive and healthy. In past lives, these people gave others all their golden eggs and then started giving away the goose! Now they are learning to keep the goose strong and well so they can give away the golden eggs without depleting the source.

In one-on-one relationships, avoiding co-dependence means not seeking to "fill in" when the partner has a need, but rather to encourage her in knowing that (1) she has plenty of talent and energy to handle things on her own; and (2) there are others she can work with to get support. For example, the partner may want to have her paintings displayed in local galleries. Rather than "pitching in" and calling the galleries, Aries North Node could suggest that she ask a friend to help or hire someone, or get an agent. This leaves Aries North Node free to pursue his own interests.

The transition from co-dependence to interdependence is a three-stage process: (1) *co-dependent stage*—two people totally tuned in to each other and compensating for each other's weaknesses so that the team can survive; (2) *independent stage*—each person being completely self-reliant; each person taking full responsibility for his or her own projects, money, and day-to-day survival; (3) *interdependent stage*—one person, independent and self-sufficient in his or her own right, uniting with another independent, strong individual to form a mutually supportive relationship and work toward shared goals.

When Aries North Node people reach the stage of personal growth where they are ready for interdependent relationships, they really start to shine!

HEALING THEME SONG *

Music has a unique power to emotionally support us in taking risks, so I have written a healing song for each nodal group to help shift its energy in a positive way.

GOING THROUGH THE JUDGMENT DAY!

The message of this song is meant to encourage Aries North Node people to shift from co-dependent tendencies toward reliance on their own impulses—which are firmly grounded in love—to lead them in the right direction.

Selected lyrics:

> *You can read all the books that ever have been written*
> *You can ask of those around you to show you the way*
> *You can study the mysteries, a long time hidden*
> *But you're the only one who can take you through the*
> > *Judgment Day!*

> *And you can't rely on anyone else for glory*
> *Don't depend on the outside to show you the way . . .*
> *Put away the books—go beyond the brain*
> *Trust the Light within to guide you through the pain, and*
> *You're the only one who could ever know*
> *What it takes to make you whole . . .*
> *And it's the Light within you that'll guide you through*
> > *the Judgment Day!*

---

* These lyrics are set to music and sung in their entirety on the CD and cassette tape "Unfolding As It Should."

North Node in Taurus

and North Node in the 2nd House

OVERVIEW

Attributes to Develop

Work in these areas can help uncover hidden gifts and talents

- Loyalty
- Awareness of boundaries
- Taking things one step at a time
- A sense of self-worth
- Awareness of personal values
- Patience
- Honoring expressed needs of self and others
- Enjoying the five physical senses
- Gratitude
- Awareness of nurturing from Mother Earth
- Forgiveness
- Persistence

Tendencies to Leave Behind

Working to reduce the influence of these tendencies can help make
life easier and more enjoyable

- Attraction to crisis situations
- Overconcern with other people's business
- Impatience
- Inappropriate intensity
- Judgmental tendencies
- Preoccupation with the psychological motivations of others
- Resistance to cooperating with what others want
- Overreacting
- Destroying something in order to eliminate one part
- Obsessive-compulsive tendencies

ACHILLES' HEEL/TRAP TO AVOID/THE BOTTOM LINE

The Achilles' heel Taurus North Node people need to be aware of is seeking
self-worth through others ("I can only feel okay about myself through the
validation of others"), which can lead them into the trap of an unending
search for a soul mate ("If I have this one special person's energy, I'll feel
complete"). In truth, Taurus North Node people can only achieve a sense of
completeness within themselves—it will never come as the by-product of a
relationship, even with a soul mate. No matter how much support and
validation they get from others, they always think they need more. In fact,
for them, others' validation is a false barometer of whether they are on the
right track. Living according to standards they *know* are right for them,
regardless of what others think, will help them develop a sense of self-worth.

The bottom line is that at some point they must stop being enmeshed
with others and involved in others' business, and simply walk their own

path instead. The irony is that when they begin to do this, others will support them, both financially and on an energy level.

What These People Really Want

What these people really want is to merge with someone else's energy and feel mutual empowerment. They are looking for total, permanent commitment. They want a partner whom they can count on to take care of all their material needs, and they will take care of all the partner's emotional needs (or vice versa)—a synergistic relationship that is mutually empowering and completely dependable. To successfully establish this type of relationship, they must be discriminating and find someone with similar energy and values. The shared goals must be innately valuable to each of them as individuals.

For this to happen, Taurus North Node people must first get in touch with their own values. They must become strong within themselves, aware of what *they* want, and tune in to what is real and meaningful for them. The challenge is to establish their own energy systems and figure out who they are as individuals. As their energy becomes stronger, they will automatically attract mates of similar energy with whom they can form successful partnerships.

Talents/Profession

These people are the master builders—whether it's a home, a relationship, or a business. When they're willing to follow the rules, they can successfully build anything. They excel in professions that are in alignment with what they consider to be truly valuable. For example, if they consider massage to be a tool for healing others that could also be profitable for them, then they would be successful in that field. They also have talents with money; focusing on ways by which they can make money on their own and be comfortable will also lead to an appropriate profession.

Any field that emphasizes appreciation of the physical aspects of life and the five senses would be enjoyable and profitable: farming, construction, engineering, cooking, or teaching physical education. Generally, Taurus North Nodes' best bet is to "do their own thing": either manage their own project or business, or work for a company where they can feel autonomous. They need to learn to forego immediate results and build one step at a time, becoming comfortable with each step before moving on.

Taurus North Node people also have the gift of being very effective in crisis situations, and they have a natural affinity with psychology. Their awareness of the needs and desires of others can help them further their own aims. By openly acknowledging and using the energies of others in mutually empowering (win/win) ways, Taurus North Node people can help achieve the results that both are seeking. However, if they involve themselves in professions that focus on psychology or crisis management, they are generally not satisfied and end up feeling empty. They are better off using their talents to establish something of tangible value, which gives them an increased sense of stability.

HEALING AFFIRMATIONS SPECIFIC TO TAURUS NORTH NODE

- "To win, I need to proceed slowly and persistently, step by step."
- "When I live by my own values, I feel good about myself."
- "Mother Nature supplies me with the energy I need."
- "When I satisfy my own needs and the expressed needs of others, I build a stable base for relationships."
- "If I'm comfortable, I'm 'on path.'"
- "What others think of me is none of my business."

PERSONALITY

PAST LIVES

MERGING WITH OTHERS

In past lives, Taurus North Node people entered inseparable, bonded relationships with people in positions of power and influence. They were the Queen or Courtesan behind the King and were privy to the "inside scoop," but in the end the decisions were made by the other person. They were the Counselor to the Chief, Prime Assistant to the President, or Confidant to the General. They fed all their power, energy, and charisma to their more powerful soul mate and in exchange received validation and appreciation from that one person as acknowledgment of their worth.

In past lives, the person of power clothed, fed, and pampered Taurus North Node. All Taurus North Node had to do was stay bonded to that person and help fulfill his or her desires, and the native would experience the finest of lifestyles. So now Taurus North Node tends to be careless with money (as though someone else is going to pay off his credit cards), but in this lifetime it's not set up to work that way! Taurus North Nodes' past life dependence on another person robbed them of the knowledge that they could earn their own way with their own talents. Thus, in this incarnation they need to assume financial responsibility for themselves as a way to regain their self-confidence; when they are not conscious of how they spend money, they can create disastrous debt.

Other past lifetimes relevant to this one were spent in "ill repute"—the business of prostitution in one form or another. In those lives, Taurus North Node people's success was dependent on not having their own boundaries so they could successfully merge with another's energy field in ways that generated more power than either person could have done alone. They developed a sensitivity to others' needs, which worked very well for them in those lifetimes. However, such intense merging with others caused Taurus North Nodes to lose a sense of their own needs and values as a separate entity. In this incarnation, therefore, when they merge too closely or quickly with another person, they experience betrayal as a warning that they should keep their own boundaries, values, and spiritual ethics.

These folks were experts at psychology in past lives as strategists and counselors, penetrating the psychology of others to understand their motives and needs and predict their behavior. They were around people who were unstable, helping them uncover their mental or emotional dysfunction, healing them, and receiving financial protection in return. Their psychic sensitivity enabled them to predict the mindset of the enemy, as well as attend to the unspoken needs and desires of their soul mate. However, in this incarnation their attunement to others distracts them from effectively pursuing their own direction in a solid, consistent way. Now it is in their best interest to pull back from deep involvement with other people and to be more focused on their own business.

Some Taurus North Node people have had past lives in which they abused power and reacted with violence. In this incarnation they are learning not to abuse power, and for some this may mean being victims of abuse themselves. Lessons in this lifetime are not easy for these folks. They can experience real extremes in life—ranging from periods of drug or alcohol abuse, to dealing with severe psychological problems, to sitting in boardrooms in corporations, to being on a strict spiritual path. Their lives run the spectrum from the depths of darkness to the highest place of light.

CRISIS CONSCIOUSNESS

Lifetimes of power struggles with others have resulted in a consciousness that attracts crisis, trauma, and "living on the edge." Taurus North Node people are addicted to the adrenaline rush that comes from crisis. In order to experience that "high" they disregard their bodies, their health, and the peacefulness required to sustain a state of well-being. Time after time, even when it's unnecessary, they take risks that throw them into a state of crisis. Then they thrash and struggle and allow their destructive intensity to wreak havoc in all areas of their lives. Sometimes they abuse drugs or alcohol, which creates new crises on a daily basis. Or they may have a partner in that situation—a person who they saw was wounded and thought they could heal.

When confronted with an apparently inflexible situation that runs counter to what they want to create, Taurus North Node people often overreact with so much intensity that they create a crisis where none existed. These overreactions are most likely to occur when Taurus North Node people face a possible separation from a symbiotic relationship, or feel that the other person may not be 100 percent bonded with them. Lacking a sense of their own self-worth, they are utterly dependent on the constant approval of their "primary other" (the person who provides money or energy)—the dependence means survival. They keep "close tabs" on the other person's psyche so they can mitigate their own behavior according to what the other person considers important. In this way, they feel they will become indispensable and their survival will be ensured.

If they fear the other person is doing something to hurt them, their first response is to take action based on revenge. However, if revenge is their motive, they always lose. They need to focus on getting their needs met by approaching people and situations in a practical way. Then they can drop their defensiveness and say to the other person: "Look, this is really important to me." Rather than resorting to power, following the humble approach will work for them.

The idea is to stay focused on the positive results they want to create. To take care of their needs is valid for these folks; and if they fear being wounded or betrayed, they need to do something to protect themselves. The problem is that they have a tendency to overreact and blow the whole thing out of proportion.

Taurus North Node people are so passionate that their drive to experience intense emotion sometimes blots out awareness of what they're doing. One of their challenges in this lifetime is to take charge of that passionate energy and redirect it in constructive directions. Passion pursued for its own sake and taken to its limit results in destruction. In this incarnation they are learning to build rather than destroy, and successful building takes more time than the intensity to which they are accustomed.

When they are coming from fear, they destroy; when they are coming from love, they build. They are learning to dedicate their passion, energy, and mental power to create something worthwhile—and when they do that, they feel *great* about it! They are learning that there is more to life than a stubborn indulgence in taking risks (financial, personal, or sexual) that lead them into crisis and destroy their bodies. It is not necessarily *what* they do but their drastic *approach* that wreaks havoc in their lives. They need to slow down and recognize that by working on themselves, slowly and steadily, they can establish the sense of grounding and substance that has eluded them.

These folks have a tremendous need for peace after so many lifetimes of power struggles with others. They are learning that when they indulge in a desire to force a situation, the entire situation will collapse. Conversely, when they add the ingredient of peace, the situation will shift to their advantage in a way that works to the good of all concerned.

SELF-ESTEEM

In this lifetime, Taurus North Node people are learning to experience their own self-worth. In past incarnations they gave up what was important to them in order to integrate their power with another. They used validation as a barometer of whether they were "on track" in successfully empowering the other person—and this worked in past lives. But they became attached to receiving validation and began doing whatever was necessary to get it, sometimes violating their own personal morals and ethics.

Because they have extinguished their own value system, they came into this lifetime with no sense of self-worth apart from the feedback of others. This makes them incredibly vulnerable to adopting the values of those around them.

Although it was correct in the past, in this incarnation it is not set up to work when they focus on empowering their partner with the silent expectation that the partner will take care of them financially or validate them in some other way. In this lifetime they are learning to build a sense of self-esteem *directly,* by living according to their own value system. They need to empower others only when it is what *they* want to do, it fits with their own values, and they have no expectation of getting anything in return.

VALIDATION

Taurus North Node people have a tendency to toot their own horns. They often jump in and use something another person says as a springboard to focus the conversation on a past victory, a way they have helped another, or a story illustrating how powerful they are—then they talk incessantly! Subconsciously, what they are seeking is validation.

During interactions with others they begin to feel insecure, so they try to compensate by focusing attention on themselves in order to gain outward validation. They hope that others will see their worth and appreciate and respect them so that their insecurity will subside. Unfortunately, it's a "temporary fix." They have to keep doing it; and in reality, the habit of focusing on themselves turns other people off. The irony is that Taurus North Nodes' feelings of inadequacy only arise when they begin to judge themselves or compare themselves with others.

These folks carry a lot of anger. However, if they take a deeper look, they will see that their anger is really based on fear: fear of not being respected, not being liked, not being treated like a human being. So when they feel angry in a specific situation, they can ask themselves: "What am I afraid of?" This will help put them in touch with a resolution.

Taurus North Node people often become frustrated and feel robbed of self-worth when they do not get the validation they think they deserve from others. All their fears are around the issue of: "How am I going to be acknowledged or recognized?" They feel afraid and angry because they're giving and they're not getting back what they need. But this need can never be satisfied externally. They can never get enough validation from others— no matter how much wealth, prestige, and power they have—to feel good about themselves on a deep level. The resolution to their anger involves beginning to live in ways that are self-validating, in accord with their own values. When they stop looking to others to provide their sense of self-worth and start looking inside *themselves,* suddenly their anger becomes productive energy.

Sometimes Taurus North Node people pursue careers that are not really what they feel called to do, but are what they think will draw validation from other people. They are vulnerable to pursuing professions that others view as "lofty" so that they can get applause. Then if they're not feeling appreciated, it can poison their enjoyment of their job. In such a situation, their best bet is to reflect on what aspect of their job makes them feel good: Is the job furthering values that they think are important? Are they using skills that make them feel good about themselves? Are they doing an out-standing job that gives them confidence? Are they making the money they think their work deserves? They need to get in touch with what they appre-ciate about their job and consciously validate themselves for being "on path" with those values. This is validation they can count on consistently— appreciating themselves for being themselves rather than for meeting some-one else's needs.

Validation from others is "energy food" for these folks. They always enjoy a phone call or visit from a friend because it's an acknowledgment of their existence. They need to establish ways of feeding themselves energy so that they become self-contained. Then they can interact with others because they want to, rather than out of neediness.

One positive, self-validating action would be to set up a financial plan for themselves. In addition, spending time each day putting energy into things that are personally meaningful for them is self-validating—such as preparing good meals. The idea is to engage in regular activities that nurture and help them feel good about themselves, regardless of the input of others. When they do this, they are "on track."

BOUNDARIES

In childhood, the parents of these natives sought to impose their values on the Taurus North Node child. This is "normal" parental behavior, but most children simply discount parental values that are noticeably different from the internal values they are born with. However, Taurus North Node children have no preestablished internal values, so they are totally open to absorbing the values of their parents. They cannot see that they are separate from the parents. Breaking the subconscious bond with their parents is one of their major life challenges.

These folks are learning to express what *they* need and to avoid thinking about others' needs first. They often feel they are moving through life reacting to other people's situations and "falling into" things, as opposed to consciously recognizing where they are and where they want to go. They tend to be too focused on the motivations of others—subconsciously seeking what they need by first defining what the other person wants. However, they often go off track when they do this. They may think they fully understand another's motivations, and take action or respond to the person on that basis, only to find that their appraisal was incorrect.

It works best when they avoid tuning in to the desires and opinions of others, and instead focus on their own needs: "This is what *I* need. . . . These are *my* reasons." To build an unshakable sense of security and successfully reach goals, Taurus North Node people need to keep in touch with their level of comfort and determine their boundaries. When they are considering a goal, they need to ask themselves: "Do I feel comfortable about this goal? Does it feel right?" They can also use their internal sense of comfort to determine when they are moving too quickly; if they are, they need to slow down and continue at a pace that is comfortable for them. When they stand firm within their own boundaries, progressing in the development of what is truly important to them, they will find others more willing to make adjustments to accommodate what these folks deem important.

SELF-SABOTAGE

Taurus North Node people have a tendency to "shoot themselves in the foot"—to do things that keep them from experiencing success. Their goal is important to them, and they're pledged to it wholeheartedly. But they also feel unworthy and subconsciously put up roadblocks so they can't achieve the goal. And then they keep banging against the door, knowing that it won't open.

The motive for defeating themselves is generally something they are not aware of; thus, some introspection or psychological probing is necessary for these folks. Sometimes it is self-punishment for a real or imagined experience, or something they feel guilty about, that pulls them back from successfully reaching the goal. For example, when they were five years old, they may have pushed their little brother, who hit his head and had to go to the hospital—and subconsciously they *still* feel guilty.

Reaching goals involves taking tried-and-true, systematic steps for getting there. But these natives have so much inner resistance that they leave out the one obvious thing that would ensure their success. If they want to go to medical school, are fully qualified, and have good grades, they may apply to several top medical schools but not also apply to an easier-entry medical school. Then if they don't get accepted at any of the top schools, they've blocked their entire path.

Another way Taurus North Node people subconsciously defeat themselves is by going too far out on a limb without a safety net. It's like jumping without a backup parachute or driving without a seat belt: They take unwarranted chances. The bottom line is that they need to rely on their own energies to reach the goals they seek. They can hope that the promises of others will come through, but in the end it's up to them to ensure that all the bases are covered regardless of what unexpected things may happen. They need to use more than logic: They have to use common sense and *strategize* their lives.

The key is a practical, step-by-step approach focusing on the next step they need to take rather than becoming fixated on the exact means of reaching their goal. Since they don't have a lot of practical past life experience, it's fine for them to check out their strategies with others who have successfully created results similar to what they want.

These folks sometimes want to be "more" than they are (they like to impress other people), and this can lead to problems. They are learning that they are okay just as they are. The self-sabotage comes from wanting to move too fast or to be "bigger" than they are at the moment. They need to stay with themselves, grounded in their bodies.

Making Judgments

Taurus North Node people are largely unaware of the serious damage they do to others when they make harsh judgments. Without regard for the other's feelings, they thoughtlessly rip to shreds another's belief system with a great deal of righteous enthusiasm. They hold nothing sacred and therefore have no qualms about destroying what may be sacred to another.

Needless to say, being judgmental does not win them any friends. In fact, it alienates them from those who would otherwise want to be close. People don't trust them because they fear being judged. These folks are learning to stop destroying what others have built, and instead focus on building what is important and valuable to themselves. The best way to fight "evil" is for them to make energetic progress for "good."

In fact, the things that upset them about others' behavior can be a clue to finding their own values. For example, if they are criticizing another for having two sexual relationships simultaneously, perhaps it is a clue that they themselves value monogamy—and "monogamy" should be written on their "Values Important to Me" list. As they begin to live by those values, they will start to build a sense of self-worth. As they remain consistently true to their own values, they will become less judgmental about others who have different values.

Taurus North Node people also tend to be highly judgmental of themselves and undermine their own self-worth. They have a code of correct conduct against which they measure everyone—and most harshly themselves. They can be their own worst enemy. When things don't work out in the way they expect, they blame themselves for being out of alignment. Therefore they suffer twice: once with the momentary bad mood, and again by casting themselves as wrong for having had the bad mood.

They often compare themselves to other people and feel jealous of what others have—this makes their lives much more complicated and much less happy! For any of us, if what we are doing in our lives is making us happy, then we're on track. But the moment we compare ourselves to others, we lose. Someone is always higher or lower, depending on the standards we use. Taurus North Nodes are learning that it's not their job to judge; it's their job to simply walk through life handling each situation the best they can and moving step by step in the direction they feel is personally meaningful.

MINDING ONE'S BUSINESS

Because they are often unclear about their own boundaries, Taurus North Node people have a tendency to meddle. These folks feel free to get involved in other people's business but are shocked when others get involved in *their* affairs—and they can be terribly opinionated! When they speculate on the subconscious motivations of another, they form all kinds of conclusions about the other person. Then they become upset because they've decided what the other person ought to be doing, and he's not doing it.

The problem is that these folks are projecting their own values onto others and then judging them when they don't measure up. The other person's goals may be totally different, and the path she is traveling may be exactly correct for her. For example, if the Taurus North Node person wants marriage and commitment, she may be extremely judgmental about a friend who enjoys dating men who are not "marriage material." However, the friend may not want to settle down at this point in her life, so dating men with whom she has nice, short-term relationships may be correct for her. Taurus North Nodes must have the humility to understand that others may have different values and goals. They need to stay out of other people's business and focus on their own self-development.

Taurus North Node people also tend to inadvertently communicate their ideas in an intense and judgmental way that causes discomfort for those around them. They are pointing out others' dysfunctions without admitting that they have that same tendency. Because they have not yet "owned" these qualities in themselves, they are unable to make comments without heavy emotional overtones. The key is to recognize that trait or behavior in themselves and forgive themselves for it—then they won't have to justify themselves by trying to define Right Action for others.

As their personal conduct becomes grounded through exemplifying the qualities they value, they will feel at peace. They will no longer be tempted to be judgmental when they see qualities they *don't* admire in others, because they will have gained the knowledge they need: They will know who they are and what they stand for.

Another aspect of Taurus North Nodes' tendency to get involved in others' business comes from past lives as mental healers (psychiatrists, psychologists, counselors, witch doctors) specializing in exploring the depths of another's subconscious. However, in this lifetime it is in their best interests to separate themselves from the energy fields of other people's minds and focus on their own business instead.

These folks are very sensitive to the judgments of others, and if someone affects their energy field in a negative way, it's okay for them not to spend a lot of time around that person. In past lives, they developed attunement so they could be as close with the other person as possible. They became very aware of how that person viewed them so they could adjust their behavior instantly to better accommodate the unit. However, in this incarnation, using their sensitivity to pick up on how others may be viewing them will disconnect them from the power of just being themselves. Their job is to *stay out of other people's minds and business.* A good affirmation for them is: "What others think of me is none of my business!"

THE DARK SIDE

Sometimes Taurus North Node people are drawn into positions of great influence. They become attorneys in high-powered law firms, executives in large corporations, and so on. Holding these positions sometimes triggers an unscrupulous side of their nature. When that aspect emerges, they are not loyal to their employees, their own ethics, or themselves—they become attached to ego gain. When they opt for full ego involvement they are willing to do anything to get ahead, and they begin to think they are "selling their souls" to progress in the world of money and power. Often they "sell out" by allowing other people to give them things *with strings attached.* Pretty soon they're going along with someone else's game, living according to others' values.

These folks are so accustomed to giving their power to others that when temptations arise in this incarnation, it's easy for them to yield in order to gain power and special privileges. And they have a lot of power in that position: They hire, they fire, they can make or break people. This inflates the ego. They may abuse that power by letting employees "sweat it out," worrying about whether or not they still have a job. However, these tactics lead to a breakdown of employee morale, and Taurus North Nodes lose the goodwill, trust, and loyalty of the workers.

They are learning to resist temptations to abuse power. After all, "what goes around, comes around"; when they abuse power, it always comes back to haunt them. They are learning that they cannot go against their own values without severely undermining their self-worth. And that's pretty serious, because self-esteem is what Taurus North Node people are aiming for in this lifetime.

Even when these folks have chosen the path of Light, they are aware of their "dark side." For example, I had a Taurus North Node client who worked as a waitress. Her Higher Self was very aware that the most difficult customers are those who need love the most. When she consciously gave them love and positive energy, in most cases they became more agreeable. But she would go back to the kitchen and pantomime punching somebody! That action was her past life tendencies being released. She would then go back to the customer and come from the loving place she knew was "correct." But sometimes these natives' instinctive response is to let their past-life side "beat the heck" out of someone.

Taurus North Node people sometimes live on the dark side, suspecting others' motives and projecting evil (*looking* for it) on those around them. They will learn much about themselves by viewing the evil they see in others as a reflection of their own subconscious. Also, when they look for evil they become vulnerable to negative energy that holds them back. To avoid being victimized by this tendency, their best bet is to stop focusing on the "dark side" in others and pay attention to the strength they are building in their own lives. They need to be like a horse with blinders, focusing on the positive things they want to manifest. As they use their powerful psyches to focus on the Light, they will attract positive forces.

NEEDS

ESTABLISHING A COMFORT ZONE

The reason Taurus North Node people become so dependent on another person is because they have moved out of their own internal sense of comfort. Then they have nothing to hold on to except their connection with the other person—a vulnerable and unstable position at best. If they consciously stay in touch with their own comfort level, their relationships work much better because they have created something solid and stable within themselves. They've been through so many radical changes in past lives that in this incarnation they are scheduled to rest, accumulate possessions, and enjoy the simple pleasures of life: good food, good sex, and a comfortable, stable home environment. An inner feeling of "comfort" is an accurate barometer of being on path. They will win if they remain true to the boundaries of their own comfort zones.

WANTS VERSUS NEEDS

From time to time, jealousy arises as an issue for Taurus North Node people. They see others' possessions and covet them. These folks often have an endless chain of "wants" based on longing for others' possessions. They see a neighbor's new car and right away a mechanism inside says: "I want that." But when their wanting is based on insecurity, it never works out for them—it's a bottomless pit. To gain the sense of substance they seek, their best bet is to turn their focus away from what they don't have and begin appreciating the bounty of what they already have.

This is a lifetime of material accumulation for Taurus North Nodes, so desiring things is not a mistake. However, they have to be willing to earn the things they want through their own efforts. When jealousy arises, they can use it to identify whether or not it's triggered by something they actually need; then they can decide whether it's worth striving for. Rather than be victimized by "wanting," they are learning they can have whatever they want if they are willing to earn it.

Taurus North Node people have a tendency to be distracted by others' wants and motives. Underneath, their issues around survival motivate their concern with others. They need to simplify things: to stop "getting into other people's minds" and just get in touch with themselves. "What do *I* need here? What do *I* need in order to feel comfortable with this situation?"

What these folks really want is for their insecurity to be resolved—to know that all their needs will be met. This is a lifetime of appreciating the bounty the universe is offering, not grabbing what others have. If they panic and try to speed up receiving bounty in their lives, they lose touch with the comfort of their natural timing.

Taurus North Node people are destined to accumulate that which increases their inner sense of substance. Their challenge is to slow down long enough to receive the gifts that life offers. By taking the emphasis off of specific people as their "source," and by partnering directly with life itself, their insecurities over survival can finally be healed. They will find that life sends the right people—who often show up unexpectedly—to ease their journey as every new need arises.

Timing and Value

Taurus North Node people are "in a hurry" about everything. Even when they are taking a drive, instead of enjoying the scenery they just want to get there, and they wonder why it's taking so long. These folks want instant results. They are incredibly intense and are learning to rein themselves in, remain within their comfort zone, and stay connected to their own strength.

These folks are learning to build slowly so that their foundations are secure. It's tough for them to go slowly because they are not accustomed to it; however, in this lifetime they are destined to replace fast intensity with slow and steady progress.

To give an example of the transition required of them, when a skyscraper needs to be replaced, there are two teams of people involved. One team destroys and removes the existing skyscraper with dynamite, crane, and bulldozers. They may take only a week, but the process of rebuilding the new skyscraper may take a year. In past lives, Taurus North Node people were on the team of destroyers—but now they are here to build. Building takes much more time, and no stages may be hurried or skipped or the entire structure will collapse!

These folks are learning to slow down and carefully build what is important to them—without rushing: a relationship, a business, or manifesting a dream. If they feel uncomfortable, it is a warning that they have missed a necessary step in the building process. They are learning to trust themselves and to appreciate the peaceful feeling they gain from slow and steady progress, accomplished on their own.

Although they need to go slowly to create successful results, Taurus North Node people also require a certain amount of stimulation to get themselves going. In a crisis they are motivated to action, and not having that crisis energy can keep them from progressing with their projects. When there's no crisis surrounding their goals, one thing that could help them is to establish time limits for themselves.

Time limits can act as an "artificial crisis." Taurus North Node people can look at the steps they need to take and write them down. For best results, the process should be in black and white: what the goal is, what the steps are, and the completion date for each step. This gives them built-in "crisis energy."

These folks need to make their plan a top priority: Reaching that one goal has to become the most important thing in their lives, and everything else needs to be subject to that consideration. For example, if they want to lose 30 pounds, they need to make that the most important thing—their "first value"—for a predetermined time. Everything else takes a backseat: job, recreation, everything. At work, their diet comes first; regardless of what others are doing, they eat precisely what is on their diet because that is their first value. If they feel low energy in the afternoon, they have a cup of coffee or take a Chinese herb—anything except break the diet. If they are tired, they go to bed early—but they do not break their commitment to the diet. Everything revolves around that.

It's important for Taurus North Node people to be realistic and choose practical times for attaining their "first value" goal. For example, if a Taurus North Node works in an accounting firm, it would be a mistake to make losing 30 pounds his first value during tax time. His job will probably be first value, and rightly so, during that time. So he needs to choose a time for reaching this goal that will not be unusually stressful. Once Taurus North Node people are committed to a direction, they can use their obsessive energies from past lives to fixate on their first value, and then they'll get there on schedule no matter what!

SELF-ACCEPTANCE

HONORING NEEDS

The first step toward self-acceptance for Taurus North Node people is to acknowledge that there is a needy person inside and to take personal responsibility for filling those needs. If they try to appear self-sufficient and suppress that needy part, it will come out full-blown to make itself recognized. They have denied and postponed their own needs in so many incarnations that now the needy part is overenergized. And that is to their advantage—they have earned the right to embrace and encompass that part of themselves.

They cannot hope to experience truth and honesty in human relationships if they do not demonstrate this behavior in their own lives. This includes no more "sins of omission" (for example, letting what someone says pass by without acknowledging feelings of hurt, or pretending to be in agreement). These folks must start communicating their discomfort or hurt with what another has said or done. To discern and build healthy new patterns of behavior, they must release the old. Self-revelation will enable others to see who they really are, discern their needs, and help them further their aims.

Taurus North Node people are tuned in to the hidden desires of others. They are often very perceptive in helping others become more self-aware and less victimized by self-defeating, subconscious motivations. But these folks have a blind spot: They can see clearly how others "shoot themselves in the foot," but they can't see how *they themselves* do it. Worse, they strongly resist feedback about their own subconscious motivations. It can be vividly clear to those who care about them that they are hurting themselves or holding themselves back. But when the behavior is brought to their attention, they tend to go into denial. To progress in this lifetime, they must bring into awareness—and release—subconscious guilt and self-defeating behaviors.

Part of their resistance to help stems from the fact that they are accustomed to being the ones doing the helping. These folks are not used to accepting that others have power to recognize and help perfect what is valuable in *them*. They are also so sensitive to criticism that they often interpret the input of others as invalidating their worth, rather than as encouraging their fuller self-expression. The key is to focus on what they want to build: their own ideas and aims. Taurus North Nodes' job is to allow others to empower *them* for a change.

A major turning point is when they focus time and energy on projects that are important to *themselves,* not being diverted by what they think is important to another person. For example, I had a Taurus North Node client who loved to buy people books in their area of interest. It was a very generous act, and she went out of her way to find just the right book with a message she thought would be valuable. One person she sent books to was a friend of mine who doesn't even read! This is an example of how these folks divert energy from pursuing their own goals for the sake of others who haven't asked for their help and may not appreciate it.

In this incarnation, Taurus North Node people are here to take back their power. When they stand in their power they can afford to be loving and helpful to others—not from a place of neediness but from a sense of contentment that enables them to be generous. Thus, their first responsibility is to themselves: to do things that bring recognition of their self-worth and the contentment of enjoying life. There are no more battles to fight, nothing more to give up, no part of themselves that has to be thrown away. This is a building lifetime: building a sense of comfort through their connection with themselves.

FORGIVENESS

In order to achieve full self-acceptance, these folks must release those who wounded them in the past through the process of forgiveness. This includes people in the present lifetime, as well as any feelings of suspicion and outrage that stem from past incarnations. Forgiveness is essential to keeping their own power intact. And their best motive for forgiveness is not generosity, but rather taking care of their own needs.

In past lives, Taurus North Nodes' method of protecting themselves was revenge: If someone hurled one stone at them, they hurled a stone back—plus an additional stone to make sure that the person stopped. To stand up to the power of others was enlivening in those incarnations, but in this lifetime it is a waste of energy—a distraction from their new, peaceful direction. They just want to build lives of comfort and stability and enjoy being on the earth.

To achieve this, however, Taurus North Node people need to face the necessity of forgiveness when dealing with abuse or wounding—it's the only way they can cleanse the other person from their psychic field and regain inner peace. Regardless of what the other person did to them, they need to forgive the abuse and forgive themselves for allowing the abuse to occur. It also helps if they identify the strength they gained from the experience.

If someone has wronged them beyond the point of forgiveness, they may need to confront the person before they can release the situation. One way to accomplish this is for Taurus North Node to go where he won't be disturbed, close his eyes, and imagine the person he is unable to forgive sitting in a chair, facing him. Through visualization, he can confront that person and let her know how he feels. Then he needs to listen intuitively for a response from the other person.

If in his mind the person responds with sincere apologies, Taurus North Node can forgive. However, if the person responds with arrogance or justification—or obviously is still not aware of the gravity of the injustice—vindication may be in order. In his imagination, Taurus North Node can take the perpetrator through the experience of abuse and allow her to experience the pain that she caused him. Then he will be able to forgive and release her from his life.

Forgiveness is essential for these folks; it is the key to their release from painful early memories. If they are angry with someone and haven't forgiven him or her, it binds them into a negative psychic connection with the other person.

One reason they withhold forgiveness is fear. If they forgive the other person, they don't know what that person may do to them, and they're afraid they will no longer be shielded from attack by their angry memories. They think they might be vulnerable again to someone who has abused them. But actually, if they truly forgive, they break the bond with that person. Then, whatever the other does, Taurus North Node is totally invulnerable.

GROUNDING

Taurus North Node people have spent so many incarnations enmeshed in the bonded energy fields between themselves and others that they have lost touch with their sense of physical grounding: being in touch with their bodies and enjoying the physical aspects of life. In past lives they wanted to experience higher realms—to "fly"—so they took one foot off the ground to experience other realities; and then they took *both* feet off the ground! Thus, in this incarnation they have no sense of grounding or inner stability. Their challenge is to get their feet back on the ground and regain a sense of their own inner strength.

APPRECIATION

One of the main keys for satisfaction in this lifetime is for these folks to consciously evoke the feeling of appreciation. This practice alone will make a significant difference in their lives. In past lives, taking time to feel appreciation was the last thing on their minds. Their consciousness was geared to crisis management, and they had an addiction to excitement. Their desire was never satisfied, always wanting more. To balance overactive desire in this incarnation they need to exercise the antidote, which is appreciation for what they already have.

Part of cultivating the energy of appreciation involves acknowledging the bounty that is already present in their lives. As they feel gratitude for what life has already brought them, they relax and feel peaceful and loved. The energy of appreciation pulls them back into themselves, and when they are centered in this way they open to life bringing them more.

For example, no matter how much or how little money they have, Taurus North Node people can say: "Thank you, Universe, for providing enough money so that I can afford [whatever they do have: a roof over their head, food on the table, etc.]." If they don't have a partner, they can say: "Thank you, Universe, for the friends, family, co-workers, children, pets, etc., you have sent into my life to love me." This is the key to the fullness they have been seeking. It has nothing to do with what is happening externally; it has to do with graciousness in accepting and appreciating what they have. As they take the time to appreciate what they do have—with openness and feeling—they begin to experience the fullness of love inside them, which replaces the agitation they have so often felt.

CONNECTION WITH NATURE

Everyone needs to receive nurturing energy in order to feel renewed and satisfied. In past lives, Taurus North Node people became dependent on soul mate relationships to provide that nurturing. In this lifetime, whenever they depend on others to fill these needs, they feel let down. It's set up this way, because their lesson is to become independent in meeting their own needs.

In this incarnation, these folks have a magical relationship with Mother Nature and with the earth, and that is where much of their nurturing is destined to come from. Their attunement to Mother Nature empowers them to connect directly with her energy and absorb it in a healing and re-energizing way. For peace of mind and inner strength, Taurus North Node people need to spend time in nature on a regular basis, consciously appreciating the support Mother Earth is giving them. This process will magically shift their basic emotional state to one of serenity. Situations with others that evoke insecurity will occur less frequently when these folks are consistently reinforcing a base of calm support inside themselves.

Some of these folks have a green thumb, and they may find working with plants or spending time gardening soothing. It is in their best interests to fully absorb the energy from Mother Nature—to touch a plant or tree and let the earth nurture them. Hugging a tree can evoke the same energy and happiness for them as hugging a person. Hugging a person is also good (sensual affection is always beneficial for them), but if they feel any reservation about whom to hug or what their motives are, a tree will always provide the "connectedness" they need.

Their ability to receive energy from nature is a gift they can share with others. For example, if they're walking in the park with a friend and share their knowledge of "tree energy," the friend will be more aware of the gift of nature's energy while in the presence of the Taurus North Node person and will be permanently enriched by the experience.

SENSUAL ENJOYMENT

To keep themselves focused on furthering their aims requires facing the issue of self-worth. These folks may feel unworthy spending time and energy on themselves; however, such feelings are totally off track. Taurus North Node must spend time doing things that *they* consider to be important, as this will build the resources they need to experience life and relationships from a foundation of self-sufficiency.

The fact is that for spiritual balance, their destiny in this incarnation is to experience the sensual enjoyments of life, to become grounded, and to regain a sense of their own earthy substance. In past lives, Taurus North Node people developed a deep enjoyment of the spiritual/psychic senses. Now it's time to develop a deeper awareness of the five physical senses. In this incarnation, their senses are generally quite sensitive and well developed. The idea is to pay attention to the pleasure their physical senses offer them: the smell of springtime, the taste of a good meal, a perfume they enjoy, or the touch of their lover. Even lifting weights or other physical exercise can be sensual—anything that gets them in touch with their bodies in a way that results in pleasure and/or self-esteem.

Music is an excellent source of enjoyment for these folks that eases their mental frequencies into harmonious patterns; they may benefit by having music playing regularly in the background. They are attuned to the sounds of nature—waves crashing on the beach and birds singing. To enjoy their sense of hearing is altogether "on path" for them. They also gain pleasure from their sense of sight—noticing beauty around them, appreciating artistic creations, or taking time to enjoy a sunset.

Taurus North Node people generally have well-developed taste buds; fully enjoying the pleasure of a good meal and going to posh restaurants are totally "on path." To become aware of their sense of touch is also beneficial. Taking the time to touch a tree, a leaf, a piece of wood, or fabric—and to experience physical comfort—is altogether appropriate. Even being aware of the sensation of snow crunching under their feet can be a sensual pleasure.

Another way to enhance their sense of grounding is to become more conscious of their clothing in terms of how it feels on their bodies. Does it feel sensual or comforting? Do they like the touch of that fabric? These are the clothes they should put on their bodies in order to take care of and pamper themselves. Clothing can also be a powerful vehicle for establishing self-worth. For an important appointment, if the choice is between an outfit in which they are comfortable and confident versus an outfit they think will impress the other person, their best bet is to wear the clothing in which they feel comfortable. That way, regardless of the other person's response, they feel comfortable within themselves.

Other sensual experiences that are "good karma" for these folks include giving or receiving a massage or being pampered with a manicure, facial, body wrap, sauna, or Jacuzzi. When they spend time giving themselves physical rewards and sensual pleasure, they won't need as much from others.

RELATIONSHIPS

SEARCH FOR THE SOUL MATE

Taurus North Node people are born looking for their soul mates. This can lead to promiscuity during their youth, with a tendency to jump into relationships too quickly because they want the bonding so intensely. Their challenge in this lifetime is to focus less on bonding and more on building their own values—then they will attract the right mate.

From past lives, these folks are accustomed to giving everything and having the other person reciprocate. But in this incarnation, much to the natives' surprise, it's not in their charts for others to take care of them in the same co-dependent way. This is the universe's way of helping them break abusive co-dependency and learn to be more self-contained. Deep in their hearts, more than anything in the world, they want a soul mate—that special person to travel with through life in a state of mutual vulnerability, commitment, and empowerment. To have this dream come true, they need to first experience being complete within themselves. When they no longer need another person to make them feel whole, only then will they attract the right life partner.

Taurus North Node people feel acutely lonely sometimes, aching for their mate. They long for the comfort of consistent, dependable companionship, and this *is* a lifetime where loyal companionship is their birthright. But as with everything else in this incarnation, they must earn it. As they work to experience their own wholeness and direction and become a powerful river in their own right, they can merge with another powerful river that is going in the same direction, and together they can flow to the sea.

INVASIVE MANEUVERS

Yearning for the soul mate causes Taurus North Node people to probe the psychology of others. In past lives this technique worked for them: Their understanding of another's psychological makeup facilitated a bond of mutual empowerment. However, they became so accustomed to stepping into other people's psyches that they lost touch with their own boundaries! Now, when they enter another person's force field they go too far and become invasive—and both people begin to lose their sense of autonomy. Also, the other person can sense that Taurus North Node wants the bonding energy, rather than simply appreciating and empowering the other as a person in his or her own right.

These folks think everyone wants the same emotional things they do: love, acknowledgment, appreciation. So they give others this emotional support and encouragement. But if they rush in and try to change another's mood, sometimes they are surprised when that person responds with anger because he feels his boundaries have been invaded.

Also, Taurus North Nodes often inadvertently become too enmeshed in another person's force field and begin to feel uncomfortable. If they get too absorbed in another's moods it dissipates their own energy. When this happens, their best bet is to excuse themselves and take a break to get grounded—walk around the block, or touch a tree and allow nature's nurturing energy to pour into them. Then, when they feel calm, confident, and centered in their own energy, they can again approach the person or situation and know what to do.

In this lifetime, Taurus North Node people need to be able to maintain their own psychic energy field as a separate entity before they attempt to bond with another. When they do bond, they need to create "space" in their relationships. They tend to do anything in front of their partner that they would do in private, which isn't necessarily a good idea because the partner may begin to feel like a part of them rather than a separate individual. Establishing boundaries that support their individuality and self-worth is essential in creating the space Taurus North Node people need for their relationships—and themselves—to thrive. Being unaccustomed to boundaries, at first they have difficulty recognizing other people's boundaries and establishing their own. Yet if they stay calm, they will gain the awareness to define their own so that their lives can be strong and they can have a greater sensitivity to the boundaries of others. Healthy boundaries promote self-respect and respect for others.

ABUSE

In Taurus North Nodes' previous incarnations, abuse was a factor—both giving and receiving—owing to the power struggles that resulted when bonded relationships became too consuming. One of their primary challenges in this lifetime is to separate their identity from that of their parents. They have to establish boundaries for themselves in order to break this bond, otherwise it continues to create a power struggle.

These folks are learning not to abuse power; sometimes they learn this lesson by being victims of abuse themselves. By being victims in early life, they have a choice: They can abuse others when they become adults, or they can break the pattern and not retaliate for the abuse they have received. They are learning about love and forgiveness; those lessons may follow on the heels of having been wounded unfairly themselves.

Sometimes Taurus North Node people are in denial about their difficult childhoods, even when the abuse was blatantly apparent to others. They tend to portray their parents as good and see themselves as having evoked abuse as rightful punishment for being "bad." They are all too willing to carry guilt. I had a Taurus North Node client with two children whose parents had severely abused her during her childhood: sexually, physically, and emotionally. Yet she thought they had been good parents. This woman eventually sought psychiatric care, and one day the doctor asked her: "What would your children have to do in order for you to feel they deserved the punishments you received as a child?" This stopped her dead in her tracks, as she realized there was nothing her children could ever do that would justify being treated in that way.

When Taurus North Nodes experience abuse as adults, they have to first acknowledge that it's happening. Then they need to extricate themselves from the situation and break the psychological bond through forgiveness. Often they do very well with psychotherapy or some other form of intervention that enables them to uncover and release past-life and early childhood memories of abuse and feelings of guilt. Their tendency to perceive themselves as intrinsically "bad" and disliked by others is actually their oversensitive probing to evoke validation from others. When these folks stop seeking validation, they will no longer be so vulnerable to feeling disliked. Sometimes the people who have abused them do shun them, and the reason is understandable: When one has abused another, there's a lot of guilt involved.

Taurus North Node people are the master builders. When they focus on building a relationship and do it their way, in tune with their own level of comfort, it will last forever. Their challenge is to not allow other people's energy to disturb their sense of what's comfortable—it's not to their advantage to allow themselves to get "knocked around" in any way.

DISCRIMINATION

Because they were not born knowing what is important to them in life, Taurus North Node people tend to investigate others' values. But this never works because when others share what is important to them, Taurus North Nodes say to themselves: "*That's* not important because of _____," and the other person feels invalidated. Not only do Taurus North Nodes lose out on what they are seeking, but the process throws the other person off track in pursuing his values, and he often ends up feeling upset.

Taurus North Node people have spent so many incarnations being subject to the value systems of others that they sometimes hide what they want if they think it's not socially acceptable or not okay with those close to them. But in this incarnation in order to build a sense of self-worth they need to discriminate between others' values and their own and honor what *they* want. Only when they go after what they really want do they feel good about themselves. For example, if making lots of money is important to them, their tendency is to allow the values of others to invalidate them:

"Oh—that's so materialistic, and you're a spiritual person." Then they feel badly and try to suppress that desire in themselves. This is typical of how they undermine their own self-worth.

However, if these folks try to suppress their desire for wealth because of someone else's disapproval, they will end up with money problems. If they try to solve their money problems, something will work against them—because they feel guilty about financial success. Then they will be "stuck," not knowing why they can't get that aspect of their life together, and feeling badly about themselves. Thus, if they desire wealth, their best bet is to openly pursue it.

Discrimination is also an issue in that Taurus North Node people attract "troubled" types as candidates for close relationships. Perhaps owing to past lives of working with emotionally disturbed people, or their attraction to "living on the edge," Taurus North Nodes tend to be drawn to people who are poor risks for closeness. When they bond with and put their trust in one of these people, they always end up being disappointed.

These folks are aware; they know when they are dealing with someone who is so troubled that she doesn't have the ability to give anything back, but they are attracted nonetheless. They think they can help heal the other person, and then they expect the other person to be grateful and offer reciprocal support. But this equals "how to lose" for Taurus North Node people! Their job is to discriminate and form relationships with those who are already psychologically healthy.

One way they get involved with the wrong people is when they seek to gain validation from others by taking on their values. For instance, even if they don't take drugs, they may talk about them and put up a front if they think it will make them look good. This confuses both themselves and others: They repel those who would normally be attracted to them, and they attract those who have the same values they are espousing. If they get in touch with what is really important to them and clearly represent those values, then they will attract people who truly resonate with them.

In this incarnation Taurus North Node people need stability, not crisis. To achieve this in the context of relationships, they must not let their partner invalidate them. If the partner says something that they are not comfortable with, they can let her know: "I'm not comfortable with that."

In this way, they make the other person aware of their boundaries, giving the partner an opportunity to accommodate them and come into alignment with what they need. As the relationship evolves, it will become apparent whether or not this person is an appropriate partner.

BONDING

Taurus North Node people love the energy of bonding with another person to accomplish far more than either one could do alone. This process, in itself, is fine. The problem is that Taurus North Node "got stuck" on one end of the teeter-totter being person B—the one who notices the worth of person A and helps person A reach his or her goals.

This no longer works. It's time for Taurus North Node to be person A— the one who allows person B to be attracted and help person A reach his or her goals. Taurus North Node people are not selfish. When others empower them in manifesting their dreams, they make sure the others are taken care of. But to achieve successful bonded partnerships, Taurus North Node people need to be the ones that others support! This means clarifying their values and goals and allowing others to rally around them.

Because these folks are so accustomed to shared energies and mutual empowerment being the key to their survival, subconsciously they think they need another person's energy in order to live. This is why they often make poor choices in their early relationships—they rush into highly charged bondings and consummate them as soon as possible—their desperation blots out their ability to accurately appraise the other person.

These folks aren't standing on solid ground when they are caught up in the intense energy early in a relationship. When they allow that to happen, they become vulnerable in a way that requires total trust. Then, if the other person pressures them for a decision, they are tempted to commit to the relationship too quickly. However, doing things quickly does not work for them; in this lifetime they have to take the slow and steady approach to ensure positive results. Relationships they just "plunge into" are almost predestined for failure because their basis is a temporary energy connection, rather than a true fit with the other person. Furthermore, if Taurus North Nodes go too fast, the relations between themselves and the other person that *could* fit (if given time for slight adjustments) don't fit because the partners have skipped the necessary stages of gentle adaptation.

To achieve successful long-term relationships, Taurus North Node people need to first recognize that their energy is enough—they can live off their own energy. As long as they feel incomplete they will continue to attract people who also have low self-esteem. But without untamed neediness driving them, they can take their time in discovering whose energy will actually increase them and bring them joy!

SEXUALITY

Taurus North Node people are generally highly sexual. They seek the intensity and excitement of sex and the bonding that is possible through a sexual connection. Early in life, they may be promiscuous. If they feel a connection with a person, right away they want to get in bed to start the bonding process. Then the relationship ends as quickly as it begins because there wasn't a stable base to support the passion.

These folks spend much of their lives looking for a soul mate—that one "piece of the puzzle" that goes together perfectly with their "piece." When they are impatient and become sexually involved at the onset of a relationship, without allowing time for a connection to be established, it's because they want a soul mate so badly and think sex will tell them who that person is. The irony is that if they take their time, the sexual energy will be much more intense and satisfying because they have established a meaningful base for the relationship.

However, they have had so much past life experience merging with people mentally and emotionally that they often leave the aspect of enjoying their bodies out of the sexual process. They can "burn out" sexually in relationships and not understand why. In this lifetime, it is scheduled for them to pull back from the energy fields of others and establish a sense of "home base" inside their own bodies; this is their key to a happy sex life. They need to deliberately take their time in relationships, not rushing the sexual aspect until they have fully developed a sensual connection with the other person.

Taurus North Node people need lots of physical affection: kissing, hand holding, touching, massaging—really tuning in to how the other person's hands feel on their skin and how their nervous system responds to the other person, strictly on a bodily level (without the aid of their imaginations). Then they need to see how the other person's body feels to them and if they feel a physical response in the other's body when they touch. Building this body-to-body sensitivity will bring their full sensuality into play and will provide a stable base for their sexuality. If Taurus North Node's body does not resonate with the other person, that is important knowledge: He will not want to pursue a romantic relationship that has no lasting substance on the physical level.

Over time, Taurus North Node people may begin to have sexual problems with their long-term partner. When this occurs, it is generally because they are using sex to barter for something else. For example, if a Taurus North Node woman wants flowers or jewelry, she may use sex as a way of manipulating her partner so he will buy her those things. If a man wants certain behavior from his mate, he may withhold sex or use sex as barter to get what he wants.

In this way the sexual urge becomes diluted by other motives, and over time the sexual part of their union becomes less intimate. The other person feels the attempt to control through sex and begins to lose interest. As a result, relationships that were once highly passionate may end up as platonic friendships, or cause a feeling of impotence or frigidity. By seeking to mentally manipulate their sex drive, Taurus North Node people lose touch with their own natural potency.

In this incarnation, these folks are learning to appreciate the gift of sharing sexual pleasure with their partner, without any other motive. They are learning the value of the simple, natural pleasures of life: food, sex, being comfortable—enjoyment of the physical pleasures that are the gifts of having a human body.

LOYALTY

Loyalty and commitment are very important to Taurus North Node people. They do not generally "play around"; they want someone to go through life with, a partner who feels the same way. They want to feel fulfilled, so when they marry they tune in to their mate psychically and begin feeding him or

her power, validation, and energy—expecting that their mate will reciprocate. This doesn't work because Taurus North Node doesn't first discern
what his partner's needs actually are, from the partner's point of view.
Instead of tuning in to his partner's needs, he projects his own values onto
his mate. He projects what he thinks she wants and needs—and then he
fulfills those needs—but his partner's actual needs and desires are seldom
even recognized.

For Taurus North Node people, solid relationships are based on each
person taking responsibility for filling his or her own needs and gaining
energy from activities outside of the relationship. Then a healthy bonding
can take place that is based on mutual strength, giving energy rather than
draining it from one another.

They are learning that loyalty between two people in a relationship is
based on both people being loyal to themselves. They need to establish a
bond of loyalty to self before they can expect to be loyal to another in a
healthy way. For example, loyalty to self implies honestly communicating:
"I don't feel comfortable with this" rather than invalidating personal needs
to adapt to the partner. It implies taking a position of integrity—based on
an inner feeling of what is correct—and standing in that one place, rather
than standing in different places depending on where the most validation
seems likely.

Through living by their own values, these folks allow the right person to
respond to them and support them. This means being willing to risk losing
their partner. If they remain true to themselves, honestly revealing what
their inner comfort level is telling them, either the other person will validate
them by coming closer or the other will leave and make room for someone
more appropriate.

When difficult times create stress in a marriage, Taurus North Node
people view loyalty as the quality that keeps two people together, working
on the marriage, until they can get over the hump. Loyalty involves integrity
and a commitment by both people to work on the issues rather than giving
up. Taurus North Node people need to feel that the other person will be
there, so when they become fully invested in the bond they won't have the
rug pulled out from under them.

Because this is an important issue for these folks, when they begin a close
relationship their best bet is to acknowledge: "Loyalty is important to me—

knowing that my partner is going to be there through thick and thin. Is it an important quality to you in a relationship as well?" By making it clear from the beginning, they allow the other person to see the type of relationship they are offering.

This is one of the most effective ways they can take care of the needy part within: discovering for themselves what their needs are, acknowledging that those needs are important, and then clearly communicating those needs to see how the other person responds. The idea is to move the give-and-take of relationships out of the realm of expectations and into the realm of open disclosure, verbalizing what is important as the relationship progresses. Then they can determine whether both partners want to meet each other's needs and make each other happy on the consistent basis that they need.

WITHHOLDING

Taurus North Node people tend to withhold what the other person needs, because they are judgmental about what they think the person really needs. For example, the other person may say she needs to play bridge with her friends one evening a week. The Taurus North Node partner may resist: "You don't need that; those people aren't up to your caliber." But by invalidating his partner's expressed needs, he undermines the relationship. His best bet is to truly empathize with the other person without the overlay of his own desires.

Because Taurus North Node people are so aware of their own needs, when the partner asks for something their first response may be resistance. They don't want to keep giving because they feel empty, so they deliberately withhold what the partner has asked for and defend their position by becoming judgmental of what the other person wants. In this situation, both people lose. The other person feels deprived, so she retaliates by giving *less* to Taurus North Node or giving with resentment. This seriously undermines the very bond they want to build.

It is to these folks' advantage to release their tendency to withhold from their partner. Often, the key is discrimination. Does the other person's expressed need violate Taurus North Node's sense of self-worth? If not, it behooves him to give the other person what she needs. Just as it is inappropriate for him to live by someone else's values, it is inappropriate for him to expect others to live by his values. Other people are simply being themselves.

AWARENESS OF NEEDS

There is a difference between expressed needs and unexpressed needs. An *expressed need* is something the partner *says* she wants (one hour alone every day, time to do a project, dinner together once a week, etc.). When Taurus North Node people generously cooperate with those needs, their partners are happy and respond with an outpouring of love and appreciation. An *unexpressed need* is something projected onto the other person. This doesn't satisfy what the other person *actually* wants and leads to dissatisfaction for both parties.

Sometimes these folks are afraid to reveal what they need for fear of appearing selfish. Actually, when they don't reveal what they want, they deprive their partner of the opportunity to make them happy. Also, if they don't communicate their boundaries and let others know what they need, people begin to lose respect for them. These folks don't object to anything; they don't say: "No! This is not okay!" Others tend to take advantage of them because they don't feel enough self-worth to stand up for themselves.

To Taurus North Node people, others can seem like gods who hold the key to meeting their needs. But they overvalue others and undervalue themselves. This is the imbalance that leads to heartbreak. Once they recognize this, instead of trying to figure out if the other person can fill their needs, they begin to let their partner know how they feel and what they require to be happy. No justification, no compromise—just simple revelation of what they need in the relationship. By overtly saying: "This is what I need to be happy in this relationship," they give others the opportunity to adapt to them. The irony is that when Taurus North Node people are true to themselves in this way, the changes others make in their behavior are generally beneficial for Taurus North Nodes as well.

These folks sometimes feel they've given and given and just don't have any more to give. This stems from being constantly aware of their partner's needs—it takes a lot of energy to keep part of one's concentration always attuned to the other person! The feeling of emptiness is actually to their advantage: It reminds them of the necessity to turn inward and meet their own needs first. Otherwise the emptiness persists, no matter how much their partner gives.

EXPOSURE

In the history of humankind, many negative thoughts and emotions have been generated as a response to life experiences: especially inadequacy, guilt, and shame. These feelings are not personal; they are part of the collective unconscious. Although they do not accurately describe us as individuals, if we identify with one of these feelings we have a tendency to hide it. Then we think we're the only ones with these terrible feelings.

The process happens in the extreme with Taurus North Node people. A negative emotion floats by and they grab it, hold on to it, and try to hide it. In order to hide it, they have to bury it deep inside. It takes tremendous energy to hide these feelings from others, and the fear that someone will find out how they feel generates a lot of anxiety. These folks are so sensitive and psychically bonded with others that they think everyone knows what's going on with them all the time anyway, so they *really* become intense trying to hide these feelings!

Their best bet to get past this anxiety is to simply expose what they're feeling, one layer at a time. When they expose it, they can release it—the Light will dissipate it. They should practice revealing their feelings in non-threatening situations where they feel a certain level of trust with the people involved—although any situation will seem threatening when they first take the risk.

They may start out: "There's something I want to share with you, and I feel a certain amount of fear in saying it." That peels off one layer. Then: "I feel anxious inside, and I'm not exactly sure why. It's like there's some kind of feeling going on underneath the anxiety, and I'm not sure what it is." That peels off another layer. As each layer is exposed and released, the next layer makes itself apparent: "Gosh, I guess what's going on is that, for some reason, I seem to feel a sense of inadequacy in this situation." Period. That's it. Once it's exposed, it dissipates—there's no more anxiety, no more feeling inadequate, the whole thing is released. Through this process, Taurus North Nodes' inner negative feelings are permanently discharged, and they begin to experience less anxiety in all their interactions.

GOALS

SELF-RELIANCE

Taurus North Node people are not allowed to rely on others for success in this lifetime because they need to learn to rely on themselves. Thus, when they count on another person's energy to create what they want and it doesn't turn out according to their high expectations, it's one more reminder from the universe that they are not allowed to rely on others for their sense of self-worth. The irony is that once they learn to rely on themselves, others rally around to help them reach their goals! Their confidence comes from knowing that because they built success on their own, step by step, no one can take it away.

ESTABLISHING SELF-WORTH

When Taurus North Node people look to others to acknowledge that they have power, they won't feel like they have any. When they realize that their power is within them, they have a lot. Part of claiming their power involves understanding their own value. They don't have to work to become something valuable; their value is inherent—who they are is a gift they bring to the planet. Their own sense of self-worth is the one thing they can hang on to amid the constant shifting of public opinion. When these folks let others determine their worth, they are on a roller coaster.

I had a client with this nodal position who was working with endangered species. She had to bring a change of clothes each day, because in handling the animals her clothing would become soiled and smelly. One day she forgot her other clothes and had to wear her work clothes home, and she had to bring a caged animal with her that day. As she waited to catch the ferry boat, she noticed that other people gave her a wide berth and treated her with disdain.

Then a friend who was in the new car business and needed to transport three autos on the ferry asked if she would drive one of them on board. When she climbed into a brand-new Lincoln Continental, she noticed that the attitude of the people on the ferry shifted: They were friendly, smiling and waving to her. Yet her worth (who she was inside) stayed the same. She could recognize how invalid it is to let other people determine her worth.

In this incarnation, the most important goal for Taurus North Node people is to pledge themselves to their own values and build a sense of self-worth. They are learning that they can't establish self-worth by going along with others' values to gain validation, nor can they attain self-worth through resisting others' values. Either way, they lose. They win when they discover what is truly important and precious to them: their own values. Self-worth will come as a by-product of living according to those values.

They recognize the truth of this but may still feel lost when it comes to knowing what their values are. And that's fine. They have a clean slate—a unique opportunity to get in touch with what is in the deepest level of their souls. The idea is to *consciously discover* what is important to them; what values give them a sense of being grounded, confident, and able to face the world without anxiety. They need to ask themselves: "What principles can I live by that will make me feel good about myself, give me a sense of my own self-worth, and give me a solid path to follow?"

For example, if Taurus North Node people decide that honesty in communication is a value for them, they need to begin letting others know when they feel uncomfortable. If they decide that starting their own business is important, they can begin systematically allotting time to it. These folks have discipline, once they're clear about their direction. As they travel through life, if they are uncertain about which road to take they can ask themselves: "Would taking this action make me feel good about myself, regardless of the consequence in the outer world?" If the answer is yes, they can proceed with confidence.

To further discriminate, they can ask themselves: "Does choosing this direction make me feel comfortable, or anxious?" When they choose to move in alignment with their comfort zone, they win; if they opt for anxiety with no safety net, they lose. "Is this path leading to inner peace, or will it create more crisis?" Inner peace will lead to victory for them. "Is my motive self-validation, or to gain the validation of others?" Those pathways that validate the principles they think are inherently valuable and that give them a sense of self-esteem help them win.

SELF-EMPOWERMENT

Taurus North Node people are so accustomed to empowering others that they have forgotten how to empower themselves. In this lifetime, their challenge is to turn the spotlight around and make themselves powerful. They can discover how to do this by noticing what they do that empowers others, and then applying those same tactics to themselves. For example, they sense what the other person really wants and encourage him or her to go after it. They add to what is inherent in the other person. Thus, turning it around, what project or direction gives *them* energy? What do *they* want to build? Once they know what it is, they need to feed themselves support and encouragement.

This is a lifetime to take their power back, to use it for themselves rather than giving it away or sharing it in ways that are not responsible to themselves. For example, if they spend their energy on charitable projects when they have trouble coming up with the mortgage payment each month, that's furthering the cause of another without first providing a secure financial base for themselves.

These folks are learning not to waste energy, whether in the form of time, money, or personal talents. They are learning to use their resources *consciously*. It's very easy to divert their energy away from building comfort and security. They may even distract themselves, spending time doing anything else, because they don't feel confident in doing things to fill their own needs. Yet when they approach it on a practical level and proceed step by step toward their goal, they gain self-assurance.

Taurus North Node people tend to be unwilling to give 100 percent of themselves. They hold back because they are afraid of failure and don't want to further undermine their sense of self-worth. Actually, if they do give 100 percent and don't attain their goal, they still feel good about themselves because they know they did their best. But when they hold back and fail, they're never sure: "If I really had done my best, would I have succeeded?" and that *does* undermine their self-confidence.

Sometimes the best thing that can happen to these folks is to encounter a situation in which they are *forced* to do their best. When it's all or nothing and they're forced to open up the valve all the way, that's when they truly get in touch with their own power. And tremendous self-worth is born from it.

Taurus North Node people are learning to recognize their own power— that it comes from within and is not dependent on anyone else. The idea is for them to do things that allow the power within to come forth naturally. Devoting time to projects that make money for them or provide comfort or security is empowering for them. They gain power when they have the courage to walk through difficult times and experience a positive outcome. They gain power when they communicate what is truly important to them, regardless of others' opinions, and see the situation turn out well. When they step outside of society's values and get in touch with their own values, they find their power every time they are true to themselves.

PRACTICAL APPLICATION

A SENSE OF PURPOSE

Taurus North Node people are the master builders. Once they learn how to take their time, work out each step so that it's solid, and not move faster than what feels comfortable, the things they build will last forever.

These folks' past lives revolved around the projects of others, so in this incarnation they are learning to make the decisions and steer the project. The strength required to see the project through will come from being clear about their purpose. If, with each step they take, they clarify their purpose ("What is my purpose in making this call? In having this meeting?"), it will help focus their direction and they will make steady progress.

One of their first jobs is to find a project that makes them secure and happy. If it's a financial project, their strength will be in seeing a public need and figuring out what they can do to fill the need that will also make money for themselves. Then, because it's *their* project, when they take responsibility their energy soars. And the energy that comes from success nurtures them and creates a positive feedback loop that helps them remain clear about their purpose and focused on their goal.

Owing to so many past lives of empowering others at the expense of their own self-worth, Taurus North Node people can be skittish about allowing the ideas of others into their world. But the fact is that now the tables are reversed: In this lifetime, after they have chosen their goal, they are supposed to allow others to help them. They tend to make the process of success unnecessarily hard on themselves. They think others are supposed to give them everything, support them, and take care of all their material needs; or they have to do everything on their own without any help. This "all or nothing" approach is neither accurate nor practical.

It is true that Taurus North Nodes need to earn their own success. However, once they have decided on a goal and are willing to put forth the effort to get there, step by step, then it is fully appropriate for other people to support them, empower them, and help them reach the goal. Others can make their route easier by opening up opportunities, pointing out pitfalls, broadening their approach, and helping them cover their bases in a practical way.

They shouldn't rely on the help of others, but they need to learn to accept it when it is freely offered.

A STEP-BY-STEP PROCESS

When Taurus North Node people see how far they have to go to reach their goal, they panic. All the work involved, the hurdles to overcome—how can they ever get there? So they pull back from their larger goals owing to fear of failure. It all seems too overwhelming.

Seen from their point of view, it would feel overwhelming to anyone! The only way long-range goals are reached is by breaking the process into individual steps. The idea of being a doctor is intimidating to a high school student. And yet, if that is a true dream, it's worth working through the hurdles. First the aspiring physician has to complete a four-year college education, then four years of medical school, then residency. It's a long process, but it can be accomplished in stages one step at a time. And the goal will be reached if each step is completed with total attention.

It's the same in an important relationship. If these folks meet someone who "rings their bells," the idea of reuniting with their soul mate is so overwhelming that they don't want to think about it; they want to jump right into it—and the result is disaster. What they dreamed of isn't accomplished because they tried to bypass the necessary steps. Sometimes when they think about their goal, they forget that getting there is solely up to them and their willingness to do the work. They can feel a lot of emotional intensity worrying about whether they are worthy of the goal.

But this is like looking at a mountain and wondering if they're worthy of reaching the summit, when the only thing that can *make* them worthy is actually climbing it. If they have the proper equipment, choose a realistic route relative to their experience and ability, and are willing to put one foot in front of the other, they'll get there.

Taurus North Node people are not accustomed to formulating a strategy for getting to the goal, since in past lives defining the steps was the responsibility of another person. Now they are learning to determine the goal they would like to accomplish (a camping trip for the family, starting a business, etc.) *and* to formulate a practical plan for achieving it. As they take the steps, they're very efficient and have a feeling of confidence that "it will work"—and it usually does as long as they systematically follow the steps.

Even so, it is not always easy for these folks to be clear about what they want in life. They may need a lot of self-reflection and soul searching to determine what they want to build. And when they do decide, it is important that they remember to tune in to their inner feeling of comfort as a barometer of whether or not a decision is "on path" for them. Regardless of what their mind tells them, if they have an inner feeling of discomfort about something and proceed anyway, they always lose. When they remain true to that inner sense of what is comfortable (which is a reflection of their own unique boundaries), everything works to their advantage.

Taurus North Node people need values and ethics to live by, a path they can walk step by step to achieve serenity. When they find spiritual principles they resonate with, their best bet is to apply them on a practical basis in their daily lives. They are much better off with application rather than theory. For example, 12-step programs are great for them (Alcoholics Anonymous, Adult Children of Alcoholics, etc.), as these programs focus on a practical, step-by-step approach to spiritual principles.

To build a solid sense of self-worth, these folks need to follow a path of doing the "right thing" according to what they feel is morally correct, rather than "going along" with the values of others. Their means of guidance may not always be the most pleasant; but if they follow it, it can lead them out of the dark—being lost without a sense of integrity and self-worth—into the Light. Shame or guilt may be an indication that they should re-evaluate their behavior. Regardless of the opinions of society, they know what makes them feel good about themselves. When they follow their own internal guidance system, a solid sense of self-worth is ensured.

MASTERING MONEY

From the charity work they performed in past incarnations, Taurus North Node people have gained the right to earn personal wealth in this incarnation. Charity work is natural for them because, in past lives, other people paid their bills. So they put their energy into things that were good for the community. However, in this incarnation it is better for them to pursue activities for which they are paid, since the process of earning money helps build their self-esteem.

These folks sometimes are too trusting with money. They know that "trusting the universe" is a principle that works. However, it is also true that "God helps those who help themselves." Trusting the universe does not mean avoiding personal responsibility and doing irrational things out of blind faith. If a friend says: "Will you loan me $3,000?" and $3,000 is all Taurus North Node has to cover his own expenses, "trusting the universe" does not mean thinking: "Well, I trust the universe, so I'll just give away my money."

Taurus North Node people need to accept responsibility for taking care of their own finances. Only then can they include others without fear of losing their personal power and self-worth. When they feel secure, they can trust the universe in a way that empowers them to see what life is offering.

TAKING CHARGE

To accept responsibility in terms of money and open the doors to personal wealth, Taurus North Node people need to deliberately begin paying attention to money: writing things down, keeping track of what they're spending and where their money is going. This is empowering: It enables them to channel their money in meaningful directions. Accumulating money is a game, for which these folks have a real talent. Once they put their minds to it, they can make a little money go a long way and can easily become wealthy.

Sometimes they feel resentful about having to take charge with money. They are angry about not having the "easier life" they were accustomed to in past incarnations. Yet it's healthy when they *do* take care of themselves: a steady job, a stable income, a savings account, and financial plans for the future. The idea is to create a secure financial base that will allow them to take risks in other areas. This gives them a feeling of ease and confidence about life and makes them feel good about themselves.

Although some folks do very well with inherited money, Taurus North Node people are not in that category. It's not to their advantage to be dependent on an inheritance, the financial goodness of others, or a state or federal assistance program. Any situation in which they are financially dependent on another debilitates their sense of self-worth. In this incarnation, it's crucial that Taurus North Nodes earn their own money and are paid for their energy.

If they have inherited money, it is in their best interests to use part of it to start their own business or in some way promote a cause that builds their sense of self-worth. If they are financially dependent on a spouse, it is healthy for them to start a small business of their own or take a job outside the home, even if they don't need it or it's "not much money." They need to build a sense of self apart from their connection with another person. Regularly setting aside blocks of time for working toward an individual goal or project that is important to them is another way to build their self-esteem.

If these folks are on a state or federal assistance program, they can begin taking side jobs to make money. If the Taurus North Node is a parent with children, perhaps she could start a child care service. The issue is not how much or how little she makes, but the sense of self-worth that is gained.

Taurus North Node people have a natural understanding of how money works and the necessity of circulating money. Their challenge is to circulate it *consciously*. Once they start using it to build with, they can become very wealthy. In past lives they were so accustomed to using other people's money that they lost respect for the value of money; they didn't have to earn it themselves. In this lifetime they are learning to respect money and to use it wisely in ways that help it multiply. Money is their teacher. Once they tap into their intuition of how money works, money itself will show them how to make more.

DEBT

Taurus North Node people may have a problem equating wealth with debt. I've had many clients with this nodal position who accumulated enormous debt owing to this misunderstanding. For example, I had one Taurus North Node client who, with her husband and another couple, started an innovative cosmetics business. It took off faster than anyone expected, and orders came in fast and furious! To keep up with the unexpected rush, my client borrowed against her credit cards to hire more employees, order more ingredients, and so on—until she had accumulated a debt of nearly $60,000.

Then there was a falling-out among the partners, the company collapsed, her marriage ended in divorce, and she was left $60,000 in debt. It took her ten years to pay off the debt. To do it, she lived in a cheap apartment, allowed herself no luxuries, cut out her social life, worked two jobs, and endured incredible stress and deprivation.

When the business first got off the ground, my client jeopardized herself by trying to respond instantly to an outside demand. She could have allowed the universe to unfold the business organically, using the profits to expand the business from its modest beginnings.

I had another Taurus North Node client who wanted to make films showing New Age encounter groups—especially those dealing with the emergence of new feminine and masculine roles in our society. She thought the films had a noble mission, and she "trusted the universe" to provide money for the project. She borrowed money (thereby accumulating an enormous debt) to make these films.

My client trusted that the money would be there because "the universe wanted the project to succeed." Her life became total chaos trying to raise more money, do the project, and come up with "delay tactics" in paying back the money she had already borrowed. Eventually the entire undertaking collapsed and she had to declare bankruptcy—for the second time in her life. This time, not only were the financial institutions hurt but friends and family who had loaned her money as well.

The accumulation of debt does not work for Taurus North Node people. They are master builders when they use common sense and don't take "leaps of faith" or try high-wire maneuvers without a safety net. But in some ways they don't respect money and tend to be careless about it. Although they don't think about it much on a conscious level, they have a lot of fears around money owing to lack of experience in providing for themselves financially in past lives.

Once these folks realize they have to deliberately be more conscious about money, they accept the responsibility. However, sometimes they lose control and go on a spending spree—buying something they don't need that they have to pay for later. In past lives, money was a tool for distraction. Thus, in this lifetime when they get bored they may have the urge to go shopping, with the subconscious feeling that they deserve it and someone else will pay. Rationally they know this is not true, but they almost can't help themselves.

Taurus North Node people can't stand feeling restricted financially. Yet the irony is that once they put their nose to the grindstone and accept responsibility for earning and budgeting, they can easily accrue the kind of wealth that will allow them to spend without worry. But once they have made it, they need to continue to be responsible about handling it—they are not allowed to be "unconscious" about money in this lifetime.

HEALING THEME SONG *

I have written a healing song for each nodal group to help shift its energy in a positive way, since music is a potent vehicle for emotionally supporting us in taking risks.

SEEK YE FIRST

The message of this song is meant to effortlessly shift the focus of Taurus North Node people toward turning within themselves to connect with the wealth of reassurance and peace in their own nature. Thus the bonding they need for security and a sense of self-worth can happen within themselves.

Selected lyrics:

> *My guy got sick, needed attention*
> *So I put on my nurse's hat . . .*
> *My heart fell when he called it "distraction"*
> *That's not where I was at!*
>
> *And I remembered:*
> *Seek ye first, the kingdom of heaven*
> *And I turned within—*
> *And before too long, my heart felt strong*
> *The outside got in order again!*
> *So seek ye first . . .*
> *Because inside of you's the kingdom of heaven!*

---

* These lyrics are set to music and sung in their entirety on the CD and cassette tape "Unfolding As It Should."

North Node in Gemini

and North Node in the 3rd House

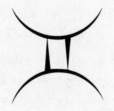

OVERVIEW

Attributes to Develop

Work in these areas can help uncover hidden gifts and talents

- Healthy curiosity
- Asking questions to learn how others think
- Seeing both sides of a situation
- Tact
- Logic
- Communication of internal dichotomies
- A positive approach to life and other people
- Purposely cheering up others
- Using a nonthreatening approach when expressing ideas
- Listening
- Openness to new ideas and experiences
- Seeking factual information before making decisions

Tendencies to Leave Behind

Working to reduce the influence of these tendencies can help make life easier and more enjoyable

- Self-righteousness
- Aloofness
- Assuming others know "where they're at"
- Thinking one knows what others are saying without really listening
- Needing to be right
- Espousing "Truth," without taking others' views into account
- Careless spontaneity
- Taking shortcuts
- Taking oneself too seriously; having a ponderous approach to life
- Acting on intuition without checking the facts
- Resisting ideas that are foreign to one's belief system
- Prejudging present situations on the basis of past experience

ACHILLES' HEEL/TRAP TO AVOID/THE BOTTOM LINE

The Achilles' heel Gemini North Node people need to be aware of is self-righteousness ("If other people would just acknowledge that I am right and appreciate me for it, I would feel understood and accepted"), which can lead them into the trap of an unending search for Truth ("If I have all the right answers, everyone will value me; then I can relax and feel connected to people"). But it's a bottomless pit: Since it's impossible to be "right" all the time, they never feel good about themselves. And when they argue and try to convince people that they *are* right, others don't want to connect with them.

However, if they have enough humility and openness to really listen to a variety of viewpoints—even those that don't fit with their previous experiences—they can get to know people in a way that helps them feel more connected. The bottom line is that at some point they have to release their preoccupation with absolute Truth and simply begin to relate to people as they are, listening to others and learning from them. The irony is that in the process of this more equitable and relaxed interaction, Truth is more successfully communicated. And when Gemini North Node people really listen to what is important to others, their responses are more appropriate and helpful. Then people *do* appreciate them and want to connect with them.

WHAT THESE PEOPLE REALLY WANT

These people really want to be totally free to pursue Truth, have adventures, be spontaneous, and be right 100 percent of the time. They want to speak completely from their Truth and their intuitive processes, and to have everyone understand them, learn from them, and appreciate their help.

To attain this goal, Gemini North Node people must stop focusing on "their Truth" and begin to focus on the people around them. They need to listen to—and understand—the information that others share about their lives. When Gemini North Node people listen in this way, sometimes they have an "aha!" insight that is *exactly* the perspective that the other person needs. And because this information accurately addresses the other's problem, it will be gratefully accepted.

TALENTS/PROFESSION

These people have the ability (when they *listen*) to tune in to the specific thought process of others and supply information that allows others to view problems from an expanded perspective. Selling, writing, teaching, and communicating in all forms can bring them happiness as well as material success.

Gifts in the areas of philosophy and religion, and an innate awareness of ethics and morality, are also available to Gemini North Node people. They can use their spiritual and intuitive awareness to understand the thinking of others without losing their own Truth. However, if they involve themselves professionally in the pursuit of Truth or religion as a final aim, they may ultimately feel isolated. They are better off when they use their natural talents to deeply connect with others on a day-to-day basis.

HEALING AFFIRMATIONS SPECIFIC TO GEMINI NORTH NODE

- "This is a people-oriented lifetime."
- "I can slow down and take the time to connect with others."
- "When I tune in to how others think, I know what to say."
- "When I am willing to listen and learn about the other person, I win."
- "If I don't understand, it's okay to ask questions."

PERSONALITY

PAST LIVES

Gemini North Node people have had two very different kinds of past life experiences with one common denominator: the pursuit of truth. They have had incarnations where they pursued Truth on their own—as traveling sadhus in India, wandering nomads in the desert, hermits, or simple people going into the wilderness alone to learn nature's secrets. They have also had many incarnations seeking Truth as a collective ideal, becoming absorbed in religious organizations. Either way, seeking after Truth, spirituality, ethics, and enlightenment has motivated their entire lives, and society and human relationships were neglected.

THE PHILOSOPHER

These folks have had many incarnations as Philosopher Kings. Lifetime after lifetime, whether Buddhist, Hebrew, Moslem, or Christian, they left everyone around them to pursue Truth. This is why, in this life, they still tend to leave everyone and go off on their own. All throughout their previous incarnations they sought enlightenment—climbing to the top of the mountain to reach the pinnacle of Truth. But after so many incarnations with the same focus, they found it! There's no need for them to continue the search in this lifetime. In the end, on their mountaintop, they became isolated and lonely. Now, in this lifetime, the challenge is to share their Truth, rejoining society and staying connected with others.

Self-righteousness can be Gemini North Nodes' biggest stumbling block to effectively relating to people and feeling the peace and love that are inherent in true connectedness. As they were philosophers and priests in past lives, other people followed their instructions. They are used to being regarded as always being "right" without question, so it is understandable that they enter this incarnation with a certain arrogance. However, other people can sense this superior attitude, and this prevents them from listening to the Gemini North Node person. As a result, Gemini North Node people start to feel that other people are undervaluing their intelligence because they won't listen. This is an example of how they suffer from a communication problem.

COMMUNICATION PROBLEMS

Due to the loneliness and isolation of their past lives, Gemini North Node people may seem like they can carry on hours of conversation all by themselves. They may remember to ask the other person a generalized question such as "How's it going?" but if the other person turns the attention back on them, they take the opportunity and run with it. They can go on and on about everything that's happening in their lives, recount their memories, tell a dozen stories and emerge the hero in every one . . . without the other person adding a single word to the conversation. Never getting a chance to interact or share his or her own story, the other person loses interest in the Gemini North Node person.

After so many lifetimes of being lonely, these folks feel a need to talk constantly. They are not comfortable with silence because they associate it with isolation. Now they want to relate to other people; so if there's a silence in the interaction, they feel like there's a "problem" and will talk about anything simply to fill the void.

They are learning that conversation is a process of skillful interaction: It has to do with sharing one's point of view with a sensitivity to how the other person is hearing it, inviting response, and being open to feedback. These folks need to remember to shine the spotlight on other people from time to time, asking them questions about their lives and sharing a point of view about the others' lives that might be helpful. If Gemini North Node people keep the spotlight on themselves for too long, they lose the energy the other people add to the interaction. When they feel this loss of energy, it should signal them to let the other person talk. Conversation is like breathing—an inhale *and* an exhale; Gemini North Node is learning that both people should have a chance to participate regardless of which person is the focus of attention.

For example, when telling someone about a confrontation they had with a co-worker, they could say: "What do *you* think about that? Do you think I judged the situation correctly?" After the other person responds, they could ask: "How was *your* day? Was it peaceful or did you also have confrontations?" If they think the other person doesn't want to talk, they need to check it out by asking: "Would you rather not talk about this, or do you have something else on your mind?" To keep the vitality going in a conversation, both people must be actively involved. Once these folks get the idea of how conversation works, they become experts at it.

Gemini North Node people are learning to see communication as a vehicle for curiosity—wanting to learn about the other person. They need to welcome input from others because, when combined with their own ideas and insights, it can produce a truth that is more powerful than either "truth" by itself.

Sometimes these folks appear combative. They think they have something important to say and are afraid that they will not be understood. So they put a lot of enthusiasm and energy into the communication to be sure they get their point across. They can become so fiery and adamant that others may feel attacked and respond defensively. Then, because the other person appears to be resisting their communication, they may become even more adamant until the interaction escalates in an irrational, overly emotional way. But they need to recognize that it's their *presentation* that is being resisted, not their point of view.

Gemini North Node people have a tendency to speak in a very direct manner—delivering their opinion as unalterable Truth—and any discussion of their Truth can lead to an argument. They may actually enjoy this and consider it a stimulating interchange of ideas, whereas the other person may see it as an empty battle of wits. This can keep them from interacting with friends on a daily basis, because people get tired of the battle after a while. Gemini North Node people need to learn to pull back and listen more carefully to the other person. They need to recognize that their strength is in clear quiet thought, not emotion. Their insights (when they have heard the correct question) are often powerful, accurate solutions, and when they speak them in a nondramatic way, the power of the idea can really be heard.

These people need to credit the intelligence of other people and trust that they will recognize Truth without it being jammed down their throats. Gemini North Node people are learning the importance of replacing impatience with respect if they wish to truly get *their* point across and connect with people successfully.

Another reason these folks are so ardent in the delivery of their ideas is that they want acknowledgment that their Truth is "right." It validates their self-esteem and helps them to relax to know that their viewpoint is accepted. But these folks need to recognize that Truth stands on its own merit and doesn't need energy from their egos to propel it, or fanfare to signal its accuracy. In fact, the more quietly Truth can be delivered, the better, so that the other person feels the serenity to receive it. Regardless of how noble their motive is, these folks may not use the fiery energy of personal ego to enforce their point of view. Others simply won't listen.

PATIENCE AND FRUSTRATION

Gemini North Node people are learning to be patient with themselves and others in working out glitches in communication. They're not used to talking. After all, they've been on mountaintops; what do they know about communication? It's as though they're speaking Latin while the people around them are speaking English. They need to have patience and slow down, take a few extra moments to translate, and really listen to what the other person has said.

Most of their problems in communicating are caused by inappropriate responses, which stem from not really hearing what other people are saying. Here is a simple example: Gemini North Node has a friend working in a booth at the County Fair who needs to count out exactly 100 apples. As she's counting—"67, 68, 69, 70 . . ."—people keep stopping by and interrupting her, and she loses count. Well, the friend has a problem, so naturally the Gemini North Node person will magically show up because he is a person with all the answers! The friend says: "These apples are for the County Fair. I need to count . . ." but the Gemini North Node person will hear the first few words and not the rest. He assumes he knows what the problem is, so he drifts off. He "comes back" when he notices the other person has stopped talking, but since he never truly *heard* what the problem was, he is likely to give an inappropriate answer: "Oh, don't worry about it—apples are two for a quarter down at the fairgrounds!" The friend will be irritated, because she had a genuine problem and wasn't given the answer she needed. And the Gemini North Node person will be frustrated because he went out of his way to help and his friend didn't appreciate it. Both people lost.

Instead of getting frustrated, the Gemini North Node person needs to stop and think: "Okay—since she didn't accept my answer, that means I didn't communicate effectively. Perhaps I didn't fully understand the problem." He needs to return to the friend with an apology: "Gosh, I'm sorry—maybe I didn't really understand your problem. Would you tell me again?" The friend will appreciate that he cared enough to come back, and when they start communicating again: "I need to count 100 apples for the fair," the Gemini North Node person can listen carefully and see the problem accurately. Then he may suggest: "Well, why don't you make ten piles of ten apples each?" Instantly the friend will be relieved: "Thank you! That's the answer I was looking for!" When the other person gratefully accepts the answer, there is a "high" for both parties and both people win.

BEARERS OF TRUTH

Often, these folks don't realize the full impact of the messages they deliver. In the above example, the friend may go home that night and suddenly realize: "You know, that's the reason my whole life doesn't work! I have it all jammed together, and what I need to do is to organize it into smaller segments that I can deal with!" Gemini North Node people must never judge any subject to be not worth talking about. If someone is sincerely interested and seeking information, these folks should always try to help the other person find it. Gemini North Node people are bearers of Truth, and in helping others find the information they seek, they often reveal a larger Truth.

"Freedom Tapes"

In past lives, freedom was very important for Gemini North Node people—to discover their Truth they had to be free. Now they have "tapes" in their subconscious that say over and over: "I've got to be free; I've got to be free." But in this lifetime, listening to such tapes is not to their advantage. If they're in a relationship, really understanding what the other person is saying and creating tremendous rapport, and all of a sudden "I've got to be free; I've got to be free" comes on in their mind, they will pull themselves out of the interaction. Then they go off by themselves and think they will feel free, but instead they feel lonely (one more mountaintop!) and say: "What's going on? There's no energy here at all."

But it's healthy for these folks to go back and say: "Gosh, I've changed my mind." This is not a lifetime where they have to be right all the time. They need to be honest when they have two different responses to something. For example, they may want to stay in a relationship and at the same time fear that by staying they won't be able to do what they want to do. At that point, Gemini North Node people need to honestly communicate their dichotomies: "To tell you the truth, I've got two things going on here. On the one hand I want to stay, on the other hand I'm afraid that if I get really close I won't be able to do the things on my own that I need to do." Or with their children they might say: "I understand what's going on with you and that you need a lot of space, but we need to have a certain amount of discipline in this family to make the unit work." When they share both sides of the issue, the answer will present itself. The person will understand what they are saying and come into alignment with them.

Just being aware that they have "freedom tapes" is a big part of resolving this issue. The tapes are like a muscle in the subconscious that got over-exercised, and now it's going to assert itself at the most inopportune times. So if they tune in to where the voice is coming from, they can *choose* to not take it too seriously.

INTERNAL CONFLICTS

DOUBTS AND FEARS

In many past lifetimes as spiritual counselors, mentors, or advisors, Gemini North Node people have had to be in positions of certainty when others expressed doubts and fears. Their subconscious tells them: "You're supposed to know all the answers." Their goals required complete faith and trust; so in this lifetime, their subconscious tries to invalidate any fears or doubts that come up.

They tend to rationalize by comparing themselves to others in ways that invalidate their own feelings. For example, a Gemini North Node person may say: "You know, I'm really not happy in my job . . . but I don't know what I want to do right now . . . and I'm lucky to even *have* a job! And *nobody* likes their job!" These folks present themselves as having it all figured out. They won't say: "I have no clue what I want to do with my life." They'll say instead: "I'm planning to go to law school" and then give six reasons why they're doing it. They'll even list the disadvantages: "I've already thought about the negative side of it, but I think that's what I want to do." When they present themselves to others as having all the answers, this attitude cuts off—rather than invites—the communication, interaction, and sharing that could provide them with new information and insights.

They are hesitant to elicit the ideas and opinions of others because they don't want to feel weak—they don't want to face the fact that they actually don't have all the answers. Because they are afraid that the other person is going to tell them something they don't want to hear, they inadvertently converse in a way that discourages others from having any input in the conversation. These folks also fear that true communication with others might expose something deeper about themselves, which would allow their fears, doubts, and inner confusion to begin to rise.

LIVING IN SOCIETY

Gemini North Node is learning that in society there is freedom of choice. Not everyone is following the same set of rules. As each one of us pursues our individual pathway, it's okay to be uncertain and have doubts and to have the humility to ask others for their opinion—in fact, it's encouraged.

Cooperation empowers people to use their talents to express themselves, achieve their desires, and do things that benefit not only themselves but other people and society as a whole.

On the mountaintop Gemini North Node people were on their own, but in society we all have strengths and weaknesses. Folks get together and share information—the plumber knows about plumbing, the lawyer knows about law, and so on. However, Gemini North Node people are not accustomed to seeking help. They think it shows a lack of intelligence. Yet society operates from the basic assumption that *nobody* knows everything. We're all in the same boat, so the person with the most expertise directs the ship.

Gemini North Node people may isolate themselves from the comfort and camaraderie of interdependence because they are resistant to other people telling them what to do, especially if the others seem to know less about Truth than they do. However, in this incarnation they must learn to live successfully in society—and there are plenty of people who know more about that than they do! Gemini North Node people should remember that humility is beneficial because it allows them to listen to and learn from others. They need to find out how to "be themselves" and still be a coopera- tive part of society. Moreover, humility allows them to learn that Truth is a universal energy that can come through anyone, so they should be open to all points of view.

DUALITY

These folks are learning to accept duality: the contradictions in others and the duality of their own natures. By pursuing only Truth in past lives, they became isolated from the experience of being human. In this incarnation, their mission is to learn about human nature all over again.

Planet Earth runs on the principles of yin and yang, night and day, cold and hot, receptive and creative, female and male—seeming opposites that make a whole. Gemini North Node people will better understand life, people, and situations when they see the "flip side" of the coin. They are still learning to see, accept, and be interested in both sides, rather than take the attitude that "It's just a coin; big deal." Rather than discounting inter- nal conflicts, they are learning about the peace of mind that comes from honestly and lovingly accepting the contradictory parts of their own nature. Therefore, Gemini North Node people shouldn't worry about having the total picture. It's okay for them not to "know"—in fact, in this lifetime it's *preferable*! Thinking they already know everything blocks their openness to new information that might improve their understanding of the situation.

These folks are also hesitant to tell people things because they project that others don't want to hear difficult truths. So when someone tells them "I left this job," "I broke up with so-and-so," or "I decided not to go to law school," then the Gemini North Node person will say: "I didn't want to tell you, but I never liked him." Or, "I didn't think law school was a good idea for you." The other person may say: "Why didn't you tell me a long time ago?" But these folks are afraid of hurting others by "speaking the truth." They need to recognize that simply expressing *their own opinion* might be helpful to the other person.

However, the motive behind offering their opinion plays a vital role in how their advice is received. If their motive is to offer love and support, the other person will feel their good intention and be open to their input. But if their motive is to be judgmental or to be "right," the other person will respond defensively. If Gemini North Node people truly want to *help,* the interaction works smoothly. They should offer their perception as another point of view, a gift of caring, and let the other person figure out whether or not it's right for the situation at hand.

OPTIMISM

Gemini North Node people have a tendency to blind optimism that can lead them to jump into things without thoroughly checking all the facts. Sometimes they intuitively feel that someone is being dishonest with them, but they may override that feeling with high hopes for great returns and the attitude that "everything is going to work out." When they become aware of this imbalance, they need to force themselves to acknowledge their other options. This will restore their self-confidence.

When they recognize that they are not in a logical situation, they need to fall back on their own strength. But they don't always feel capable of handling things. They tend to blindly trust people they feel are better able to take care of themselves in the real world. And because they are trustworthy, they project that others are trustworthy as well—and this can get them into a lot of trouble.

These folks *should* rely on others to help them; however, they should not do this blindly. Their challenge is to understand the people around them, and not to trust just anyone out of fear that they have no other choices. They need to listen to the other person's words, and because Gemini North Node people are basically truthful, they can tell when others are not being truthful with them.

INTEGRITY

Gemini North Node people don't necessarily expect the people they're with to tell them the truth. They think that other people work from some other point of reference where it's all right to be dishonest, tell white lies, hide money, and so on. And since they themselves would never do these things, they feel that others are operating from a lesser level of integrity. Once again their past life experience with its strict moral code comes into the picture, and these folks have a tough time dealing with what they perceive to be the "dishonesty and games" of other people.

These folks need to recognize that their function is to reinfuse spiritual ethics and Truth into the mindsets of others. If they cast others as being "wrong" for not being "moral," naturally others will resist their insights— no one wants to feel like a sinner! So they need to support people in integrating the spiritual path into their daily lives. At the same time, they must be open to other views and temper the rigidity of their own position.

When Gemini North Node people give their word, they keep it—it's a matter of morality to them. And they expect those around them to play by the rules both parties have agreed on. When other people talk about doing something and then don't do it—for whatever reason—these folks can get extremely upset. They want the initial agreement to be acknowledged, and they want to be consulted about any changes.

For example, if they agreed to clean the attic with someone and then something came up, they would say: "We said we were going to clean the attic today, but it's looking like we're not going to have time. Is everybody okay with that?" They hate things to be said and then not followed up on.

Yet they don't know how to bring this trait to other people's attention—they don't want to upset the others or have them deny that the discrepancy is happening. It can be an area of serious confusion for these folks.

When such discrepancies occur, it is usually for one of three basic reasons:

1. It may be the result of an initial misunderstanding that the Gemini North Node person let pass without clarification, even though he didn't feel good about it at the time. If he has to clear up something from the past, he needs to stay with the facts of the situation: "Yesterday I heard you say _____, and now I hear you say _____. I don't understand the discrepancy. Will you please explain this to me so I can understand better what you're saying?" If his motive is truly to understand, and not just wanting to make the other person appear wrong, this approach will work. Otherwise, the other person will become uncomfortable and respond defensively.

2. The other person may not have really said what Gemini North Node heard—there's a lot of miscommunication in these folks' lives. If Gemini North Node can remember the words closely, he can say: "Yesterday I heard you say _____. Did you *mean* _____, or did you mean something else?"

3. It is also possible that the other person felt strongly about a situation one day, and then—due to a change in circumstances, perception, or feedback—changed her mind and felt just as strongly in another direction the following day. Part of living in society is learning how to adapt and change direction in response to feedback from others. People put an idea out into the world, and depending on how others respond to it, the idea is continued or changed to best accomplish the goal. For example, someone might be convinced that advertising in Magazine A would increase business. Then, after getting

a limited response, he or she might be equally convinced that Magazine A was *not* a good advertising bet,
put an ad in Magazine B, or use an entirely different
media outlet.

Gemini North Node people might see these situations as discrepancies,
but they simply represent the process of intelligent adaptation to feedback
from the environment. From past lives in religious environments, these folks
are used to seeking eternal truths: absolute universal laws that never change.
But in this incarnation they are learning to move about in a social environment, and they need to have the humility to listen and learn about how the
rules work in this environment. Such recognition will also help them be
more open to others. Others' responses can help these folks determine
whether or not they are truly making a contribution and effectively adding
positive energy to the situation.

NEEDS

ACCEPTANCE AND SHARING

Gemini North Node people feel a sense of urgency about getting their point
across and being "heard." Underneath this urgency, however, what they
really want is to feel accepted. Acceptance is an accurate barometer for them
of whether or not they are "on path." When other people accept what they
are saying, it's a signal that they are communicating effectively. If others
don't accept their words, it's a signal that they need to pull back and recast
their message in words that the others can understand.

For these folks, truths are like sacred stepping-stones—the very foundations of their perceptions. They hesitate to share their truths because they
are afraid that others will think they're crazy or judge them for pondering
Truth instead of thinking about making money or other material concerns.
They want to reveal themselves to others, but their sacred Truth is so
intangible that it's difficult to talk about directly, and the other person often
loses interest. Then Gemini North Node gets frustrated because he doesn't
know how to communicate his philosophy in just a few words.

It's like walking into a dentist's office with a toothache. The patient wants to know: Shall we fill the tooth, pull the tooth, cap the tooth, or do a root canal? She does not want the dentist to tell her about all his experiences in dental school. Because all the years the dentist spent studying support his view of what should be done with the tooth, the patient will feel the learning behind his simple, factual opinion. Likewise, Gemini North Node people need to learn to answer the immediate need of the other person, giving what may seem to be a temporary or simplistic answer rather than an entire philosophy. This is what is scheduled to work for them in the present incarnation.

Truth is an energy, not a concept. These folks are actually seeking the energy of Truth, but they need to remember that it is not scheduled to come in a ponderous way. As they exchange ideas with others in order to solve problems in their daily lives, they will get in touch with the Truth they are looking for. When they help others break through even a superficial problem or misunderstanding, the energy of the Truth will come through and everyone involved will share resolution and peace of mind. In this incarnation, Gemini North Node people are scheduled to access the Truth through simple, daily interactions and genuine connections with others.

STAYING IN THE PRESENT

HERE AND NOW SOLUTIONS

Gemini North Node people have a tendency to be so concerned with distant, overall solutions that they don't allow themselves to feel the joy of the moment. They are still looking for "eternal truths." However, in this incarnation they need to be more concerned with "here and now" solutions and recognize that if they (and those around them) are happy in each moment, the moments will add up and the happiness will last.

The same is true in their business affairs. They can be so concerned with the "larger picture" that they lose sight of how to create an immediately successful situation. They need to be more aware of time, budgeting their projects into specific blocks for completion, instead of feeling that they have "forever" to handle material concerns.

For example, I had a Gemini North Node client who owned a duplex rental property. When one of his tenants moved out, some minor plumbing repairs were required. Rather than handle that and rent it out again, he decided it was a good time to do a thorough plumbing overhaul. Then he decided it would be a good time to shore up the foundation—which required a major expenditure of time and money (which he didn't have) as well as lifting the house off its present foundation ("in order to do a thorough job"). He kept thinking that somewhere down the line (these folks always think in terms of eternity!) it would have to be done, so he might as well handle it now. Since he didn't have the resources to finish the job immediately, the vacancy continued for month after month. When the family on the top floor moved out, he expanded the project to include the upstairs plumbing ("it would have to be done eventually"). The property had been completely vacant for nine months when he came to see me; due to lack of rental income, he was in danger of losing it.

These folks are learning the value of temporary solutions, handling problems when they arise and not projecting too far into the future. Otherwise, they lose the strong foundation that provides a base for future expansion. Life on planet Earth is temporary—eternity only exists in consciousness. They need to shorten their view and put their current affairs in order. They need to look at all the salient *facts* of a situation—the upside and the downside—and use their *logic*.

SENSE OF PURPOSE

While in some areas of life Gemini North Node people are too patient, they simultaneously try to take shortcuts in other areas. But illogical shortcuts always result in more work in the long run because these folks will have to go back, slow down, and do it all over again. They rush to get everything and everyone out of their way so they can be "free" for more important things. Often this inner restlessness is associated with feeling lost. In fact, they *do* need a purpose to give their life direction. However, it's up to them to define that purpose—and it has to be more than the pursuit of Truth. They must have an individual, "in the present" purpose that connects them to society; until they define that purpose, they will feel lost. This is one reason these folks change jobs so frequently. If their current occupation doesn't satisfy their inner sense of purpose, they have no qualms about leaving and trying something completely new to see if it "fits." They are willing to go through as much formal education as it takes to prepare for the job they think might "do it" for them.

The search for "purpose" that calls Gemini North Node people is a carryover from past lives of seeking Truth. But in this lifetime, their purpose is to learn the process of connecting with society. For example, if they're sitting at a table with four people, these folks are great at the beginning of the conversation. But if they're with the same four people day after day, they become nervous. They think they've already said everything they had to say. Indeed they did, but they haven't heard what others had to say in response—and that's the next step! These folks need to *listen* to others and learn how to build on their responses so the relationship can grow. This kind of sharing can generate tremendous energy that leads to new realms of mutual discovery. When the four people at the table have new experiences, they have new insights to share with one another.

CHANGE

Gemini North Node people have spent so many lifetimes "trapped" in religious organizations concentrating on Truth, that in this incarnation they resist limiting themselves to only one thing. They are starved for worldly adventure: to taste life; to experience different kinds of relationships, different occupations, and different places. They are hungry for the benefits of living in the world.

Yet they can be envious of people who settle down to just one job, marriage, or lifestyle. They wonder: "Wow! What would it be like to just completely put myself into one life choice?" But their subconscious knows that when they were dedicated to one thing life got pretty boring, and they can't do it! In this lifetime, they need to have plenty of options to keep their lives interesting and to keep the energy moving.

The potential drawback of always seeing life as an adventure is that it can give them a superficial experience of the people they encounter. They tend to miss out on the others' depth—their history and character, how they arrived at where they are now—they just share an adventure with them and then move on. But only when they take the time to find out about other people will they experience the connectedness and peace of mind they are seeking. Thus, it is to their advantage to slow down and be patient with those around them—taking the time to ask the other person questions and really connect.

SPONTANEITY

These folks love to be spontaneous—it makes them feel light and happy! Spontaneity works for them sometimes, but it can also be a hindrance in more intimate relationships. For instance, they have a tendency to try and get together with others at the last minute, and often the people they want to see are not available. It would be to their benefit to recognize that a lot of people live with more planning; if they really want to get together with someone, they need to let that person know in advance. Often they figure if that person can't get together with them, it wasn't "meant to be."

These folks prefer spontaneity over planning because they don't know in advance if they're really going to want to be with a certain person. They prefer to be free to go in any direction—wherever the energy is and wherever their sense of adventure takes them. But they are learning that there are times when their love of spontaneity doesn't work for them, such as in business matters or when dealing with people who don't choose to play on a spontaneous wavelength.

RESTLESSNESS

Gemini North Node people are somewhat restless. But from past life training, they still have the ability to focus 100 percent on whatever occupation they are in—even if it won't be long term. For them, this is healthy. They feel they can't afford to spend this whole lifetime on any one thing, because it's through a variety of experiences that they are learning how to live in the world.

However, sometimes they get "stuck" in a profession. They may be successful and make a good living, and on one level they're satisfied. Yet they know the best time to make a change is when they're feeling really good about themselves and when everything is going well. Since this is a lifetime of learning and growing, and of gathering and dispersing information, they think that if they don't voluntarily make a change when it's time, life will assist them in making changes. Yet these folks don't lack boldness. They usually have the self-confidence, optimism, and trust in life to take the gamble and make the change themselves.

Often the changes Gemini North Node people make are based on intuitive knowing. They have a sense of the next adventure that they need to experience. Although their intuition guides them, they also need to consider the logical route to follow in making these changes, including others' input. Otherwise their journey can be a lot more difficult than necessary. This is not a "do it yourself" lifetime for them—they need input from people who have had more experience operating in society to help them reach their goals.

These folks must be wary not to get "bogged down" somewhere because of their tendency to be more thorough than the situation requires. They are learning to be content with a "temporary fix" rather than the permanent solutions they sought in past lives. In society, everything is continually changing. The idea is to keep life moving in a positive direction by operating in a helpful way with other people. If there is no motion in their life, they need to lighten up and solve their problems in logical ways that may be suggested by those around them. That will bring back the energy!

Solitude used to bring Gemini North Node people comfort in past lives, but they know that this is incorrect for them now. That's why they're coming back to society: to bring that internal harmony they found by themselves into their interactions with others. They're learning how to *maintain* that harmony while being in relationships with others, to extend the harmony outside of themselves.

But they are so introverted socially that this is difficult, and they're trying to evolve just through their *internal* computer. In other words, they aren't asking questions of others; instead, they're trying to formulate some kind of continuity through the thread of connectedness that, in past lives, they firmly established within themselves—the thread of inner peace and harmony.

Now they have re-entered society, and they are trying to maintain that inner peace while interconnecting with others. This is why temporary, superficial relationships can sometimes be good for these folks. By only going to a certain depth, they can more easily maintain their own sense of harmony when they are with another person. Once they learn how to do it on a superficial level with many different people, they can learn how to get more deeply involved and still maintain the energy and harmony.

SLOWING DOWN

Gemini North Node people feel they have so much information to give to others that all the messages to be delivered seem like a burden. Yet their lives are not operating at the same speed as their past lives when they were traveling alone. They need to slow themselves down. After all, this is a people lifetime.

If these folks try to take shortcuts, they will end up taking the long way around because they will have to go back and repeat things. They should keep in mind that right where they are is where they're supposed to be, and the person right in front of them might be the one who needs to hear their message. This can greatly relieve the pressure they feel; but if they're going too fast in order to get to the *next* person, they won't effectively deliver the first message, and the weight of it will still be with them.

Another problem is that Gemini North Node people feel a responsibility not only to *deliver* the message but also to see that the other person *understands* it. In a way, this is correct. They are Teachers in this lifetime, and their job is to deliver the message in a way that others can understand. But if impatience takes hold of them, they inadvertently try to force others to receive the message rather than slowing to present it in the other person's own "language." They need to focus on the fact that twelve messages effectively delivered to a dozen people is worth hundreds of messages that are not understood.

RESPECT FOR WORDS

More than any other nodal group, Gemini North Node people have a tendency to stutter in their youth. This is because their minds are traveling so fast and they've had so many lifetimes of silence and meditation that they're not used to talking. Their minds are going ten times faster than their vocal apparatus. They're enthusiastic to communicate because they haven't been in society for so long and they're happy to be part of it again, yet they're fearful because they don't know how to relate. All that can contribute to a tendency to stutter. Once again, slowing down to meet another person's "wavelength" facilitates transmitting a lot of information in a short time with fewer words.

Stuttering can have a useful purpose in other ways. It forces these folks to find alternative words in case their first choice doesn't come out right. This makes them more aware of slowing down and accurately saying what they mean: It teaches them to respect words and the art of using them to pinpoint exactly what they mean. By forcing themselves to use exact words to convey their meaning, these folks are channeling their highly creative mental energy constructively in their relationships with others.

They have so much mental energy that if they don't have respect for the power of words, the result is frustration. It's very important for them not to blurt things out; taking the time to find the correct words channels their energy and gives them the focus they need. They know exactly what they want to say, but it can be difficult to make themselves understood. These folks see others communicating clearly, and they don't know why they have so much trouble. In fact, they enjoy movies with interesting, involved dialogue, since they learn from watching what people say and how they say it.

The most important thing for these folks to remember is to "slow down." They need to be sure that what they say is being understood by all concerned, point by point, rather than blurting out a series of ideas before the first one has been accepted. For example, if they say: "I have not had happy experiences in foreign travel," they should pause and see how those around them respond. If others invalidate their statement by pointing out how much fun the Gemini North Node should have had in Tahiti, they need to stop and clarify what they said originally.

Perhaps they could say: "I'm not saying that foreign travel is unpleasant for everyone, but it's not where I, personally, have the most fun." No one can invalidate another's *personal* experience, as long as they make it clear that they are not saying it is the truth for everyone. After taking the time to clarify the first point, they may realize that they can learn from others' different experiences. They may ask: "What have your experiences of foreign travel been like?" These folks are better off when they try to see how others view life in order to expand their own perceptions.

TIMING

Gemini North Node people are learning to think before they speak. They are also learning how important it is to wait for the proper timing to make their point. Even if Gemini North Node offers the other person the perfect answer to a problem, it won't do any good if that person is not ready to receive it. And if the other person is not receptive, these folks need to let it go until the next opening presents itself. They should focus on rapport and goodwill, which they can offer only if they have no personal investment in the communication. When they are invested in the other person accepting and acknowledging what they have to say, that investment translates into an intensity that defeats them and may seem like preaching or combativeness to the other person. These folks are caring people who want to help, but sometimes their greatest caring shows in their willingness to support the other person—even in moments when that person does not seem to understand them.

RELATIONSHIPS

NEED FOR FREEDOM

Gemini North Node people feel a tremendous need for freedom in this incarnation. If this drive is prompting them to meet new people, it is healthy for them and will result in an increase in their vitality. However, if the urge for freedom is based on listening to their "freedom tapes" or running away from the challenge of connecting with others, the result will be restlessness and loneliness.

FEAR OF CONNECTING

When others "push their buttons" and upset these folks, their reaction is to turn off completely and retreat to their "mountaintop." They feel it makes them weak to connect with people, and subconsciously they fear being deeply understood by another person. Also, it's frustrating for them to go through the work of sharing their truths. Although truth comes all too easily to them, they have great difficulty translating it for others in a way that can be understood and appreciated.

Since Gemini North Node people are learning how to listen to others, asking questions is a good habit for them. Being a good listener is all about asking questions and being interested in the other person's life; when these folks are engaged in this process, they are happy and peaceful. They have a fear of deeply, genuinely connecting with others; but when they *do* it, the feelings of acceptance and completion are deeply satisfying. They can reconnect with the tranquility they worked so hard to attain in past lives.

For success in close relationships, they need to start by admitting they have been in a "cocoon." They need to rise above fear and declare their intention: that they want to come out of the cocoon to connect with the other person—not only on the level of hopes and dreams, but also fears and doubts. Then when they reveal themselves in conversation, they can truly be honest. They will not just share their buoyant, optimistic outlook about the way things should be—they will share how life really is for them on a day-to-day basis and talk about their own challenges. Being receptive to others can really help them achieve victories in their daily lives that they could never have accomplished alone.

COMMITMENT

Most of these folks want to "settle down" in a permanent, committed marriage relationship, but one part of them simultaneously fears this kind of permanence. They want to be free to grow and change, move around, and do different things. If they could connect with another person who has the same temperament, they might have the best of both worlds. But if they enter a relationship that limits their freedom, it generally doesn't work out.

Gemini North Node people do not relate easily to the word "commitment" in their relationships. What they are committed to is the thread of Truth and harmony within themselves. They do not want their philosophy tampered with, and they are not sure how to become fully committed to another person without merging their beliefs. They feel their truths are what make them who they are. However, they can live with a person of dissimilar beliefs as long as both people are open and accepting of each other's philosophies.

These folks are also reluctant to do anything that limits their interactions. They are learning how to relate and how to reintegrate themselves into society, and they need to experience a lot of different people in order to expand their awareness of how to do this. They want to bring the awareness of Truth and that feeling of inner harmony into society, and to expand that thread of continuity to include others. As they "practice" with different people in different situations, they gain more confidence in their ability to maintain their own inner happiness while interacting with others. Then they can allow people to get closer, because they know they'll be able to maintain their harmony.

Thus, for Gemini North Node people, entering a committed relationship can take longer because they lose their inner sense of peace if they go too deep, too quickly. Marriage or a commitment that would restrict them from interacting with others is actually counterproductive to their larger goals. They need a partner who supports their need to move through society. They need a lot of "in the field" experience to fully manifest their potential. This does not mean that monogamy is counterproductive for them—it is the need to interact *mentally* with a variety of different people that must not be limited.

ACTING ON ASSUMPTIONS

Of all the "tricksters" in their subconscious, the one that most often sabotages relationships for Gemini North Node people is the tendency to assume. When they act without gathering facts or sharing information with others, they set themselves up for disappointment. When in doubt, they need to talk to the other person and listen without judgment. When they assume others know that "all is well," they often get into trouble. When they check things out on a daily basis—finding out how the other person is and giving information about how they are—they will be much happier. To experience successful relationships, they must go out of their way to keep the lines of communication open.

LACK OF COMMUNICATION

When these folks are in a relationship, they tend to assume that others know what they are feeling and experience what they are experiencing. For example, I had a client who spent an absolutely beautiful, perfect night with a man. He never contacted her afterwards, and she assumed that he had experienced something different than she did. But the fact is, she doesn't know! There could have been a hundred reasons why he didn't call her: He may have lost her phone number; he may have been in another relationship that he hadn't completed; something may have come up that he had to take care of first and then he felt embarrassed to call after so long; or her conclusion may have been correct. But her best bet would have been to pick up the phone, ask him how his life was going, share with him how much she enjoyed the evening, and find out why he didn't call her. These folks need to apply some of their faith in positive outcomes and take charge of creating positive results in their own lives.

When they're in a relationship, Gemini North Node people often don't call the other person for extended periods of time. If they're going through anything negative or are unsure of something in their life, they don't want to get in touch because they don't want to have to say: "Actually, my boyfriend just left me," or "They took my credit cards away." They want to wait until they've "got it together" so they can share the positive—they don't want to communicate when they're not at their best.

Naturally, a lot of people interpret this lack of communication as a lack of interest. These folks have lost in many a romantic relationship due to lack of communication, when the other person assumes they aren't interested and gets involved with someone else. If they are truly interested in maintaining a relationship, they cannot assume the other person knows that "all is well." They need to pick up the phone or send a card on a regular basis to maintain the connection. If they are going through a period of doubt or uncertainty, they could communicate that: "Well, I hesitated to call you because I'm not ready to see you right now. I need to complete some things in my life, but I wanted to let you know I'm thinking about you and I wanted to see how you're doing."

If there's a misunderstanding, these folks need to take responsibility for straightening it out. They might also find it helpful to alert others to potential problems: "Sometimes I don't hear what people say because my mind jumps ahead. If you think I haven't understood you, please let me know because I want to communicate clearly with you." Gemini North Node people can be thinking something and assume it has been understood by other people. It's a shock to these folks to find out that the way *they* interpret the world is not the way everyone else interprets it. It's essential for them to double-check with others and be conscious of verbalizing what is on their minds. If they tactfully make others aware of their various thoughts and ideas, they will find their relationships shifting in new and positive ways.

COMMUNICATING FEELINGS

When Gemini North Node people take the time to accurately share their point of view about their own personal experiences, others are deeply moved. As a result, Gemini North Node people experience the joy of acceptance and empathy. When they share things without having to be "right" or prove a point, the results will be heartfelt. To reach others on a soul level, they must speak the truth about what they are experiencing.

For example, I had a client with this nodal position whose girlfriend made some unexpected charges against one of his credit cards at a clothing store. He confronted her, and even though he already knew it involved clothes, he wanted her to confess what she had spent the money on. When she said "household items," he became so obsessed with making her tell him the truth that she ended the relationship. These folks hate lies, and they tend to respond with self-righteous indignation when they think they have been lied to. However, in this case the man's response was also not the truth. He should have said: "There's something I'd like to discuss that's very important to me. I found some unexpected charges on my credit card, so I checked to see if there had been a mistake. There were three credit slips for clothing with your signature on them. You know I've always been generous—I want you to have nice clothes—but I feel hurt and betrayed because you didn't ask before using my credit card."

Then, from that honesty, the next level of truth could have emerged. By putting forth the facts and his honest feelings, he would have opened himself to see her character more accurately. Either she would have changed to be in greater ethical alignment with him, or he would have seen that she was an inappropriate partner for an intimate relationship. These folks have to give others a chance to grow ethically. They can open space for this only by being willing to act with integrity themselves—honestly revealing their feelings instead of trying to force the other person to be truthful.

SELF-RIGHTEOUSNESS

Gemini North Node people have a strong resistance to other people's "truth"—especially the people they deal with on a daily basis. This can be one of the reasons why people feel they have to lie to them—these folks may not really want to hear what is going on with the other person. But their disinclination to listen can result in painful misunderstandings with those they care about most.

Even though they say they want "the truth," they become upset when others tell them. But if they don't really want to listen to the truth, it will have the effect of encouraging people to lie to them. No one wants to be "made wrong," and these folks can be so self-righteous about who is right and who is not that others don't want to be around them.

Gemini North Node people are learning to value happy rapport with others above the compulsive pursuit of philosophical Truth. This also requires that they suspend judgment. When these folks judge another person, they are not taking into account the other person's code of ethics. To understand this person better, these folks need to ask questions: "What did you study in school? What was your first job?" These folks have a tendency to see things so much in the present that they assume people's lives have always been the same—yet it's fascinating to them when others share what brought them to their present circumstances.

If they are seeking "truth"—or factual accuracy—from another person, they should always be very clear with themselves first about their own motive. Is it to learn about the other person and help that person reveal himself or herself more clearly? Or is their motive to "be right"? If their underlying motive is to listen, they will win; if their motive is to be right, they will lose.

Gemini North Node people must grant others equality if they want them to communicate honestly. And honesty evolves—it doesn't necessarily happen in the first few encounters. As these folks allow people the space to become more honest with themselves, the honesty they are seeking will emerge. In personal relationships, they need to communicate how important honesty is to them in a constructive way that does not alienate the other person. For example, they could begin in subtle but clear ways: "We have more fun when we are honest with each other than we do when we are trying to deceive each other. Honesty brings us closer together and helps us accept each other."

COMMUNICATING DICHOTOMIES

If these folks force themselves to give someone a yes or no answer when actually there's a conflict going on in their own minds, whatever they say will be a lie because the truth is that they haven't found the answer yet. So the "answer"—and the correct thing to communicate to the other person— is that they can see two alternatives and don't know which one to choose. Once the other person understands this, the Gemini North Node person can experiment with one path and keep the option to choose the other if it doesn't work out.

For example, I had a client with this nodal position who was offered the choice of working in an office or at home. She wanted the peace and solitude of working at home but was afraid that if she didn't go to the office her level of productivity might drop. She needed to tell her boss exactly what she told me: "I would like to work at home, and keeping my productivity level high is very important to me. So I would like to experiment with working at home, and if my productivity level drops, I would like to come back to the office."

In this incarnation, it's perfectly fine for Gemini North Node people to change their minds. They were not allowed to do this in past lives, so they have a sense that they are supposed to say: "*This* is the way it is." But now they are learning to see more options, and as they get more information they will naturally alter their course to take advantage of the new input.

So when these folks express their decision (or their opinion at the moment) they should try not to present their views too rigidly, so that they have the option of changing their minds. Instead of saying: "This is incorrect and it's always going to be incorrect," it's better if they say: "This is incorrect. I might change my mind, but this is the way it appears to me now." Their views may change, so it's okay for these folks *not* to have a final answer.

ROMANCE

VARIETY

Gemini North Node people have the karma of connecting with a variety of different people: nerds, jocks, high school dropouts, college graduates. The people they get involved with are a mixed bag. Sometimes they wonder who their "type" is because they relate on a surface level with all these various people! When they gain a greater sense of their spiritual identity and figure out how to share messages with people, being with so many different kinds of people begins to make sense to them. When their "truth" is bounced off so many different surfaces, they can see it in many different ways. This helps them know when a concept is really "right," and they gain joy from seeing that concept work through the varied perceptions of others.

For example, they may ask themselves: "What is 'Poor'?" Then they watch people who are financially poor and discover that in some cases, being poor gives a person better values than if they were rich. Their exciting discoveries stem from their openness to compare their ideas with what is actually going on in the environment. The harmony they seek comes from integrating the other person's views with their own truth. Their challenge is to acknowledge an energy that *encompasses* variety.

When Gemini North Node people begin experiencing their sexuality, their tendency is to seek a variety of people to interact with. They have been deprived of the warmth of human relationships for so many incarnations that they can be like a kid in a candy store: They want to try it all! Actually, in their case and within reasonable limits, this is not a mistake—especially during their early years. They are learning how to relate with others while maintaining and sharing that thread of Truth within themselves. Variety can help them learn to share it without losing it.

These folks have a well-developed sense of integrity from past lives and would never say anything to mislead another person. They don't say "I love you and I'll stay with you forever" with the motive of getting the other person under the covers. However, due to guilt from their religious training in past lives, they are plagued by a voice that says: "I know this is wrong—I should only be with one person." There may come a time when that path is correct for them, but that decision needs to be based on maintaining their truth while they are with the other person without allowing themselves to slip into isolating self-righteousness. When dating a variety of people, they are charming and maintain their "good behavior" to keep the connection progressing. When they can retain that same "good behavior" while being with only *one* person, then they are really on track.

While they are still in the process of dating a variety of people, their motive needs to be clear. If they are only trying to ease their loneliness through sex, the result will be temporary satisfaction that night, but an exaggeration of the empty feeling the next day. To avoid that destructive cycle, they need to keep expanding their mental connection with the other person as a foundation for physical intimacy. They should establish an emotional connection prior to a physical relationship. Then the physical interaction will be a joyful expression of that truth, and they won't feel empty or guilty.

OBSESSIVENESS

Gemini North Node people can be obsessive in their attachments to others, particularly in romantic/sexual relationships. If they become overly committed to one idea or one person, they should deflect their obsession in order to regain a peaceful, constructive state of mind. If they are obsessed with an idea, they need to consider another point of view to balance their thinking. If they are becoming obsessive about another person, they need to find a platonic friend to spend time with as a balance for the more intense relationship. Then they can create success in the primary relationship. Realizing they have options always works for them.

Conversely, these folks can also go to the extreme of nonattachment. In this lifetime, they tend to want to be the Philosopher King again—but when they get to the top of the mountain, who else is going to be there? One of their most dangerous obsessions is the tendency to internalize their thoughts, which causes their relationships to become secondary. They can fail to even acknowledge other people because they are too intensely focused on their own thought process. "My thoughts are so justified, so meaningful." They may totally disregard other people's input, and that's where they can really be hurt. They won't find the variety they need if they aren't open to the viewpoints of others.

Gemini North Node people need to learn to give greater weight to human relationships; they need to spend more time and energy getting involved with people, rather than focusing on goals. The people may in fact end up *being* the goal, if they can just stop overthinking.

SUPERFICIALITY

These folks are great with first meetings: the introductory small talk, the charm, the superficial connection. But they are like a professional greeter in a restaurant—they know how to make the other person feel welcome, say the first few lines that everyone will relate to, make the first gestures and smiles; but after that, they're lost. In a romantic situation they often get nervous and either go off by themselves or try to move things to the physical level right away. These folks are very comfortable with their bodies, so once they start connecting physically they feel at ease again. Unfortunately, if a mental affinity and mutual understanding haven't been established first, their sexual connections are often brief and only temporarily satisfying; they do not lead to deep and rewarding relationships.

These folks have had a lot of past lifetimes of high adventure, as well. When they were headed toward some mountaintop to look for Truth, an attractive person would come across their path and they would have a sexual adventure with them. But these folks weren't interested in settling down— they were in pursuit of Truth. To develop nurturing human bonds or take romantic relationships deeper would have been contrary to their goals. In this lifetime, such behavior leads to isolation, but these folks continue to run from deep connections with others. They want to be close to others, but they don't know how to do it. And this awkwardness can be very frustrating for them, especially in romantic situations.

However, Gemini North Node people need to know that they have a tremendous gift for making connections with people once they get the idea. The key is to become genuinely interested in—and curious about—the other person. How do they think? What is important to them? What are their interests? What message does the other person have for them, and what message do they have for the other person?

Conscious Interactions

Gemini North Node people have a tendency to be too direct, and this gets them into trouble. They need to remember to look more deeply at what they really want to convey, and then communicate in a responsible, sensitive way.

For example, I had a client who had been married for twenty-six years to a Gemini North Node husband. One day he came home and said—with no prior warning—"I've met my soul mate and I want a divorce." He had met this woman only two weeks earlier! The message totally shocked his wife. It took them more than a year of intense confrontation and soul searching to find out what the problems were that led to his drastic pronouncement. In fact, the encounter turned out to be a diversion—what this man really wanted was to revitalize his relationship with his wife. They had a good marriage based on mutually strong feelings of love, and as of this writing they are still together. He got what he wanted: His relationship with his wife was transformed. However, his wife has never recovered emotionally, and she is unable to completely forgive him for what he put her through.

Gemini North Node people are learning that when they speak without considering the effects, they can be unnecessarily hurtful to others. This is especially the case when what they say isn't really the underlying truth, but simply an attempt to hurt the other person or get attention. They must clarify in their own minds what they're feeling and *then* decide on the best way to say it. Is their motive to rekindle the relationship, or to make the other person feel guilty? Often, when these folks speak with harsh directness they are not really communicating how they feel. They need to focus on resolving problems in a more responsible way.

In the above example, rather than blurting out a conclusion he hadn't thought through in advance, the husband could have talked with his wife and said: "Look, a woman I am attracted to has come across my path. I haven't become involved with her yet, but I'm considering it because I'm so unhappy in our marriage." Telling the truth in a factual, logical way would have gotten him what he wanted—a revitalization of his marriage—without devastating his wife. They could have worked together to resolve the underlying problems in their relationship. And although they did end up staying together, the shock and anxiety were so great that the relationship was never completely healed.

Gemini North Node people need to put themselves in the other person's place and see what approach would make the other person feel comfortable. Using words with respect helps these folks connect in positive ways with other people; it is a key part of maintaining happy relationships.

GOALS

DELIVERING AND RECEIVING MESSAGES

Gemini North Node people are learning how to deliver the messages that they are meant to pass on, and how to hear the messages they need to receive. To do this most effectively, they must discriminate between the different functions of the mind and emphasize that aspect which promotes a factual, logical orientation.

INFORMATION VERSUS INTUITION

These folks have spent many past lives developing their philosophies and relying on their intuition. In their private, solitary search for Truth, intuitive knowing was their best guide. However, now that they are back in society, factual information will help them connect in a way that restores their inner peace. If they make decisions based solely on intuition, it almost always results in isolation from others. If they feel uncertain or upset about a situation, they need to seek more information. It's easy for these folks to misunderstand, and they are quick to feel rejection when none was intended.

However, if they have a strong intuitive feeling about something they should not just push it aside. Their best bet is to take the time to ask questions that will ease their mind: "I heard what you said, but for some reason I have an uneasy feeling about this. I want to get some more information so I'm sure what I'm getting into." These folks always benefit from gathering the information that gives them the reassuring, warm feeling of "truth" inside.

LOGIC VERSUS SPONTANEITY

In this incarnation, making decisions based on spontaneous impulses does not work for Gemini North Node people. If they have a spontaneous urge to get on a plane and go to Peru, they need to stop and consider the idea from a logical base. Decisions made from a logical base, rather than from trust or high hopes, will work out best for them in the long run. In this lifetime, Gemini North Node people cannot take shortcuts without taking all the facts into account.

These folks are also learning the value of applying logic to daily situations. For example, if one of their truths is a belief in the value of friendship, they need to hold their goal in mind—"creating friendship"—and then logically observe what kinds of behavior create friendship. How does a friendship develop out of a casual acquaintance? What common denominators exist in successful friendships? Logic will tell them what behaviors work best to create the friendships they seek. Above all, logic is *soothing* for them. It provides them with a sequential process through which things can work out, and this is calming for them. When they use logic, they feel connected and see how they can maneuver effectively through society. In new situations, Gemini North Node people can deal with their anxiety by logically strategizing how to proceed, because planning gives them the feeling of continuity that they need.

LISTENING

Gemini North Node people are here to circulate the energy of Truth through society. When they are unable to spark another person to see a higher truth, it's often because they're not listening to what that person is really saying. They aren't responding appropriately. When they accurately perceive where the other person is coming from in the conversation, then they can match their words and timing to connect with the other person on his or her level to translate their truth so the other person can hear it. When they respond appropriately, the feeling of disjointedness will evaporate. This requires patience on their part. It also requires them to be sufficiently excited about the possibilities in the potential connection to invest the time and energy.

But sometimes these folks are judgmental about who is "worthy" of their patience. The irony is that they have the capacity to create true communication with almost everyone they meet! They are accustomed to looking for people who are also seeking Truth, but in this lifetime they cannot speak exclusively with other philosophers. They need to listen to everyday people: the mail carrier or the clerk at the grocery store. There is an endless variety of people they can connect with and they must find those for whom *they* have messages.

But they have to trust the universe to bring the right people to them. Whenever there's a miscommunication, that's the person with whom they need to have patience. Miscommunication is a red flag for these folks, signaling them to slow down and pay attention to whoever is right in front of them.

DIPLOMACY

The main purpose for Gemini North Node in this lifetime is teaching. When others are not aware of the importance of Truth on a daily basis, it gives these folks an opportunity to gently teach what they have learned. The operative word here is "gently" . . . or "tactfully," "lovingly," "diplomatically," "humorously," or "sociably." They need to share their message in a way that does not cast the others as "wrong." Then the others will not feel defensive and will be able to successfully receive the message.

Gemini North Node people are naturally helpful; when they see someone in trouble, they are among the first to offer assistance. However, their tone of voice and their delivery can sound like "preaching" when they don't realize that the certainty behind their ideas has a self-righteous quality. They truly want to give the other person the answer to the problem at hand. But they are learning that even if they do have the solution, the other person won't be able to hear it if their delivery is offensive. Just like trying to give medicine to a child, coating it with sugar makes it easier on everyone. These people need to learn tact: how to package their ideas in a brief, informative way that others are willing to swallow.

SEEKING ADVICE

Gemini North Node people are reluctant to seek advice, because they fear it will show they are unsure and they think they already know what the other person will say. Actually, the other person may tell them something totally different from what they expect, and it may be the very thing they need to resolve their quandary! Other people can indeed help these folks to see things from different angles and give them an opening for new insights.

They are always surprised to discover that others are aware of what's going on with them even though they haven't divulged the fact that they are having a problem. They think if they show an optimistic face, others will accept that everything is fine. In truth, others are often quite sensitive to these people's moods and may have just the piece of information that will be helpful.

EXPANSION AND INTEGRATION

EDUCATION

Formal education is good for Gemini North Node people, and they enjoy acquiring new knowledge and new information. This kind of broad learning helps them to see the "big picture" and puts them in touch with the way society thinks. It offers them structure and exposes them to various points of view, which keeps them from remaining stuck in their own "truth." Reading also enables them to practice seeing life from the perspective of someone else's mindset. These folks are like empty hard disks on a computer: They are hungry for information. They like their reading to cover many different subjects; otherwise they might get bored with it. As well as expanding their knowledge, reading gives them a variety of subjects to talk about with others, which makes them more confident in their ability to relate.

NEW ENVIRONMENTS

It's healthy for these folks to put themselves in situations where they are surrounded by different people, because each one teaches them something new about themselves. They often see things in a moralistic or spiritual way, so they are willing to take lessons from others to heart. New situations force them to question who they are and what they believe in. So they have to start meeting people, asking questions, reading: in other words, doing everything they can to learn about each new situation. It's another chance for them to see the world from other people's points of view.

If Gemini North Node people try to settle down and avoid personal growth, something will happen externally to propel them toward a new challenge. Since "the writing is on the wall" in this respect, it's wiser for them to *choose* to go where their intuition is pointing and willingly move through life. But these folks can be stubborn about learning the lessons they are scheduled to master. They need to be aware of this tendency and be *consciously open* to changing—so as to avoid the unnecessary mental or physical pain of getting a "wake-up call." When they choose change, the new situations motivate them and put them back into the flow of life.

WRITING

One of the best ways Gemini North Node people can experience the integration they're seeking is through the process of writing—a journal, books, articles, etc.—on a regular basis. The physical process of taking pen in hand and writing down what they are thinking *grounds* them in a confident, stable way. Writing calms their internal restlessness, releasing the tension and anxiety in a form that brings them peace.

These folks are extremely talented writers, although they may not recognize this until much later when they look back over what they have written. They have an ability to clarify thoughts on paper in a simple way that actually communicates far beyond the words. Also, when they begin to write about their problems or experiences, it focuses their subconscious and the answer they were looking for comes through them and onto the page!

Writing is a tremendous release for them. If they are upset with someone, or feel misunderstood, one of the best therapies is to write the other person a letter. Even if they never send it, simply writing it makes them feel much better. They can even write: "It's been a tough day—I feel so stressed out." The simple act of writing down whatever they are noticing in that moment will discharge some of that intense mental energy. In this way they release heavy mental stress and open themselves to solutions that bring them peace.

For these folks, writing can even be a good profession. There's so much flexibility and room for growth that it can be the "one thing" they are looking for. They needn't rely on a corporation or a structure; they can be anywhere and be themselves and do their life's work—and that appeals to them.

SPEAKING

Gemini North Node people are so used to silence that in large groups they may be shy about sharing their message—yet they can make the very best of orators. After they have listened to the ideas of the other group members, they may notice a discrepancy between what is being stated and what is actually going on. In this case, it is their job to share the truth of their factual experience. They may feel such energy and passion, that they aren't sure they've said the right thing. But if they are compelled to say something to put things into alignment, they should go ahead and share it.

The key for successfully doing this is to first acknowledge that they have heard and understood what the other person said, and then respond positively about it to validate the other person (for example, "You spoke eloquently, with heartfelt sincerity, with courage," etc.). It can also help if these folks use the other person's own words to form a connection with them. As long as they first acknowledge what the *other* person has said, the other person will be able to acknowledge what *they* say.

TEACHING

In this incarnation, Gemini North Node people are here to teach. They are here to bring the Truths, principles, and practical application of ethics into society. They understand universal law and want to help others learn to apply it in practical ways in daily situations.

They are learning that Truth lies behind the words, and that they must listen carefully to others' words in order to understand the questions that others are asking. If they let go of their ideas of Truth and really listen, they will automatically tune in to the other person's belief system and spontaneously say—through a sincere question or a new piece of information—those words that will shift the perspective for both of them to a fresh recognition of Truth.

When Gemini North Node people view themselves as teachers, rather than as philosophers, their entire experience of sharing Truth shifts and becomes a total joy for them. As teachers, they don't expect others to know what they know, which gives them more patience in relaying their messages. When they assist another person in discovering his or her own truth, they experience harmony and share the warm feeling that comes when Truth is present.

As teachers, these folks have to divorce themselves from prejudicial viewpoints and allow the other person to think freely, without trying to guide the other to a conclusion that's identical with their own. It's the difference between a true question and a rhetorical question. A true question prompts the other person to answer in harmony with his or her own *inner* truth, whereas a rhetorical question maneuvers the other person into reaching certain pre-established conclusions. Rhetorical questions do not work for these people; true questions and logic are gifts that Gemini North Node people bring to help others find a higher level of perception. When they act as true teachers, these folks behave in a way that creates a win/win situation for everyone.

FITTING INTO SOCIETY

Gemini North Node people are learning to value human relations and the importance of maintaining goodwill in their daily interactions with others. They have a tendency to be so aware of their own Truth and their own aims that they are likely to forget the importance of treating others gently.

Drawing on their many lifetimes of spiritual truth, these folks can open the doors to honest, self-revealing communication. When they do, a feeling of timelessness blesses and enlightens everyone involved. The atmosphere is charged with what feels like a soul-to-soul communication. Afterwards there is a feeling of: "Let's celebrate tonight . . . let's cry and laugh over the past . . . let's plan and dream about the future . . . let's just *be* right now and share together." Gemini North Node people have the gift of opening an entirely new level of communication when they are willing to reveal their intimate selves—without having to be "right" or be the hero.

QUESTIONS

Questions are an invaluable tool for these people. It can be better for them to ask a question than to come up with the answer. If they're not able to develop rapport with someone, they should ask the other person a question (not a rhetorical question, but a true question), honestly seeking to understand what the other person is thinking. The other person will often stumble into his or her own truth in the process of answering the question, because Gemini North Node people have Truth in their energy field!

As long as their motive is to connect, the right way of communicating—what to say and how to say it—automatically becomes clear to them. Until they get the hang of it, this can be difficult and requires a conscious effort. They must force themselves to listen and to ask questions—and it can be hard for them to control that restlessness inside. Yet for Gemini North Node people, asking questions to gain more information is very important. It helps them feel "in the moment" and involved in the interaction.

The misunderstanding that causes difficulty for these folks is the idea that there are two kinds of talking: regular conversation in which people simply talk about their daily lives, and much deeper connections that can only occur while discussing a subject that is soul searching and significant. The irony is that Gemini North Node people can have *real* communication—deep and meaningful sharing with another person—without talking about life and death, philosophy, or major decisions. The connection can occur through talking about the simple things of life, but these folks must be engaged and asking questions. When they do engage in this way, they suddenly find that everyone wants to be around them—because it's such a joy for others to talk with them. In turn, they want to be around lots of different people because they enjoy the variety of experiences they can tap into.

However, the process involves giving up control. Gemini North Node people are very good with small talk, but if they ask a friend: "Why are you going to Chicago?" they don't know what the other person is going to say. That means they won't know how to respond. Because the other person is going to give them new information, they're essentially giving control of the conversation to that person. It feels good to them on one level, but they're always afraid they're not going to know what to say next! Yet when they do let go and allow the other person to control the conversation, what they want to say comes naturally, and their real selves come out in a positive way.

When these folks take a chance, release control, ask others questions about their lives, and remain open to connecting—somehow the connection happens. They can call on their natural trust that the universe knows what it's doing when it moves energy between two people. Ironically, they feel no fear at all when the other person asks *them* questions—it gives them a chance to share their truth!

Gemini North Node people want to achieve a higher level of interaction with the other person. They want to expand beyond where either could have gone on their own. But only through really communicating with others can new, expanded ideas and resolutions become apparent.

SOCIAL GRACES

These folks have been isolated for so long on mountaintops that they have forgotten the nuances of how to relate with others. They can be like a bull in a china shop, rushing to accomplish their purpose with a total lack of awareness of the delicate feelings of those around them. They are unaware of social graces and good manners because they are not used to living in society, where people generally get their way in a manner that evokes the support of others. Caring and taking the time to *not* alienate others is valuable, as isolation would create unnecessary obstacles to meeting one's needs. These folks are learning: Social graces will empower them to live in society and gain the benefits.

BODY LANGUAGE

These folks benefit by being aware of others' reactions and body language. They are often more intent on their message than on the effect of their words. They may say something and then notice that the other person looks shocked. Rather than let it pass, they should check with the other person: "I noticed that you just stepped backward. Did I say something that hurt or offended you?" If the other person says "yes," the Gemini North Node could say: "Well, my intention was not to hurt you, so I think we've had a misunderstanding. What was it you thought I said?" Nearly all the problems they have in relationships can be traced back to careless communication.

In this lifetime, these folks are learning about themselves and about what it means to be human. As they experience themselves in different situations, their understanding of human nature grows. Moreover, all their different life experiences teach them something about themselves. As they understand themselves more deeply and recognize the contradictions that are part of the human experience, they come to accept the different facets of their own nature. This opens the way to understanding and accepting the contradictions within others, and they are welcomed back into the family of humankind.

HEALING THEME SONG*

As music is an empowering medium for emotionally supporting us in taking risks, I have written a healing song for each nodal group to help shift its energy in a positive way.

BETWEEN YOU AND ME

The message of this song is meant to effortlessly shift Gemini North Nodes' attention from their own concept of Truth to the bond they naturally share with those around them. From that base, a joyous combination of mutual understanding and genuine connections with others becomes possible, and they can finally experience the energy of Truth they have been seeking.
Selected lyrics:

Between you and me there's a memory of trusting
And being let down in the end
Between you and me there is misunderstanding
Ready to come up again . . .

Yet—between you and me there's a magnet that draws us
Between you and me there's a path and a promise
Between you and me are the feelings that bond us
Between you and me—there is Love!

---

* These lyrics are set to music and sung in their entirety on the CD and cassette tape "Unfolding As It Should."

North Node in Cancer

and North Node in the 4th House

OVERVIEW

Attributes to Develop

Work in these areas can help uncover hidden gifts and talents

- Noticing and validating feelings
- Empathy
- Nurturing and supporting others
- Building one's own foundation and security
- Honest disclosure of feelings and insecurities
- Humility
- Accepting others' foibles and fluctuating moods without judgment
- Staying centered in one's own feelings

Tendencies to Leave Behind

Working to reduce the influence of these tendencies can help make
life easier and more enjoyable

- Needing to control everything and everyone
- Compulsion to take charge without fully
  understanding the situation
- Ignoring the process; being too focused on the goal
- Feeling completely responsible for everything
- Hiding feelings and fears in intimate relationships
- Doing things to gain respect or admiration from others
- Taking care of others' feelings and neglecting one's
  own
- Doing what is "socially acceptable" rather than what is
  totally honest
- Thinking that things have to be difficult in order to be
  important

ACHILLES' HEEL/TRAP TO AVOID/THE BOTTOM LINE

The Achilles' heel Cancer North Node people need to be aware of is their
need for control ("If only I can make them get their lives together, then I
can relax and be vulnerable"). But the truth is that they can never control
situations—or other people—enough to feel that it's safe to be themselves.
When they try to take charge of situations in other people's lives without
being invited, they are inappropriately usurping others' responsibilities.

The trap they need to avoid is an unending search for acknowledgment
("If only others will recognize my contribution in a respectful way, I can
begin to feel good about myself"). But it's a bottomless pit: Others can
never give enough recognition for them to feel satisfied. Only when they
acknowledge *within themselves* the importance of the contributions they

make (through nurturing others in a supportive way) will they begin to feel fulfilled.

The bottom line is that they will never have enough authority to feel that it's safe to be vulnerable. At some point they must take a chance and let others know the truth of who they are and how they feel: their insecurities, fears of rejection and abandonment, and feelings of inadequacy. The irony is that when they risk letting others see who they truly are, they finally gain total safety—because in revealing their feelings they've taken charge of themselves on a deeper level.

What These People Really Want

What these people really want is to be in absolute control of every area of their lives all the time. They have an insatiable need to think they have the power to succeed. To attain this goal, however, these folks must stay in touch with their feelings and insecurities and share the truth about themselves with others.

Acknowledging their insecurities will give Cancer North Node people a stable base from which to create success in the outer world, for they are no longer fighting themselves by trying to hide or suppress their feelings. This gives them a calm, inner certainty from which to accomplish their goals. And by acknowledging their own emotions, they will develop an awareness of other people's feelings. As long as they remain aware and supportive of other people, they will gain the support they require to help them on their own path.

Talents/Profession

Cancer North Node people have the gift of being able to nurture and support others; therefore, any profession that gives them the opportunity to nourish others (physically, mentally, or emotionally) is a joy for them. Good choices would include dealing with food (restaurants, hotels, hospitality, etc.), house repairs, and working in the home. They also do very well selling or investing in real estate. However, they must use their instincts in such investments and follow their "hunches."

Cancer North Node people also have a solid and accurate business sense and an excellent capacity for bargaining and shrewd negotiating. They instinctively know how to accomplish things and succeed in business. However, when their profession involves using only their business acumen, they are not happy because it is too "dry." Their profession should make use of their business instincts only as a backdrop to nurture others in a practical, financially viable way.

HEALING AFFIRMATIONS SPECIFIC TO CANCER NORTH NODE

- "When I try to control, I lose."
- "When I share my feelings, I win."
- "I win when I acknowledge the capacity of others to take charge of their own lives."
- "It's okay to let my feelings show."
- "It's okay not to manage everything all the time."
- "No one can invalidate my feelings."

PERSONALITY

PAST LIVES

DEPRIVATION

Many Cancer North Node people have had past incarnations in highly structured monasteries, convents, or other places where they were participants in strict, community-oriented religious environments. They were separated from the normal flow of family interactions. Because of limited experience with interdependence, dealing with people's moods, and acceptance of their own and others' natural human urges, they lack the instinctive ease of family relationships that is common to the other nodal groups.

In past lives these folks were trained to repress their feelings, instincts, sexual urges, and enjoyment of the physical senses. Abstinence and discipline were foremost, and deprivation of the joys of being human was rewarded with respect and promotion. In this incarnation they still tend to put up a wall between themselves and easy, earthy interaction with others.

They are accustomed to postponing the pleasure of life, and often postpone-ment leads to permanent denial.

These people have a "lofty goal," and everything else is put on the back burner until that goal has been realized. A feeling of righteousness is at-tached to this goal, and they do not allow themselves to be distracted by human temptations. The only problem is that the goal is perpetual, an endless quest arising from the subconscious desire to achieve spiritual heights. However, because the goal is insatiable, these folks end up con-stantly striving, with no time for relationships, fun, or really *living*.

Cancer North Node people have been trained throughout past incarna-tions to suppress their "feeling" (that is, emotional) responses to life to remain focused on the higher purpose they were serving. But their hearts long to connect with the rest of humankind. They yearn to belong and experience a sense of family with those they love—but they feel awkward. They have had so many lifetimes of disciplined training that they don't know how to do it—they're ashamed to let their feelings out. Their insensi-tivity to others is a product of their ingrained insensitivity to their own feelings. However, in this incarnation, repressing their feelings in the name of a higher purpose is contrary to the direction their souls need for comple-tion and fulfillment.

RESPECT

In past lives these folks achieved positions of public authority, social promi-nence, and prestige. They were feudal lords, politicians, businesspeople, and heads of households. Cancer North Node people functioned as "the boss"; they managed others and took responsibility for behaving in a way that epitomized social correctness.

Owing to many incarnations of enjoying the spotlight, they are still looking for their audience! Respect is important for these folks. They tend to act from a motive of seeking respect from others. They make tremendous personal sacrifices, stand for principles they believe in at the expense of their own personal needs—and still get no respect. They're accustomed to being in authority, yet now no one is following their directions—and they can't figure it out. They become frustrated because they don't understand what is happening, and over time this can harden their hearts.

In reality, their accomplishments stand on their own merit and are their own reward. But Cancer North Node people are subconsciously seeking recognition for the nobility of their sacrifices. This makes completing any task unnecessarily difficult. If they simply release the need to "get credit," they can reach their goals and enjoy personal pleasure along the way.

This lifetime is simply not scheduled for them to win respect for making personal sacrifices. When they use respect as a barometer of whether they are "on path," they get "off track" every time. In past lives, respect was a valid indication for them. But they played those public roles and held positions of authority in so many lifetimes that they became lonely and isolated: so much responsibility and so little personal nurturing, over and over again! Now their birth chart is set up to *not* allow them to put accomplishment, respect, and honor above other more personal aspects.

Cancer North Node people need to pay more attention to organizing their lives in a way that meets personal needs as well as long-range goals. In this lifetime these folks don't have to maintain an image for others. In fact, as they work to reach their goals just because it makes them happy to do a good job and because the work fills a public need—whether it's for their own family or the entire world—the recognition will be there. But if they go looking for it directly, it takes them off track.

They are still masters of accomplishment. But if their motive for accomplishment is to gain the respect of others, they will never be happy with what they obtain because their need for respect is insatiable—they never gain enough to be satisfied.

Ironically, the key to satisfaction for these folks is to learn to *give* respect rather than *demand* it. When success in any area comes too easily, these people tend to become ego centered and carried away with their own importance. They may become careless and unwittingly push away the very prize they were so eager to obtain. It is essential for them to greet success with humble appreciation. This will slow them down and put them in touch with the energy of new beginnings. They need to learn to honor this time—the new relationship, the new job, the new opportunity, the new home—and to treat the initial stages with tender awareness. This will create a solid foundation upon which success can be built. Once they slow themselves down, they are naturally aware of the correct way to do this.

When Cancer North Node people consciously respect and honor something beyond themselves (the opportunities life brings, the people who help them, etc.), a shift in their orientation occurs and they approach people with a new attitude. They treat them with care, attention, empathy, and meticulous clarity—creating a situation that is positive for everyone involved. Rather than seeking to gain respect, these folks need to orient themselves to giving respect. If they are able to do this, their lives will shift in a magical, mutually nurturing way.

GOAL ORIENTATION

For the sake of reaching an important goal, these folks will sacrifice without complaint. Hard work is not foreign to them. They are perfectly happy working 12-hour days, foregoing personal pleasures and postponing relaxation. Moreover, they will personally see to it that the job gets done successfully, regardless of the effort required. However, they are used to being in authority, and as a result they like to delegate details as soon as they are in a position to do so. It's not that they look down on "detail" work; they simply want their attention clear so they can focus on the larger goal.

Cancer North Node people are masters at achieving goals. The talent is so innate that it is almost subconscious. When they have a goal in mind, they are continually alert for opportunities. They view everything as a stepping-stone to the goal. However, if they do not have a goal that they can commit to, their natural abilities are likely to degenerate and the goal becomes one of controlling others and maintaining the status quo.

These folks need to be more clear about what they want to achieve to keep from subconsciously manipulating others in an attempt to avoid getting what they *don't* want. To do this, their past-life goal orientation can be used to advantage. For example, if they are renting out a house and don't want the rent to be late, they can tell the tenants what they *do* want: "I'll do everything I can to make your living here enjoyable; the only thing I'm inflexible about is that the rent must reach me by the first of each month. If I don't make the bank payments on the first, we're all in trouble. So I have to have the rent payment by the first—is that acceptable to you?"

In job situations, if they don't want the employees to be late or slack in their duties, they can make an impression by saying: "Look, we're all a team here. If we don't do a good job, the company won't make a profit and we'll all be out of work. This is the structure we're going to follow to make sure we achieve our goals so we all prosper: Everyone comes to work on time (etc.)."

Because in past lives Cancer North Node people were rewarded for attaining goals with high social status, in this lifetime they may have a subconscious desire to choose goals that will bring them prestige rather than ones that are truly the desires of their own hearts—and this gets them into trouble. In this lifetime they must redefine what is truly important to them. Their devotion to purpose is fine, but not if it's at the expense of their relationships; otherwise, when they reach the goal they will not be happy. This is why they need to put their own needs above "performing" for someone else. It's time to release their image. Attempting to gain respect through "role playing" for others costs them their own satisfaction and emotional well-being.

MANNERISMS

SERIOUSNESS

In this lifetime, Cancer North Node people tend to take everything very seriously. Because they have carried the "weight of the world" in past lives, they come into this incarnation feeling like they're shouldering grave responsibilities. They are drawn to people and situations that trigger their powerful urge to take charge, and they end up feeling totally responsible for the fates of everyone around them. Even as children, they often take on the responsibility for the well-being of one of their parents, usually the mother. They are born "old and serious"—even taking jokes seriously; usually only later in life do they realize it might be to their advantage to "lighten up."

With their serious demeanor, they inadvertently send out an energy that causes others to think they are unapproachable. Much of this is due to past lives in which they *were* unapproachable, and they continue to subconsciously project that attitude. Now their manner makes others see them as aloof, "on top of things," and not needing or wanting anything from anyone else. However, once you get past the "keep away" exterior, you find that they are very vulnerable and down-to-earth. Unfortunately, the people who could most deeply appreciate Cancer North Nodes for who they really are can be "put off" by their cool exterior; sometimes Cancer North Nodes end up attracting social climbers and less genuine folks who want to manipulate them. Their deepest longing is to feel close to others with whom they can relate on a genuine level, so it is to their advantage to recognize and release the aloof attitudes that keep others at a distance.

These folks are learning to take life—and themselves—less seriously, but this is not easy. They are attached to the serious approach, thinking it will help them to accomplish their goals. Actually, it may surprise them that they get the job done more easily when they are not so serious. When they lighten up and take a more playful, open approach to life, it balances their energy and they actually become much more effective. Others want to "go along" with them—and they have a lot more fun!

INSENSITIVITY

Owing to past lives of being in authority, Cancer North Node people are accustomed to taking charge. It was their responsibility to see that the fields were tilled or that the business was successful, and others depended on their ability to reach the goal to ensure everyone's survival. Therefore, they tend to rise to positions of authority, see how to achieve the goal, and then delegate tasks to others without always taking the time to explain the importance of everyone's role.

These folks often are so focused on reaching the goal that they forget that true success is based on more than just running promotions or bringing in accounts. The people who are helping them can't be treated like objects. Cancer North Nodes must take the time to understand the other person's situation and forge an emotional connection. The other person will support their goals if they have taken the time to show interest in that person. For example, rather than chastising an employee for being late, it would be to their advantage to ask what's going on at home—is something causing the employee to be repeatedly late? They have to continuously remember to put themselves in the other person's place and treat the other with sensitivity, the way *they* would like to be treated themselves.

Cancer North Node people hate to look as if they're not "on top" of everything, but they often feel inept at handling emotional upsets. They discount the importance of feelings, viewing them as a distraction from getting the job done. When their own moods interfere with achieving practical results, they judge themselves harshly. When other people's problems interfere with getting the job done, they may judge them harshly as well. This makes them seem uncaring and makes it difficult for others to relate to them.

Sometimes Cancer North Node people respond to their frustration at not knowing how to handle people by "blowing up"—which overpowers and invalidates the feelings of everyone involved. Others become afraid to be themselves around these folks, because people never know what might trigger Cancer North Nodes' anger. Others "walk on eggshells" until Cancer North Nodes can learn how to relate to people's feelings in new ways. These natives are discovering that all they need do is recognize and acknowledge the emotional upsets of others, in a caring way, and they will have healed the problem. Then they can help refocus the other person on the task at hand.

Cancer North Node people lack consistency in their sensitivity to feelings—their own and others': They are either hypersensitive or utterly insensitive. If they are conscious of emotional rapport with others on a more consistent basis, they will be less likely to speak or act in ways that hurt others' feelings and thus avoid situations that ultimately hurt their own feelings. They are learning to integrate a consistent awareness of feelings with the rest of their personality.

RESISTANCE

Cancer North Node people resist taking suggestions from anyone—they like to do their own thing. They're a little bit cocky because they think they already know everything. To earn *their* respect, someone has to come up with something they haven't thought of—and that makes a big impression on them. They feel they have finally found someone who can offer them something. When they do take a suggestion, it's when someone who is successful at something shows them how to do it. They only have respect for people who are doers—not talkers! This is one reason they are such good businesspeople. They are not distracted by others' ideas or lured by "get rich quick" schemes; they always look beneath the surface.

Perhaps because of their past-life religious values, Cancer North Node people are generally not victimized by greed. Once again, this makes them good businesspeople because they are not lured by promises of big returns with little investment. They are practical and willing to work hard, seeing how to reach the goal step by step. They have an accurate instinct and an innate talent for organizing all the pieces of the puzzle to realize the larger goal.

Because these folks are so innately goal oriented, when they face a challenge they figure out where they want to go with it before sharing it with anyone else. And they often become fixated on it. They want to make the decisions, because they are going to accept full responsibility for the results. It is also difficult for them to accept help from others because they think others don't grasp the whole picture. However, the best managers elicit feedback from others, factoring everyone's perspective into the equation before making a final decision. These natives must remember that no one sees all the possibilities, and life would be a lot easier if they sought others' input before taking action.

PRINCIPLES

THE WORK ETHIC

Cancer North Node people sometimes have difficulty managing others. They follow a strong work ethic, and they want others to live up to it as well. The problem is that by holding up themselves as the ideal, they don't bring out the best in other workers. People can never measure up; these natives are willing to commit "whatever it takes" to get the job done, and others simply aren't willing to do that. Others feel defeated from the beginning—they don't give their best because they know they can't measure up to Cancer North Nodes' ideal.

These folks have been in authority in so many incarnations that they came into this lifetime with a strong instinct to tell everyone else what to do. They have a very strong sense of rules, discipline, and goal orientation. For this reason, they frequently end up alone.

"The boss" often does end up alone—it's "The Buck Stops Here" philosophy. In past lives, these natives played the role of the boss so well that they lost touch with their own humanity and a sense of belonging to the world and with everyone around them. Thus, in this lifetime, their highest goal is to figure out a way to regain their connectedness.

To begin to feel connected and to bring out the best in their employees or co-workers, Cancer North Node people can experiment with many approaches. Most important, they can try to be a friend to others in the workplace—soliciting others' opinions, becoming interested in their lives, and taking the time to get to know them on a personal level. It doesn't seem logical to Cancer North Nodes, but getting to know their fellow workers will strengthen their business tremendously. Also, they could give others "a little slack." By giving others approval and noticing what they do well, Cancer North Node people feed others' positive energy. This includes acknowledging others' value and letting them know the job can't be done without them. Employees who are treated with respect are more inclined to listen and follow through when there *is* something they need to correct.

"MY WAY OR THE HIGHWAY"

Cancer North Node people have an idealistic view of how other people should perform. If others don't measure up, rather than pampering them or coaxing them along, these natives may decide they don't want them around—reflecting a "get it done, no excuses" attitude. They don't understand that most people don't operate in this way. These folks need to develop sensitivity to others' feelings—especially at work. They must be aware of their tendency to ignore feelings because of their own standards of performance, which are often very rigid. They need to allow people to *not* live up to those ideals; they are learning that others have their own methods of operation.

Sometimes, reacting to their frustration of not knowing how to stay in control of a situation, these folks become angry and walk out. Later, after thinking about it, they usually come back to make amends. They may apologize in some way: "I know I get short-fused, but once I get it out I'm through with it." Or they may try to make it up in some other way. It is healthy and valid for these folks to apologize when they have made a mistake or run roughshod over others' feelings. Making apologies is healthy because it gives them a new sense of humility and relatedness, and it gives others the insight that these folks aren't made of iron and can make mistakes. This endears Cancer North Node to others, so *any* excuse for a sincere apology is a good one!

Cancer North Node people have had lifetimes of assuming "ultimate responsibility" for getting the job done—so in this lifetime they must let others be responsible and have the experience of management. One way to accomplish this is by taking on the role of the person who has the need (which is a learning experience for Cancer North Nodes), presenting tasks as problems they need help with.

When they take a "My Way or the Highway" approach, it's because they don't really know how to find a middle road. They feel awkward. They don't know how to elicit a positive response. Because they already know all about goal orientation and goal achievement, in this incarnation they are learning to convey that knowledge in ways that empower others. Through this process their greatest happiness—and their own goals—are achieved.

COMMITMENT

Regardless of their role (boss, lover, employee, friend, etc.), Cancer North Node people are highly dependable—they always keep their word. They pride themselves on an unwavering devotion to taking responsibility and keeping commitments. However, in this incarnation, attachment to commitments can be carried to extremes. These natives make commitments when they are not even necessary and hold on to them even when it is no longer appropriate. They may sacrifice taking care of themselves and discount their own need for security simply for the sake of honoring a commitment.

For example, if they have agreed to attend a certain event, they are likely to show up even if they don't feel well and going out worsens their condition. Or they may remain in a destructive marriage rather than choose a nurturing relationship because the marriage was their original commitment. Their word is their bond, and they don't understand when other people don't manifest the same value. Thus, they are often afraid to make agreements with other people, for fear that they will be trapped once they have given their word.

The *idea* of standing behind their word is valid, but *attachment* to that idea may put them out of touch with their instincts and the natural Flow that brings experiences that are emotionally satisfying and promote their personal growth. Cancer North Node people must not postpone pleasure for the sake of commitment. When the two appear to be at odds with each other, they must rethink the situation, deciding what is most important for *them* to experience. Ironically, when these folks follow their instincts and go for what they truly want, the situation ultimately works out better for the other people as well.

NEEDS

EMOTIONAL VALIDATION

Cancer North Node people have a tremendous need for their feelings to be validated, to strengthen their awareness of feelings, and to give their own feelings a voice. These folks have come into this incarnation with the past-life habit of suppressing emotions. They may subconsciously set up their early environment so that it appears as though one of their parents is invalidating their feelings and discouraging them from letting others know how they feel. For instance, in the American culture nearly all little boys are told: "Be a man, don't cry"—but Cancer North Node boys take this *very* seriously. Their parents may give them a hundred different instructions, but this is the one they hear the loudest. (This is an example of how past life patterns are brought through the form of the present life to cause a resurgence of traits that must be balanced and resolved in this incarnation.)

RISKING VULNERABILITY

These folks must not neglect their personal needs or pretend their feelings do not exist. Their emotions have been repressed for so many lifetimes that now they constitute a huge mass of not-to-be-denied energy! Cancer North Nodes are scheduled to experience a personal life of caring and being cared for by others on an intimate level. Yet they've spent so much time suppressing their feelings that the idea of being emotionally vulnerable to others is frightening. "What? I should let others know how I feel? You've got to be kidding! Why should I expose my feelings and give others power over me?" They're petrified because they're accustomed to being in control. Yet honestly revealing their feelings is exactly what is scheduled to work for them. In this lifetime, in order for a rounding and softening of the personality to occur, their feelings must be validated.

Further suppression makes their feelings more insistent and more intimidating. The longer they avoid expressing their "feeling" nature, the more crippled they become. Cancer North Node people are learning to integrate their feelings with the other parts of themselves. One of the best techniques to do this is to walk through situations that are intimidating and experience the feelings that are evoked. In the process of acknowledging their feelings, the magnified intensity will dissipate.

The problem, however, is that Cancer North Node people have developed instinctive responses geared to avoid their feelings at all costs, so their emotions have become somewhat frozen. Life can be dry and boring, filled with outer achievements but devoid of inner meaning and satisfaction. Thus, in this lifetime one of their greatest challenges is to find the courage to get in touch with their feelings and *communicate* those feelings to others—honestly revealing their feelings without having to "do something" about them. This validates the natives' emotions and allows them to be integrated with the rest of their personality.

Also, owing to past lives of suppressing their emotions, these folks came into this incarnation with a certain shyness. They feel unskilled in relating with others on a "feeling" level because they have had so little practice. However, once they get used to it, they realize they have more talent than any other nodal position for responding to others' feelings in a way that is both nurturing and strengthening. It just takes a while for them to unfold to the point at which they are comfortable with this part of themselves.

NURTURING AND PASSION

Perhaps owing to past life monastic experiences, Cancer North Node people have a tremendous resistance to passion and an enormous capacity for self-control. They are programmed to "never lose control, never let themselves go." Therefore, emotionally passionate relationships represent a tremendous challenge for them—and ultimately can set them free. They have spent so many lifetimes disassociated from natural human drives that when passion—the most intense of human sensations—confronts them, they react with fear. An automatic "disconnect" button is pressed, and they turn around and run the other way because they don't want to lose control!

When these folks interact with someone who stimulates their passion, their primal urges become activated and threaten to take over. Since these urges have been suppressed, they now seem overwhelming and out of proportion in intensity. The irony is that what Cancer North Nodes fear most is also what they most want and need. They long to experience the nourishment and fulfillment that comes from a deep connection with another person. Nothing else in life will ultimately satisfy them. Sooner or later they must let go and allow their emotions to be stirred by another to experience completion in this lifetime. Passion can be their greatest source of pain and frustration, or the challenge that takes them beyond the limitations of internal controls and heals the painful boundaries they have erected between themselves and others.

Cancer North Node people have a tremendous need for a stable foundation from which to know they are loved and secure. They need to feel there's something—someone—they can depend on and "go home to." Deep down, they are looking for someone as strong and reliable as themselves to love them and take care of them. However, they need the nurturing and reassurance so much that when it's offered, they are often afraid of losing it and seek to control it so they can keep it. The irony is that in trying to control it, they end up pushing away the very thing they need most.

As long as they seek that source of love and security outside themselves, they court disappointment. This is why, ultimately, they need to develop a sensitivity to their own needs. They need to "hug themselves"—give themselves nurturing and love before wanting it from someone else. They need to reassure themselves that "it's going to be all right . . . don't worry . . . I'll take care of you." In the process their energy (which is outer directed and goal oriented) begins to sink back inside themselves, and they are able to feel satisfied and nurtured.

When their own energy is centered, they can be vulnerable and sensitive toward others because they have taken care of their own needs and now are emotionally secure. When they don't desperately need to be loved, other people are able to love them. When they give themselves reassurance, they gain enough inner confidence to be with others quietly without having to control, "look good," or feel they have to "do something." When they can simply "be," they nurture others just from the fullness of being who they really are.

RECOGNITION

Owing to past incarnations of success and recognition, these folks come on the planet with a strong sense of *inner pride*. They're used to considerable recognition for their achievements, and they want other people to feed that pride. The only problem is that they can never get enough recognition to feel satisfied. It's always the *next* goal that, when achieved, will finally make them happy. They cannot win if they continue down this road.

At this point, their pride from past lives has become a wall of isolation around them. They are so accustomed to reaching their goals that they subconsciously look down on those who have not yet learned the art of achievement. This feeling of superiority alienates Cancer North Nodes from others. Their purpose in this lifetime is to teach others how to achieve their own goals; then they are "on track" and incredibly happy.

MAKING THINGS DIFFICULT

Cancer North Node people often are so attached to gaining respect from others that they subconsciously make life harder than it has to be—just so they can win recognition for their sacrifice. They often think that a task has to be hard in order to be worthwhile. They tell themselves how difficult it is until the whole situation becomes overwhelming and unmanageable. This is a self-defeating pattern.

The truth is that achievement is not difficult for these folks. Even as children, they reached their goals so effortlessly that they got no recognition from others. So they re-evaluated. Perhaps if the task were more difficult, others would give them more attention, sympathy, and recognition. So now, as adults, they may have problems they can't overcome (weight, habits, finances, etc.). They truly believe these problems are insurmountable even though they are trying their best, and they may even feel victimized by their circumstances.

For example, I had a Cancer North Node client who was in her early forties. Her battle against being overweight had become a problem in her early twenties, but up to that point food hadn't been an issue for her. Then, after a disappointing love affair, she gained 10 pounds. She immediately went on her first diet, followed the rules, and lost the weight effortlessly. She didn't know it was supposed to be hard. Six months later a peer, whose respect she had been hoping to gain, pointed out that the diet this woman had followed was found to be a fraud. The peer talked about how difficult it was to lose weight. My client immediately regained the 10 pounds, added 20 more, and was 30 pounds overweight nearly all her young adult life. For years she felt utterly frustrated because, to her, being overweight had become an insurmountable problem.

As soon as this woman thought of her goal as "difficult"—and tied it in with wanting to gain respect—she lost her power of accomplishment. Fortunately, when I saw this woman again she had lost the 30 pounds and had maintained her weight for more than two years. She had simply decided to take charge of the problem and make reaching a desired weight her number one priority—and she put all her past life power of accomplishment behind it. She saved her money, spent her vacation at a "fat farm," and followed its regimen to the letter after returning home.

When these folks finally decide to do something, they always have the discipline to rise above the problem. They must stop taking themselves so seriously, begin to take charge, and put their lives in order. It's easy. They need to just "do it" and not make such a big deal out of it—regardless of whether anyone else respects them for it or approves of their method. Once they have taken charge, they are automatically on the alert—drawing in the people and ideas that can assist them in attaining their goal. And it's to their advantage to achieve goals they have had for a long time, because it frees them to pursue new goals as they arise. These people will never run out of goals!

BOUNDARIES

Cancer North Node people have very clear boundaries—in their own minds—beyond which others may not go. Their limits are not unreasonable. They need to be treated with a certain amount of consideration to feel good about themselves. The problem is that others don't know where these boundaries are and thus may encroach on them unintentionally.

In response to feeling violated, these natives generally remain silent in the presence of the offender and then complain about it to everyone else. They need to learn to respond directly to the person they think is treating them disrespectfully. They need to say: "Stop! This is my boundary!" and let others know how they feel. This can be difficult, since they fear others' emotional reactions and are afraid they won't know how to respond if the other person gets upset. This may intimidate them and keep them from speaking directly, since they don't want to have to justify their feelings. It's enough to say: "Look, when you said that, it hurt my feelings." Or in business situations, it's enough to say: "Look, that's how I want it."

Cancer North Node people are still learning not to let anyone invalidate their feelings. Feelings are a personal matter; each person is the only one who can accurately describe what he or she is experiencing. For example, if I stub my toe among a crowd of people, I might say: "Gosh, I just stubbed my toe. It's really throbbing." One person might respond: "It doesn't really hurt that much; I've stubbed my toe before." But the fact is that I'm the authority: It's my toe and I'm the only one who knows how it feels.

In the same way, no one can invalidate how a person feels emotionally. Only that person knows if he or she feels disappointed, hurt, insecure, or left out, just as only I know how much it hurts to stub my toe.

SECURITY

FOUNDATIONS

These folks need to focus on connecting with their own foundation. In this way they will have a secure place to "be," which is essential for them to experience authentic, deep sharing. Once they are in touch with their own foundation they can venture out and successfully interact with others. If the other people's energy becomes too intense or disruptive, they can pull back into themselves. But if they haven't connected with their own "home base," they may inadvertently identify with other people's foundations and try to control *them* in order to stabilize the relationship. When Cancer North Node people are in touch with the "home" inside their own body, they become more comfortable being around other people.

Purchasing a home is another avenue that can strengthen these folks' sense of having a foundation. Sometimes, when we do something on a material level, it also produces emotional healing. This is the case with Cancer North Node people owning a home. Once their home environment is secure and comfortable, they feel more confident in accomplishing what they want in the world. Having a stable home is empowering for them. They feel more secure, more grounded, and safer just being themselves.

Actually, these people have excellent real estate karma and would do well in this field. As brokers or salespeople they gravitate to "good deals" and have the business acumen to know how to make the sale workable for everyone involved. They can see homes objectively, as a business, and are not distracted by the emotional considerations and feelings others have around "their homes." They locate homes that fill their clients' bottom-line needs (close to good schools, within a realistic price range, etc.). They sense what is important to the other person. They are also good at structuring deals creatively so that the purchases can take place, even when it seems impossible.

On a business/investment level, they are great at finding a "good real estate deal," fixing up the property, and renting it out. In this way they are able to start a business that can grow as far as they want to take it. They know how a property can be used to its greatest financial advantage (for example, dividing a large home into separate apartments and renting them). However, their good real estate karma applies only to properties that already have a structure on them—not necessarily to bare land.

BELONGING

These folks have spent many lifetimes standing for causes outside themselves; now part of them feels nomadic. They are always on the go, looking for the next goal to achieve or project to undertake. Their deepest need is to feel comfortable and to feel they can relax because they belong. But it is difficult for them to think they truly "belong" anywhere; even with their families they often feel they don't really "fit in." The first step toward changing this is to gain a sense of belonging within themselves, which they can do by remaining true to their inner impulses.

For example, if Cancer North Node hears potentially upsetting gossip about a friend, his best bet is to get in touch with his instincts. Does he "feel" that the information is true or that there is any reason to be upset? If his gut feeling is calm, then he can trust it. Indeed, Cancer North Node people gain a sense of belonging when they trust themselves and follow their instincts. They also need to experience a feeling of belonging with others, which they can gain by letting others know when they feel vulnerable. This gives others the opportunity to open their arms and let these strong Cancer North Node people know how much they're loved.

In this lifetime Cancer North Nodes' feelings demand attention; they need to be around others who are sensitive and supportive. It is important for these natives to develop a technique for discriminating between those who care enough to be emotionally supportive of them and those who do not. The best technique is to honestly reveal how *they* feel when others take actions that affect them, and then see how the other person responds.

For example, if one of Cancer North Node's friends has a party and doesn't invite her, the best bet would be to tell the friend directly: "I felt left out when you didn't invite me to your party." No justification, no manipulation—simply an honest disclosure of her emotional response to the incident. If the friend says: "You shouldn't have felt left out—I invited you to three parties last year!" and invalidates her feelings, that gives her a clue that she is dealing with someone who does not really care about how she feels. On the other hand, if the friend says: "I'm sorry you feel that way, and I can understand it, but in this particular case . . ." (and explains what happened), then Cancer North Node knows this is a person who responds to her feelings.

These folks tend to hide their feelings from others in intimate relationships. The irony is that this prevents them from developing the intimacy they seek and hinders them in establishing the interactions that would help them feel fulfilled. Intimacy is a by-product of revealing personal feelings and having those feelings understood and accepted by another. Feelings add fullness to life, and it is the birthright of Cancer North Node people to open themselves and experience the satisfaction of mutual caring on a deep, personal level.

RELATIONSHIPS

CONTROL

For Cancer North Node people, the tendency to control is the major pitfall in their intimate relationships. It's so automatic, they don't even know they're doing it. They are always two steps ahead, attempting to manage the other person's behavior by mitigating their own. For example, if they sense that their partner feels trapped and is about to leave the relationship, they may take a vacation to give the other person more space so he or she will stay. They are all too willing to sacrifice their own feelings and needs for the sake of keeping those around them satisfied and "under control." But when they do this, no one wins.

CONTROLLING SELF

These folks are actually extremely sensitive to emotion, both their own and the emotional reactions of others. Others perceive them as being insensitive, but in fact they are *too* sensitive and don't know how to handle the feelings that arise in themselves and others. Until they have developed a system that allows them to experience their "feeling" connections with other people with confidence and ease, their automatic response is to try and control either themselves or others because this eliminates the issue of how to deal with feelings. They try to organize their partners so they can control the relationship, but this bypasses the element of caring. Ultimately they feel alienated.

When Cancer North Node people are operating unconsciously, they often give more importance to maintaining a smooth working relationship and getting their way than to the moment-to-moment interplay of what's actually going on. They may place severe limitations on their own behavior—acting the way they think their partner wants them to be—in order to control the situation. Their subconscious thinking is: "I'm allowing you to control me; therefore you will be what I want." It's all geared toward creating predictable, stable situations they can count on—at the expense of the vitality of true emotional sharing, connection, and intimacy with the other person.

Sometimes these folks perceive emotions as a weakness. When others become emotional, they close down and feel cold inside, as the emotions trigger their instinct of wanting to take advantage of all opportunities! When this occurs, their best bet is to consciously *not* take advantage of the situation. Their challenge is to simply *be there* without trying to assert control. Then, after they have relaxed, they will instinctively know what to do that will be genuinely helpful.

They are so accustomed to taking responsibility that they tend to think they are responsible for other people's feelings. They think everything depends on them. Again, this can lead to suppression of their emotions so as not to upset the other person. But they are doing no one a favor by hiding who they really are and what they feel. In fact, hiding their feelings and fears prevents full restoration of the health of the situation. One of the greatest lessons Cancer North Node people are learning is to *not* suppress their own feelings for the sake of another person.

In fact, these folks must make sure their feelings are being acknowledged and their needs are being met. If they don't take care of their own needs, they won't be able to help others. In fact, when they do what they need to find happiness and fullness within themselves, they set their partners free and their relationships thrive.

CONTROLLING OTHERS

Until Cancer North Node people have established their own emotional identity, they internalize the emotions of others: When those around them become upset, they become upset as well. Then they seek to control the other person so they can feel in control of themselves. They respond to a crisis with instant advice; in fact, they have a talent for helping others get on top of things. But owing to their habit of suppressing their own feelings, they tend to suppress others' feelings as well. When someone becomes upset, their first instinct is to deny that person's feelings and urge him or her to be calm and rational. These folks have compulsive tendencies to take charge and restore order—often before they have a full understanding of the situation. They need to avoid the temptation to give advice before they're asked and instead focus on the nurturing, emotional energy they can share with others. They need to recognize and accept people's fluctuating moods as part of the larger picture.

Sometimes these natives indulge in emotional outbursts—getting angry, "blowing up," becoming insulted—as an avoidance of feelings and a way of bringing the situation to an end. Subconsciously, they use the outburst as a defense against feelings that are surfacing within them. They blow up and get over it right away, but in the meantime they've intimidated everyone and got them all back in line, so they don't have to deal with the underlying feelings. Emotional outbursts can be another way of staying in control. Others don't want to get into conflict, so they walk on eggshells around these folks—and once again, the natives feel lonely and isolated but don't know why.

Subconsciously, Cancer North Node people are trying to avoid emotions because they don't know how to handle them. One of their challenges is to learn to deal with situations in which they feel inadequate without becoming angry. One thing they can do is to consciously be more patient with the person facing them. They could be curious about the other person and ask questions to better understand the situation. When they begin to see the larger picture, they are usually able to reach an agreement without running roughshod over everyone's feelings in the process. Sometimes their caring about the other person's position relaxes the resistance, and the other person will help them figure out how to get what they want. Because in this incarnation Cancer North Nodes are learning to relate to others on a "feeling" level, rather than a mental level, they need to slow down. In order to offer suggestions that others will be receptive to hearing, they first need to establish emotional rapport. This takes time. Once the other person feels understood emotionally, he or she will be open to the advice these folks have to give.

Cancer North Node people are long-standing achievers who give excellent advice. When they hear a problem, their focus on success and resolution is so strong that they automatically see a successful, practical solution. Ironically, they often attract people who have the problems *they themselves* need to learn about in their own lives. By listening to the answers that flow through them to nurture others, they will know what they must do themselves. This also helps them feel connected.

The choice facing Cancer North Node people is one of control versus caring. Whenever they respond to a situation with the motive of control, they lose. Whenever they respond from a position of caring and wanting to be supportive, they win. Thus, an important thing to do before making a telephone call about which they feel insecure, or before interfering in a situation, is to take a moment and identify their motive. In this way they can know if they are on solid ground in taking action. If they are coming from a place of genuine concern about the other person, when they interact the other person will feel it and respond accordingly.

GOAL FIXATION

Cancer North Node people don't realize how controlling they appear to others. They come into this lifetime fixated on accomplishing whatever needs to be done, and they often are so absorbed in the task at hand that they are unaware of the feelings of the people involved. Then, when others become upset, these natives feel isolated and don't understand what happened.

For example, I had a Cancer North Node client who bought a home in a condominium. She wanted to help make sure her community was running smoothly, so she volunteered to be one of the grounds supervisors. Her job was to "walk the grounds" once a week and issue citations to residents who were breaking community rules (parking where they shouldn't, playing the radio too loud, etc.). She took her job very seriously, and soon she had lots of enemies. She was so focused on doing the job that she forgot to consider how people might feel about receiving citations. Cancer North Nodes are learning to consider the other person's perspective and think about how they themselves would feel if positions were reversed. This helps them gain confidence in knowing how to interact with others in ways that bring successful results.

Owing to past life authoritarian experiences, they sometimes appear to be "all business" to others. This is a loss for both sides: Both people feel uncomfortable relating to each other. The problem is that Cancer North Node people assume that everyone wants the same things they want, so they don't care what it takes as long as the goal is accomplished. But other people *don't* think that way—much to these natives' surprise—and may not be clear on how the "order" they just received fits into their plans. They may need an explanation of how their task is part of the larger picture. Others have not been as goal oriented as Cancer North Nodes in past lives, and they may not see the strategies that are so obvious to these natives. Therefore, Cancer North Nodes must slow down and take the time to communicate; and sometimes they must be willing to *not know* the answer.

For example, in the case of the woman with the condominium, rather than issuing a citation right off the bat she might have gone to the "offender," made sure the rule had been understood, and discussed why the rule was to everyone's advantage. She might have asked how the "offender" would enforce the rule. Cancer North Nodes need to be willing to *not* come from an "on top" position; they should allow others to offer suggestions for getting the job done. In this situation the "offender" may have said: "Don't worry, I'll move the car right now so you won't have to issue a citation. Thank you for letting me know!" The idea is that there's more to life than "getting the job done"—there's the satisfaction of connecting with others in mutually helpful ways.

EMOTIONAL RISKS

What Cancer North Node people really want in their relationships is to feel secure and know they are loved for who they are. Yet they make this almost impossible because when they don't reveal themselves, how can others know them and love them? The greatest challenge for these folks is to allow themselves to be vulnerable. Taking the risk of revealing their feelings establishes their emotional identity for themselves as well as for the other person, but to them it feels as if their very survival is on the line—it's overwhelming! Yet these are the very steps they must take to be happy, relate successfully with people, and feel at home.

COMMUNICATING FEELINGS

These folks can be real loners. They're so afraid to acknowledge their feelings that it's hard to risk letting other people get close. They don't want to get hurt. What they are learning, however, is that *fear* of getting hurt is far worse than actually experiencing their most intense feelings. They shy away from their feelings because they are unfamiliar; but as they practice revealing them, they'll find a new depth to their life and a tremendous sense of satisfaction. Feelings add color and substance to life—a whole realm of personal enjoyment without which life on this planet would be dry, flat, and forlorn.

Cancer North Node people fear being overcome by feelings and losing control. However, they never have to worry about being permanently overpowered by their feelings because they have no desire to be irresponsible. Even if they were to find themselves swept in a negative direction, they could always escape by simply exercising their innate ability to take charge.

They are learning to trust that feelings are temporary—like the tides of the ocean. If experienced and released, they offer a constant variety of moods and sensations.

Feelings add a dimension to life that makes possible a complete connection with others. To connect with others only through the mind leaves relationships painfully lacking. In this lifetime, these people are learning that when they take others' feelings into account, they gain an expanded appreciation of all the subtle facets of the other person. And by sharing their own feelings, Cancer North Nodes give the other person a more complete appreciation of themselves.

For example, if a Cancer North Node person is feeling very affectionate toward someone but doesn't show it, there is no communication. But if she does show it, then both people have the opportunity of connecting on the same wavelength. Feelings are conveyed through body language as well as words. If these folks are feeling affectionate, it is not a mistake to follow their impulse by hugging the other person or taking his hand.

Their subconscious urge to control often keeps them "in check," always doing what's "correct," but this only postpones the reality of what they are feeling. They may spend a lot of time in manipulative thinking: "If I do this, this will happen; if I do that, that will happen"—it all becomes strategy. But they ultimately out-manipulate themselves and miss opportunities to enjoy the "feeling" side of life until they learn to trust their feelings to guide them in their relationships.

In this incarnation, Cancer North Node people must let honesty be the bottom line, rather than what is "socially acceptable." These folks are learning that when feelings are not communicated and acted on, there is no "endless opportunity." Emotions must be acknowledged when they arise. These folks must not think themselves out of acting on their feelings. This may be a solitary path, in that most people would not recommend that anyone always honestly communicate what's going on. But for these folks, authenticity is the only correct path.

INTIMACY

Cancer North Node people need to ask themselves: If a relationship isn't based on a truthful connection, what is at the core to see the partners through the tough times? These folks want and need to experience intimacy; the way to create it is to be vulnerable rather than controlling. It may be easier to express positive feelings, but they need to remember that their intention in communicating fear, sadness, concern, frustration, anger, or insecurity is not to justify or prolong these feelings, but to expose them so they can be released. When these natives suppress such feelings, it doesn't work.

Other nodal positions may not have a problem being themselves and letting others see how they feel, but for Cancer North Node people it is a challenge that requires a great deal of courage. They need to reveal and communicate their true feelings. They must express feelings verbally, with no other motive than disclosing their inner selves. Then, if the other person invalidates them in any way, they will know it is a person with whom they cannot share a true affinity. However, this approach gives those with whom the natives *can* develop nurturing, warm supportive relationships a chance to know them.

In past lives, because Cancer North Node people were always the responsible ones, they had to be able to justify everything they said or did. They became wary of speaking before they had considered all the possible repercussions. The good news is that in this incarnation these folks don't have to justify anything—they have permission from the universe to simply be who they are and share what they feel, without taking responsibility for how others respond. They don't even have to know *why* they feel what they feel; yet sometimes the process of communicating feelings gives them insight into what is going on or gives the other person an understanding that promotes constructive feedback.

All Cancer North Node people have to do is communicate what they know at the time. For example: "I'm feeling uneasy with what you said, but I'm not sure why." "When you said that, I started to feel angry. I don't know why, but I just wanted to let you know what's going on." "I feel nervous, and I seem to be responding by talking a lot." "I know this is what we agreed on, but as the situation has unfolded, I feel uneasy with the agreement." Regardless of what they fear will happen, when these natives actually risk sharing their feelings and let others see where they're coming from, the situation will resolve in a mutually empowering way. Cancer

North Node people had a complicated pattern of past lives, yet it's a simple path of Right Action for them in this lifetime.

SUPPORT AND EQUALITY

PARENTAL ROLES

For these folks, security and confidence come from a conscious motive of supporting others. When this support is clearly based in equality, their relationships thrive. However, they had so little traditional family experience in past lives that they tend to get "stuck" in playing one role only: the authoritarian/dictator/"father" type. They are so accustomed to responsibility, organization, and control that they think others can't take charge as well as they do. Thus, when an emergency (or even the hint of an emergency) arises, they jump right in and start organizing everyone—it's automatic!

Cancer North Node people always want to know where others are going and what they're doing because they're so accustomed to taking responsibility for every situation. But they're learning that there's a difference between support and usurping the responsibility for others' lives. One of their challenges is to understand the foibles of others without making judgments or trying to correct the situation.

To counteract the tendency to play the "father" role, one of their best bets—male or female—is to allow themselves to assume a nurturing, supportive "mother" role. For balance, these folks need to learn from the feminine role: receiving energy and responding authentically from the heart. This softens them and allows others to receive and benefit from their energy. Cancer North Nodes need to understand other people in terms of their insecurities, not just in terms of their authority; then they won't feel intimidated and can relate as equals.

Here is an example of the father/mother contrast. When others become upset, the "dominating father" aspect of Cancer North Nodes tends to tell the other person what to do to dispel the negative feelings. They inadvertently invalidate others' feelings (this is also the way they treat themselves), but it causes others to feel unacknowledged and unnurtured. In this lifetime, Cancer North Node people are learning to develop empathy. They must listen to others and understand their pain, just as a mother understands the pain of her child; their understanding will help heal the wound. To say to the child "I'll kiss it and make it better" is not as logical as saying: "Next time, avoid putting yourself in that situation and you won't get hurt." Yet the first message of comfort is what others need, and what they need from themselves. After acknowledging the pain, so the other person knows they care, they can make practical suggestions that will be useful.

In past lives, others gave them recognition and acknowledgment for their achievements. In this lifetime, they need to turn the process around and give *others* support and encouragement. These folks are here to fill other people's needs; as they do so, they grow and gain security themselves. In going out of their way to help others, they automatically meet their own needs. They are nurtured and fulfilled in the process of nurturing others.

Above all other feelings, Cancer North Node people absolutely cannot handle rejection. Although they are learning to be sensitive to others' feelings, they came on the planet being overly sensitive to their own feelings. Thus, they have an exaggerated reaction to any hint of rejection, and they take everything very personally. The key is to be more objective—less focused on self and more aware of how to respond to other people's immediate needs.

For example, I had a Cancer North Node client who was part owner of a steakhouse. If a customer sent back a steak that wasn't cooked well enough, he took it personally. His position was: "Well, I cooked it right; what's wrong with the customer?" When these folks focus on the issue of their adequacy in any situation, they are always on the defensive. They must sidestep the ego and be more receptive to what they can do to nurture the other person. When their focus is on doing their best to make others feel supported and cared about, everyone wins and the energy soars.

Feelings are an important part of our identity. What makes you cry may be very different from what stimulates tears in your sister or your friend. Our feelings are a personal characteristic, and when Cancer North Node people express their feelings, they begin to let others know who they truly are. Often they think others don't see who they are or allow them to be themselves. Actually, they are the ones who don't allow others to really know them, because they are afraid they will seem different. The amazing thing is that when they finally reveal themselves and risk being ostracized, they discover that they truly belong.

When these folks speak from their hearts—from the overflow of emotions welling up inside—it is endearing to others, who inevitably respond with empathy and support. The irony is that what feels the most personal to Cancer North Nodes is actually the most impersonal. How the world views things and how they look to others seems very personal to them because ego gets into the middle of it. But when they express their feelings and gut instincts, the ego isn't involved at all. It's instinctive—so how can they take credit for it? It's not emanating from their thinking process; it's just an honest reaction.

GOALS

TRUSTING FEELINGS

TUNING IN

Cancer North Node people have tremendous integrity from past lives. They need to hold on to this honesty in terms of revealing their inner process and letting others know how they feel. Owing to many incarnations playing a prominent role in society and being on display, these folks are used to "being someone"—pretending to "have it all together" in order to fill a social need. However, in this lifetime their feelings are so strong that they demand recognition. They may seem cold or businesslike to others, but this is because they are subconsciously trying to deny their feelings in order to appear "on top of things." By now, blocking their feelings is automatic; but to be happy in this incarnation, they must reprogram that response.

One way to accomplish this is to slow down and take time to listen to themselves. Generally, when they feel something they ignore it or act directly against it. Now they need to deliberately retrain themselves. The idea is not to be pressed into communicating feelings immediately, but to take enough time to let the feeling come and *then* to communicate it. This is new for Cancer North Node people—like learning to walk or talk—so they need to be patient. As they experiment, they'll find the people around them magically supporting their new behavior. It stimulates others and brings more closeness to their relationships, creating true intimacy rather than shallow, long-term connections.

Owing to many past lifetimes of being rewarded for suppressing their feelings, Cancer North Node people tend to perceive feelings as a weakness. But feelings have nothing to do with being weak; they simply reflect a reaction in the body. Can Cancer North Nodes say: "Because I'm incredibly happy, I'm weak"? No; it's just another feeling.

Instincts will never lead these folks astray. Often their emotional responses promote unity in their interactions or are an accurate prophecy of times to come. Cancer North Nodes' fear is that they're not in control—they might be wrong. But they shouldn't let that fear stop them. They have to say: "This is what I'm perceiving right now; this is what I'm feeling." Their instincts are always correct. It's also "good karma" when they allow themselves to show emotion publicly. For these people, emotion is positive and healing; when they let their feelings show, it endears them to others and often heals the situation for all concerned.

COMMUNICATION

Cancer North Node people have an instinct for achievement, so they can use it to their advantage by making their goal the thing that challenges them the most: honest disclosure of their feelings, fears, and vulnerabilities. They must learn to do this in order to create a bond of empathy with others. If at first they are too shy to let someone know how they feel, they can begin by writing a letter. Or, if at the decisive moment they suddenly "forget" what they wanted to say, they can write notes to prompt their memory.

Their aim must be honest communication of their "feeling" responses in a responsible, nonblaming way. For example: "When you didn't keep your promise and call me yesterday, I felt insecure and frustrated—I had turned down another invitation because I told you I would wait for your call." These folks need to communicate the facts of what happened and then relay the feelings they experienced in response to those facts. Then they need to stop talking and give the other person an opportunity to respond. They must slow down the process and give the interaction an appropriate beginning—a space in which two people can tune in to each other—rather than immediately focusing on results.

Often Cancer North Node people are annoyed that they always have to be the strong ones—the ones others rely on for help. They may be resentful because they have no one to turn to for advice in their own times of need.

To allow themselves to always be "on top" becomes an ego trip that makes them feel separate from others. The key is to allow themselves to be helped, as well as helping others.

However, when they do accept help, it's usually in a dramatic way: "Okay—I would like to use your car today, but don't worry—I'll have it back to you in exactly two hours, not a moment later!" Subsequently they overemphasize how responsible they were in getting the car back, rather than accepting and appreciating the other person's support. They are learning to accept help and caring from others with thankfulness and love. They are learning that interdependence is not a form of weakness but, rather, that it promotes a sense of belonging with others that adds depth to their lives.

If these folks don't reveal their insecurities, they deprive others of the opportunity to support them and give back to them. Only when they communicate their fears and feelings of inadequacy do others become aware of their needs. Then people have the opportunity to help them, take care of them, and pamper them—all valid experiences for Cancer North Nodes in this lifetime. For many other nodal groups, being taken care of would be an ego trip. But for Cancer North Nodes it is actually more of an ego trip to *not* allow it. Changing this is a healthy experience of humility and an exchange of energy that is empowering for all concerned.

In accepting help, Cancer North Node people may feel uneasy because they think they are not being completely responsible. Actually, by including other people and allowing them to help, they validate the worth of the other person. Once they learn that people like to help, their entire worldview will change.

FOCUSING ON PROCESS

Cancer North Node people have had so much past-life experience in reaching goals that this lifetime often becomes a series of achieving one goal after another, without experiencing the joy of the process. No matter how much they attain, it isn't satisfying. They are overachievers, postponing appreciation of the moment and the abundance around them in lieu of striving to reach the next goal.

In past lives they achieved maximum success, so it is not set up in this lifetime for them to find happiness through reaching goals. Now the process is important; happiness will come through the enjoyment of getting there. They must pay more attention to beginnings, nurturing things and seeing them grow. They still may reach goals that are far beyond the accomplishments of others, but they will have done it in the right way—in a way that was fun and nurturing for themselves and for those around them.

ENDS VERSUS MEANS

This is not an "ends justifies the means" lifetime for Cancer North Node people. To feel secure, they need to stay in touch with process rather than striving to reach the goal. This will also prevent them from inadvertently abusing, exploiting, or hurting people emotionally. There still may be times when the instinct for control sets in and they try to manage their lives from their minds, but they need to remember how much pain it causes.

Cancer North Nodes' tendency to sacrifice the process for the end result also leads to a lack of energy, vitality, and personal enjoyment. For example, rather than focusing on the goal of having a successful marriage, they should focus on the process of creating a successful marriage. They need to take time to notice whether their partner is enjoying the relationship. The goal may be to have a mutually supportive, happy marriage through the means of revealing feelings and creating closeness, with each partner letting the other see who they really are. Then the end result (a successful marriage) is the natural outcome of their day-to-day process.

They are learning that if they take care of the little things, the big things will take care of themselves. Others may not understand their preoccupation with integrity in each step of the process (others may be learning about achieving long-range goals), but Cancer North Nodes, who are masters at worldly achievement, must be true to themselves and to their process. When they take care of the "little things" (for example, honest communication of feelings; awareness of others' feelings; staying emotionally connected with the situation; proceeding one step at a time in a caring way), they are truly on the path of Right Action.

Cancer North Node people must remain aware of the fact that whether or not what they are doing is understood, validated, or respected by others, they are spiritually correct. Only they know how difficult it is for themselves to be vulnerable; when they are true to themselves in this way they gain self-respect regardless of others' opinions. This fosters a new strength that brings them an incredible, calm courage in dealing with worldly life. When they maintain integrity in their process, what they accomplish will be emotionally satisfying far beyond their expectations.

GOALS FOR SATISFACTION

Because Cancer North Node people have such ability to attain goals, it's important that they distinguish between their own goals and those imposed by society or early environmental conditioning. Their goals make them happy through the process itself. One goal that will help replace frustration with happiness is to recognize that "a bird in the hand is worth two in the bush"—to learn to appreciate what life has already brought. Their subconscious goal orientation always prompts them to seek satisfaction in "the next thing"; as a result, they don't enjoy the bounty they already have. When they consciously recognize and appreciate what they have, it provides energy for further achievement in a balanced way.

Another goal that can bring deep satisfaction to Cancer North Node people is to focus on achieving emotional connectedness and intimacy in relationships. This empowers them to slow down their process and keep their awareness on themselves and the other person. It means maintaining awareness of the importance of feelings as part of the fullness of life.

One way they can do this (which will also bring greater security in unfamiliar situations) is to focus on shifting the center of energy in their bodies. Cancer North Node people usually keep their vital energy centered from the shoulders up to the top of their heads—they are "top heavy" and lack a sense of inner substance. These folks need to bring the energy down into their lower abdomen (the area below the belly button). Walking through the day with an awareness of the power center within will make their sense of value an internal, quiet factor that is sustaining, nurturing, and complete within themselves, regardless of others' opinions. When they move the energy down to the lower abdomen, centering occurs and their hearts begin to open.

This allows them to learn an entirely new way of responding to the emotional frustrations of others. They have always felt uncomfortable with negative emotions and at a loss to comfort the other person. Their first response has been to ignore or suppress the feelings and go right for the goal of resolution—so the person will be back "on top" of things. But the magic is that if they make their goal to validate what the other person is feeling, to acknowledge the emotion and empathize, then they will see the appropriate response that will actually support the other person and deepen the bond between them.

For example, I had a client with this nodal position who was dating a man she liked very much. They both lived in New York, where there was a lot of social activity. He once called her in a state of boredom and frustration while on a business trip to Minneapolis. She didn't know what to say to cheer him up, and it was a short conversation. What she might have said in response to his restlessness was: "I'm sorry to hear that." Immediately— as soon as these natives validate and empathize with the other person's feelings, the right thing to say occurs to them. In this instance, it might have been: "Maybe I should fly right out and join you for the weekend." In this case, the response would have created a win/win situation. But these folks will never know the "right thing" to say in emotional situations until they first acknowledge and validate the feelings that others share.

THE LEGACY

Cancer North Node people are learning how to communicate with others in ways that are comforting and supportive. They must learn to give people the benefit of the doubt, thereby bringing out the best in them. For example, I had a Cancer North Node client who was part owner of a large restaurant in the Southwest. His chief chef turned out to be an alcohol abuser (which wasn't apparent when he was hired), and after several months on the job the cook ended up in jail for three days. Following his release, the cook returned to the restaurant. Good chefs were hard to come by, and my client needed him. The other owner greeted him enthusiastically: "Hey, John—nice to have you home!" But my client was aloof. As long as he was going to take him back, why not make the cook feel valued? These folks are working on acknowledging when they need someone.

TEACHING

Cancer North Node people are so innately aware of how to accomplish their goals in the material world (what it takes, how the world works, how business works) that they often assume others have the same knowledge. But there is no other nodal group with as great an awareness of how to accomplish a goal, no matter how lofty. One of Cancer North Nodes' purposes on the planet in this lifetime is to teach others how to attain goals.

With their lifetimes of experience in this area, these natives immediately notice when others are subconsciously sabotaging themselves, indulging in counterproductive behavior, or allowing themselves to be distracted by lesser concerns. They also see clearly how the problems can be resolved— how others can position themselves to reach their goal. When they see another person's needs, they can use their innate practicality to help make that person's dream come true.

When Cancer North Node people see someone acting in ways that are counterproductive, rather than "punishing them" their job is to teach them in a nurturing way how to reach their goals. One of the best ways these folks can participate with others is to help them identify their goals, and then encourage them to "go for it." When they are sensitive to others' needs in this way, they shift from a "dictator father" role to a "nurturing mother" role and can reach people far more effectively. When they are more understanding and supportive, their confidence brings out the best in the others.

In the example of the chef, my client could have taken the time to get to know him better. Why was he a chef? What did he want to accomplish? What did he want to gain by working at that particular restaurant? If the chef's motive was to make a good living for his wife and child, and his reason for being at that restaurant was to build a good reputation, my client would have known how to motivate him in a supportive way.

Patience is another attribute that Cancer North Node people are cultivating. Their job is to teach by demonstrating—cheering the other person on. They are such master achievers from past lives that when they take on the role of an understanding teacher, others listen.

SENSITIVITY AND SHARING

Owing to past-life suppression of personal feelings, the "feeling" nature in Cancer North Node people has become purified. There is no "hidden agenda"; their emotions are an innocent, natural response. Quite often when they express themselves, everyone else heaves a sigh of relief. Their "feeling" nature is quite open, and often they "pick up" the feelings of those around them. This is why it is healthy to share their feelings in a responsible way: "I'm feeling uneasy in this situation"; "I felt uncomfortable when you said that—it didn't feel like a fair response that took everyone's needs into account." When they risk verbalizing their feelings, everyone is healed and released from emotional inhibition. In group situations, others may come up to them and say: "I'm so glad you said that! That's exactly what I was feeling, but I didn't know how to verbalize it." When that happens, it's the universe validating that they are "on path"—that responsibly verbalizing their feelings in a nonblaming way was exactly the ingredient needed to clear the way for their goal to be reached.

In disavowing their emotional bodies in past lives, Cancer North Node people disconnected themselves from the advantages of being human. In some ways, they may not even feel part of the human race. They understand purpose, accomplishment, responsibility—but for what? Where is the reward—the true value—in the experience of being human? It is in the nurturing and delicate feelings one experiences from the emotional self. Every outer experience is empty without the inner emotional charge that results from it. And to share those feelings with another is the most exhilarating and exquisite of experiences.

In dissociating from their feelings, these folks are missing the contentment and sense of belonging that are inherent in recognizing—and claiming—an emotional connectedness with humankind. They have earned the right to claim the benefits and pleasures of being part of the human family, rather than being responsible for it. It is perfectly appropriate for them to slow down and reap the most nurturing reward of having a human body: the experience of feeling.

HEALING THEME SONG*

As music is an empowering medium for emotionally supporting us in taking risks, I have written a healing song for each nodal group to help shift its energy in a positive way.

ON THE ROAD

The message of this song is meant to inspire and encourage Cancer North Node people to take risks and be vulnerable, reveal their feelings, and thus open themselves to the emotionally fulfilling interactions that they desire.

Selected lyrics:

Seems to me the only way I can
Find out just where I stand
Is to be honest about how I feel
With the people I hold dear
The change will make it all so clear
Take the risk and watch magic appear!

It's a long, long way back home
Back to where I'm coming from
But I'm on the road!
Growing used to breaking through
All the things I thought I knew
To rejoin the flow . . .
On the road back home!

---

* These lyrics are set to music and sung in their entirety on the CD and cassette tape "Unfolding As It Should."

North Node in Leo

and North Node in the 5th House

OVERVIEW

Attributes to Develop

Work in these areas can help uncover hidden gifts and talents

- Individuality
- Willingness to take "center stage"
- Following one's heart's desires
- Strengthening one's willpower
- Enthusiasm
- Self-confidence
- Taking risks
- Relating to the childlike quality in others
- Enjoying life—having fun
- Looking at life as a game
- Developing an "It's up to me" attitude

Tendencies to Leave Behind

Working to reduce the influence of these tendencies can help make life easier and more enjoyable

- Yielding to peer pressure in order to "belong"
- Detaching from emotional situations
- Aloofness
- Waiting for others to prompt one's own action
- "Overlooking" what's really going on
- Waiting for "more" knowledge before taking action
- Excessive daydreaming
- Running away from confrontations

ACHILLES' HEEL/TRAP TO AVOID/THE BOTTOM LINE

For Leo North Node people, the Achilles' heel they need to be aware of is the overriding need to feel the acceptance of peers ("If I just cooperate with life and 'go with the flow,' my peers will automatically support me and bring me happiness"). But it's a bottomless pit: Their friends can never give them enough support for them to break out as individuals and take advantage of the exciting opportunities life brings. They need to become their own best friend and encourage themselves to go after those things that will bring them happiness.

The trap they need to avoid is an unending search for knowledge ("If I have enough knowledge, I will feel confident to take creative action"). They will never feel they have enough knowledge to ensure successful creative action, so they continue to "go with the flow," waiting for happiness to find them. The bottom line is that at some point they must take the risk and start creating their *own* happiness. The irony is that once they take action and begin creating happiness, the knowledge they need to succeed will come to them effortlessly.

What These People Really Want

What Leo North Node people really want is to receive love. Their need to experience the loving energy of others is nearly insatiable. To successfully bring this energy into their lives, they need to first give love by cheering people up—they know how to use the limelight to make others happy. By exercising their creativity to contribute to the happiness of others, they create an "audience," or a peer group that will support them, accept them, and love them. The best barometer of being "on track" for Leo North Node people is the applause and approval of others. In the process of giving happiness—as long as they stay in alignment with their own humanitarian ideals—they gain the reward of knowing they are an important participant in the stream of life.

Talents/Profession

These people belong in professions that reward individual creative effort. Entertaining (singing, acting, etc.), entrepreneurship, or some other way of being at center stage releases their tremendous creative energy in constructive ways that bring joy to all. Other good options include activities dealing with children, speculation, games, and sports.

Leo North Node people also have the gift of objectivity—they can accurately see what the "game" is. When this skill is used as a backdrop for achieving goals that are fun for them, their ability to see things objectively becomes an asset. However, if they involve themselves in professions that have objectivity itself as a goal (scientist, inventor, engineer, X-ray technician, etc.), their lives may become devoid of vitality and joy. They are better off using this natural talent in intensely creative projects.

Healing Affirmations Specific to Leo North Node

- "The only person who can create my happiness is me."
- "If I'm having fun, I'm on track."
- "When I follow the impulses of the child within, I win."

- "I win when I actively create the results I want."
- "When I relate to the child in others, everybody wins."
- "When I bring joy to others, I feel included."

PERSONALITY

PAST LIVES

Leo North Node people have spent many lifetimes living on the sidelines watching others interact. They were the scientists, the observers, those who sacrificed personal identity to promote humanitarian causes and ideals. They are accustomed to linking their creative energy to the dreams and aspirations of others, without taking into account their own needs and desires.

Thus, in past lives they lost touch with the vital energy of their inner child. In this life they have again subconsciously chosen environments that negate their inner child, in order to work through this issue and regain the connection with their vital energy. They may be born into a violent household where objective observation of a parent's behavior is a matter of survival. Or they may be born into an alcoholic household in which the emotional responses of one or both parents are unpredictable, and since they are not able to trust their caretakers, the only safe route is to suppress their feelings. Or perhaps the loss of a parent at an early age gave them an added sense of responsibility, and they felt it wasn't okay for them to "just be a kid."

These folks have had so many past lives of being objective and watching from a scientific point of view that in this lifetime they have a real fear of getting involved. They're afraid of losing their objectivity; subconsciously they feel it's the only thing that has kept them safe in the past. But this lifetime is about becoming involved and learning how to play! They've taken the stuffy, scientific approach for too many incarnations—they have *not* been having fun on this planet—so this time they need to go in the direction of enjoying themselves. When they are around children, their own inner child is reflected back to them. When they see children playing and simply being themselves, it inspires these natives to play and become involved in life. And this is their challenge—to step back into the center of life's vitality.

Owing to their past-life scientific orientation, Leo North Node people enter into this incarnation with a "laboratory objectivity"—continually observing without seeking to change, or in any way interfere with, the data. This allows them to be very clear and accurate about what is going on. However, if they become overly identified with the role of "Important Observer" it can become an ego trip, where they stand back and pass judgment on other people and feel superior.

They may take the approach: "We're going to cut through all the nonsense and tell it like it is!" and then, when they see the look on the other person's face, they feel badly. But their minds say: "Well, I said it! I'll stand by it!" and they settle into the rigidity of their position. However, in this lifetime these folks have the challenge of pointing out to others what is going on in positive ways that make them laugh and/or help them change their perspective and lighten their burdens. This time Leo North Node people need to not only *see* what's going on but *actively participate* in transforming "what is" into something positive for all concerned, including themselves. In this incarnation, their life purpose is to learn how to get what *they* want, not through detachment but through intense involvement.

OBSERVATION VERSUS ACTION

Leo North Node people sometimes feel as if they are being swept up in other people's dramas and they themselves are just sitting back—powerless—even though they can clearly see the writing on the wall. They think that other people can adjust their course of action, "sail their boat into the wind," change direction, and win from prevailing conditions. But Leo North Node people often feel as if they watch the wind change and are aware of the waves, but can't seem to hook up with the energy and take advantage of the situation.

These folks get "stuck" on one side of the creative pendulum. To successfully manifest a dream, the process involves both observation and action. Sometimes it's necessary to pull hard on the ropes to physically maneuver the boat, regain equilibrium as the boat shifts, move heavy objects into balanced positions in readiness for the new direction, and "batten down the hatches" to prepare for the change. A lot of energy has to be exerted. Accurate observation of the prevailing forces is an equally important part of the creative process so that all the energy is expended in the right direction. Leo North Node people are great on the observation end, but they must remember to swing into action in order to create changes in the physical world.

THE SCIENTIFIC APPROACH VERSUS CREATIVITY

Sometimes Leo North Node people can practically "think themselves to death." They analyze everything, think of all the things that can go wrong, check the moods of the people around them, and gain all the knowledge they can so that they won't make a mistake once they decide to act. However, there are so many different things to think about that they become overwhelmed and paralyzed. This tendency to seek security through "certain knowledge" can keep them from taking the risks that could increase their vitality, and it often locks them into stagnant, passive lives.

These folks are learning to become more fluid; they must start trusting their intuition rather than clinging to their logical strategies. They need to be willing to consider that their basic premise might be in error. However, they often assume they possess superior knowledge; even though that "knowledge" blocks them from manifesting their dream, they may stubbornly hold on to it. "In order for me to follow my heart and take a chance to create what I want, x, y, and z conditions must first be met." But they never are. These folks need to *release* the idea that they can be totally in control of the success or failure of their dream. In fact, life is their partner; when they put aside their concerns and begin doing whatever they can each moment, little by little they will make their dreams real. If they are not willing to do this and their "right conditions" are never met, these folks may postpone taking a risk until it is too late and the window of opportunity is closed.

Leo North Node people are learning how to transcend the limitations of the scientific approach and be truly creative. Creativity can't be planned or put on a schedule. It is a process of working hand in hand with the intuition and energy available in each moment and with the materials at hand. It involves deciding where to go and then cooperating with the universal Flow to accomplish that objective. The end result may not be exactly what was expected, but the *energy* of that expectation will be joyously and successfully manifested.

Leo North Node people must accept what the universe brings to help make their dreams come true. When they say to the universe: "I want an answer on this," and every time the universe *brings* them an answer their mind says: "No, that's not it," they invalidate their own answers by not acting on them. They go in circles and feel estranged from their life force. When this occurs, it is a signal for these folks to take action. They need to contribute to life in some way: pick up the phone and call a friend, send a loved one a gift, or sign up for a sport or activity that will reconnect them with their energy. When they are linked with their own energy they feel articulate, able to connect with others emotionally and intellectually—they feel terrific!

GOING WITH THE FLOW

Leo North Node people lack recognition of their personal power to make creative changes in their lives. They think the Flow has all the power, so they feel powerless. Often they even put up with abusive situations—believing "that's just how it is"—because they don't think they have the power to change it. One of their most important lessons in this lifetime is to recognize that they *do* have the power—in fact, a special talent—to enact constructive change based on their own view of the larger picture.

In past lives these folks would tune in to the Flow of Universal Energy to guide them, and that worked perfectly. In this lifetime, as long as they are actively pursuing their own goal (one that resonates with their inner child), they can again trust that the Flow (with a capital "F") is guiding them in the right direction. The danger lies in when they do *not* feel an inner connection to their goal. Then, because their destiny in this lifetime is to learn how to relate with others in a creative way, the flow they pick up is actually *other people's energy,* not Universal Guidance. At these times, when they're "going with the flow" (small "f"), it's really the flow of other people's desires and wants, which may be based on very selfish concerns.

Leo North Node people also go along with the flow to appease people. It's their way of cooperating and being accepted without having to get in the middle of things and risk emotional disruption. The only problem is that when these people go along with the flow, they frequently end up playing second fiddle to other people's willfulness. When they feel this maelstrom of other people's desires, their best bet is to simply step back and temporarily withdraw so they can recognize and validate their own feelings in the situation—then simply trust what they want. Their job is to follow what makes their inner child happy. As those feelings grow stronger, these folks will know they are on the right path.

Their minds—which use "scientific appraisals" of what's best for everyone—are not good barometers for Leo North Node people in this lifetime. They need to focus on the joy of the child within. When they choose to walk in this direction, someone who was counting on them for his or her own needs may feel hurt or disappointed. But they should keep in mind that in the larger scheme of things, this may be exactly what the person needs to learn in terms of his or her own personal responsibility. Leo North Node people have no idea of what everyone else's lessons are. All they can know with certainty is the feeling of pure happiness inside themselves; that feeling is their only sure beacon toward right action.

When Leo North Node people follow their minds rather than the longings of their own hearts, they avoid what they are here for in this incarnation—to do what makes them happy. For many lifetimes these people have served humanitarian purposes, so their inner child has been very purified. Whatever makes that happiness inside them "ring true" is what they need to follow—it is the only voice that will lead them out of the confusion of other people's ego energy and into the light of their own radiant individuality.

Most folks would give anything to be given the following prescription in this lifetime: Play and have fun! These folks are free to do this because they automatically act in ways that are responsible. Their pathway of Right Action now is to pursue their individuality and to manifest their own dreams without allowing others to stand in their way.

PEERS

These folks may have unfortunate "group karma" in this lifetime, which contributes to their confusion with other people's energy. In past lives they were very involved with groups of people, but they lost touch with their own individuality. In this incarnation they tend to decide which social group they'd like to be a part of, and then "make themselves" belong. They act out the part: They start dressing like those people, using the same expressions, emulating their behavior, and adopting their perspectives. When the group does accept them, they lose their identity in the effort of being just like everyone else. The problem is, they did the process backwards! Instead of being themselves (that is, expressing their own individuality and choosing friends based on true inner affinity), they used their *minds* to decide whom they would be friends with. Even as children, these folks have a tendency to fall in with "fast-lane" peers and then get into trouble because they are following their friends rather than their own judgment.

In all group situations, Leo North Node people face the challenge of expressing their own individuality. Often they end up being part of groups where others think they belong—but sometimes their "disguise" breaks down at a decisive moment because the people around them recognize that these folks are not really being themselves, and thus feel a lack of mutual trust.

It would benefit these folks to understand the true nature of a group. Groups that one can really count on for support are based on a natural coming together of individuals who are in touch with their intrinsic natures and have their own personal sense of what is important. These groups form spontaneously out of the natural affinity. That is why, in order for Leo North Node people to have healthy group relationships, they must stay in touch with their inner being. In the process of asserting their individuality, they will truly notice and respect the individuality of others. Their alliances will be based on mutual respect for one another's unique inner nature, rather than yielding to one another's wills and expectations.

DAYDREAMING VERSUS MANIFESTATION

Many times, Leo North Node people lose themselves in daydreaming about the future. This is owing to the sadness they feel because they have not created the vitality they seek. They daydream about everything: how it's going to be "later," someone they're going to run into again, someone they know and how it *could* be—perhaps how it *will* be . . . until dream after dream fills their consciousness. However, spending too much energy in daydreaming dilutes their creative fire. They need to spend less time in daydreaming and more time in taking action.

In this lifetime it works for them to decide: "Well, what would I like to create? What would be fun for me?" They get many different ideas, and their inner child says: "Yeah, let's do *that* one!" The only problem is that they can sit back for years thinking about it, doing nothing. It creates a deep sadness within when they waste years never realizing their dreams.

The issue of manifesting dreams is a crucial one. In this incarnation Leo North Node people have the power to create their own destiny, but it's up to them to take charge of their lives and do it! They must choose one dream that resonates deeply for them and take the steps in the outer world that will turn that dream into reality. Sometimes this can be a frustrating process. There can be such a gap between their dream and reality that it seems almost impossible to bring the two into alignment. Yet these people have a unique talent for manifesting in the material world whatever they dream about. The first step is to recognize that participating in the game of creativity can itself be fun and satisfying. They need to enjoy the process of creating their dream, and not postpone happiness until "later."

Leo North Node people have a tendency to become impatient with their dreams and try to *force* them into reality. Sometimes the gap between their dreams and current circumstances seems too wide, and they give up in defeat. Yet this is not in their best interest, for in their hearts they continue to long for their dream and feel dissatisfied with the reality around them. They must slow themselves down and allow the creative process itself to lead them. As they successfully complete the first step toward their goal, the next step will occur to them. If they wait to see the whole picture before taking action, they will never gain enough "knowledge" to have the confidence to act. For them, vitality lies in taking risks.

FOCUS VERSUS DISTRACTION

Leo North Node people are learning to keep their goal in mind. They are so easily distracted by life's multitude of opportunities that they have trouble staying "tuned in" to the goal that originally excited them. They are learning to develop their will and stay on path regardless of distractions and obstacles. To do this, they need to see themselves as players instead of observers.

Sometimes, when they first see an opportunity to experience their dream, they get caught up in the happy energy this creates and start moving in that direction. But then they realize there isn't a straight, easy road from where they are to where they want to be. If things start to become shaky and are not turning out as they imagined, they tend to give up, or they get distracted on some other path that holds less energy for them in the long run.

Leo North Node people are learning that to create the happiness they envision for their lives, they won't always be able to forge straight ahead. As they move toward their goal, a "second force" is often introduced—a resistance to their dream. Then they must pull back and rise above that resistance—experience a growth in character that takes them to a new level. It's somewhat like a fairy tale: The Prince has to go through tests of character (slaying the monsters, etc.) before he wins the prize. The second force that these folks encounter is actually a part of their character that has always been in their way but that only becomes apparent when it stands between them and getting something they want. If they want to win the prize, they must go through these tests of character—gaining in strength and self-discipline and overcoming their greatest fears—and not back down.

CREATIVITY

One of the main lessons Leo North Node people are learning is to become involved in the joy of the creative process. But their greatest frustration can be the discrepancy between their dreams and the stark reality they see unfolding around them. Although these folks are accustomed to "going with the flow" of what others have created, in this lifetime they are supposed to create the situations *they* want. But they don't know how. How does someone so used to following an objective, uninvolved path suddenly turn around and create something? How does he even begin? The fear of not knowing is what leads Leo North Node people into the trap of pursuing more and more knowledge, seeking an answer that they hope will empower them to act. Ultimately, the answer is intention. When they are totally focused on what they want to create, the knowledge they need will come to them in the process of going forth to actively create what they want. In this incarnation, their job is to create their dreams now.

KNOWLEDGE VERSUS EXPERIENCE

Leo North Node people are always hoping that they will gain enough knowledge to feel confident in taking action. But these folks could be 200 years old and still think they didn't have enough knowledge to act! They must stop using knowledge as an excuse to postpone action and admit that it's okay to be wrong sometimes. In fact, it's through making mistakes that we gain more "real" knowledge about what actually works in life.

In certain ways, Leo North Node people have lots of solid self-confidence. However, their self-confidence is founded on trusting their own information base. They have total confidence in what they *think* they know, but their sense of "knowing" is based on past experience and observations. When they form rigid ideas based on knowledge only of the past, they limit the potential of their future. Their challenge is to be willing to *not* know—to be childlike and experiment. They need to follow their hearts—to try things even though other people aren't doing them—and find out what happens. This will bring vitality back into their lives, and they will see that even though they don't "know" how to do it, they *can* create positive results here and now.

These folks like to wait for the certainty of knowledge in order to avoid the pain of making mistakes. But they need to learn to follow the dynamism of their inner child, which will take them into new, uncharted territories of pleasure, excitement, discovery, romance, and creativity. If they don't, they will become discontented, disassociated, and confused about why the drummer they were following didn't lead them to a happier place. Any stubborn attachment to "knowledge" or "conditions" as a guide will be a stumbling block. For example, a Leo North Node client of mine had spent the past twenty-two years trying to leave his wife so that he could begin a new life. But he became fixated on the idea that in order to leave, he had to amass enough money to take care of his wife financially. For twenty-two years the more money he made, the more she spent, and he could never accumulate enough money to meet his prerequisite. However, his wife was creative, independent, and highly intelligent. By not allowing her the power to make it on her own, and by continually striving to meet his "conditions" before acting, he trapped himself in an unhappy marriage.

To increase their vitality and enjoyment of life, Leo North Node people must step out into the unknown, and find their truth directly through experience. To take risks without knowing all the repercussions requires trust, and to gain innovative knowledge requires the innocent courage of a child. These folks must trust the vitality within themselves. If they keep their goal in mind, they will see what adjustments to make along the way in order to get where they want to go.

GAMESMANSHIP

Leo North Node people are excellent at games and can play out any role they choose. Their objectivity allows them to construct excellent strategies. Once they have a goal firmly in mind, they can see how to play their role with the other people involved to make their dream come true. This talent can be particularly useful in situations where they feel insecure. If they allow themselves to view it as a "game," their natural ability to role play will kick in.

Once they discern their role, they can create a strategy for winning. The strategy may call for them to play different roles as the situation progresses. At one stage they may need to be "Jim the Healer" and at the next stage "Jim, the Man of Your Dreams." The idea is to see the role they need to play to further their goal at that time, and then to play it to the hilt. They're very good at it, and it's immense fun for them at the same time! The only word of caution is for them to remember the importance of fairness and to only enact roles that work for the best interest of everyone involved.

Leo North Node people would do well to recognize that they can also use their sense of drama to emphasize a point so that others hear them. Because of their tendency to go along with things, people often take advantage of their easy-going nature. Then they resent that others aren't taking them seriously and giving them the respect they deserve. So they must be firm in making a point: "I have an important phone call right now; I can't talk, I'll be out in fifteen minutes." It's not what they say, but how they say it, that gets others' attention. They can use their dramatic flair to meet their more immediate needs in day-to-day situations as well.

These folks are also excellent gamblers, because they are not immersed in "winning" on an emotional, ego-centered level. Since they are aware of the larger forces and prevailing energies of the Flow, they know when to press forward and when to pull back in placing their bets—and in reaching their goals. In this lifetime, they are learning that even a "wrong" action—if they are following the energy of happiness in their heart—is better than inaction. However, it's important that they continue to think of it as a *game*. They must continue to reassess their strategy before making a new move if they want to win.

NEEDS

PERSONAL GROWTH

These people desperately need the energy of approval. They have had so many past incarnations of being detached, of being "nobody," that in this incarnation they are terrified of being "somebody"—and of being them-selves. Through many lifetimes of sublimating their identity to a larger cause, they have lost track of who they are. This makes them exceptionally good actors and actresses; they are willing to play the role of somebody else in order to get the approval they so greatly need. In fact, the approval of being validated and applauded for positive participation is healthy for these folks—it grounds them in their own active personality.

DEVELOPING THE EGO

The function of ego (as it is discussed in this chapter) is to articulate desire, to interweave the individual's wants and needs with the rest of the world. The ego verbally communicates the direction the individual wants to go. It is the decision maker and activator of the will. Leo North Node people have had many past lifetimes of being immersed in a "superego" mindset based on "shoulds" and "oughts"—morality as dictated by society, family, reli-gion, or an awareness of humanitarian ideals. As a result, they have lost contact with their personal ego—a sense of themselves as individuals, with individual needs and directions. They are aware of their id—their spontaneous "gut reactions" to things—and their superego mind, but they are not in touch with their ego as a mediator between the two. Thus, they tend to swing between being too accommodating and allowing others to walk all over them, and erupting in anger that their "line of fairness" has been violated. Often they don't even understand what is happening, and they find it difficult to explain their anger to themselves or others.

Without a sense of ego to help them make good decisions, these folks can become extraordinarily stubborn. If they think they can't leave a situation for knowledge-based reasons (shoulds, oughts, moral or spiritual beliefs) even though their gut tells them it's not healthy, they'll stay no matter what. This stubbornness can work to their advantage if they convert it to determination in actively pursuing their goals, but it works against them when they remain in a stagnant, limiting situation. Their motive in remaining can also be safety, security, and fear of change. Usually they try to turn their inertia into something positive by finding a new challenge within the old situation to make them feel creative. But the fact is that if there's only so far they can go, ultimately it will end up as self-limitation. They might find the courage to break free if they set a time limit for themselves. They can use the predetermined time to prepare themselves for leaping into a new life. When they make up their mind and refuse to consider any other options, they activate their will and suddenly have the power and energy to change.

In this incarnation Leo North Node people are here to consciously develop a healthy ego. Their challenge is to strengthen the ego by validating it, verbally communicating what they perceive from a superego point of view, as well as what they are experiencing in the id (their gut reaction). For example, they could say: "I know I shouldn't be angry about this because you've had a hard day at work; you're tired, and you just want to forget about dealing with people. But I get very upset when you come home, pick up the newspaper, plop down in front of the TV, and don't talk with me. I'd like to create some time each evening for taking care of each other and regenerating our relationship."

Once these natives have voiced their own truth and expressed what they feel and want without censoring themselves, they begin to develop a sense of their unique individuality. This takes tremendous courage, but it is the only way for these folks to ground and integrate themselves on a vital, solid level.

When they communicate both their superego and id point of view in a loving but firm way, creative solutions become apparent, their egos grow stronger, and others begin to pay attention to what they say. If they don't strongly communicate their feelings to others, how can people really know them and give them what they want?

By consciously developing their ego through their accomplishments, these folks can stay on the path of Right Action and also give the gift of putting other people more in touch with their superegos. By sharing the larger picture that they see and by communicating gut reactions from their id, they help others have a more expansive outlook that takes everyone's best interests into account.

DEVELOPING THE WILL

Leo North Node people also have a mission in this lifetime of developing their will—evoking and building the strength within themselves to actively pursue their dreams. They have more inner strength than they realize, and they are learning to recognize and integrate this. Part of the process involves acknowledging the amount of time it takes to manifest things of value. If they want a dream to come true, they must be willing to give it time. The other people involved need time to come into alignment with Leo North Nodes' dream, and the preparatory steps must be completed in the physical realm. All these things require time, so these folks must have endurance for the long haul.

They will create the dreams of their heart if they are willing to go slowly—step by step—in completing each stage of the process and allowing the next step to be revealed. If they focus on the goal and stay in touch with their inner feeling of happiness, the process will build the strength of character required to handle—and fully appreciate—the fruits of their labor. To connect with their inner power, however, Leo North Node people must push through a mountain of self-doubt: "What if I fail? What if I can't?" The idea is to not think about failure. Instead, just try it. It can take these folks a long time to begin recognizing their inner power, but once they accept it, nothing can stop them!

Will is the instrument they need to manifest their dreams. They will also be strengthened by remembering that what they are looking for is also looking for them. At the same time they are persistently taking steps to reach their dream, the dream is beckoning them and pulling them onward.

SELF-MOTIVATION

In order to feel motivated, Leo North Node people often have to be "propelled" in a certain direction. They feel a pull from a person or situation—and when they follow that pull, they find that they're on track. But in this incarnation they must remember to stay in touch with their own inner motivation, not just what others want them to do.

Sometimes these folks become so detached and inactive that they pull back from being involved in anything. This can be especially difficult for those with whom they share reciprocal responsibility (such as a spouse or a business partner) because when a crisis hits, these folks tend to disappear and let those around them handle it. When there is a family crisis, they may not want to be involved—they really don't want to do anything. Others feel they have to prod them, knock them over the head, or threaten them to get them to help.

Instead of responding to this, Leo North Node people often pull further away. They feel all the emotional energy in those around them—and they don't know what to do. What they should do is pull back for just an instant and get in touch with their own heart. What would they like to see happen in the situation? What would make them happy? Once they can see it, they must take responsibility and do their part to create that positive outcome.

When they're following their *inner* prompting, no one needs to force them or prod them because they are already actively pursuing their own course. As an individual, they may want to handle one area of a relationship and not another, or resolve one type of crisis and not another. To be helpful and fair to everyone, they should define the areas in which they are willing to participate and let others know when they can—and cannot—be counted on. For example, they may be happy to play with the children, but need an hour every evening right after work to be by themselves and get centered. They should find out what their spouse needs and then find a way to meet both partners' requisites.

Because these folks are learning to get in touch with their inner selves and clearly define what they want, they need to remember to make only those commitments that are in alignment with what they want or with what they truly feel is fair—and keep their word! If they say they're going to become involved on a certain level, they need to follow through and do it. On the other hand, if they choose not to participate in something, they need to discuss that honestly with the other people involved. In the process of opening up communication, a higher degree of order is created that brings more joy for all concerned.

INVOLVEMENT

Leo North Node people are dependent on receiving love from others. When they risk sharing their feelings and desires, they tend to give up if others don't immediately provide validation. They quickly become silent again. But they may have to put some energy—some drama—into their communication so that others understand that it's important to them. They must be firm in expressing their needs so that others take them seriously. And their motive should not just be "getting their way," but expressing the integrity of who they are so that their character and ego can develop. Their self-expression is the natural architect of the boundaries within them. When they are not honestly and firmly expressing their true inner reactions, they are inadvertently being unfair to others: They are denying others the opportunity to really see who they are, interact with them, and meet their needs.

These folks have an incredible talent for stimulating enthusiasm in others and making them happy. They can apply this talent to both business and personal arenas. The key is to be willing to participate—to become involved with others and to communicate with their hearts as well as their heads. When they become disappointed in a situation and withdraw, everyone loses. When they increase their interest and continue to put constructive energy into the situation, everyone wins.

Leo North Node people are very attuned to the emotions and wills of the people around them. They feel what others want, the different directions of each person's will in the situation, and what they are striving to create. When they get into the middle of all that emotional energy, they don't know how to handle it. They often detach themselves rather than participate. But actually, these folks have incredible abilities to deal with the wills and emotions of other people. Because they don't have an ego attachment to the will, they have the objectivity to see how a given situation can work out fairly so that everyone's divergent needs and wants are acknowledged. They need to learn to detach only *momentarily*—just long enough to see what is going on—and then use their power to accurately appraise the situation. Then they can use their emotional energy and ability to act out a role to create positive results.

They must be willing to step into the middle of a situation and begin to *play* with people. In this way they can create the right energy so that everyone's divergent wills align for the good of the whole, bringing justice, fairness, equality, and harmony to the situation. This is the happiest use of their ability to detach—to turn it into conscious involvement where they exercise their will in a truly creative way. They also must remember to include *their* will—what they want—as part of the equation, or the solution won't work out in the long run.

Leo North Node people can be self-conscious, and this is debilitating for them. Actually, they are happiest and most confident when their attention is focused outward, uplifting the spirits of those around them. However, when they become self-reflective, they get "stuck" in feelings of insecurity; their energies begin to circle around themselves instead of moving forward. Involvement, then, is a key ingredient for their happiness and vitality.

COMMITMENT

Leo North Node people tend to have serious issues around commitment. The issues usually arise when these folks allow themselves to become deeply involved in something—especially a romantic relationship. All of a sudden someone may enter their life who is so attractive that they say: "Okay, I'm going to take the risk and get involved." And they really want to. The energy of romance is healthy for them—it stimulates their basic vitality, makes them want to be alive, and fills them with joy. So they "go for it" and get right into the middle of all the emotional energies that are stimulated.

Being very perceptive about what the other person wants, these folks go about playing the role of the other person's ideal mate. They charm the other person and say all the things she wants to hear. They create much happy romantic energy, and the other person responds with love and affection. There is mutual joy, and things go well for a while. But at some point the partner starts to relax, be more assertive, and exercise her own will—and the Leo North Node person becomes irritated. He feels that if he is going to embody the "ideal mate" for his partner, the partner should do the same for him. He becomes very upset when his partner starts to be herself; often he may simply withdraw and drift on, never really making a commitment to create a relationship that feeds energy back to both partners over the long haul.

The Leo North Node person's commitment needs to be on a deeper level—not just when things are going well. It isn't fair to the other person, who responds to his advances and becomes open and vulnerable, only to have her heart broken when the Leo North Node person changes his mind and leaves by detaching either emotionally or physically. And since these people *do* have a strong sense of fairness, they must be willing to monitor the relationship carefully and use their creative power to make it work.

Their challenge is to interweave the strong picture of the situation *they* would like to create and the creative will of the other person. The first step in doing this is to find out who the other person really is. What are the other person's ideals, dreams, and goals? What is important to him or her to create and experience in this lifetime? Also, where is that person willing to yield to accommodate the individual needs of the Leo North Node person? These things need to be discussed to ascertain whether or not the two personalities can blend. If the Leo North Node person can align himself with his partner's values and aspirations, there can be supportive mutual involvement. Both individuals can move together toward fulfillment of their common goals. These folks need to recognize that the vitality of romance is not always found only between two people with identical ideals, wants, and needs. In fact, often the fire they are seeking is created by two temperaments that, in some ways, are very dissimilar; it is through the process of encouraging individuality that the fire burns hotter.

TAKING RESPONSIBILITY

Leo North Node people may overlook a lot of what is going on around them, because they are receptive to so many distractions. The biggest problem is that when they are overlooking certain aspects of a situation, they do not tune in to how things are affecting them. Instead, they ignore anything unpleasant. This allows them to avoid taking responsibility and clearly stating their feelings. Some situations remain unresolved because these folks have not been honest and clear. The worst impact of this tendency is usually on their intimate relationships. When they overlook what others want and the others become disappointed or upset, the Leo North Node people may feel overwhelmed by incredibly fierce emotional responses from others that were not anticipated. And then these folks are crushed—they can't figure out what they did that evoked such wrath. After all, they just ignored the whole thing and went on with their lives!

But looking back, they always feel they should not have overlooked what they were feeling, and they wish they had given the other person the chance to respond by communicating honestly.

To avoid problems like this, they need to pay special attention to what the other person *truly* wants—not on a quick, what's-going-to-charm-or-appease-them basis, but real understanding of the other person's values and dreams in the relationship. They can learn to open up their hearts and take personal responsibility.

TRUST

Many problems with taking responsibility have to do with trust. Leo North Node people violate other people's trust without intending to or recognizing when they have done it. This is why other people sometimes react violently against them. If these folks can see the child in other people, they will recognize that everyone operates from a certain level of trust that others are going to keep their word. They cannot discount or violate this trust without experiencing severe repercussions. Once they give their word, they must keep it as they would with a child—to reinforce the trust that others give them. If they change their plans, they must let those who were counting on them know in advance what is happening, and not just go their own way.

They also need to be aware of the "game" that they have given other people the impression they are playing—and know what the rules are. Once they have agreed to the rules—or let others *believe* they have agreed to the rules—they need to take responsibility and play by those rules. For example, if they're involved in a relationship and one of the rules is monogamy, they have to be monogamous. They can't just "go with the flow" and let momentary distractions take them in some other direction. They must be true to their word and create what *they* say they are going to create.

Since they have learned about detachment in past lives, they may not recognize how attached others are to them; but when they act carelessly, others react vehemently. Leo North Node people are learning to recognize that those in the other nodal groups often take life much more personally than they do.

RIGIDITY VERSUS VITALITY

Leo North Node people have a tendency to get "stuck" on what they think they "know." They take in a few objective facts and then reach a conclusion based on their perception of the situation, their goal, and their own needs. Often they become rigidly attached to their position, refusing to budge. Then they begin to plan for the future based on their decision, which they consider to be "objective, irrevocable truth."

The problem with this process is that these folks tend to reach their "conclusions" and "certain knowledge" without discussing anything with the others involved. They may remember something the other person said and base their "knowledge" on that, rather than sitting down with the other person and allowing new truths to emerge from the interaction. They should be willing to share their feelings, their fears, and the conclusions they are drawing with an open mind and a willingness to receive new input.

A sensitive awareness of how others feel will empower Leo North Node people to act without provoking unexpected resistance. If they understand in advance how others feel—by being aware of others' attachments to them and putting themselves in another's place—they will be able to present their decisions in ways that others can accept. If they are willing to abandon logic and enter the realm of feeling and enthusiasm, they will discover that they are uniquely equipped to present their plans in a way that shows others how they also can win.

For example, if Leo North Node is dating a person and the fire dies out—or was never really there to begin with—his instinctive response may be to leave the relationship without explanation. This can cause emotionally distressing reactions in the other person: confusion, distrust of the opposite sex, feelings of personal inadequacy . . . sometimes Leo North Node people don't realize how unfair or hurtful they can be. Taking the responsibility to openly acknowledge the direction their individuality is taking can be mutually empowering: "I just don't feel the fire anymore, so I'm interpreting that as an indication that it's time for me to move on. I'm being honest with you because I want you to know what's happening. This way, it opens the door for someone new to come into your life who can make you much happier than I can."

These folks have an incredible ability to "raise the mood" by tapping into other people's feelings. When they present things in a way that evokes others' enthusiasm, the resulting energy motivates *them* into action. Other people's feelings and emotional energy can actually be a source of power for them—a fuel that motivates them to put their dreams into action. Thus, rather than overlook or ignore people's feelings, their best bet is to be aware of them and work *with* the emotional energy.

RELATIONSHIPS

DYNAMICS

PARTICIPATION

Leo North Node people don't like to fight. They may be experts at provoking fights, but when it comes to getting into the trenches and hashing out an emotionally charged issue, their tendency is to withdraw. They either sit in silence, "tuning out" the other person (which makes their partner mad), or they leave the situation to avoid dealing with it. They can be like ostriches—sticking their heads in the sand, hoping the problems will simply go away. They think that because they are not participating in the drama around them, it's not their fault if the relationship becomes negative. Yet their lack of participation often breaks the hearts of those who want to love them.

When these folks pull out of a situation, they become inaccessible. Then, when they think the emotional intensity has diminished, they return and act as though nothing happened. The problem is that they begin to accumulate a bad history with the people around them. The unresolved problems build up, and eventually their partners withdraw emotionally or physically from the relationship because of the unresolved tension. Others may think that these people don't care about them because of their lack of generosity in responding to others' emotional needs.

Sometimes this occurs because of their ideals of how relationships ought to be: "without any drama, nothing to discuss, no issues to resolve; relationships don't have problems." They fail to recognize that crisis can actually be a focal point that draws two people *closer* in an intimate bond of understanding and empathy. Willingness to help another person through upsets and frustrations can result in a depth of mutual appreciation, open giving, and loyalty that could not otherwise have been forged. Indeed, an alchemical process occurs when two people make a commitment to share in the process of giving and receiving on a deep level, being willing to create something positive out of what may first seem to be a negative situation. If these folks take the energy they put into withdrawing and being miserable, and put it into becoming involved and creating happiness, it becomes a win for everyone concerned!

FAIRNESS

For Leo North Node people, part of their detachment springs from their innate sense of fairness: They support the individuality of others and don't want to interfere with—or suppress—the other person. But in this lifetime these folks are learning to draw boundaries, to say "no," to say: "That behavior hurts me. If you continue to do that, I will leave." They are taking a hand in their own destiny and giving the other person an opportunity to change. This simple, honest expression of their *own* individuality is much healthier for them than just leaving a relationship without notice.

Because they have the gift of being aware of what pleases the other person, these folks assume that others also have the ability to know what pleases them. So when others don't "give back" (by doing things to please them) they think the situation is unfair and begin to withdraw. In fact, others are *not* as objective and observant as Leo North Node people, and are often unaware of how to please them unless they give some clues.

Leo North Node people have had so much past-life experience being aware not only of their own desires but of the desires of others that when they want something, they have already established that it will be a positive thing for those around them as well. Because we all tend to feel that others are just like us, they assume that others' desires also take everyone's best interests into account. But this is not the case. Others generally do not check the "fairness" of their desires relative to those involved, and many of their desires may be selfish and shortsighted. So when Leo North Node people just go along with the desires of others, they often end up losing—and then they resent the other person for not having looked out for them. They are learning to look out for themselves; and if they are in a situation that is not fair, it's important to let other people know how they feel.

DEALING WITH EMOTIONAL ENERGY

Leo North Node people are not comfortable with highly charged emotions. They may evade communicating because they don't want a confrontation. Once they have made a decision (about not pursuing a relationship, etc.), they just do it. They may even avoid contact with the other person, who is then left hanging, not sure what happened and why the Leo North Node person is no longer involved.

Inwardly, these folks can be so aware of the intensity of their partners' feelings that it's hard to express what *they* are feeling. When they remember to objectively share their larger view of what's going on, as well as their feelings, it will help them communicate. They have a reticence to tell the other person what's "wrong." They're afraid it may devastate the other person, whereas in actuality their honest communication gives the partner the benefit of their objective view.

But everything depends on motive, and their intention must be clear. If their motive for sharing thoughts about a partner's behavior is an expression of love, genuinely wanting to benefit the relationship, their partner will feel the loving intent. But if they are bringing it up out of anger, they will lose. Their objective view really *can* be very helpful to the other person. But problems will arise if these folks become rigidly attached to their insight, insisting they are "right" regardless of feedback from the other person.

Leo North Node people have a tendency to not put energy into their relationships. They go into denial about what is actually going on. Even if the relationship becomes abusive, they tell themselves: "This is how it is;

everyone goes through this." They continue to hold on to their ideals, dreams, and expectations of how they would like the relationship to be, without putting energy into creating what they want, until one day they become so disillusioned that they give up. Then they "turn off the switch" and leave. Instead, they must learn to use their creative energy to change things into what they want rather than detaching from how things really are.

These people miss tremendous opportunities in life when they neglect romance, play, and giving love to others. They have the potential to be surrounded by love throughout their lives, yet often they end up without love. When they lose out on love and romance, it's usually because they are not willing to put enough energy into the relationship to make it work.

For Leo North Node people, the answer is commitment to active participation. Particularly at the beginning of a relationship, these folks must be willing to commit 100 percent to creating a true combining of their ideals and the other person's ideals. They must speak up about what they want *after* they find out what the other person wants. Particularly in romance, they need to find out what the ideal romantic relationship would be for the other person. Then the Leo North Nodes person can determine if the other person's ideas are compatible. If so, the Leo North Node person can confidently enter the relationship with his or her tremendous talents for creating happiness.

CHILDREN

Leo North Node people are wonderful with children, and children are "good karma" for them. Being with children puts them in touch with the child within. In fact, one of the main purposes for Leo North Nodes in this incarnation is to get in touch with the inner child and to allow that child to play and openly express itself. The joy and vitality they feel through play pulsates through them and resonates with the children, who have more fun with the Leo North Node adult than they ever would on their own.

These folks recognize the individuality of each child and are aware of how the child is responding to outer stimuli. They treat children as people in ways that encourage discipline while allowing for individuality. They have special talents with children. It would benefit if they shared their knowledge of how to treat children through the written or spoken word, or if they chose a profession in which they could work with children. This would help others learn how to treat children, and make everyone happier.

GIVING AND RECEIVING

Leo North Node people can seem aloof, yet they long to be involved in romantic, passionate relationships to feed their vitality. Romantic relationships are based on giving—indeed, giving to one another keeps the flame burning. The giving can take many forms: compliments, encouragement, gifts, approval, understanding, cheering up the other person, and countless other ways both large and small. These folks are experts at knowing what and how to give—when they remember to go out of their way and pay attention to that "special other" in their life.

KEEPING SCORE

For Leo North Node people, motive is all-important. If they are giving with a pure motive—to make a contribution and to keep the energy flowing—then happiness is a natural by-product. But if they are giving with an expectation of payback or "keeping score," then they are courting disappointment.

Accepting gifts and support from others is easy for Leo North Node people. They were accustomed to receiving in past lives, when their job was to allow themselves to graciously receive love and help. However, after many incarnations in this process, an inertia set in. They became bogged down, "overnurtured," and lost touch with their personal initiative—the vitality, excitement, and creativity that come with being on the giving end of love. In this lifetime, these folks want their creative power back. And it is through giving that they can experience high energy.

The problem is that the process of giving without thought of return is not instinctive for them. Yet such giving can free them to *receive* more. When people focus on giving what they can in whatever situation they're in, they leave the channels open to receive beyond their wildest expectations. But when they give in order to receive, they can only receive according to *their* expectations, which are naturally limited.

Having rigid expectations of what others should be giving back creates a situation in which others can give and give, but the Leo North Node never notices. For example, she may take a friend out to dinner. A month later she has a serious problem, and this same friend may spend hours on the telephone comforting her and helping her see the situation in a more positive way. But if she does not acknowledge the time and energy involved, she may still expect her friend to take her out to dinner and feel hurt if the friend doesn't. Alternatively, giving freely (without expectation of return) would leave her open to the goodness of life that flows from unexpected sources. It would also help her appreciate all the little things that others do for her that she may not have previously recognized.

These folks may also begrudge the way others receive what *they* give. If they give in spurts, giving can seem like a big deal to them and they want the other person to appreciate it. They are learning to cultivate a consistent, giving spirit—giving in all the little ways that, in the end, are usually the most important.

If Leo North Node people keep track of how much they are giving without recognizing that in the process they are also being uplifted and revitalized, then they begin to feel like martyrs. When they become aware of themselves as giving or loving, then these actions become an ego trip rather than a true extension of themselves. Sometimes they see themselves as going out of their way to feed energy to the other person and make him or her happy. This is just another form of keeping score. The truth is that when Leo North Nodes *do* receive things, it never really excites or fulfills them. What truly, deeply satisfies them is *giving*, and the other person's response of love and appreciation. This is what they need in order to feel energized. As they learn the art of giving for its own sake and feel joy in the happiness they evoke in others, they begin to experience the satisfaction of living in a truly nurturing environment.

ACKNOWLEDGING OTHERS

Sometimes Leo North Node people exhibit a cynical reaction when people offer to help them. They tend to undervalue assistance from others, often to the point of repelling those who could further their cause. But others are not encouraged to give more if what they offer is not appreciated and acknowledged. These people are so attuned to the idea that the Flow is bringing them everything they need to create their dreams that they may forget to acknowledge the special contribution of those around them.

These folks can be greedy in terms of accepting favors without true reciprocation. They need to generously acknowledge and praise the people who help them; in this way they will establish a bond that encourages others to be there for them when they need further support. Rather than being preoccupied with what others *aren't* doing for them, they could balance this aspect by deliberately taking time each day to acknowledge the ways that others give to them. This includes the small things like holding a door open, wishing them a happy day, or simply smiling at them. Leo North Node people need to see what *is* being given to them, since this mindset will bring them a lot more enjoyment and love in their relationships.

Leo North Node people sometimes forget to acknowledge the specialness of the people who trigger their energy, and think they can create successful bonds with anyone who fits their basic guidelines. They are learning to recognize this inner affinity of a "special"—rather than simply universal—nature. Acknowledging these special bonds also helps Leo North Node people appreciate their own specialness.

Their tendency to undervalue those with whom they feel a special connection often leads these folks to be careless with their romantic partners. They may think that "all of them are the same" (the opposite sex) and that it doesn't matter who they are with. Then, rather than make the effort of working it out with someone who generates the feeling of "aliveness" within them, they may choose someone who is geographically more available, has a more compatible background, and so on.

On the other hand, when Leo North Node people summon their energy and commit 100 percent to making a relationship work, they give so much that the other person may be overwhelmed. The other person may "fall in love" with them but may also seem to take them for granted, not understanding the energy these people put into making the relationship work. These folks need to receive the energy of appreciation to validate their efforts and inspire them to keep their creative juices going.

ROMANCE

Romance is very important and healthy for these folks. However, they can't expect any one person to supply the amount of stimulation they need to keep their vitality and joy alive. It is up to them to cultivate a variety of creative interests and projects that help energize them and keep them happy. Working with children can supply this stimulation, as can acting, painting, sculpture, music, or anything else creative and fun. Their greatest joy comes with the process of full creative involvement—whether through a project or a love affair!

Owing to so many past incarnations of objectivity and observation, Leo North Node people are very aware of what brings them joy and how they resonate inwardly to the people who cross their path. They are instantly aware of true romantic connections. When they meet someone of deep affinity, their heartstrings are activated—they can almost feel it physically; there's no thinking about it. Usually they are attracted to a special vitality in a person—a certain life spark. Because they have the gift of instantly recognizing true romantic affinity, they assume that others have the same gift . . . but this is not the case.

Usually, when they feel a tugging in their heart they look to see if the other person feels the same—but if it wasn't mutual, these folks wouldn't feel it. Generally, the other person is less aware of the intensity of the attraction and may initially seem less interested. If Leo North Nodes give up too soon, before the other person has had time to become aware of the connection, both people lose. Thus, these folks need to trust their gift of accurate recognition of a true love connection, and slow down long enough to give the other person time to recognize the depth of the connection. Their best bet is to approach the other person on a nonthreatening friendship basis and spend time establishing a genuine relationship.

These people love romance and actually need it to activate their vitality and creativity. They know how to play the game, how to get a romance started, and how to stimulate passion and make it fun. The problem is that after the romance has been going for a while, they may run out of steam. They grow tired of always being the one to spark the fire and bring out the best in the other person. They are so busy acknowledging the other person's specialness that they forget to create situations in which their own specialness can be acknowledged. They keep the other person at "center stage" and neglect their own needs for creative expression and attention.

In their romances, these folks must take responsibility for creating relationships in which they not only give love and honor the specialness of the other person, but in which they are also honored and loved, so that the flow goes both ways. If they neglect to express their own needs, they inadvertently create an imbalance. When they realize that the relationship revolves totally around the other person, with no energy coming back, they lose interest. Worse yet, they may create a monster out of the person they initially admired: The other person may develop a "divine right" attitude and a puffed-up ego!

For example, I had a client with this nodal position who went out of her way to make her boyfriend happy—doing the things he liked, having little surprises for him, and so on. She encouraged him to let her know what he needed in a relationship and then yielded her own identity to accommodate his needs. He was totally in love with her, but she noticed she was beginning to lose interest because the energy wasn't "coming back." Rather than detaching from the relationship (a normal tendency for these folks), she decided to take the initiative and let him know what she needed to be happy.

She had a need for romance, so she bought him a book of "101 ways to say I love you." She let him know that romantic cards and flowers were important to her to keep the love energy going. She told him how to react if she got in a bad mood: "Just make me laugh and I'll pop right out of it." She practically gave him an instruction manual for how to keep her happy. She was on track, taking a straightforward approach to create the happiness she needed. In this case, however, her boyfriend still didn't "get it" and she ultimately left the relationship. But since she had "done her part," it was the first relationship she ever left where she felt completed with it.

MAKING CHOICES

Leo North Node people think that half the process of having a happy marriage is choosing the "right mate." The only problem is that they try to choose their mate mentally, rather than trusting the energy connection they feel with another person. This can postpone their having *any* marriage, or leave them stranded in an unhappy marriage because they overrode what their hearts said and chose with their heads. They say to themselves: "This person has a good social background, they're financially secure, they have the qualities I would like to have in a mate, they are attractive, they will make a good father/mother, they are about the right age/height/weight; generally they 'make sense.'" And that's it—they get married. Yet when they make personal relationship choices based on mental "logic," their choices rarely make them happy in the long run.

Later in life these folks are generally more open to a relationship based on the happiness they feel on a consistent basis with the other person. When they find such a relationship, the other person may be very different from what they thought they wanted; yet that is the person who makes their heart sing with joy.

The romantic interaction that Leo North Node people seek in relationships is perpetually available to them when they are linked with a person who truly inspires their creative fire on a vital, authentic (not mind-based) level. In such a relationship, where the body helps decide the attraction, they are experts at keeping the romance alive—they need this to feel involved with life in a happy way.

On a deep level they know what is making them happy and what is not, but they have to be willing to let go of their image of what will make them happy and become more open to what they are actually *experiencing*. When they take the risk and pursue what genuinely makes them happy, they may feel a bit insecure at first if people seem to resist. But others will eventually see the wisdom and come into alignment with their choices.

FRIENDSHIP

Leo North Node people have had many past lifetimes in which friendship was a major factor. In these relationships, mutual dependencies were inadvertently created. In the process of becoming so identified with their friends, these folks lost touch with their own individuality. In this incarnation, when they first look for support from their peers with similar interests, it's not there. This is because they need to learn *not* to rely on their friendships at the expense of their own individuality and creativity.

While these folks are learning to be themselves, friends can actually be a detriment rather than an asset. For example, if they are having a problem in a love affair and ask a friend for advice, often the friend will suggest they go in a direction that doesn't work out. It's not that the friend wants them to be unhappy; it's just that others often give nonobjective advice: a reflection of how *they* would handle the situation, and not necessarily what is best for the Leo North Node person. These folks are learning *not* to depend on the advice of others. They themselves are the master strategists; when they follow their own instincts, they always win.

When these folks rely on friends and their friends let them down, or they feel taken advantage of, the universe is saying: "You can't do that. You're not going to compromise yourself. You're going to start being who you really are!" They identify so closely with their friends that they give beyond the boundaries of what is appropriate in a friendship. Then they expect the other person to give back to them equally; when it doesn't work that way, they are disappointed. They are learning the boundaries of friendship; to give what they can—without expectation of return and without violating their own essential strength and energy. As they grow in the direction of their own individuality, choose to express their own creativity, and stand on their own, they will find that more reliable friends are drawn to them.

One of their most important jobs is learning to credit others with the strength and potency to create victories in their own lives. If they do this, they will not fall into the trap of allowing others to become unnecessarily dependent on them. When they hang on to the idea that others can't get by without them, it's an ego trip. But when they validate the individuality, strength, and confidence of others, they gain confidence in their own potency to be an individual and follow their own dreams—to be led by the little child within that likes to play and have a good time. They must follow and express *that* part of themselves, regardless of group pressure or the acceptance of their peers.

GOALS

SELF-DETERMINATION

In this lifetime, Leo North Node people are not enacting someone else's dream. They are learning how to create their own dream, and it is solely up to them! It's not that they can't enlist others to help . . . but no one else is going to take the helm.

They know what's going to happen—they "see the writing on the wall" and think others see it too. But this is not the case. Often people are so involved in the drama that they are unaware of the patterns that cause unhappy outcomes for themselves and others. But when these folks take charge, it works for everyone. They have a special talent for seeing what's going to happen and translating it into constructive leadership. Rather than sitting back and allowing the potentially disastrous circumstances they foresee to come about, they must participate—use their input to alter the course of events to achieve a more positive outcome.

SELF-ACCEPTANCE

Leo North Node people are learning self-acceptance: to accept and embrace the child in their own nature. They are learning to acknowledge that they, too, have needs and to recognize and pursue what makes them happy. Once they accept themselves by acknowledging their wants and needs, then others can accept them and help them get what they want.

These folks tend to be very hard on themselves, because even though they can see what's going to happen, they tend to feel totally unprepared when it does. They need to recognize that this is normal. It's impossible to be prepared for a new situation—that's where excitement, joy, and the zest for life come from! That's how knowledge is gained—from dealing with circumstances that are totally unfamiliar! The best opportunities for testing one's strength and ingenuity are the unfamiliar situations we encounter along our path.

ENLISTING OTHERS

Once Leo North Node people have established where they want to go, it's just a question of getting the folks around them to join the party. The best bet is to be straightforward in stating their direction, sharing the basis from which they made their decision and then inviting others to join them. For example: "In the larger scheme of things, this is what I see going on. Therefore, I have decided to go in this direction. Now, given the circumstances, do you feel you would like to join me, or do you feel there's another direction you would rather go on your own?"

I had a client with this nodal position whose job was to bring his industry into the computer age. To do this, he had to enlist the cooperation of the plant managers. So, he went to each plant to convince the managers that the age of computers was inevitable and there was no choice but to computerize. They agreed in theory; but when it came to actually installing the computers and changing procedures, the managers voiced all their objections and continued to do things in the old way. He met opposition and struggle at every turn.

It would have been much simpler had he spent less time explaining and more time asserting his will. For example: "I'm sure it's clear to everyone that the age of computers is here. Therefore, this plant will be fully computerized by June of next year. Now we are going to need plant managers who can work with this. Do you think you will be able to adapt and learn the new systems? Do you think you will be able to come into alignment with what we need so you can continue on board with us?" Then the plant managers' energy would have been geared in the direction of cooperation rather than opposition.

FUTURE ORIENTATION

Leo North Node people have an innate capacity to recognize things before they happen: to appreciate an art form before others see its value, to see real estate opportunities before the idea occurs to others, to notice trends before they become popular. Their challenge is to take advantage of the opportunities they see. This is why they seem to have "good timing"—they see how things will unfold, and when they are on "on track" they put themselves in a position to benefit as the situation develops.

However, their tendency to withdraw can tempt them to resist using their potential. An opportunity may inspire their enthusiasm, but they may pull back because they can see the "hype" or think the people involved have less than noble motives. What they are learning to recognize is that their unique capacity to see the "game" gives them an edge in winning it! And because of their ethical, clear approach, their participation can improve the quality of the game for everyone.

This is a leadership lifetime for these folks. Their job is to become involved and, through healthy leadership, prevent the injustices that would otherwise occur. They consider a situation and say: "This is how the game works. If I play, they are going to try to do this . . . and this . . . and this." Leo North Nodes are learning to exercise their strength and realize that when they see these things coming, they can intercede and change the course before it overtakes them.

USING CREATIVE ENERGY

ENERGY TRANSMISSION THROUGH ACTING

Leo North Node people are natural actors and actresses. Because they do not have a strong sense of individuality, they do not form a strong ego attachment to—or identification with—any particular role. Their natural objectivity allows them to notice all salient details of the character they are playing; they can get into the role and become fully involved. Whether as a career or a hobby, acting is definitely a healthy release for these folks and a moving, enriching experience for their audiences.

Any kind of performing is wonderful for Leo North Node people. They are born entertainers. When they are onstage their whole being lights up. They love the energy that comes from making other people happy; indeed, that's what they're here to do in this lifetime—to give love to others on a personal level. Because the relationship between entertainer and audience is personal, they thrive in this arena.

As long as they find a way to be at "center stage," the situation will work for everyone involved. Yet they often resist it because they are afraid of looking foolish, or of what their peers will think. These folks have had lots of past lifetimes watching other people take center stage; in this lifetime they fear being successful because they haven't done it themselves. Yet someone has to be the person in the spotlight, receiving the applause, and when they do it everyone has a good time. This is their lifetime to take center stage *because* their ego needs development—they need that energy to balance them, and they are actually hindering their development if they don't get out there and do it.

Leo North Node people have the capacity to sway an audience by virtue of the emotions they transmit. They can feel the audience's energy and can make the audience feel their own energy. Whatever is in their heart, they can project outward. They can control the audience's emotions and take them in a new direction, almost physically feeling the energy move as if the audience's emotions were tied to their own. It's a feeling of control and power—but a positive one that generates enthusiasm, empathy, and emotional connectedness. These folks are tremendously energized by the process. Although they may feel drained afterwards, they will also feel alive! When they give these emotional experiences to others, both sides feel the vitality and healing power of the connection, and everyone wins.

When they apply this talent to a smaller arena—with a child or a partner—they can be equally successful. Even in daily life, Leo North Node people have the capacity to play out a role that cheers others and lightens their loads through inspiration or humor. Yet sometimes they undervalue their gifts. They may think it's more important to be the person writing the songs—but it is the singer who chooses the songs and directly affects the audience, and they love doing it! When they inspire positive energy and enthusiasm in others, they become excited and involved themselves.

HIGHER CONSCIOUSNESS: THE ANGEL CONNECTION

Leo North Node people have the gift of being in touch with their Angels—a level of consciousness that shows the next step in creating their dream. Suddenly, ideas occur to them about what their future could be and what they could create—because these folks have a clear, objective view of the future and can see things in advance. They must choose one thing they would like to do and then make the decision to actively create it.

As soon as they make that decision, a host of ideas occurs to them about how to successfully create their dream. The proper sequence seems to spontaneously appear; as they follow one step, the next step unfolds. The timing is absolutely miraculous. As they take each step, doors open and the right opportunities for success are presented to them. But it's up to them to respond to this angelic help by taking each step.

The process is a lot like surfing. The surfer begins in a calm place with broad horizons. Then a large wave begins to form around him. He becomes aware of the wave only moments before he must decide whether or not to ride it. If he makes the decision in time and catches the right wave, he has a heck of a ride and a whole lot of fun! If he catches the wrong wave, he may not have as smooth a ride but he still finds himself intensely involved and having an adventure. However, if he sits on his surfboard all day long and never catches any waves, he has a safe but boring time filled with memories of missed opportunities.

Leo North Node people have clear vision, but it's up to them to take the chance and catch the wave. Do they have the talent and skill to successfully rise to the occasion? They'll never know unless they take the risk, and then they will find they have creative talents that they never even suspected—talents that arise *only* when they ride the wave. They must put themselves in an intense situation of risk, excitement, or romance to really express their creative talents. That's when they feel most alive.

But even if they catch every wave, Leo North Node people need a principle or ideal to live by that extends beyond their personal life. They need a star to follow—a spiritual pledge that will empower them and lead them through the creative process to their goal. This ideal or value needs to be a moderating principle in all their actions. For example, it could be the commitment to "follow their bliss" regardless of fear or insecurity. It could involve speaking their truth regardless of others' reactions, or furthering causes such as human rights, world peace, or healing the environment. Their correct "goal" will not engender feelings of sadness or tight-lipped perseverance; it will be emotionally uplifting. By aligning themselves with a cause that extends beyond the personal arena, they become bigger than the personal arena and are willing to take risks and make real changes.

Leo North Node people have an incredible ability to create through the power of their imaginations—their use of visualization and their connection with Angels. They can attract the people and situations they want simply through the power of their wishes. If they truly make up their minds, whatever they ask of the universe (if it is in alignment with their good) will come to them. Suddenly their lives will shift—new people and situations will appear to lure them in a different direction that will bring about the fulfillment of their wishes. Their job is to accept the new opportunities presented. Problems arise when they try to analyze and judge these opportunities—then they miss their timing. They are learning to go in the direction of their dreams: to take the risks and put forth the creative energy to make it happen, even if they don't know the route ahead of time.

Leo North Node people simply need to keep their minds on the goal and do *whatever* it takes to push past the "second force" resistance (see the previous discussion under Personality) that is part of the creative process. Inertia is self-perpetuating; in creating something new and vital, inertia becomes resistance. Sometimes it takes incredible intensity to break through the second force and rise above the old, self-perpetuating patterns. It takes will, discipline, and a firm intention to create the new *regardless* of how much energy is required. Going through the resistance to create a new reality empowers Leo North Node people to truly appreciate the dream they manifest.

Creating the realization of a dream held in the heart is never easy. In fact, that's why we have dreams—they are the "carrots" that lure us past our limitations and cause us to grow beyond who we thought we were. When we rise out of the pool of complacency and ego to follow the path to fulfillment of the unique dream in our heart, we grow and become free. Ultimately, it is freedom and vitality that these people want. The active path to creatively pursuing their dreams will take them there.

VITALITY

Leo North Node people long to reconnect with the joy and vitality of their inner life force. They desire an experience that will make them feel alive, so the universe responds by offering them a situation that can stimulate and restore their life force. If they accept the opportunity and move through it, much growth, aliveness, and joy will be gained along the way. They instinctively reach for these vital experiences, but often their mind steps in and invalidates their creative impulses. In this lifetime, their job is not to listen to their mind but to follow the excitement of their inner child.

MAKING DECISIONS

These folks often experience a sharp discrepancy between what their knowledge base tells them they should do, and what their heart tells them they should do. The choice may boil down to creative passion versus safety—but when they choose creative passion, they win, and when they choose safety, they lose. If they look back over past experiences, they can see how it has worked out in their lives. This is because their "knowing" is actually a logical projection of the future based on their past experiences. However, they have access to many other possible futures, if they take responsibility for changing the direction of the present.

Leo North Node people should ask themselves if making decisions based on what they "know" is leading to increased—or decreased—feelings of aliveness. If following a path that they "know" to be the correct one diminishes their personal vitality, they need to reconsider before they waste years on a path they will later regret. They need to acknowledge and act on the truthful feedback they receive from their own state of being. This means trusting that their passion is strong enough to pull them through, to ensure their survival, to feed them the energy required to build a new life.

Once I lived next door to a retirement home, and I asked many senior citizens about their lives. Looking back, what was important to them? What did they wish they had done differently? Although they gave different answers on many things, every one of them told me that they never regretted the things they had tried that ended up being mistakes; what they regretted were the things they had *wanted* to do and not done—the chances they *hadn't* taken. Leo North Node people are learning to take those chances.

This is not to say that they should handle their lives in an irresponsible way. They can make decisions to follow their vitality, and then enact those decisions in an intelligent way that takes other people into account. For example, to stay in a destructive, abusive marriage "for the sake of the children" would not be wise. It would be giving the children the message: "I can endure and suffer. It's okay to be unhappy in life." However, it would be prudent to handle the departure from the marriage in a responsible way (for example, telling the children in advance that there are problems in the marriage, communicating what is going on) so that the children aren't given a last-minute shock. Leo North Node people must carry out their plans in a creative, responsible way that takes others' feelings into account.

TAKING ACTION

Sometimes the greatest challenge for Leo North Node people involves taking actions that make them happy. They are so accustomed to doing things for everyone else that they tend to put the joyous child within themselves on the back burner. In this life they are learning to do what they need to do for themselves.

The irony is that after these folks take action on their own, someone often shows up to help. If they hold back and wait, fearing to act until they have everything they need, it will never happen. The action they take may not make sense to others, but if they feel a happiness in their hearts around it, their job is to do it with or without the support of others.

For Leo North Node people, all the real knowledge accumulated during past lives was gathered into their inner child, and that is why following the child within makes their lives work in joyous ways. Conversely, when they look for "knowledge" to be sure they're going to be "safe," they never summon enough energy and the opportunities pass them by. The inner child is the sense of having fun, the sense of play, of taking a risk and doing something that makes them happy. For example, if they get the idea: "Wow! I think I'd like to go swimming today!" and they feel excitement about it, then it would be following their inner child to go and do it. Every time they follow that sense of fun and excitement and act on the prompting of their inner child, that part of themselves is validated and becomes stronger. Connecting with the inner child to gauge whether or not they are on track is their key to success.

HEALING THEME SONG *

I have written a healing song for each nodal group to help shift its energy in a positive way, since music is a potent vehicle for emotionally supporting us in taking risks.

BE THE CHILD YOU WERE

The message of this song is meant to put Leo North Node people in touch with their own inner child, from whom they can gain the self-confidence and stimulation they need to create their own destiny.

Selected lyrics:

> *Sometimes I wonder, if we saw when we were born*
> *Our destiny—crystal clear—before us*
> *Sometimes I wonder, before the world became our guide,*
> *If we knew to follow who we are inside.*
>
> *Be the child you were—be the child you were*
> *Before the world got to you*
> *Told you things that were not true*
> *Be the child you were—be the child you were.*

---

* These lyrics are set to music and sung in their entirety on the CD and cassette tape "Unfolding As It Should."

North Node in Virgo
and North Node in the 6th House

OVERVIEW

Attributes to Develop

Work in these areas can help uncover hidden gifts and talents

- Participation
- Bringing order to chaos
- Creating routines
- Focusing on the here and now
- Acting on feelings of compassion
- Being of service to others
- Analyzing and categorizing
- Gaining self-confidence through experience
- Moderation
- Taking risks in spite of fears
- Noticing and valuing details

Tendencies to Leave Behind

Working to reduce the influence of these tendencies can help make life easier and more enjoyable

- Being a victim (or having victim consciousness)
- Confusion and disorientation
- Avoidance of planning
- Escapism/addictive tendencies (drugs, alcohol, excessive sleep, daydreaming, etc.)
- Extremism
- Oversensitivity
- Self-doubt
- Feelings of inadequacy
- Withdrawal
- Vagueness (not wanting to commit)/inaction
- Giving up

ACHILLES' HEEL/TRAP TO AVOID/THE BOTTOM LINE

Virgo North Nodes' Achilles' heel is victim consciousness ("If I don't have constant, compassionate attention and understanding from others, someone will take advantage of me"). But it's a bottomless pit: Others can never give them enough reassurance to overcome their inner sense of helplessness and paranoia. Only when they look within can they discover what outer structures they need to create in order to give themselves strength and purpose.

The trap they must avoid is an unending search for a savior or mentor whom they can trust blindly and to whom they can surrender ("If only I can surrender enough, God will put things in order"). However, life has shown them that inward surrender will not make the external world orderly and productive. The only way they can achieve their goals is to organize their lives in the way *they* need them to be, so they will feel safe and strong.

The bottom line is that they'll never feel they have enough confidence to go into the world and do something productive. At some point they simply have to begin actively participating in life. The irony is that when they begin to participate and learn what leads to successful results, they will gain the confidence they seek.

WHAT THESE PEOPLE REALLY WANT

What these people really want is to be lost in the security blanket of their own personal connection with the universe. They want to "let go" into something larger than themselves that will support them and give them an expanded sense of identity. Virgo North Node people have an insatiable need to experience peace and oneness. But to successfully attain this goal, they must go into the world and be of service to others. As they shift attention from their own fears and focus instead on the here and now, they can easily see how to restore order in situations of chaos.

TALENTS/PROFESSION

These people make excellent doctors, dentists, nurses, or nurses' aides, because such professions give them the opportunity to use their healing energies while being of service in practical ways. Psychologist, healer, dietician, accountant, organizer, and craftsperson are also good choices. Virgo North Node people have "good karma" on the job and get along well with co-workers and employees. They can accomplish a task in one hour that might take another person five; they should be in a situation where "getting the job done" is honored, rather than simply working for an hourly wage.

Another reason the healing professions are excellent choices is that these jobs deal with the physical nuts and bolts of life. In fields where success is so dependent on paying attention to detail, Virgo North Node people are forced to stay in the present. For them, the process of physically creating order relieves psychological stress.

Virgo North Node people also have compassion and a capacity to remain aware of the larger picture. These past-life gifts of spiritual awareness are an asset when Virgo North Node actively participates in creating tangible results. However, professions in which the goal is attainment of spiritual consciousness and forgiveness tend to undermine the grounding these people need to feel strong and complete.

HEALING AFFIRMATIONS SPECIFIC TO VIRGO NORTH NODE

- "I'm the only person who can put this situation in order, so I might as well do it."
- "This is *not* a victim lifetime."
- "When I withdraw, I lose; when I participate in creating positive results, I win."
- "When I focus and have a plan, the whole universe opens the pathway to success."

PERSONALITY

PAST LIVES

These people have an innate awareness of the spiritual dimension of life and are attuned to the higher, lovelier realms of their own natures. They are extremely sensitive, easily wounded, and very careful to avoid causing pain to others. In fact, they are sometimes more aware of—and concerned about—other people's suffering than the people are themselves.

DISSOLUTION OF EGO

Virgo North Node people have a history of many lifetimes spent in dissolution of the ego—either through meditation and spiritual quests; drug and/or alcohol abuse; confinement and time to reflect in convents, prisons, or asylums; or losing themselves in music, poetry, or art. No matter how the dissolution occurred, in this life they must deal with the effects. If it occurred through spiritual orientation, this lifetime will be total confusion until they find a spiritual path with principles similar to those of past incarnations. If it occurred through the use of drugs or alcohol, these people will have addictive tendencies in this lifetime that may again be problematic and may have to be overcome from a spiritual perspective (the 12-step programs of Alcoholics Anonymous, etc.). Talents with poetry, music, and art may still remain as a way of connecting with lofty emotional states.

These people have had many ethereal experiences and incarnations in which they gave up bits and pieces of their own identity in order to merge with a higher energy. But they have completed that process; allowing themselves to dissolve any further in this lifetime is counterproductive. They have already yielded to being absorbed in their vision. In this lifetime, they want to manifest their vision in the physical world.

HUMILITY

In past life experiences, these people purified themselves by questioning their own motives and recognizing where they were lacking in virtue, thereby gaining a tremendous amount of insight that now allows them to be nonjudgmental toward others. In this lifetime, they don't consider themselves "superior" in any way—their introspection has resulted in true humility.

Virgo North Node people have had so many victim lifetimes that they tend to give up too easily. They don't do well with confrontation, competition, or any strong reactions against them. Their psyches are very sensitive, and life can seem harsh to these folks. In general, they don't believe that more "stuff" is going to make them happier. Since their motivation for living is not to gain material things, if the world seems to resist their efforts to participate, they have a tendency to simply give up.

Because of past lives of being taken advantage of, when these people produce a creative work it is not uncommon to find that they have allowed it to be publicly distributed without any compensation, or that someone else has taken both the credit and the money. Often they don't even mind. After all, the work fulfilled the service it was intended for. Also, in past-life monastic experiences they may have taken a vow of poverty and thus feel uneasy about accumulating wealth in this incarnation. Subconsciously, they may feel there is something "impure" about accumulating money. They need to recognize that money is a by-product of service—a barometer of the usefulness of their participation.

Virgo North Node people are truly compassionate and want to help wherever they can. In this lifetime, they need to recognize that by creating solid material bases and allowing their lives to become strong, they are in a better position to help on a wider scale. In this lifetime, to allow themselves to be "victims" does not work; *resisting* this tendency is the higher road for them.

Diffusion Versus Focus

These people have had many past lifetimes shut away from society. They are not accustomed to being in the world. Consider what it would be like to live many lifetimes in monasteries, where gongs signal the times for rising, meditation, prayers, exercise, eating, working, and sleeping—and someone else is ringing them! Monasteries function in this way so that the participants can gain an awareness of timelessness, formlessness, and the flow that underlies the mundane details of life. While this works very well in a monastery, now Virgo North Node people need to learn how to live in the world.

They must learn how to set routines for themselves—how to ring their own gongs. For instance, because they are accustomed to having someone else organize their time, they may have trouble being punctual. However, when they summon the self-discipline to live by the rules that give structure to society, they gain tremendous power and the self-confidence they need to function in the world. Thus, it is important for them to take charge and make sure they are on time for their appointments. Structure gives order and stability to their lives in ways that are nurturing and supportive.

Owing to the seclusion of their past lives, Virgo North Node people know how to entertain themselves with the power of their minds and imaginations. But what worked in the past is actually a detriment in this incarnation, where they need to produce positive, practical, tangible results in the material world. Thus, all forms of escapism are counterproductive for them. Daydreaming, drugs, alcohol, too much solitude, excessive sleeping—any form of withdrawal from life undermines their confidence.

This is not to say that they can't occasionally enjoy themselves (relax and take a "break" from dealing with the nuts and bolts of life), but they must guard against overdoing avenues of escape to the point of forming addictions.

IMAGINATION, DAYDREAMS, AND FANTASY

These people have an acute awareness of the psychic and/or imaginative realms from their past lives. If these talents are not now directed properly, they can become a weakness resulting in paranoia, fear, and anxiety. However, when Virgo North Node people work toward a goal, their mystical talents can be used as tools to get the job done effectively. If there is an outlet for their creative imaginations—a service to provide for others—their visionary abilities can be a marvelous asset.

Virgo North Node people should keep their creative imaginations flowing outward by serving others and producing tangible results, rather than inward with undirected self-examination. They need to go through the hard work necessary to make their visions real by doing the research, organizing the project, producing it, and then seeing that it gets distributed. Getting the job done is easy and joyful in this lifetime—once they've defined their goal.

What these folks need to avoid is a tendency to daydream and fantasize. Through daydreaming they can connect with delicate, ethereal states of consciousness—almost as though they were on a "bliss" drug in some billowy realm. However, this state defeats their ability to function in the material world.

If they're not happy with their situation, instead of working to change it they tend to use fantasy to escape into their own world. If used in moderation, these fantasies can actually give them a better idea of what they want. But it can take tremendous discipline to break the energy connection of the fantasy. It's so addictive that it's better for these folks to simply avoid indulging in deep fantasy. They can become so attached to otherworldly states of bliss that it prevents them from establishing the order and fulfillment in their daily lives that they need to experience *true* bliss. For example, they might become so involved in a fantasy involving family that it would prevent them from creating satisfying family relationships in their own lives.

I had a 48-year-old male client with this nodal position who had a fantasy of the "ideal woman," and given the power of his fantasies, she was almost a reality in his imagination! He became involved in many relationships but couldn't really commit, because none of the women matched the woman in his fantasy. This had been going on for thirty years, and he was still living alone and feeling depressed. Unfortunately, he deprived himself of the opportunity to learn what relationships are all about by not focusing on how he actually felt in response to the women he spent time with. In this way, fantasy can prevent these folks from taking constructive action to make their dreams come true in the physical realm.

CONFUSION VERSUS COUNSELING

Virgo North Node people sometimes lapse into a confused state of consciousness. For many people, confusion can be good: a prelude to a higher order. But for these folks, confusion is not "on path." When they become confused, they begin questioning themselves and doubting everything they are doing, which undermines their current course of action. They need to turn away from the confused energy, refocus on circumstances in the outer world that triggered the confusion, and then re-enter the situation and restore it to order.

For example, if they become confused about a backlog of paperwork, their best bet is to sit down and go through the papers, physically handle them, and reorganize them in a way that makes sense to them. If they are confused about the behavior of a co-worker, they should face it head-on: Talk to the person and find out what is altering his or her behavior.

When experiencing a problem, Virgo North Node people usually benefit from going to a therapist or talking things out with a friend, because the interaction enables them to gain a more practical perspective. Their imaginations are so active that on their own, they tend to exaggerate problems and imagine all kinds of unresolvable situations. Their imagined fears can paralyze them from taking the steps that would restore order in their lives. So it is very helpful for them to get feedback as to whether their fears are based in reality or the product of an overactive imagination. Virgo North Node people are much more successful when they actively experiment to see what does and does not work on a practical level. They should not try to figure it all out in their heads.

If Virgo North Node people feel they are losing their boundaries in a relationship and are having difficulty communicating their frustration to their partner, then they may want to bring in a third party. They can be so sensitive to not wanting to hurt their partner that they may avoid the approach that would actually "get through." The partner may need to hear: "Stop! This behavior is not acceptable! If you continue this behavior, you will push me to the point where I will leave!" A marriage counselor can be a valuable ally in communicating with their partner.

These folks actually make excellent counselors themselves, professionally and with their friends. Others feel their tremendous empathy and naturally trust them. Virgo North Node people have an energy that induces other people to confide in them; an analytical mind that enables them to give clear, practical advice; and a remarkable ability to combine intuition with common sense.

VAGUENESS VERSUS DETAIL

These people are so used to maintaining an awareness of the larger picture that they can easily overlook the details of the here and now. This can cause them to take actions that are not in their best interests. But as long as they pay attention to the actual details of any situation, they are very seldom deceived.

When they allow themselves to live in an unfocused state, they often start to feel anxious without knowing why. They may even feel vulnerable to attack, becoming overly suspicious and fearful of other people. In those moments, if they can just remember to focus on the details of what is going on around them (the clothes that someone is wearing, the details in a store window display, how the temperature of the air feels on their face, etc.), they calm down and feel secure again.

PAST-LIFE FEARS VERSUS THE HERE AND NOW

Virgo North Node people have learned the consequences of breaking the law in past lives, so in this incarnation they may have a strong sense of right and wrong, and an absolute phobia about breaking the law. They have a long history of superstition and may have many ideas about certain omens that should be followed to avoid a fearsome punishment. But looking for omens distracts them from noticing commonsense details. They have had so many past-life experiences with spiritual "messages" that they enter *this* lifetime looking for premonitions and ignore what is happening on a tangible level. Rather than watching for omens, these folks are better off observing the physical facts and getting direct feedback from others to confirm that they are on the right track. If they fear that "something is out of order," rather than withdrawing, their best bet is to step forward and participate, enlist the support of others, face the fear, and create an environment that prevents the worst-case scenario from happening. As a simple example, rather than fearing that their telephone will be turned off, it is much better to set a regular time each month for paying the bills.

These folks excel in activities that bring them into the here and now. Bookkeeping is good for them, because they know their own financial situation at any given time. It is very empowering for them to be able to pull out their records and see what they had last year, and how it compares to this year. It gives them a powerful sense of grounding, orientation, and confidence.

Whatever keeps Virgo North Node people focused in the moment becomes a labor of love for them. Their jobs can have that effect on them; if not, they should reconsider their line of work. Computers can be excellent for them because, once again, the physical involvement and details keep them focused in the present moment. They excel at—and are very happy with—anything that requires paying attention to details in order to produce successful results.

SELF-DOUBT AND ANXIETY VERSUS FAITH AND ACTION

There is an aspect to Virgo North Node people that is very introverted and introspective. When they feel anxiety, they turn inward for solace and understanding. Unfortunately, they have no external checks to this inner process, and there's no end to the anxiety, doubt, and suspicion that they can access. These people also have a tendency to go off by themselves and look back over their lives to see where they "went wrong." But this can lead to a tremendous feeling of failure totally out of proportion to the facts. When they retreat and reflect, they are trying to understand things; but this practice simply does not work for them. They need to avoid self-doubt at all costs.

One of the worst things Virgo North Node people can do is doubt the purity of their goal. By the time they have gotten a clear picture of their objective, they have already run it through a rigorous process in their own mind to make sure it has a pure motive, is harmless, and will be of service to others. In this lifetime they are finding out how their vision can work on the practical level. It is healthy for them to use a process of trial and error, as this helps them discover what makes things work in the material realm.

These folks cling to the idea that when they encounter chaos, they can work it out and rise above it *inwardly,* and the situation will resolve itself *outwardly.* This creates frustration for those who are anticipating that the Virgo North Node person will become actively involved in solving the problem. They don't understand when these folks remove themselves. It also creates frustration for people with this nodal position, as they feel misunderstood and don't comprehend why their system isn't working. However, in this lifetime they aren't able to resolve their problems by turning inward. From an astrological point of view, resolution must come through external action.

Virgo North Node people also tend to invalidate themselves with feelings of inadequacy, which can really lead to a downward spiral. Sometimes they intuitively "pick up" a problem in advance, or feel anxious about their relationship with a person or the outcome of a situation, but don't know why. If they focus on the anxiety, they imagine all kinds of "worst-case scenarios" and begin to interpret outer events selectively, in ways that validate their paranoia. Then, to regain a sense of inner balance and fight back their fear, they begin to doubt their intuitive response. Either way—using their minds to validate or invalidate their fears—does not work. What *does* work is reaching outside themselves for more objective information.

In fact, these folks' intuitions are generally correct. For example, imagine that when they went to work they left a window open (a detail they didn't consciously notice, but perhaps saw out of the corner of their eye). Suddenly it starts to rain and they become irrationally anxious about home, visualizing a burglar breaking in or a fire starting. They are fearful about their home and don't know why. The solution is to return home, where they will probably notice the open window and rain coming in. The situation around which they feel anxious is accurate; and when they check out the details objectively, they can see the problem in a way that empowers them to resolve it, such as closing the window. They should neither invalidate their intuition nor indulge their fears, but rather physically face the situation and analyze the facts, seeking more information if they need it.

Virgo North Node people need to have more faith in what they want to do—and faith, for them, is best built through action. Faith is a gift from their past lives. Through their experiences with surrender and seeing the larger vision, they gained faith in the moment-to-moment unfolding of daily living. In this lifetime, they know innately that "all is well and everything is happening as it should," and they gain peace of mind and confidence from remembering this.

For example, I had a client with North Node in Virgo who lost her job. She used anxiety to boost herself into action; although she had three months to find another position, she immediately started looking. She found two positions and chose the one that fulfilled her idealistic picture of the ease of working in the suburbs instead of the city. After ten days on the job, she realized she had made a mistake and called to reapply for the first job. After much trouble and reluctance, they did accept her, but she was glad she went through the experience. "If I had immediately worked at the city clinic, I wouldn't have appreciated it. I would wonder if I would have been happier in the suburbs. This way, I know!" The ability to see how everything is working in one's ultimate favor is based on faith that "life is on my side and everything is unfolding in a way that can ultimately lead to my greatest happiness."

A "Serve or Suffer" Lifetime

For Virgo North Node people, service is the antidote for internal suffering. These people have a great sense of connectedness with humankind and a deep compassion for the suffering of others. Even when someone wrongs another person, they usually understand both sides. They are innately nonjudgmental, and their hearts easily resonate with the suffering of others.

These folks are learning to act on their feelings of compassion. They have an inner knowledge that they are here to serve other people; yet when they start to do it, they begin to waver. When insecurities arise, they can remind themselves that their motive for helping is pure—their only intentions are to be of service and restore order. When they focus on the other person and what they can do to help, they are filled with a calm confidence. To be happy, they always have to be "fixing" something. Volunteer work or helping out friends and family makes them feel useful and fulfilled. It's healthy for them to have lots of outer-directed activities.

They are not usually motivated to help promote abstract ideas: ending world hunger, manifesting global peace, or supporting the environment. They are motivated to help people. When somebody says: "I'm hungry" or "I'm having allergic reactions to my home environment," they can't say no. When somebody enters their personal space and touches them, their hearts well up with the joy of giving. But they need direct interaction to get their "helping juices" flowing.

Sometimes Virgo North Node people focus their desire to help on *themselves*. They may become self-absorbed, which can lead to a number of problems. They might worry more about how something affects *them* and not how it affects another person. For example, if someone at the office gets angry, they might be more concerned about "What are they trying to do to me?" rather than "What can I do to help them feel better?" They assume that everyone else always knows what they're doing, and they think: "I'm in the weaker position. Others have to bend over backwards for me because they're smarter, stronger, and more worldly and should know how sensitive I am." However, the idea that they are "less than" others is not accurate. Actually, owing to many past incarnations spent in self-purification, in many ways *they* are more together!

Even if other people have a superior attitude, that doesn't mean they always know what they're doing. Thus, when Virgo North Node people assume that others know how sensitive they are but hurt them anyway, this is not correct. In truth, most other people are not as sensitive as these folks and are "rough" without realizing it. Virgo North Nodes need to stop focusing on themselves, and shift their concern to the other person. They should try to use their abilities to improve the situation, since others need and welcome their soothing, healing Virgo North Node energy.

Sometimes these people reverse their "less than" perception and see themselves as coming from a superior position. Then they feel they have to bend over backwards for others. When they see themselves as superior, they can afford to be kind; when they see themselves as inferior, they expect other people to be kind. Yet both positions are extremes, and neither one truly works because both have "self" as the center instead of service.

These folks are learning that they need to serve out of compassion and not out of duty. When they do things from feelings of love, they generate a spiritual quality that is the connection to the universe that they long for. When they are acting out of duty, they're doing it with their head; when they are acting out of compassion, it's coming from their heart. If they have to think about helping another, something is wrong. The genuine desire to help comes spontaneously from knowing themselves and being connected with their feelings. This gives them insight into human nature, a familial bond with others, and a connection to all humankind. When Virgo North Node people are in this spiritual, compassionate mode, incredible things happen to the people around them that are magical and healing.

GIVING VERSUS BEING DRAINED

These folks are by nature very sensitive, vulnerable, caring, compassionate, and forgiving—and this does leave them open to being taken advantage of.

In relationships, Virgo North Node people can gauge the right path by whether they lose or gain energy from an interaction. Other people feel their compassion and are attracted to them like moths to a flame. They listen to others' problems nonjudgmentally, with empathy, and then often find their own energy drained. The lesson is to be discriminating about who is really interested in finding solutions and who is just looking for a shoulder to cry on. They need to allow into their lives only those who are truly seeking productive solutions. These folks will be good for Virgo North Node people, giving them confidence in their problem-solving talents— which they have in abundance in this lifetime. When they share their ideas with people who are really looking for solutions, everybody wins.

However, when they allow people into their lives who are only looking for sympathy and whose conversation is a one-way list of endless problems, these folks begin to lose energy and self-confidence. The other person usually walks away feeling great (temporarily), but the Virgo North Node person may have incurred such an energy loss that he can barely drag himself to bed because he has not been successful in finding a productive solution.

This lessens his ability to help those who really are looking for solutions. Everyone loses when Virgo North Node people allow themselves to be exploited in this way.

Allowing their energy to be drained gives the message: "It's okay to take advantage of another person by making him or her feel worse so that you can feel better." When they do not allow this abuse, they are giving the other person the opportunity to stop, examine his or her behavior, and learn to become more sensitive to others.

These people may have a secret motive in allowing themselves to be abused. They have had many past lifetimes of suffering, self-abnegation, and pain, and they think that "no one really knows how much I've been through." On an unconscious level they are looking to have their suffering recognized, and may put up with other people dumping problems on them because they are awaiting "their turn" to talk about their distress and anxiety.

However, others don't generally "give back" by listening to them. And when they finally do find someone who will listen, it leads them into a bottomless pit of fear and anxiety. Moreover, they take the other person with them. Indeed, dwelling on unresolvable problems—either their own or someone else's—is just not scheduled to work this lifetime. All the past-life feelings of pain, martyrdom, and suffering are best kept in Pandora's box: *Don't open the lid!*

TRANSLATING LOVE INTO SERVICE

In past lives, Virgo North Node people gained a lot of understanding and love that they want to share. Thus, in this lifetime they need to focus, participate, and make their wisdom available to others. They are learning how to translate love into service—and how to reconnect with the feelings of boundless love and compassion within themselves.

They also have healing talents stemming from a tremendous power of faith, once they tap into it. Not infrequently, miraculous healing has occurred in their own lives. They truly understand that physical ailments have a deeper psychological basis or a higher spiritual dimension. Once they understand the "reason" behind the ailment, often the healing occurs spontaneously. It is the power of their faith, combined with their perception of the bigger picture, that precipitates these cures. They make great nurses and doctors, as their very presence can evoke faith in others.

They are also "hands-on" healers. That's why it's best for them to be physically involved in life, touching objects, pets, or people to help themselves get grounded. When they are fully present in the physical realm, all their psychic, spiritual abilities can come forth.

As they start healing people—staying in the moment and watching the details of where the energy is going and how the other person is responding—their psyche opens and they see exactly where to put their hands for maximum effect. When they do this healing work, they can tell where the other person is out of touch with his or her inner energies. They long to activate those energies so that the person can open to his or her own wholeness.

Through deep introspection and self-examination, these people have become truly nonjudgmental of others. They have a deep understanding of the common plight of humankind, knowing that everyone is doing the best they can with the Light they have right now. This understanding gives them compassion and acceptance of others. However, these folks must learn to separate being nonjudgmental in the moral realm from the necessity of practical discrimination. Many times, out of compassion or an effort to bring about healing, these folks withdraw and yield to the wills of more assertive personalities.

For example, I had a client with this nodal position who was severely harassed on her job for nine months. She was an assistant nurse and had a problem with one man at the hospital. She kept silently sending him love, trying to heal the situation, but much to her surprise it didn't do any good. She became so distressed that she decided to quit the job she loved. Then one night the man threatened her life, and she finally let someone know what had been going on. Eventually the man lost his job, but it cost my client nine months of severe distress.

This is a perfect example of what does and does not work for Virgo North Node people. This woman allowed herself to be victimized for nine months rather than actively participate to correct the problem, silently sending the violator Light, compassion, understanding, and love. In past lives the method worked, but not in *this* lifetime. Of course it's always a good idea to send others Light, but what works for these folks is taking *physical* action to correct negative circumstances.

NEEDS

SELF-CONFIDENCE

Virgo North Node people need to build self-confidence in this lifetime. Because of their sensitive natures, they are operating with underlying feelings of helplessness and constant vulnerability. This can all too easily lead to free-floating anxiety. They can't release these feelings until they can determine the cause. Then they usually recognize that their worries have little connection with reality, or they see how to avoid falling into the circumstances that subconsciously provoked the anxiety. This process generally goes more smoothly with outside help from a counselor or trusted friend— another point of view will steady them and keep them from turning inward.

For example, I had a client with this nodal position who was extremely anxious about accepting a job that looked very good on paper. It was exactly what he wanted, and the person making the offer promised him the world. However, he felt anxious about it without understanding why. While explaining it to me, he mentioned that he had previously worked in that part of the country with bittersweet results: He had made lots of money but felt very isolated socially, as there was a strong bias against his particular lifestyle. He was now at a time in his life when his social life was as important to him as his financial success. Once he understood where the anxiety was coming from, he connected with reality and made a confident decision not to accept the job.

Self-confidence is not innate for Virgo North Node people. They have a deep anxiety owing to their lack of practical experience in the world. Confidence is a by-product of successful experience, and these folks haven't had enough past-life experience in the world to know how truly effective they can be. However, they will find their confidence growing by leaps and bounds in every area of their lives where they consciously set goals. When they bypass their emotions and use their powerful abilities to focus on reaching an objective, they can be masters at discriminating between what works and what doesn't, and they can succeed in an amazingly short period of time. Once they get the idea, there is no stopping them.

BUILDING CONFIDENCE THROUGH WORLDLY EXPERIENCE

Since Virgo North Node people don't have a lot of "worldly success memories" in their subconscious, worldly things are not second nature to them. Sometimes they're afraid that if they "do something wrong," they can't have what they want. Actually, that's true, but it's not a moral or ethical issue—just a practical one! For these folks, a hands-on approach is best: learning by doing, experimenting, finding out what does and doesn't work through their own process. Virgo North Nodes are not "theoretically based" people who regard books as the final authority—they want practical results. They want to implement their vision and make it work in the physical world—and only they can do it.

They have no ego attachment to "being right" and are willing to make mistakes in the process of finding out how to do things successfully. This natural openness and humility works to their advantage, since mistakes are a necessary part of learning. Successes tell a person that he or she is correct in pursuing the present pathway with the techniques he or she is using; mistakes indicate being "off track." These folks are usually "quick studies," and it doesn't take them long to get the idea of what works and what doesn't in any situation.

Past-life experiences in asylums are also very connected with the karma of Virgo North Node people. This is why in the present incarnation they may fear "losing it" or going crazy—it is possible that parts of their psyches went out of balance in the past. Work is an excellent antidote for them in this lifetime. When they focus on their job and positive results, whatever part of their psyche was out of balance will come into permanent alignment through the practical necessity of getting the job done.

These people must be willing to take what may seem to be enormous risks to gain the confidence that comes from actively participating in life. For example, they may have all kinds of fears about looking for a job, but as soon as they move their feet the forward motion cuts through their fears. There is no way they can think their way beyond the anxiety; it is activity that gets them past an innate lack of confidence.

VULNERABILITY

Virgo North Node people are extremely sensitive, and they tend to think that others are just as sensitive. When they look closely, they can see beyond the masks that other people present into what is really going on: the others' motives, desires, and insecurities. They can do this because they are nonjudgmental. The resulting compassion allows them to see the inner worlds of others.

Because they have this ability, they assume that others can do the same. Thus, they feel very vulnerable when they are out in the world. What they must recognize is that others cannot see into them, for others have not yet experienced the self-purification required to look deeply behind people's masks. They worry about others judging them, yet holding judgments and preconceptions are the very traits that block others from this ability! Understanding this can be very liberating for these folks—they can act as if they have loads of self-confidence, and others will believe it.

When Virgo North Node people look at others they can see into their very souls, and thus feel tremendous compassion for others. But when others look at them, they only see the self-portraits painted by these folks. In this way, Virgo North Node people can control much of what happens in their lives in a constructive way by putting up a strong "front."

These people also assume that others are aware of how sensitive they are, of how much they yield and withhold to avoid hurting others, but this is not correct. This is why these folks must establish well-defined boundaries and let other people know when they get hurt. Rather than cry and give up, they should clearly define what is going on for the other person and set a clear, constructive course of mutual action.

OUTWARD FOCUS: PARTICIPATION

Virgo North Node people tend to have too much inward focus. One of my clients with this nodal position frequently said: "I can overcome this if I just go inside myself and think about it." My counsel was always: "No! Actively participate to bring order to the situation."

It can be tough to find out what is going on in these folks' minds, since their first instinct is to withdraw. It may not be easy for others to understand them, so sometimes their feelings don't get taken into account. To effectively enlist their participation, it may be necessary to ask them specific questions to determine what the situation looks like to them, how they feel about it, and what they want. Once they are clear about what they want to create, they will initiate action.

Their tendency to inward focus especially works to their disadvantage in social interactions. When they are relating with someone, if they become conscious of themselves and lose sight of the other person, they become anxious and withdraw. Their purpose in this lifetime is to serve others; when they stay focused on the other person and what they can do to help, they feel confident because they are "on path." But when they begin to question their own intent or how they are coming across to the other person, the focus shifts to themselves and they become anxious.

The key for Virgo North Node people is in connecting and problem solving *with others*. By helping others actively take steps to bring order to the situation, they help themselves. As long as they remember that their motive is to be helpful, they are filled with the confidence they need to interact joyfully. After all, if their primary motive is to be of service, they have nothing to lose. Keeping this in mind is very empowering for them. By concentrating on the other person and solving the problem through an orderly structure, their powerful focus helps create productive results.

These people have a tremendous ability to translate the flow of life into organized form. Once they have a specific goal, everything seems to "fall into place." The key for them is focus—by simply focusing on their objective, the steps unfold before them in a perfect, orderly sequence that proves to be the most efficient way of reaching their goal. In difficult situations they can see the areas of volatility, and by putting energy into creating a more stable base at the beginning, they prevent things from blowing up later on.

The ability to perfect things in the physical realm is a gift they were born with—and they are far better at it than anyone else on the planet. Yet it is a new gift, and they may not know they have it. It is like finding a "new room" inside themselves that holds talents for restoring things to order, analyzing, and successfully applying spiritual ethics in the material world. If they can open the door to that new room, they will find they have gifts for bringing a vision of spiritual love and order into their environment.

DISCRIMINATION

In past lives, Virgo North Node people gained a spiritual understanding of life. Although much of what they learned was accurate, some of the teachings were inaccurate or incomplete. They can learn to discriminate by experimenting with what actually works on a tangible level. For example, they may have been taught that having a compassionate love for all beings is Truth, but they may not have been taught the nuts and bolts of how to apply that Truth in the world, as it currently exists, in ways that are not harmful to themselves or others. It's up to them to learn how to do it—and they are experts at practical application once they realize that this is what they need to do.

These people are learning the lessons of clarity and discrimination in every area of their lives: what is real and what is fantasy; what is beneficial and what is destructive; who really needs their help and who just wants sympathy; when they are serving and when they are being victimized. They need to differentiate so that they can clear their consciousness and begin to create an efficient order that brings strength, stability, and confidence to their lives.

The folks in this nodal group usually are accurate in their intuitive sense of a situation but don't trust themselves until they have the details to back up their intuition. This process can lead to "selective viewing"—only seeing information that will substantiate their hunch. For example, if they project that a person is a certain way, eventually the person will do something that—taken out of context—supports their theory. But the whole process is really in their own minds.

If, on the other hand, they feel uneasy with someone but are able to put aside their feelings and watch the *reality* of that person, they can find out what is actually going on. But they must be objective. For example, if they think that someone keeps putting them down, the best thing is to stand aside and watch how that person behaves toward others. If that person is putting others down, then they know their feeling is justified.

TAKING ACTION VERSUS GIVING UP

Virgo North Node people must fight against a tendency to give up. Overcoming opposition is part of the process necessary for them to gain inner strength and self-confidence. All of us lack confidence in areas where we lack experience. The difference is that most people don't surrender when faced with opposition. In this lifetime, Virgo North Node people are learning not to give up.

One resolution to the habitual pattern of withdrawal and surrender is to realize that their life doesn't get any better when they pull inward and give up. The universe keeps bringing them the same situation—with different people—so they can break through it and experience the vitality of life. People who are involved with these folks need to recognize that when Virgo North Nodes pull back, they don't mean to be hurtful. Sometimes they need their partners to pry them loose from their self-imposed isolation. However, this must be done gently, with acceptance and love, rather than in a condemning or harsh way. At times, rescue is nice for these folks.

When a crisis occurs, they must fight their tendency to not interfere and instead increase their participation in a constructive way. Then they win, and so does everyone around them. For example, I had a Virgo North Node client who had been head over heels in love with a man, and he with her, for five years. They seemed the perfect match. However, she was seven years older, a factor that—unknown to her—troubled him. One day he came to her in great pain and broke off the relationship, explaining that the only reason was the age difference. My client was devastated, but rather than object she pulled back and allowed him to leave. He went to Europe, married a woman younger than himself, and had a child. He came back on business and took my client to dinner. He was miserable, still in love with her, but it was too late to turn everyone's lives around. Rather than withdraw, my client should have moved forward and participated in creating the results she desired by saying: "Wait a minute, we can work this out." The results might have been a victory for them both.

EXTREMES VERSUS MODERATION

Virgo North Node people sometimes respond to others in extremes, being overly focused or totally unfocused; too trusting or too suspicious; a complete doormat or totally aloof and invulnerable. They can be very intense emotionally. To avoid problems they need to concentrate on the practical aspects of each situation, make accurate evaluations of the people involved, and then decide on the "appropriate" energy and the most productive approach.

This problem with extremes is also related to their tendency to daydream rather than to focus on the changing details of the here and now. For example, if Virgo North Node people are involved in a relationship where they are getting hurt, it takes them a long time to recognize what is happening. They're lost in their daydreams about the relationship, rather than being present on a moment-to-moment basis. When they "come to" and realize what is going on, they withdraw. But they tend to withdraw too far, for too long, and not notice if the relationship changes to better accommodate their needs. They inadvertently give inaccurate signals to their mate or co-workers, first giving the impression that they can be taken advantage of without objecting, and then suddenly becoming totally unreachable. By staying present in the situation as it unfolds, these folks can adapt their responses to the reality of what is happening and have more positive relationships.

Virgo North Node people are learning to act with moderation in every aspect of their lives. This is easy when they take circumstances into account objectively. They only go to extremes when they are absorbed in their *own* reactions to outside stimuli. The path of moderation is found by taking other people into account, focusing on the details of what is going on, and working out a practical resolution to the situation at hand. These folks must learn to deal with life on a practical, goal-oriented level.

For example, if they own a business and are upset with their employees, they should *not* overlook what is happening out of compassion, or react with self-sacrifice and become a workaholic, or get angry at the employees. They need to objectively observe the details of the situation, and put together a set of rules and regulations that become part of the work environment. Only those employees who follow the rules will be allowed to stay. Actually, these folks have great job karma, and their employees and co-workers invariably love them. Yet to prevent being taken advantage of, they must define job boundaries and put them in writing. This translates their vision for their employees and allows everyone to work together toward a common goal.

ORDER

RESTORING ORDER TO CHAOS

Virgo North Node people gravitate to situations where something needs to be done to correct an existing problem. Since they have the ability to solve problems in situations of chaos or neglect, their job is to create order by participating in the physical world to set things right. When these folks see chaotic situations around them, their first reaction (past-life tendency) is to withdraw, and the whole thing falls apart. In this lifetime, when something isn't working, they need to roll up their sleeves and get further into it. When they give up, everybody loses—because others are counting on them, subconsciously, to get involved. When there's a problem, it's the universe saying to them: "Hey—we need some help here in the material world!"

It is also very important for Virgo North Node people to keep an orderly environment, both in the home and at work. Having order and organization around them gives them clarity and strength in their daily lives. It is essential that these folks, more than any other nodal position, take the time to keep themselves organized on the physical level.

On the psychological level, chaos and confusion are especially detrimental; these things undermine their confidence to operate in the world. Having their physical environment in order gives them a sense of psychological order, which empowers them to function confidently.

Actually, the process of ordering the environment is healthy for Virgo North Node people. When they feel a sense of inner anxiety—whether they are male or female—sometimes the best thing is to pick up the vacuum cleaner. Going through paperwork, doing the dishes, dusting, putting the environment in order—simple tasks can be therapeutic for these folks. Physically moving in a constructive way transforms their inner anxiety into productivity.

STRUCTURE AND PLANNING

In the area of planning, these folks sometimes go to extremes. They can spend so much time *planning* their lives that they forget to *live* them. This may appear as an overly conscientious, workaholic phase. Then they compensate by not planning anything at all, lose their strength, and dissolve into a life with no boundaries. It is two sides of the same coin: the desire to become lost—either in activity or formlessness—and not to take responsibility for creating the structures that would give balance to their lives. Much of this tendency is owing to past-life experiences when other people were responsible for creating their routines. However, in this lifetime it's up to them.

To give their lives proper structure and meaning, Virgo North Node people need to consciously define their goals and be able to adjust their use of time accordingly. What works best is to allot time (whether it is one-half hour each morning, or two hours once a week) for consistently re-evaluating their schedules. For example, they may determine that they need time for work, exercise, friendships, play, romance, meditation, music, and so on. It is to their advantage to make a list of the various aspects of their life that are important to them and consciously structure their weekly routine to allot time for each. This can help them considerably in achieving a fulfilled and balanced life.

Also, as they organize themselves in a physical way, they gain a clearer picture of exactly "where they are" in different areas of their lives. For example, I had a client with this nodal position who felt vaguely suspicious about her stockbroker. To settle her fears, she took all her records of stock sales since she had been working with him and calculated exactly how much money she had made on the transactions, and how much money he had made on the commissions. Once she had the facts and figures in front of her she could determine the reality of the situation, and her feelings of anxiety dissolved.

RELATIONSHIPS

This is not a victim lifetime, and Virgo North Node people are learning how to say "no" and not allow themselves to be abused in their relationships. Sometimes they say "no" very gently, and the people who are abusing them don't get the message. But these folks need to let others know when there is inequity in giving, or when they need more support, before they withdraw from the relationship. If someone isn't getting the message, it is simply an indication that Virgo North Node should change her approach. We all have different levels of sensitivity—some of us are very sensitive, and some of us need to be hit over the head! Therefore, if the abuse continues, Virgo North Node should keep upping the intensity of her "no" until the other person hears her.

ROMANTIC RELATIONSHIPS

In romantic relationships, Virgo North Node people may, once again, go to extremes with either total aloofness and lack of participation, or total submission to the other person. Again, walking the middle road of moderation is their key to success. One obstacle that keeps them from finding this middle road is that the minute they see a person they care about romantically, they start giving an inch and then giving a mile—before you know it, they've lost themselves. Once these folks become romantically involved and the other person doesn't give them what they want, they start trying to talk themselves out of their own limits: "All right, maybe I'm being too rigid." Then they dissolve into a confused state in which they just "go along" without standing up for themselves. This doesn't usually happen in their friendships, because they aren't so afraid of losing friends. And if their job is interfering with their health or well-being, they will make the decision to move on. But when an intimate, personal relationship is at stake, they are terribly afraid of loss.

Another trap they face is giving up their self-respect. They have a tendency to value the person they are seeing romantically more than they value themselves. They make the other person their center; once they have done that, they are lost. For romantic relationships to work for them, they must value the relationship more than just the other person.

When they fall in love, these folks also tend to create the reality they want in their minds, and then they live it. This is their "payoff" for putting the other person at the "center." They create a blissful atmosphere through a combination of psychic attunement and an active imagination—it's almost as though these folks are having a love affair in their own minds. However, this breaks down when the fantasy is too far removed from reality. They need to keep inviting the other person's input into their fantasy, for realistic grounding and for avoiding deep disappointment.

They should only allow themselves just so many fantasies, or allot only a certain amount of time to fantasize. "You can have five minutes of fantasy, and then go on to the next thing!" The "next thing" should require a focus that is the antithesis of fantasy: an activity that is mathematical (balancing the checkbook, paying bills, etc.), physical (doing the dishes, vacuuming, etc.), or something else that requires precise, objective thinking. This can help them break with the energy of fantasy and come back into balance.

Virgo North Node people also need to consistently monitor their relationships. Are they putting in too much or too little energy? Is there a balance between giving and receiving? Is their participation leading to feelings of confidence or feelings of inadequacy? They must be willing to let the other person know where their boundaries are. This fosters respect and allows them to experience the joys of participating and working with another toward a mutual goal. Once they become committed, it is helpful for both parties to write down their goals for the relationship. The clearer they are about what they want to create, the greater their chances for success. The goals should be re-evaluated from time to time as the relationship changes.

In a marriage, shared goals might include mutual support; going out for a romantic dinner two nights a month; encouragement in reaching individual aims; handling money together in a joyful way; giving each other confidence; and seeing a marriage counselor once a year to keep the relationship "tuned up." Writing down these objectives helps engender a practical approach.

If Virgo North Node people feel confused in a relationship, there may be too great a discrepancy between the reality of what is occurring and their vision of how they would like things to be. In that case, they must first clarify their thinking about their goals and what they would like to create in the relationship. Then, armed with the strength that comes from having defined their limits in their own mind, they can approach their partner to gain clarity.

In opening this dialogue, it is best for them to refrain from communicating their goals and limits first. Instead, they should actively listen to the other person's vision of the relationship. Then they can determine whether or not they fit appropriately with that person. If they communicate their goals and limits first, they set themselves up to be fooled, cajoled, or appeased, as the other person may seem to agree in order to keep them involved.

If the Virgo North Node person has determined it's a "fit" (both partners' goals truly do align), then they can define their limits and the negotiations can begin. But if in fact he determines that it is not a "fit" (their vision and their limits are incompatible), then Virgo North Node must summon the discipline to break off the relationship, or reshape it in a form that does work (for example, a friendship instead of a marriage). His inclination is to fantasize about how it could eventually work out and to "stick it out," hoping that he can change the other person. This process does not work. It leads not only to a waste of time and energy but to much disappointment and hurt.

When these folks do enter into a romantic relationship, they must pay special attention to their interaction during the first few weeks. If they realize (when they are still working toward full participation) that the relationship isn't going to succeed, they should get out immediately. They must be honest with themselves that this is not the ideal situation and determine if the limits they have defined for themselves will work within the reality of the relationship. Staying in touch with reality—in every area of their lives—will make their lives work. It is important for them not to live in a fantasy.

ATTRACTION

Virgo North Node people are often attracted to people with qualities that they feel they lack: strength, assertiveness, decisiveness, and the like. They attach themselves to the person in an attempt to emulate him and absorb these qualities. Rather than recognizing that they want that certain trait, they feel very strongly that they want the other person. They need to be conscious of this problem when entering into an intimate relationship. As part of this dynamic, sometimes they allow the other person to treat them badly in order to get what they think they want. Until they've gained the "missing" quality themselves, they are afraid to confront the other person and run the risk of loss.

By recognizing the quality in the other person that they are attracted to, they can consciously put *developing that quality within themselves* at the center of the relationship, rather than the other person. This approach gives them more objectivity and enough emotional distance to maintain their own identity, which will help the relationship work more smoothly and honestly for both partners. It also helps these folks to remain aware of supply. Just as there are many potential friendships that would fulfill them, and many potential jobs that they would enjoy, likewise there are many potential intimate relationships that they would find satisfying. Thus, if the relationship they are involved in is hurtful, they should never forget that they can afford to take the chance of moving on.

FANTASY VERSUS REALITY

In their professional lives, Virgo North Node people can be practical and realistic. If they would apply the same mechanisms to their romances, their personal lives might also be successful and run smoothly. However, in their personal lives they tend to live in a fantasy world and use their imaginations in ways that ultimately disappoint them. When they find someone who appeals to them romantically, they often begin to fantasize about what the other person is like. They create an entire fantasy of the other person, which they project onto the other person. Then when they relate to this person, it's always in terms of how closely he or she matches their fantasy, and they always feel let down. In actuality they may never have seen who the other person really was. The other person may be a *better* match for them than their fantasy person, but when the behavior of the love object varies too radically from the picture these folks have projected, they retreat. They withdraw their projection and become noncommunicative, and their partners never quite understand why they suddenly became so unreachable. The Virgo North Node person becomes confused and disappointed; the partner becomes angry and provocative.

The way out of this dilemma is through discrimination. Virgo North Node people must deliberately postpone their fantasy until they have had time to pay careful attention to who the other person really is. By objectively analyzing the partner's values, behavior, and beliefs, they can respond to how that person makes them feel in the here and now. In the long run, reality is much more satisfying than layers of projection.

Romantic Fog, Adoration, and Blind Faith

These folks often begin a romance wearing rose-colored glasses. They are in a "romantic fog" created by their connection with the other person, which insulates them from any harsh realities that might exist in the relationship. These "glitches" may be very apparent to everyone else, but not to Virgo North Nodes. They idealize their partner, fall in love with that ideal, and project a future of living "happily ever after." Their daydreams and fantasies seem so real that they even use them as a basis for making practical plans, until the discrepancy between ideal and reality becomes too great. Maybe an incident occurs that demonstrates the reality of the situation, and in an instant their entire fantasy "pops."

For example, the Virgo North Node person, seeing how smoothly the relationship is going, may assume that marriage is the natural outcome. The other person may never directly dispute the possibility and allow discussions about marriage to pass by without comment. Then, seemingly out of the blue, the other person announces that he doesn't want to marry anyone—ever. Virgo North Node is shocked and bewildered, and begins to doubt herself. The event can nearly destroy her confidence in her own perceptions, and it can take her years to get over it.

To avoid such a disaster, these folks need to stay focused in the here and now, watch the details of the relationship unfold, and make corrections when necessary. They can experience the joys of romance and fantasy once they have established the relationship on a firm and practical foundation, but they cannot indulge in the irresponsible aspect of romantic fantasy and blind dependence without repercussion.

These people have an extraordinary capacity to make their dreams come true, manifesting their visions on a tangible level. This applies to romantic life as well as professional life. They just need to approach their goals on a practical level.

Practical Strategies for Interaction

Before falling too much in love, Virgo North Node people should clearly define the goals and objectives of the other person, as well as their own. They must set limits: "What do I want? What am I willing to accept? What am I not willing to accept?" It is to their advantage to avoid the possibility of deception, even if it is unintentional, by asking practical, key questions at appropriate times. Is the other person married or living with someone? Has he been married before? Why did his marriage end? How does he feel about commitment? Some answers may change as the relationship progresses, so it is beneficial to ask these kinds of questions from time to time.

These folks need an incredible amount of space. They need alone time, to pull back from the world and simply "be" so they can regenerate and reconnect with their power, their energy, and their vision. They know they must do this even though they can't explain why, and sometimes they find it very difficult to communicate their need to those who are close to them. When they do try to communicate their need to pull back, often the other person responds by talking them out of it or *not* honoring their boundaries in some other way. Then they try noncommunication and simply withdraw without explanation. This alienates and infuriates the other person, who doesn't understand what is going on. The best bet is to focus on a plan with a time schedule: How much time alone will they need, and when can they rejoin the other person? Then they can approach the partner with a clear proposal.

Here is one practical approach:

1. *Share the Vision:* "This is what I would like to create for us . . . a happy time together in which we can really devote attention to each other."
2. *Share the Practical Details:* "Now, there are certain things I have to take care of before I can spend this kind of time with you. I need to take care of some shopping, spend time with my folks, and have some time alone to recharge my batteries before seeing you."
3. *Share the Plan:* "So, I'm going to need the next three days to take care of these things. I'll call you on Thursday and I'd like to get together on Friday."

In making this communication, Virgo North Node people must come from a "focused" place where they are in control. These folks are fantastic at making plans. They can see how to organize all the details to work in everyone's best interest. Others will go along with them if they come from an "in-charge" position rather than a helpless position.

When Virgo North Node people become too overwhelmed with the profusion of events in their lives, they sometimes react by taking a "hiatus"—extracting themselves from a situation until they can see it more clearly and handle it more effectively. However, a breach of trust can occur if they don't notify the other person in advance that they will be "on hiatus," especially if there's no indication of how long that break is going to be. No matter how difficult, forthright communication of their plans is the key to positive relationships.

Owing to a past-life residue of hermitage in one form or another, these folks were not born with a natural knowledge of how to maintain long-term relationships. As priests, they may have been privy to the private experiences of others but lack the direct knowledge of repeated personal experiences. Thus, when things go "wrong" in a relationship, they may avoid fighting or expressing any strong emotion. They don't realize that the tension is a call from their partner to draw closer and participate, using their incredible talent to create order out of chaos.

Virgo North Node people must be willing to roll up their sleeves, walk directly into the chaos, and reorganize. They must recognize that chaos in relationships is a signal that it is time for more efficiency in the "nuts and bolts" operation of daily life, and to develop greater feelings of closeness. These folks are masters at straightening out problems as soon as they are willing to participate 100 percent in creating practical solutions.

GOALS

SELF-DEVELOPMENT

Virgo North Node people are learning how to "rewire" their own internal mechanisms so that their interactions with others produce happier, more productive results. These folks love self-help programs and do well with anything involving analysis and technique. They have a special talent for successfully working on themselves so that their style of being stimulates positive results in the world. They have a natural understanding of psychology on a very deep and healing level, which empowers them to change themselves. When they exercise these talents—working on getting their own "house in order"—they are energized, happy, and productive.

To facilitate coming out of their shell, these folks should also develop their generosity. They have an innate capacity to give others the confidence of seeing that there is structure in the world.

SELF-SUFFICIENCY

Virgo North Node people need to develop self-sufficiency so that they have the confidence to create healthy, mutually empowering relationships. They have had too many incarnations of helplessness and reliance on large organizations for their survival.

In striving toward self-sufficiency, these folks create the strength that allows them to be vulnerable in a balanced way. If they are reliant on someone else for their sense of well-being, their finances, or other things, this can easily become complete surrender of their power. There is also the problem of their natural affinity for adoration and devotion. When they lived in monasteries, devotion to a spiritual ideal was appropriate; but now, devotion to the wrong human being can be their downfall. That's why it is essential for these folks to be discriminating regarding to whom or what they give their devotion. In the right hands their devotion will be understood and appreciated; in the wrong hands it could lead to victimization.

These folks are learning to depend on people to be themselves. They need to watch and see who people really are, and then depend on them to be consistent in areas that are clearly intrinsic to their nature. For example, if a person is monogamous by nature, then Virgo North Node can probably depend on monogamy; if a person does what he says he is going to do, Virgo North Node can count on him to keep his word; and if a person is insensitive, Virgo North Node can probably rely on that trait continuing as well.

As long as Virgo North Node people remain self-sufficient, they are whole. They can function as a "total" person in every relationship. For them, being self-sufficient doesn't mean that they won't rely on others—it means that they won't fall apart if others don't come through for them in the way they expect.

CREATING ROUTINES

Owing to past lives in which other people controlled their time and schedules, Virgo North Node people are not accustomed to organizing themselves so that all parts of their lives fall into order. Yet in this lifetime, they must plan how to use their time constructively. Now, they are free! They are making their own rules and voluntarily following them.

Routines are absolutely essential to keep their lives from dissolving, which for them means facing limitless fears and feelings of insecurity. They need to personally take charge and structure their time so that their needs can be met in every area.

DIET

Diet and health are important for these folks. In past lives, monasteries or institutions took the responsibility of maintaining a balanced diet for them—in this lifetime, they must do it themselves. They are extremely sensitive and easily affected by different foods. They should notice the effect of certain foods and moderate their diet accordingly.

For example, "spaciness" does not work for them in this lifetime. They need to eat foods that help them feel grounded, solid, and confident. They may do well to eliminate sugar if they notice that it causes anxiety or lack of focus. They also require a regular exercise program, which helps them feel physically strong so their self-confidence can blossom.

More than any other nodal position, these folks must be conscious of not overindulging in alcohol or drugs—they just don't have the tolerance for it. Their mindset is already unfocused, and drugs or alcohol can affect them in an unhealthy, exaggerated way.

ORDERLY ENVIRONMENT

An orderly environment is essential for Virgo North Node people. They do not do well with chaos. It is very important for them to keep home and office neat, clean, and organized. Again, the underlying issue is confidence. When their environment is neat and orderly, they feel stronger and more confident in their ability to create order in the world outside themselves.

PAYING BILLS

Paying bills on time is another "must" routine for Virgo North Nodes. Staying on top of the details creates an inner security that is essential for them to operate with confidence and ease in the world. They are actually dynamos—capable of accomplishing in one hour what it would take the average person five hours to complete. The issue is not a lack of talent, but rather soothing their psychological state so that they are up to the challenge of facing the world.

MAKING LISTS

Lists are excellent for helping these folks organize their thinking. Planning allows them to focus their mental energy and gain a sense of orderly participation and strength in the material world. In decision making, it may help them to physically write out all the pros and cons of the issue on paper, so the right path becomes clear.

Virgo North Node people do well with daily planners and elaborate organizing systems. Organizing details gives them more confidence in their capacity to implement their vision.

EXERCISE

A regular program of physical exercise is essential for these folks. Going to the gym three times a week to give the body a workout seems like a small thing—but in their case, the routine gives a feeling of solid self-worth and well-being. The positive repercussions of taking charge with a regular exercise routine reinforce their emotional, mental, and spiritual power as well as their physical energy.

PETS

Pets can be a real plus for Virgo North Node people. A pet forces them into a routine and gives them someone else to take care of on a tangible level. At the same time, pets provide a secure outlet for the unconditional love— without boundaries—that Virgo North Nodes want so much to give. With pets they are able to strike a proper balance between unconditional love and discipline. If this could be applied to their relationships with people, it would go a long way in teaching them how to have happy, healthy human relationships.

PUNCTUALITY

These folks have trouble being on time, because in past lives other people prompted them. But now it is important for them to learn to be on time. This is largely owing to the difference it makes in their level of confidence. If they are late, they feel guilty; this triggers their feeling of being "less than" others. To feel confident, they must do their part to the last detail. If they are on time, they have participated according to the rules and can deal with whatever happens from that point forward. But if they are late, their whole day may be off balance and they will carry a feeling of insecurity.

The problem is that they are so accustomed to living in a state of time-lessness in their consciousness that they have to deliberately plan when to leave in order to get to their destination on time. Otherwise, one thing after another will distract them. It requires conscious attention on their part to be on time.

One method that works is to plan in advance how much time they will need to comfortably reach their destination punctually, and then add ten minutes. Knowing when they need to leave their house helps; it also helps if they make that time inflexible in their minds: "I have to leave here at 5:07, no later."

At the other extreme, some of these folks have compensated for this tendency by becoming obsessively "ahead of time"! They pressure them-selves just to be sure that they arrive at their destination in advance. This can put them under constant stress that undermines their nervous system. It can also cause them to be intolerant and judgmental of others who are late. Once again, the path of moderation is the healthiest route.

HEALING THEME SONG*

Because of the compelling way that music can emotionally support us in taking risks, I have written a healing song for each nodal group to help shift its energy in a positive direction.

USE WHAT YOU HAVE RIGHT NOW

The message of this song is meant to effortlessly shift Virgo North Nodes' focus to the details around them, helping to ground them in the physical world. This will bolster their confidence and provide a foundation of support, arousing them to take constructive action in the here and now.

Selected lyrics:

Why be discouraged when you have to go back
It only brings you closer to where it's all at—
Life always brings just what we need
To give up and suffer, or break through and get freed!

And you . . .
Use what you have, right now
You've got the tools—you're where you need to be
Watch the One, not you or me
And take the next step in front of you—and when you do—you'll get free!

---

* These lyrics are set to music and sung in their entirety on the CD and cassette tape "Unfolding As It Should."

North Node in Libra

and North Node in the 7th House

OVERVIEW

Attributes to Develop

Work in these areas can help uncover hidden gifts and talents

- Cooperation
- Diplomacy and tact
- Increasing awareness of others' needs
- Selflessness: giving support without expecting reciprocity
- Creating win/win situations
- Sharing
- Seeing things through another's eyes
- Communicating self-identity

Tendencies to Leave Behind

Working to reduce the influence of these tendencies can help make life easier and more enjoyable

- Impulsiveness
- Thoughtless self-assertion
- Lack of awareness of others' needs for support
- Self-centeredness
- Selfishness
- Lack of good judgment regarding money
- Expecting others to be like oneself
- Indifference to how one is seen by others
- Resistance to compromise
- Outbursts of anger
- Overconcern with survival

ACHILLES' HEEL/TRAP TO AVOID/THE BOTTOM LINE

The Achilles' heel Libra North Node people need to be aware of is selfishness ("My survival depends on looking out for myself first, and others should make sure my needs are met regardless of anyone else's concerns"). But it's a bottomless pit: If they feel that others have to constantly fill their needs for them to feel safe and connected, they will find that they always need more attention and energy just to feel okay. They need to find partners whom *they* can give to, who will feel so energized that they naturally fill Libra North Node's cup in appreciation. Satisfaction lies in connecting with people who see them for who they are, appreciate them, and want to give back to them.

The trap they need to avoid is an unending search for independence ("If I can just be self-sufficient enough, I'll have the confidence to relate successfully with others and I won't feel so lonely"). Life has shown Libra North Node people that accomplishments and independence do not make them feel complete. The bottom line is that they'll never feel a strong enough sense of self to become part of a team. At some point they need to take the risk of losing themselves in supporting another person. The irony is that once they start unselfishly supporting someone else, they begin to feel the joy and glory of their true self shining through.

WHAT THESE PEOPLE REALLY WANT

What these people really want is to be their own person, to be the center of attention, to discover themselves in different life situations, and to surround themselves with people who feed them energy. To achieve this, Libra North Node people need to refocus their attention away from themselves and discover the nature of the people who have been drawn to them. Once they discern which people truly admire them and want to support them, and once they begin to feed those people energy, the energy that comes back to them will create the situation they want.

TALENTS/PROFESSION

These people are fantastic counselors, diplomats, and peacemakers. They have the gift of clearly seeing and successfully communicating the identity and concerns of person A to person B (and vice versa) in a way that prompts mutual understanding and fair, harmonious compromises. Libra North Node people also excel in fields involving beauty and art, and they make great entertainers or public speakers when their goal is to uplift, energize, and bring confidence to their audience. They are extremely gifted and can be successful—both materially and personally—in any profession involving a supportive role.

Libra North Node people have innate gifts of independence and leadership through their awareness of themselves as separate entities. When they use their past-life gift of self-confidence as a tool for peacemaking and helping establish justice for others, their innate abilities create positive results. However, if they pursue professions that have their own independence as the aim, they may become dissatisfied and feel they have never reached their goal. When they use their strong self-identity to support others, Libra North Node people gain a sense of inner satisfaction and completion.

Healing Affirmations Specific to Libra North Node

- "When I focus on supporting others, I feel confident."
- "When I successfully stimulate self-confidence in others, we both win."
- "When the team is successful, I win."
- "When I share with others, I have more."

PERSONALITY

Warrior Attributes

Lifetimes of personal achievement, self-sufficiency, and independent action result in a consciousness that is unaware of team effort and partnership. Libra North Node people have had too many incarnations enacting the role of the warrior. A warrior on the battlefield isn't concerned about anyone else, only with staying alive and killing the enemy. If he even glances at a comrade, his body can be destroyed. Thus, his entire consciousness is geared toward himself: *his* body, *his* fighting ability, *his* position relative to survival.

These people now have an exaggerated survival urge and a "me versus you" mentality. It's all they know. They are competitive, goal oriented, and tactical, always aware of how they will be affected by what they do or by what's going on. They yearn to be with others, to love others and to feel loved, but they don't know how. They are afraid to release their strong grip on their sense of self, because they fear "the battle" may begin at any time and they must be strong and on their guard to survive.

But these folks need to recognize that this is not a warrior lifetime. No one is out to destroy them or take things away from them. They need to notice that there are comrades on all sides. Their job in this lifetime is to help *others* win battles; and in helping others, Libra North Node people win.

Throughout all those warrior lifetimes, these folks lost touch with love, with the ability to work with other people. Thus, they came into this lifetime feeling awkward about cooperation and relating to others. But they shouldn't worry, because their entire chart is set up to reconnect with people. As long as they are clear about where they're going, old habits won't get in their way. In fact, this entire lifetime is about partnership for them—and there will be no lack of opportunity to get it straight, because opportunities for marriages and partnerships will come to them easily.

RUGGED DISCIPLINE

Owing to past-life warrior experiences, Libra North Node people have developed a "no questions asked—no nonsense" discipline that is foreign to those in other nodal groups. Their past lives in the military stressed orderliness with dress and personal possessions, so these folks come into this incarnation valuing organization in their environments and in their lives. They have a strong tolerance for discipline and harsh limitations, and they think others should be willing to endure the same punishment and deprivation. It's hard for them to understand when others won't accept the same restraints and sacrifices that they are willing to shoulder—a factor that undermines their relationships.

No other nodal group has the same capacity for taking constructive action under conditions of strict personal discipline and deprivation. Actually, Libra North Node people thrive on the challenge of personal survival under adverse circumstances. It's a "high" for them! The intense drama of striving to reach a goal through personal sacrifice, harnessing their resources, being put to the test, and emerging victorious gives them a sense of personal validation.

These folks have such a strong sense of self that they imagine everyone is just like them, and subconsciously, they are looking for someone who is just like them to be their partner. They can become very frustrated and feel shortchanged when the other person does not exhibit the same qualities.

One of the lessons Libra North Node people are learning in this lifetime is the beauty of individual differences. Who they are and what they have to offer in a relationship may be very different from who the other person is and what he or she has to offer. The challenge is to pay attention to individual differences and to appreciate the strengths that others bring to the relationship. For this to occur, they first must re-examine their definition of strength.

Owing to so many incarnations spent in the warrior mode, their definition of strength usually includes only the following: courage, intense effort, willingness to sacrifice and endure deprivation, 100 percent goal-focused orientation, insistence on immediate results, discipline, impulsive initiative (the hero mentality), high-energy modes, and willingness to take personal risks.

Yet there are other strengths that these folks do *not* have that partners may bring into their lives. These include the ability to appreciate the *process* of reaching the goal (which can slow down Libra North Node people and give them more staying power); communication skills (which can create rapport and understanding); empathy (which can make Libra North Node people finally feel like they belong); playfulness (which can make the process of reaching a goal enjoyable); analytical abilities and a capacity for working with details; diplomacy; sensitivity to others' needs; the ability to create synergy (which can enormously empower both parties); a sense of adventure; managerial skills; creativity and inventiveness; and the capacity for compassion (which can heal Libra North Node people).

In this incarnation, Libra North Node people need to partner with others for success and fulfillment. To receive the benefits of partnership, their challenge is to appreciate how others are different from them.

TEMPER OUTBURSTS

Libra North Node people have a penchant for angry outbursts, which they must learn to leave behind. They have a temper like that of a child. When they don't get their way, they throw a tantrum to force the other person to go along with them. If the other person resists, they escalate the situation until they get their way.

However, creating win/lose situations does not work for these folks. In the long run, such situations only isolate them from the very people with whom they want to be close. When they "win" by getting their way at another's expense, they pay the price—the other person will close down and withdraw, not wanting to be vulnerable to such violent tactics. Libra North Node people may emerge all smiles, totally unaware of the damage they have done to the other person. They think the other person should be happy for them because, after all, they did "win." They will experience many bitter lessons until they learn that nobody wins through intimidation and temper. Victories won by attacking others result in those people not wanting to be involved with Libra North Nodes anymore, and thereafter the mutual exchange, energy, and admiration that these folks so covet vanish from their relationships.

DECISION MAKING

These folks tend to be swift decision makers. They are accustomed to immediate action, since they take only themselves and their own goals into account. They are usually unaware of their effect on other people, and without realizing it they may use people to further their own goals. This has bad repercussions for Libra North Node people, however, because it's very painful for others.

When these folks make decisions without allowing other people to support them, they may fail to get the things they want because they have discounted the benefit of others' energies and ideas. Before taking action, they should remember to consciously include others in their decision-making processes. Part of their reluctance to include others comes from the former battlefield mentality that "people are basically against me." Much of this false thinking can be resolved through an understanding of proper communication—how to check in with others in a way that is mutually beneficial. I once had a client with this nodal position who confessed to me: "I'm so busy working on my marriage by myself that I can't see my husband, I can't hear him, I don't know who he is!" It would be much easier for these folks to just check in with the other person.

Lack of consideration in decision making can cause Libra North Node people a lot of unnecessary pain. They may be so afraid of not getting their way that they are ruthless in campaigning for what they want. They may fear that if they hesitate for a moment to engage another person in making plans, the other person will block their course of action. What they don't understand is that considering others does not mean abandoning their agenda. It *does* mean caring about the other person's concerns and being willing to work toward a compromise that satisfies both parties.

For example, I had a client who was in a relationship with a Libra North Node native. They had been living together monogamously for nearly a year. One day the Libra North Node said he had to leave and would be back late that night. She was very intuitive and got a psychic picture that caused her to say: "David—you're going to make love to somebody else!" He became angry with her (these folks don't lie easily, and they tend to get upset when they are caught). She started asking questions, trying to understand what was going on, but he was so intent on his goal that he refused to take the time to talk with her. He didn't want to be late for his appointment with the other woman, so he left the matter unresolved. Hours later he called her with profuse apologies: He had made a mistake, he loved her, she was the only one for him, it would never happen again. But it was too late—her heart had closed to him and she had already decided to leave.

According to my client, it was not the *event* that caused her heart to close, it was the way the Libra North Node had handled it. She couldn't forgive that he did not care enough about her feelings to talk out the situation with her. When these folks close themselves to input from their partners, everyone loses.

SURVIVAL

Libra North Node people can be overly concerned with survival, but in this lifetime such a focus is inappropriate. They've already learned how to survive; now they are here to help other people, to infuse them with the energy and confidence that will make the others stronger. In giving, the Libra North Node people gain tremendous self-confidence and peace.

These folks need to apply everything they learned as warriors and use it constructively in relationships with others. This means putting down their weapons and looking around to see how their comrades are doing. Does the person next to them need a pat on the back before going into battle? Their job is to empower *other* people to win. And no one is better equipped to help others win than Libra North Node.

NARCISSISM

Libra North Node people must guard against a tendency for narcissism. They put on a front of being in control and having qualities that others admire. Others give them compliments and they feel good, but they are always secretly afraid that who they *really* are and what they *really* like may run counter to their projected image. Sometimes they gather people around them who are acceptable for their "look." For example, I had a client with this nodal position who was attracted to very heavy women, but he would never let any of his friends find out because he was afraid of their ridicule. He kept his real desire a secret because it didn't fit the image of himself he wanted to project.

These folks like it when others compliment their looks; so they act out what they think the desired stereotype is, and expect people to see this and feed their ego. Wanting to be attractive to others, they manipulate their image to be what they think will attract the other person. But this process prevents them from gaining a true sense of inner confidence through knowing that others love and accept them as they are. They will never learn this unless they take the risk of revealing themselves.

Libra North Node people are in danger of indulging in self-love—and excluding others who could expand their true sense of security. They may have a tendency to be concerned only with their own happiness or fall victim to vanity—such as keeping themselves in prime physical condition for the purpose of winning the best that life has to offer. Their values can be naively superficial. But in this lifetime, they are scheduled to gain an *expanded* sense of their own soul by truly loving another person as much as they love themselves.

"ME FIRST!"

Overconcern with self, self-sufficiency, and self-preservation will function as Libra North Nodes' basic motivations until these folks become more conscious. They must consider who else is in the game. Often they don't even know who the other people are, because they're so used to focusing attention on themselves. Whenever they impulsively say "Me first!" other people pull away. But because of their natural counseling abilities (a gift given at birth to facilitate their transition from focusing on self to supporting others), people automatically confide in them. As they spend time listening to other people's problems, they wonder if they are getting their "fair share." If they're not, they think they are being used. Then they resentfully push people away.

Everything depends on their *motivation* in listening to others. Are they doing it to get this person "out of their hair" so they can put the attention back on themselves? Or are they listening with the sincere motivation of wanting to help, not expecting anything in return other than the happiness of knowing they participated in healing the other person?

To win, Libra North Node people need to get in touch with a feeling of internal social harmony that will help them focus on others and stop putting themselves first.

SELF-CONSCIOUSNESS

Libra North Node people can be painfully self-conscious and judgmental of what they deem to be their "negative" qualities. This is why they lose power when they focus on the self. All they see are their "unacceptable" qualities, which they focus on hiding. But this process prevents others from getting close to them. Not knowing what these folks are hiding, others don't trust them and back away. Then Libra North Node people get the feedback that something *is* wrong with them—which is exactly what they suspected in the first place!

Also, in the process of holding back they are not fully open to receive others and therefore can never fully partner with them. They are afraid to let down their guard, lest others will see who they really are and then harshly judge and reject them. Instead, by focusing on the other person and what they can do to bring out the strength and goodness in that person, Libra North Node's own self stands open to receive other people.

It is in the best interests of Libra North Node people to stop judging themselves and simply *be* themselves. If they have some attributes that are not quite "right," others can give them feedback. After all, they've had warrior incarnations—what do they know about the social graces? They can't expect to know what experience has not taught them. They need the help of those who have lived in society for many lifetimes to learn the rules. By being honest, they can learn how to change and start connecting with people and developing positive relationships. They need to become attuned to the world and to others, instead of themselves. When they focus only on themselves to see what the other person is giving back to them, they see only their own incompleteness and their confidence drops. But when they focus on supporting and healing the other person, they will no longer feel self-conscious. As they put their energy into others, they will receive the approval and energy they need. Indeed, the key to their own self-confidence lies in stimulating the confidence and enthusiasm of others.

MAKING ASSUMPTIONS

Libra North Node people tend to assume they know what is going on with others, so they often bypass communication and go directly to action. This undermines trust in their relationships, yet it is understandable in light of their past-life military experience. They were taught to view the "enemy" (that is, the "other") from a distance. They observed the enemy's actions but never interacted with him directly until the battle. Now, in this incarnation, they observe other people from a distance, making assumptions about their identity, behavior patterns, likes and dislikes, and so on. For these folks, the truth is what they see—they assume "truths" about the other person and then act on those "truths." They don't listen to the other person. They interpret the other's actions according to what *they* would be thinking if *they* were doing those things.

They can also be judgmental of others for not resolving their situations or reaching their goals as quickly, or in the same way, as a Libra North Node would. If others don't do it "their way," these folks might assume: "They're not doing what I told them. They're not taking responsibility and dealing with this." But the other person may be dealing with it in his *own* way, and Libra North Node just hasn't checked in to find out what's going on.

They also judge others when they observe them hurting themselves. They don't understand why people do things that go against their own best interests. They can't figure out why others don't have the discipline to stay in shape, or finish their projects, or maintain order in their environments. Because Libra North Node people feel that actions speak louder than words, they often underestimate other people's ability to overcome obstacles, simply because they have not done it yet.

Libra North Node people are learning that everyone has a unique style. They are so single-minded and goal oriented that they project onto others the goals that are important to themselves; then they advise others how to reach those goals by the quickest, most direct route. They become judgmental when other people don't follow their advice. They fail to take into account that others may have their own agendas and that there are other values besides reaching the goal in the fastest possible way.

In this incarnation, rather than being judgmental or intolerant, these folks need to find their own vulnerability in others. If the other person says she can't do something, Libra North Node could think back on a situation in his own life when he felt he couldn't do something; then he will feel more compassion for the other person. In this lifetime, Libra North Node people need to learn to relate successfully to others—to inspire and empower them to win victories in their own lives. But to do this successfully they need to learn to discover the *other person's* objectives, values, and style of operation.

THE RULES

Libra North Node people establish their own system of values and assume that everyone else will meet their standards and follow their rules, simply because the rules make sense to Libra North Node. This is a Pandora's box. Only negative things occur when they are inflexibly attached to "the rules." When other people don't play by "the rules" (that is, Libra North Nodes' rules), Libra North Node people experience disappointment; when others resist "the rules," Libra North Nodes' tempers rise. They don't realize the other person didn't get a chance to vote—nor was the other person notified of what "the rules" are.

Sometimes when Libra North Node people think others are being unfair, it's because others aren't following the invisible rules. However, their sense of fairness is essentially selfish because it is based only on their own rules. Libra North Node people must become aware that there are other rules. Their own rules are no more sacred than anyone else's.

In all fairness to these folks, the problem with rules isn't their fault. Subconsciously they are still in the military, where everyone is highly disciplined and follows clearly understood regulations, protocols, and behavior. The good thing about the military, from Libra North Nodes' point of view, is that it's not personal. They're not stepping on the other person's toes when they say what to do—they're just giving orders! If the other person doesn't cooperate, they feel: "Well—you're not being a team player."

Everyone has rules: standards, ideas, and values. Most people are aware of their ideas as "ideas"—not as absolutes. But for Libra North Node people, their rules are the constitution they live by—"the law." Other people can have their own standards and ideas but still be open to others' views. Libra North Node people often can't see any view except their own.

An example of how hurtful this can be is the story of a client whose father was a Libra North Node. On her wedding day, he felt that his father (the client's grandfather) should walk her down the aisle. Because of childhood abuses, my client hated her grandfather. But her father cared more about "the rules" than his own daughter, and he insisted that the grandfather walk her down the aisle "out of respect." Those were "the rules"—there was no discussion. His past-life military programming was allowed to run roughshod over the feelings of his own daughter, even on her wedding day.

Libra North Node people must sit down with their friends and partners to work out rules that both parties accept. Only when the rules are mutually accepted can these folks expect others to live by them. Also, *how* the others respond when the Libra North Node people share their rules will reveal a lot about the relationship—and whether it is appropriate.

By discovering the others' standards and rules, Libra North Node people can expand their own value systems. In fact, their ability to develop a sense of inner freedom depends on this. When there are mutually accepted rules in a relationship, the resulting unit will be powerful, efficient, and personally rewarding. And the relationship will be based on a foundation that lends permanence.

PROJECTION

Because Libra North Node people are so tied up in their own identities, they may be unaware of who they are actually dealing with in relationships. They project their own identity onto the other person and then try to relate to that person—which, strangely enough, doesn't work!

When people don't turn out to be the way these folks think they are, it surprises them. They picture the other person's role, and when the partner doesn't *play* it, they become upset. They think the other person is not being "fair" with them (that is, the other isn't being true to the role). Once again, they are relating to others in terms of their own past-life military experience, where everyone was considered an object and judged in terms of how well they fulfilled their function.

These folks have difficulty seeing the other person outside of the role they have projected. For example, I had a client with this nodal position who discovered, after twenty-three years of marriage, that her husband had sexually molested their daughter for several years. She had absolutely no idea it had been going on until her daughter went into therapy. There can be many reasons for this kind of "not knowing"; but in the case of Libra North Node people, they never did *see* who the other person really was.

As a by-product of projecting their identity onto others, they expect others to be as strong as they are, as generous, as confident, as disciplined— and they feel cheated when the partner doesn't exhibit these characteristics. They need to step into the other person's shoes. In this way, they can discover the levels of strength, generosity, confidence, and discipline inherent in the other person, and thus have more realistic expectations. Also, they will discover certain positive qualities (ones that the Libra North Node person doesn't have) that the other person brings to the relationship. They are learning that we all have different identities, and therein lies the capacity for growth in unexpected and rewarding directions.

NEEDS

APPROVAL

Libra North Node people are hungry for approval and want to be included in the other person's energy field. They feel relaxed and happy when others "feed" them love. This is a valid need: In this incarnation, love from others will give them the spiritual balance they require.

The problem is the methods they use to get others' attention and energy. To this end they may get caught up in competition, overachievement, and taking the initiative without consulting others. They show off, trying to look good to attract the attention and loving energy they so desperately need. Because they hunger for the spotlight, when other people are talking these folks will often say something about themselves so that the attention comes back to them. They aren't really tuned in to the other person—only to their own need for love and approval. These needs can also cause Libra

North Nodes to be competitive in situations where cooperation would work more to their advantage.

The resolution lies in shifting their focus from making themselves look good, to making the other person feel good. When these folks tune in and take their partners' *feelings* into account, they will know how to further joint goals in ways the partners can accept. If Libra North Node people help those around them to be happy, they will automatically feel the good vibrations. They don't have to "extract" this energy from others; acceptance, love, and approval will automatically flow to them. It's part of the natural process of being sensitive and doing what they can to make others happy. The energy these folks need is the energy they will feel when they validate others for just being themselves.

CONFIDENCE IN RELATIONSHIPS

These folks can lack confidence in relationships owing to lack of experience in partnership and sharing in past lives. Also, they tend to undermine their own self-confidence by focusing so much energy on self. For example, if there's a misunderstanding in a relationship, rather than checking in to find out what the other person is thinking and feeling, Libra North Nodes' tendency is to immediately focus on themselves—either their own hurt feelings or what they did wrong. They never look beyond their own mindset to determine what's going on with the other person, and this erodes their confidence in the relationship. They may assume that the other person doesn't like something about them, and they end up feeling "unacceptable." Or they may make a harsh judgment against their partner, which leads them to think there are very few people they can connect with in the world.

Libra North Node people actually have a lot of confidence, but they aren't in touch with it on a social level until they begin to share it. By focusing on how they can help others feel more confident, they feel more confidence as well. The ability to "do" relationships is actually an incredible talent for these people, but they don't know they have it. They become discouraged when relationships don't seem to work out. What they want is not incorrect, it's just that their methods are "off." The part of them that knows how to "do" relationships is like an interior room where they have remarkable tools for creating successful relationships—but they have to remember to open the door!

SUPPORTING OTHERS

These folks are real "people promoters." For example, Johnny may have just invented a device that takes all the pollution from exhaust emissions out of the air—but he's not doing anything with it. Others may say: "Johnny, you should sell your invention! Think of the money you'll make—think how you'll help the environment!" But Johnny has a million excuses for procrastinating: "Well, it's really not good enough yet." Then a Libra North Node person comes along, says a few words to Johnny, and something about the way he says it causes Johnny to put things in motion.

These folks have a tremendous ability to empower others to be warriors—to give them the confidence and energy that send them on their way. But they fear that others will become dependent on them. They don't want others to drain their energy, their ideas, or their life force. In fact, the other person will give back to them—but then they have the challenge of accepting the gifts that others give. This requires humility and acknowledgment that Libra North Nodes are not totally self-sufficient. It's part of learning to give and to receive—to be part of a team.

SHARING AND SELFLESSNESS

Sharing is important for Libra North Node people. They've had many past lifetimes of isolation and missing the joys of having a mate. In this lifetime, their desire to have a mate is enormous; it needs to be honored for them to feel complete and nurtured emotionally. An unselfish love, with no thought of personal reward, is the key to actualizing the closeness and rapport that will fill their hearts. They need to give simply for the sake of sharing their wealth and bringing support and joy to their partner. Then, as the other person gains strength, his or her happiness will in turn permeate and satisfy the Libra North Node person.

These folks have a tremendous love of life, and in this incarnation they are learning to expand it by including others. They need to take the other person into account, discover the other's limits, and then go out and share experiences. They need to remember that sharing experiences with that one special person is more nurturing than reaching their own goals.

Libra North Node people are learning the art of selflessness: putting their feelings aside for the sake of supporting someone else. When they give to another with no thought of return, they become a channel for giving. The universe gives more to them, because they are actively passing on the energy. As they selflessly give to other people, they clear the way for their partners—and for life itself—to give back to them. There is no need to keep a ledger for "fairness" in giving and receiving; when Libra North Node people give to others, they are truly giving to themselves.

ACCEPTANCE

SELF-PROTECTION

Owing to so many past incarnations as warriors, these folks have developed a trait of inaccessibility. They are very selective about the image they project, and if people see them differently, they become upset. They try to control how people see them: "How could they say that about me? That's not how I see myself!" This defensiveness makes it tough for other people to relate to them.

Libra North Node people may indulge in unexpected behavior, because they don't want others to be able to figure them out. It's a tactical maneuver. Fearing that people won't find them interesting, they resist being completely "known." Also, this nodal group regards all the other groups as the same, and they don't want to be like everyone else. They're afraid that exposing their emotions and checking in with people will make them like everyone else—and they won't be different and exciting anymore.

INDEPENDENCE VERSUS INTERDEPENDENCE

The warrior in Libra North Node people wants to have sharp wits, independence, and no emotional ties so that it can move on at will. In their psyches, the muscle of independence has been overexercised in past lives and now can rear its ugly head at the most inappropriate times and ruin relationships that might have been nurturing.

It can be somewhat unnerving for Libra North Node people to check in with others and support them. They are afraid that if they give to someone they'll start to feel responsible for that person, which goes against their "on the road" warrior mentality. Subconsciously, they don't want to be tied down.

These folks need to keep in mind that this is a people lifetime. Their best rewards will come through interdependence, not self-isolating independence. They've already experienced extreme independence; to rewalk that path will only result in missing the deep connection with others that they crave. When they do step past their fears and support another, they create a bond with that person and receive the appreciation and validation that they so desperately need. In supporting someone with no motive except genuine caring, their loneliness is healed.

When Libra North Node people support others, they automatically empower people. So, in reality, they are not creating dependency but are helping others achieve a higher level of self-sufficiency. However, sometimes they become resentful, thinking: "Why aren't other people already as independent as I am? If everybody were like me, the world would be a fine place!" They don't mean to be vain, but past-life habits are strong, and the discipline of the warrior is a mindset that is difficult to break.

These folks have been isolated from society and the peaceful satisfaction of nurturing relationships for so many incarnations that it's frightening for them to even consider taking the plunge and joining in. But it's not that they don't know how. Once they make up their minds, these folks can accomplish anything. In fact, once they get into it, they'll find they have a *talent* for creating successful relationships. But first they must make the conscious decision that interdependence is a higher road than isolation.

HARMONY

Libra North Node people are tired of war; in this lifetime, they want to experience peaceful relationships. Nonetheless, they have intense relationships that are highly emotional, and their lack of communication can promote that intensity. But they are ready to move on to the next level—a place of more caring, more interdependence, and more compassion. They need to choose peace, hang up their shield, and participate in relationships in which they can be vulnerable.

PATIENCE

In this lifetime, Libra North Node people are learning patience. There are other people on the planet, and Libra North Nodes' lives will unfold most happily when they take the time to include others in their plans. Temper tantrums are a symptom of their impatience. Often, if they don't get their way immediately they'll leave, when it's exactly the situation that would have made them most happy.

These folks have an excess of impulsive energy. In past lives, their rashness was seen as courage that resulted in success and self-glorification—they were heroes! However, "heroism" also created a sense of superiority and isolation from others. In this life, impulsive tendencies lead to defeat rather than victory. When Libra North Node people act on their impulses, they may trample other people's feelings in the pursuit of their own desires and seriously injure the goodwill others have for them.

Because of their impulsiveness, Libra North Node people need to nurture their patience and understand that a certain process of events needs to happen for their plans to be realized. They are often so directed and want things so intensely that the process seems agonizingly slow. They're running at high speed—but there's no war to fight anymore, and slowing themselves down and thinking things through is necessary for true fulfillment in this lifetime.

Because of their impulsiveness, these folks may not fully understand why they want something. If they could be patient, they would see the bigger picture. Then they could explain it to the other person involved, and a lot of problems would dissolve. The other person would be given the opportunity to cooperate and understand.

SENSITIVITY AND CONSIDERATION

Libra North Node people are very sensitive—in an insensitive way. They feel things very deeply themselves, but they can be shallow when it comes to understanding other people's feelings. They experience hurt on a *very* deep level. Because of these intense feelings, they think they have a wonderful understanding of everyone else. But the process fails to take other people's idiosyncrasies into account or acknowledge that Libra North Nodes' actions may affect another person in a negative way. This is behind much of the misunderstanding in their relationships. Libra North Nodes need to actively search for that deeper level in their connections with others.

Tuning in to another person means temporarily leaving oneself. It's like listening to the radio: To clearly hear the music, you have to stop humming the song in your own head. In the same way, these folks should leave their own mindset and tune in to others' melodies. After they "hear" the feelings and perceptions of the other, they can determine whether they can harmonize with the melody of that person.

These folks have to remind themselves to be aware of other people's needs and feelings. For example, if two friends are walking down the street and one is burdened with packages and the other is carrying nothing, likely the friend carrying nothing is a Libra North Node—no one else would be so unaware of the other person. Things that seem obvious to everyone else simply do not occur to these people. They don't mean to be hurtful; they are just unaware of the damaging effects their self-preoccupation has on others. In this life, if they want the joys of successful, happy relationships, they must consciously cultivate selflessness and an awareness of others' needs and feelings.

RELATIONSHIPS

LACK OF EXPERIENCE

THE WARRIOR LIFESTYLE . . . IT'S JUST ME!

Because of their past lifetimes in military environments, Libra North Node people lack experience in personal relationships. In a military setting, relationships are governed by protocol and firm, objective regulations that are understood by everyone. When it comes to relating outside of a strict set of codes, these folks don't know how to do it. The simplest things about relationships—sharing, mutual helpfulness, and interrelatedness—that come so naturally to all the other nodal groups are totally new areas of discovery for Libra North Node people. When they make mistakes in their relationships it is not intentional or malicious, but rather owing to a habit of following "the rules" instead of relating to people.

Another problem is that warriors don't usually stay in town to build a family—they move on to fight the next battle. These folks can be classic "one-night stand" people, making a conquest and then moving on to the next person. For them, love and sex can be competitive. They love the game of romance. Once they succeed (and the other person has been "captured"), they need to face the next challenge. It's all they know. Yet, as a lifestyle, this tendency for quick, superficial relationships leaves them feeling peculiarly empty.

The irony is that when Libra North Node people understand how relationships work, they can be masters at it. They have superior (latent) talents for sensitivity and diplomacy, once they understand how to access and apply them. Because their life purpose is to balance past lives through partnering with others, they will always have an abundance of people attracted to them.

Some of these folks are afraid to love anyone because they aren't accustomed to *exchanging* love. In this life, their early attempts may fail because they haven't learned how to exchange love. They close themselves off emotionally in response. However, they are learning that some people will love them for their innate individual spirit, and some will not. People are different, after all. It is not only how these people present themselves that determines how others respond to them, but also the nature of the other person. Therefore, they need to be open and let others see who they are. Then they can feel safe by knowing who loves them for who they really are, and be cautious (in terms of giving 100 percent of themselves) with those who do not accept them.

DISCRIMINATION . . . YOU MEAN THERE ARE OTHER PEOPLE OUT THERE?

These people want a partner with whom they can share the joys of life on an equal basis, who will reciprocate by feeding them appreciation. But for this energy to come back to them, they must choose the right partner. Part of a successful relationship involves discrimination—seeing who the potential partner really is and not simply how that person fills the Libra North Node's needs.

Sometimes their tendency to project aspects of their own identity onto other people is so strong that others feel uneasy around them. Libra North Nodes feel that they won't be understood or accommodated anyway, so what's the use? This problem can rob these folks of true intimacy. An example is a client whose mother was a Libra North Node person. When this client was promoted and began buying expensive suits appropriate to her new management position, she knew her mother would object to the expense. Because she didn't want to be made to feel uncomfortable, she hid the clothes in the hall closet until she had the privacy to transfer them to her room. This robbed both her and her mother of the fun of looking at the new purchases together, which could have brought them closer.

Another way these folks misjudge relationships is by focusing only on the qualities about the other person that they like. They may not like *all* aspects of the other person, and they may block out the less appealing qualities, thereby overlooking what is actually going on.

The first step for Libra North Node people is to be willing to learn about the other person. Does this person have goals and ideals similar to their own? Does the person have aims that they feel they can support? Is the other person a giver or a taker? What are the other person's values? What kind of identity do they want to build? Libra North Node people must have the humility to be genuinely curious about the identity of the other person and not project their own ideas onto them. To understand another's values, one must ask, put one's own identity aside, and allow awareness of the other to temporarily engulf oneself.

Generally it works better when the Libra North Node asks the other person questions first and *then* states his or her position. The tendency is to say immediately: "Well, *I* would like to have a marriage where there are no children and both partners work and make lots of money. What would you like?" If the other person wants to please, he or she will give a response that can be interpreted as supportive of the Libra North Node's position.

But this is how these folks get into trouble. Their identity carries so much strength that the other person may sidestep a direct confrontation because it could put an end to the connection. Others will generally yield, either by understating the importance of their own position or by "going along" with what the Libra North Node person wants.

I had a Libra North Node client whose experience illustrates this problem very well. In his second marriage he was tremendously in love with his wife, who was twelve years his junior. He had one child from his first marriage, and he and his second wife had agreed that they would not have children.

This was his idea, but she talked herself into it because she loved him so much. Once the agreement had been reached (which he considered to be "mutual"), he had a vasectomy. The marriage seemed "on track" for the first four years, and he was very happy. Then came the traumatic weekend when she asked for a divorce because she wanted children. The marriage was filling his needs, but not hers. He was traumatized, and it took him years to recover emotionally from the experience. Disappointment for both parties could have been avoided if my client had taken the time to *truly* ascertain his partner's desires. Then he could have decided if he loved her enough to compromise his original preference in order to satisfy her need for a child.

Libra North Node people should trust their own internal sense of happiness in choosing a partner. They will not be able to rely on logic, but they can trust their feelings of love and attraction to be an accurate guide. Once they identify an appropriate partner and enter a relationship, the challenge for these folks is to be vigilant regarding their partner's changing needs. When they cultivate the habit of checking in and keeping in touch, they engender such loving feelings in their partners that the results are overwhelmingly abundant.

EXPECTATIONS . . . AND THEY'RE SEPARATE FROM ME?

These folks often are disappointed in relationships because they create expectations without accurately assessing the needs, ideas, preferences, or timing of the other person. They think it's up to them to reach the "goal" through their own efforts. In relationships, they seek relevant facts that will help them reach their goal with that person. Then they pull back and plan their strategy, based on what they *believe* are the partner's characteristics, needs, and desires. The only problem is, they never ask for the other person's input!

Libra North Node people often presume to know the "character trait" behind someone's behavior. But when they are wrong, it leads to painful misunderstandings on both sides. They can also become very angry because they think others don't appreciate who they are. They expect the partner to see how their talents could add to and better the other person's life. Sometimes they become arrogant, downplaying the other person's intelligence because the partner does not seem aware of how much they have to give.

They become angry and erect a wall of judgmental thinking that keeps others away.

These folks need to expand their perspective to gain a more objective viewpoint through communication. Often, when they feel that others don't appreciate them, they haven't clearly understood the other person's concerns. To avoid feeling isolated and betrayed, they should ask the other person to define himself or herself from his or her own point of view; this will help Libra North Nodes gain an accurate understanding and far more realistic expectations.

LACK OF AWARENESS . . . AND I HAVE TO TAKE THEM INTO ACCOUNT?

These folks can appear to be very inconsiderate. They don't take the other person's reactions, desires, or needs into account when making decisions. They act without getting any feedback from the other person.

For example, I had a client whose husband had this nodal position. When they went on vacation, he would spend the entire time sight-seeing and exploring. My client would protest that she wanted some relaxation as well. When they returned home, however, she would excitedly tell their friends about all the different things they had seen. From her behavior, her husband assumed that by doing what he wanted, she was also enjoying herself. He didn't take her protests seriously because he knew "how good it was for her." The Libra North Node often assumes that he knows what will strengthen the other person, regardless of the feedback the other person gives him.

The irony is that often these folks *do* know what the other person will enjoy, but they need to temper that knowledge with feedback. In the above example, it would mean listening to the wife's protests and asking questions to determine her anxieties. Once the husband was aware of her concerns, he could work out a plan that encompassed her expressed needs, and he would be rewarded with her appreciation of his leadership. This is how teamwork works best for these folks.

TIMING . . . AND THEY HAVE NEEDS?

In the matter of giving, Libra North Node people must pay more attention to their partner's timing. When the partner expresses a need, that is the time for them to give. They should put everything else on hold and listen to what the partner needs at that time. If they wait until they feel ready to initiate giving, the opportunity will have passed them by.

For example, the partner might ask for help with a project. The Libra North Node person might say: "Oh, come on now. You can do it by yourself." He doesn't want to divert his energy and get distracted by his partner's problem. This instinctive selfishness can have a subtle but destructive effect on the relationship. Libra North Node people can't have the benefits of partnership without the reciprocity of giving. When they find someone they want to be with, they need to take the cue on "timing" from the partner if this is a person they don't want to lose. This is a relationship lifetime; when they put their primary relationship first, everyone wins.

FEARS

FEAR OF EMOTIONAL EMBARRASSMENT

As much as Libra North Node people want and need a partner in this incarnation, some part of them is terrified. They are afraid of embarrassment—but they need that special relationship with another person so badly that they simply must risk it. One of their fears is of "being stuck"—making a poor choice and not being able to get out of it. They are such perfectionists that they want their primary partnership to be perfect, too. If they choose the wrong person and it doesn't work out, then they will have to admit that they are having problems. What they're really saying is: "I don't want a relationship because I don't want to look as foolish as others look to me if it doesn't go well."

Because "looking good" is so important to these folks, it's also important that their mate "looks good." If they find some quality in their partner less than compelling, they'll want the partner to change and may start to nag the other person. This never works when the Libra North Node person's motive is to "look good" to others by having an attractive mate. Once again, the motive is self. However, if the partner also wants to change, and if Libra North Node is willing to give support and help, both people can win.

Until they lend their strength and discipline to help the other person overcome the limitation, often the partner's condition will worsen. For example, if a Libra North Node person notices that her partner has gained weight and seems unhappy, the first thing she should do is check in with the partner to determine what he wants. She could say something like: "I've noticed that you're concerned about your weight, and I've noticed that you continue to overeat. Are you upset about something? I'd like to know what's going on with you, and if there's anything I can do to help." In the process of caring and seeking to understand the other person, she can learn how to help him overcome his problem. These folks are learning to care about the relationship more than they care about their image.

Libra North Node people don't understand why others put up with being treated badly. They don't understand how much someone can love another, and they fear passion and bonding. They are afraid that if they truly love someone, it may lead them to a place that isn't good for them. They must trust their hearts and believe that in alliance with the other person, they can develop a healthy relationship. In this incarnation they can discover the joys of extending the love they feel for themselves to include another person.

FEAR OF CO-DEPENDENCY

These folks are terrified of "co-dependent relationships." The irony is that because they want to be on the receiving end all the time, they naturally become dependent on the partner's giving. But the partner cannot also become dependent, because he or she is not getting anything back from Libra North Node. When the partner leaves (physically or emotionally), these folks are devastated and can't figure out why the relationship didn't work.

If these folks want true independence in a relationship, they should always try to give more than they receive. Then they will be the "strong" one and can experience the joys of being vulnerable and *interdependent* with another person without the threat of abandonment. It's very important that they make a conscious effort to be helpful and giving in their close partnerships. They often hold back from giving fully lest they lose their identity. But not to worry—their identity is so firm, it's not going anywhere!

Libra North Node people need to be careful about using their need for independence as a defense against participating in their relationships. Their demands for independence are often poorly timed and appear abrupt, abrasive, and alienating. This causes their partners to think the Libra North Node people don't care about them, and that both parties aren't looking out for each other. Naturally, the other person doesn't want to be the only vulnerable one in the relationship, and so begins to detach emotionally. This need for time alone can be absolutely disastrous in intimate relationships. If it is not handled properly, the people closest to these folks feel unloved, unappreciated, unprotected, and without the "special mutual awareness" that makes going through the challenges of a long-term relationship worthwhile.

Libra North Node people are so used to being independent and secretive that when others start to really see them, they become embarrassed. They fear that being vulnerable to another person will make them weak. They want to be independent all the time *and* they want a relationship—and the two don't go together! When they're leading, the focus is on them and they feel good. But when someone else is in charge, it can be embarrassing because they don't understand their role. They need to recognize that usually others will allow them to lead if they'll just take the time to check in and communicate. Others do not necessarily want to be in charge; they just don't want to be told what to do without their feelings being taken into account.

Libra North Node people place a high premium on independence, but in all fairness they support their partners in being independent as well. They think: "It's fair if everybody follows the rules." But as their priorities change, their rules change and they expect everyone to follow along. They're so used to being leaders in past incarnations that they think their job in this lifetime is to lead. In fact, their job now is to help *others* grow into positions of leadership.

Fear of Compromise and Change

Compromise is an essential part of a happy relationship. Only by recognizing and acknowledging the other person's needs, as well as one's own, can a win/win situation be created. When Libra North Node people operate from a vacuum, considering only their own desires, they create a win/lose situation in relationships. Eventually, the person who is "losing" wanders off to find someone who will play more fairly. The first thing Libra North Node must do is acknowledge the individuality of the partner and understand that person's needs and insecurities.

However, sometimes these folks don't *want* to compromise. They don't want to take the time to establish a clear understanding with the other person. They may fear that if they are aware of the other person's position, they'll have to sacrifice their own. However, by refusing to acknowledge the need for compromise, they negate the importance of the other person and, once again, sow the seeds for ending up alone. Sensitivity to the other person is essential. When the partner voices an insecurity, that is the time to stop everything and do whatever it takes to re-establish rapport.

Giving from the Heart Versus Keeping Score

Tit-for-Tat Games

Libra North Node people tend to have a "tit-for-tat" consciousness. They want everything to be equal, and they want their partner to share in the sacrifices they have to make. For instance, if they have to get up at 5:00 A.M., they want the other person up with them. Rather than recognizing his partner's need for sleep and caring that the other person is balanced within herself, the Libra North Node wants her up (making breakfast or doing something to help) so that she is balanced with *him*. But true balance is each partner supporting the other 100 percent in being balanced and happy within themselves. Happiness in the relationship will be a natural by-product. The relationship will thrive if the Libra North Node stops checking to see that he's getting his "fair share" at every moment.

When they do give, these folks should do it without "tooting their horn." They have a tendency to take note of exactly how much they are giving and then expect exactly the same amount of energy in return. At the very least, they expect recognition and profuse thanks from the other person; if it isn't forthcoming, they remind their partner of how much they've done. Of course, by demanding recognition, Libra North Node people have taken the gift back and turned it into a trade—warrior style! The secret of giving is that it creates an opening to receive. Others will always give back more than these folks can imagine if their giving is pure, with no expectation of return. If they focus their energy on the other person, their partner's resulting happiness will fill their hearts and make them happy as well.

These people want to experience the joy of having a partner to interact with—and the joy of two people sharing a load. The problem is that according to *their* ideas, each person should carry 50 percent of the *same load*. They must recognize that people are stronger and weaker in different areas, and that to measure giving against the "50 percent marker" in every area defeats a relationship. When they learn to give 100 percent where it's needed, they will find their partner is giving 100 percent in an area where *they* need support. Their willingness to do more than their share will come back to them—in more than equal measure—over time.

COMPETITIVENESS

These folks are accustomed to competition from past lives as warriors, but in this lifetime their competitive spirit can hinder them in getting what they want. They are so used to fighting that everything seems like a battle to them. They create opposition where none exists, and by assuming that others are going to oppose them, they provoke the very opposition they fear. For example, they may impulsively take off for an adventure without notifying their partner, thereby provoking worry and negative feelings. Other behaviors that sabotage their relationships include carelessness, rashness, defensive outbursts, noncommunication, and other subtle (and not-so-subtle) tactics based on the idea that they have to defeat others in order to get their way.

These folks are learning that their partners want to support and help them, as opposed to thinking that their partners are going to create problems. A shift in perspective is required: viewing their partners as being "on their side" and wanting to be supportive. By definition, special relationships signal a willingness to let one another in on the deepest levels, to share from a position of vulnerability and closeness. That's what partnership is: two people helping each other overcome obstacles that neither could have conquered alone.

RECIPROCITY

Relationships should be reciprocal and cumulative. When one person continually gives to another only to contribute to the well-being of that person—with nothing expected in return—the recipient feels that purity of intent and becomes more kindly disposed toward the giver. Out of thankfulness, the recipient will spontaneously want to give back to the partner. It's a natural process—we cannot force another person to want to give any more than we can force that person to love. True giving is a loving response to the positive way another person affects us.

All too often, rather than truly giving for its own sake, Libra North Node people trade: "If I let you do this, then I expect you to let me do that." The partner does not receive a gift but something that has to be earned. This robs a relationship of the feeling of benefit and the graciousness of giving. But when Libra North Nodes put the partnership first and are genuinely concerned about helping, both partners have a heartfelt desire to give back.

SELFLESSNESS

These folks are learning that, as the Bible says, "It is more blessed to give than to receive." It is not only more blessed; it is a lot more intelligent. As a person gives, it creates a void; and nature cannot tolerate a void. Immediately life sends new energy to fill the space. The problem is that Libra North Node is looking for the payback to come in a certain form.

For example, I had a client who went out of her way to comfort a friend who was going through a divorce. She took her out to dinner twice and spent many intense hours counseling her, encouraging her, and helping restore her self-confidence. Two years later my client was moving and needed a place to stay for a week. She called this friend, but the friend was unable to offer her lodging. My client was crushed. She had been keeping track of the kindness she had shown this woman, and she only wanted help from her. Because her vision was limited to help coming only in that form, she overlooked all the other possibilities that life was sending to support her.

When Libra North Node people keep score of how much they are giving in personal relationships, they limit the vision of what they can receive and where it comes from. Sometimes they cut off their giving prematurely, even though their hearts are enjoying the process: Instead of following their hearts, they follow their scorecard. They may stop giving just at the point when the returns from the other person were about to be forthcoming. As long as they are feeling joy in the process of giving, they just need to follow their happiness.

By having a specific idea of what they want back from someone, they miss the rewards that are natural by-products of the relationship. For happiness, these folks must learn to appreciate the unexpected gifts they receive along the way.

KARMIC PARTNERS

Libra North Node people often attract partners who have tremendous potential but who lack the self-confidence to convert that potential and reach their goals. Often, these are people to whom they owe a "debt" from a past life. Perhaps the other person sacrificed self-identity and helped them to win in some way, and now it is up to them to return the favor.

On some level these folks know this is a "partnership" lifetime, and they actively seek a mate. But they keep attracting people weaker than themselves, which can make them angry and resentful. Owing to many warrior lifetimes, they have mastered self-discipline, single-mindedness, and efficient attainment of their goals—and think that other people should be the same. They tend to disdain others' weaknesses, scorn their lack of self-discipline, and look down on what they perceive to be their lack of courage. They need to recognize that if they attracted a fellow warrior as a mate, this would be another lifetime of competition rather than a time of peaceful sharing.

In fact, Libra North Node people have such strong self-identity in their aura that it operates as a barrier to other people. They need to work on dissolving that force field, and they can do this most efficiently by giving that energy to others who actually need it. They need to get rid of the excess energy around their self-identity so they attract people who need more self-identity: The other person gets a "charge" of self-confidence and the Libra North Node person gets a release. Both people win. The result is an opening in the aura of the Libra North Node person through which he or she can receive more love and energy.

INTERDEPENDENCE

Learning how to relate with others in a meaningful way is the primary challenge in this lifetime for Libra North Node people. In any area of their life where they are "winning," there is a strong partnership behind them. In areas where they are "losing"—whether professionally or in terms of personal happiness—they have not yet learned the lessons they must pass through in order to build successful relationships.

One way or another, these folks are destined to learn the value of including other people's energies as part of their plans. They can learn the hard way—through battling and disappointment; or the easy way—by acting on some of their life lessons. Each time they strike out on their own, they either fall short of their goal or, when they reach it, find it to be hollow and unsatisfying. They are learning to recognize that: "Hello . . . there are other people on this planet! Who are *you*?" They are also learning to recognize that they need the energies of others to nourish their own well-being and reach their goals.

COMRADES OR LOVERS?

These folks have such a talent for supporting and building up the strength of other people that they may experience a long string of relationships that don't last. Those close to them become strong in their own right and then, for various reasons, a parting of the way occurs. This sometimes happens because—subconsciously—Libra North Node people work to build the autonomy of the other person so that they can be "equals," rather than building a team. They can see where the other person lacks confidence, so they reinforce the partner's strength. Once the partner becomes self-sufficient, he or she doesn't need the Libra North Node person anymore. And because the focus has been on building mutual autonomy, it is only natural that both individuals go their own ways. But Libra North Node feels crushed—it seems unfair that as soon as the partner became strong, the partner left.

For Libra North Nodes, relationships should not be based on the concept of two fully self-sufficient comrades sharing experiences in the context of their own self-contained, separate identities. That system is based on barter, trading, 50-50 sharing, and sensitivity only to self. It leaves out the magic ingredient of emotional sensitivity that is so satisfying in a long-term relationship.

When the emotional interconnection—the sensitive awareness of the other person and the desire to make him or her happy—is lacking, Libra North Nodes' partners often leave them. For the partner, the alliance can become dry and loveless—based on systems of expectations, rewards, demands, and "fair play"—so the partner leaves to find nurturing elsewhere.

The key for these folks is to notice and act when their partner needs support. Then the partner will be happy to stay because of feeling connected, and the Libra North Node will be getting all that happy energy back. It's a win/win situation.

LISTENING AND SENSITIVITY

Putting awareness and consideration of the other person first is essential if Libra North Node people want to have a successful relationship. To maintain a consistent base of communication and understanding takes more time than they are accustomed to giving, since they are used to only having to take themselves into account. But if they want a relationship to last over the long haul, these folks must learn to be sensitive and listen to their partner's needs.

They also need to be careful not to injure others (physically, psychologically, or emotionally). Their partners may not make a lot of demands, so Libra North Node people may ignore them. They are shocked when the seemingly accommodating partners walk out. They hadn't taken the others' identity—their idiosyncrasies and needs—into account.

A team is two individuals taking care of each other, being aware of one other, compensating for each other's strengths and weaknesses, and helping each other instinctively without being asked. For example, if I injure my toe, I put a Band-Aid on it. I don't think about it or ask: "What has my toe done for me lately?" Nor do I expect the toe to recognize how wonderful I am for putting a Band-Aid on it. I take care of it instinctively. It's the same with teamwork—you are sensitive to your partner and instinctively step in to help when there is a problem, because the partner is a part of you.

Libra North Node people must be sensitive to their partners' insecurities and, sometimes, respond just to ease their fears. Not all questions are asked with the intention of receiving an accurate, factual answer. Sometimes, in partnership, a person may ask a question with the motive of gaining reassurance or a feeling of closeness. For example, if a newlywed asks: "Do you think we'll always be in love this way?" he doesn't want to hear: "Well, I hope so, but I guess one just never knows" (which would be a typical Libra North Node answer); he wants to hear: "*Of course* we will be!"

GOALS

These folks can be selfish. They can act impulsively and with total disregard for others' situations. They tend to take over unexpectedly when their goals aren't being met quickly enough. They are prone to acting on their assumptions without checking in to find out what is going on with the other person. Even though their motive may be to promote the best interest of everyone involved, others feel stripped of power and resentful because they weren't part of the process. Trust—a key issue for these folks—is undermined on both sides in the relationship.

Although checking in with a partner is an easy resolution for many obstacles, these folks fear doing it. A part of them thinks: "If I check in, they'll think I don't trust them." Actually, it's *not checking in* that leaves the other person questioning their trust, and once again, Libra North Node people end up feeling isolated, misunderstood, and unappreciated.

For example, I have a client with this nodal position who is in the restaurant business. In the typical warrior "chain of command" approach, he gave his manager the instruction: "There's a special party coming in, I want the table set up by 7:00." At 6:40, the table was not set up and the people started to arrive. My client thought: "Oh my God! He's not going to have it done!" So he set the whole thing up himself. He was shocked and angry when the manager approached him later and instead of thanking him, said: "You didn't trust me." The old warrior had forced a result without considering the timing and feelings of the other person.

These folks need to take the time to communicate instead of forcing their way. My client could have said to his manager: "Stan, I'm a little worried that this table isn't ready. Is everything okay, or can I do something to help you?" By *checking in* with the manager, he could have assured himself that the job would get done and created the bond of teamwork that these people so desperately need. When they take the time to access it, these folks have a rare gift for diplomacy that can create tremendous affection on both sides, while at the same time accomplishing the goal.

Libra North Node people need to relate with the other person in the process of giving orders. It is not enough for them to simply "state the facts"; the other person needs to gain a sense of their power in the situation. These folks must explain why the orders are important in the context of the overall situation and impart their confidence that the other person can do the job successfully. Libra North Node people think they've made the instructions so simple that anyone could do it, but the truth is that what would be easy for them might be a very difficult assignment for others.

Before giving the orders, these folks should also notice how the other person is feeling. For example, if the other person is already flustered, getting more orders might push him or her over the edge. Their best bet is to acknowledge the other person, emotional frailties and all, *before* giving the orders. Taking the time to establish a solid base for the relationship makes carrying out the orders joyous for the other person and is added insurance that the job will be done correctly.

Another good approach—especially in goal-oriented situations—is to say: "This is where we're going, this is how I want it done . . . but how would *you* do it? If you have a different idea, please let me know."

ACKNOWLEDGING INDIVIDUAL DIFFERENCES

Libra North Node people find it difficult to fit freedom and creativity into their lives. They like things to be direct and orderly, and it can be hard for them to go with the flow. Other areas of conflict can stem from the fact that these folks like to "test the fates." On some level they believe: "I'm the center of the world! Nothing can touch me!" And generally they don't get hurt, even in high-risk situations. This unique style of operation works for them. The problem comes when they decide that other people should have the same approach. "Just press through your limitations" is their recommendation. But what works for them is not necessarily going to work for another person. Their job is to support the other person in reaching his or her own goals, taking into account that person's unique style.

Experiencing Expanded Identity

Synergy

Consistently, the solution for these people is partnership. Even in reaching personal goals, their success is ensured if they approach that goal with a partner. For example, if a Libra North Node person is having an impossible time losing 20 pounds, his best bet is to find a friend with the same problem and lose the weight together. In the process of helping the other person stick to the diet or exercise program, the weight will simultaneously start dropping off the Libra North Node person. The same holds true for any personal goal he is having difficulty reaching: If he finds another person to do it with, both will win.

These people have the ability to "transplant" courage into others, giving them confidence to take the initiative and do things that—without their help—the other person never would have attempted. They have the ability to validate others' identity with so much confidence that others start to believe in themselves. They are great successes as business consultants, psychologists, teachers, coaches, or any other role that brings out confidence and courage in others.

However, Libra North Node people need to be certain there is no selfish motive involved, or the process will backfire. Thus, the ability to be objective is essential: They need to discern the *other person's goals*.

Intimacy and Vulnerability

Libra North Node people need to develop their capacity to be vulnerable. They are learning to be sensitive to others: open to others' feelings and perspectives. They are learning to allow others to experience them: sharing their feelings and fears. These folks have strong defenses against being vulnerable. Their strong programming says: "Never let anyone know your weaknesses." But they are learning that there is great strength in vulnerability—indeed, the best warrior is one who knows when to fight and when to make peace. But if they don't check in with the other person, they won't know which is which.

For their relationships to work on a lasting level, they also need to learn how to become more intimate. Intimacy is a by-product of being more sensitive to the other person's insecurities and more open to revealing their own vulnerabilities. When they are more intimate, they are able to grow. But when they don't become more intimate, they remain unapproachable and inaccessible.

When they are hurting, Libra North Node people's first instinct is to pull back and not let others know they have been affected. In this lifetime they are learning the value of opening up and allowing others to take care of them. In sharing their vulnerability, what they were originally ashamed of becomes something they can celebrate, and they find themselves bonding with others in an authentic way. Now they can allow others to know them—rather than the image they project. These people have innate honesty, courage, and directness. It can be a leap forward in self-discovery when they allow themselves to be vulnerable with others.

Libra North Node people are afraid that if they expose their vulnerability—if they don't have it "all together"—they're going to lose the people they want to impress. Instead, exposing their vulnerability endears them to others. Further, it helps others know how to support them and give them confidence. They include the other person in their lives on a deeper level and feel accepted by that person at the same time. The old feelings of isolation melt away.

When these folks allow others to share their fears, their innate courage inspires everyone to make deeper connections. They find that others have been through similar situations and made even more drastic mistakes. Making mistakes, learning, and growing is part of being human—quite different from the "war machine" Libra North Nodes experienced in past lives. For these folks, pulling down the wall between themselves and others can be like a warrior putting down his shield—it's scary. But to be fulfilled, they must be willing to set that shield aside and be vulnerable.

TEAMWORK

Libra North Node people don't have a sense of teamwork. They've had no past life experience with it. As warriors, they take on the entire job themselves. They become annoyed with others who want to share the responsibility. They want to manage the job on their own because they're afraid the other person will "mess up"—and they won't attain their goal because someone else didn't do their part. Also, they have no patience for somebody taking two or three days to do what they can do in one day—and better!

Yet in this lifetime they are not here to do the job by themselves—they already know they can do that. They have tremendous confidence in achieving short-range goals. But now, when they do reach a goal on their own, they don't feel the happiness they expected. In this lifetime, their job is to accomplish their own goals within the context of a team effort while transferring confidence to other people who need it.

Thus, in working with a team of six other people, they need to remember that there are seven of them. Libra North Node people have an incredible ability to empower others and can see in those six people where each one needs confidence. They welcome the "glitches" that highlight where others lack confidence because it shows them where they can "boost" others, making themselves an invaluable and beloved part of the team.

They always need to first consider what's best for the team. It doesn't work for team members to fall out of communication; it works for them to go out of their way to stay in touch with one another to foster positive feelings of interdependence. To this end, each member must be willing to express his or her needs objectively—not as a resentment or a "tit for tat," but as a means to empower one another in partnership by being open about his or her needs. It's another way of being vulnerable.

PARTNERSHIP

For Libra North Node people, the strong parts of their identity are the qualities they bring to benefit their relationships. The other person brings different gifts that may be exactly what the native needs. Through the partnership, these folks find their balance with others and can access parts of themselves that would otherwise be inaccessible. With a partner, life is no longer drudgery but a positive exchange of energy that makes self-discovery and self-actualization a lighter, happier process for both people.

Since the other person is bringing qualities to the relationship that the Libra North Node person may lack, it behooves Libra North Node to see objectively who the other person actually is, what that person is offering, what talents and qualities he brings to enhance the team. He may not bring confidence or initiative, but perhaps he brings the gift of emotional sensitivity and nurturing, or playfulness and fun, or seeing life as an adventure, or compassionate forgiveness. If Libra North Node can understand what the other person is bringing, she can be more open to accepting and being energized by the gift.

What Libra North Node people truly want is to unite with someone else and *empower* that person's dreams and plans. Thus, it is their responsibility to carefully discern the details of what the other person is seeking so they can discover if it resonates within their own soul. These folks are learning to recognize that their personal survival is based on doing what's best for the relationship. As they take care of their partner with a whole heart, they finally begin to experience joy and fulfillment.

RESISTANCES

These people are tremendous fighters from past lifetimes and are accustomed to the energy of combat. In relationships, they may actually *provoke* fighting simply because they are used to the energy. They want to win at all costs and thus sometimes push away the very relationships that are most dear to them. They fight when there is no need to fight and often end up losing in the end. Their relationship can become a contest of "your needs versus my needs" if they view it as two separate individuals, rather than recognizing that a partnership is actually an entity itself. In fact, the very thing that makes the partnership strong actually feeds both people involved.

They need to learn to put the goal of the relationship ahead of their impulse for conquest. They are much more likely to attain what they want through diplomacy, tact, and consideration of the other person's position. But these folks are also learning not to use diplomacy to manipulate (that is, making something seem "fair" to the other person just to get their way). They are discovering the value of being a true diplomat: listening to the other person and sharing their own point of view to see if they can reach a compromise. This will satisfy both parties in a lasting way.

Libra North Node people are also learning to consider how to express their impulses. They must weigh what they want to say and the actions they are considering taking, and think about the effect on other people. They are learning to think before speaking.

CREATING WIN/WIN SITUATIONS

Libra North Node people are the natural peacemakers of the zodiac. They have a talent to clearly see both sides of a situation or conflict and effectively communicate person A's position to person B, and vice versa. Harmony is established through objective understanding of the other's position. This ability qualifies them as marriage and family counselors—or any role that requires balancing two different points of view, including diplomacy. As a side benefit, when Libra North Node people help others become objective, they enhance their own ability to respect the identity of others. They exercise the muscle in their psyche that helps them find personal balance, peace, and happiness.

These folks have the talent to make a relationship work successfully with rapport, understanding, teamwork, and satisfaction. When they remember to exercise that talent, they almost always create a win/win situation. For example, a Libra North Node man may love to ride fast motorcycles. He has a wife and three small children, and his wife worries about the risks he takes. Rather than understand her point of view, he becomes angry, feels his independence is being threatened, and throws a temper tantrum (a "me versus you" mentality). The issue becomes an "impasse" in the relationship. Over a few years, the situation becomes one of many impasses in which there is no reciprocal communication, and thus no resolution. The couple drifts apart and the marriage is over (emotionally, if not physically).

Let's look at a win/win alternative. The first time that his wife voiced concern about his motorcycle, the Libra North Node man could have taken a deep breath and sat down to talk with her. He could have asked her questions to find out *exactly* what she was concerned about. Just the fact that he took the time to sit down with her and wanted to know her point of view would have created an atmosphere of rapport, caring, and support. Once he understood her concerns, they would have had the opportunity to work out a resolution.

The key is in finding a resolution *together*—after all, this is not a "do it yourself" lifetime for Libra North Node people. If the wife feared he might have a fatal accident and she would be left with the financial responsibility for their three children, perhaps they could take out a hefty life insurance policy that would give her a greater sense of security and allow her to support him in the joy of riding his motorcycle. They have the innate ability to face things head-on. They must develop a willingness to understand their partners' concerns and work with them to turn each challenge into a win/win situation.

HEALING THEME SONG*

I have written a healing song for each nodal group to help shift its energy in a positive way, since music is a potent vehicle for emotionally supporting us to take risks.

COME ON, PEOPLE

The message of this song is meant to gently shift Libra North Nodes' attention to a deeper awareness of others. It will subconsciously inspire them to help others in ways that give them the feelings of love and fulfillment they have always longed for.

Selected lyrics:

Your brother's trying, but he's getting weak
Pushing his rock up the mountain peak
His rock is heavy, about to break through
He needs some help for a moment or two
Can you take one hand from the rock you bear
To help him with his load, his breaking point is near . . .

Come on, People—step into his shoes
Wake up, People—to see his point of view
Come on, People, help all you can today . . . 'cause
All you can take with you is what you've given away!

---

* These lyrics are set to music and sung in their entirety on the CD and cassette tape "Unfolding As It Should."

North Node in Scorpio

and North Node in the 8th House

OVERVIEW

Attributes to Develop

Work in these areas can help uncover hidden gifts and talents

- Self-discipline
- Choosing constructive change
- Releasing whatever causes stagnation and low energy
- Eliminating nonuseful possessions
- Enjoying things without having to own them
- Accepting support from others (ideas, money, opportunities)
- Enjoying high-risk situations that make one feel alive
- Awareness of others' psychology (their desires, wants, needs, and motives)
- Openness to partnering, supporting, and merging power with others

Tendencies to Leave Behind

Working to reduce the influence of these tendencies can help make
life easier and more enjoyable

- Attachment to comfort and the status quo
- Possessiveness
- Overconcern with accumulation and ownership
- Questioning past decisions
- Stubbornness
- Getting bogged down in sensual appetites
- Repeatedly doing things one way (the hard way) even
  though another way is easier
- Resistance to change and others' input

ACHILLES' HEEL/TRAP TO AVOID/THE BOTTOM LINE

Scorpio North Nodes' Achilles' heel is comfort ("The goal of life is to be
comfortable; I need lots of possessions to survive"), which can lead them
into the trap of an unending search for accumulation ("When I finally have
enough money and possessions, I will feel good about myself and can relate
to others"). This thinking leads to stagnation on all levels: material, physical, mental, emotional, and spiritual. Life experience has shown that Scorpio North Nodes never get enough "stuff" to feel comfortable in making
the changes that will add vitality to their life. Scorpio North Node people
need to be willing to risk losing their current level of comfort to gain a
higher state of power and vitality.

The bottom line is that they will never have enough money and personal
property to think they can afford to bond with another and feel that there is
enough to take care of all their needs. At some point they simply have to let
go of self-concern and put their full power into the partnership. The irony
is that when they finally bond with another, the mutually empowering
relationship can make them rich!

What These People Really Want

What these people really want is money. They want to accumulate financial resources and material possessions to gain a sense of comfort and stability so they can begin to "really live." To achieve this, these people need to be willing to form partnerships with others, finding those who have similar values and resources (money or talent) that they can share.

If Scorpio North Node people use their talents to enhance their partner's energy, truly linking with the other as a team rather than maintaining a sense of separation (my money/your money, my resources/your resources), the result can be great financial rewards for both parties. With the contractual understanding that they will get a percentage of the profits, Scorpio North Node people are free to focus on enhancing their partner's energy and power in ways that the other person feels will increase the success of the team. In terms of financial arrangements, Scorpio North Node people are better off asking their partner what would be fair, because others appreciate them more than they value themselves.

Talents/Profession

These people are great editors, since they have the ability to delve into the minds of others, discern their intentions, and bring the material to light in a clear way. They have a talent for empowering the projects and businesses of others, and when they do so, the other person tends to generously reward them. This can be especially true in working with other people's money—as in banking, insurance, or investments. They also excel as psychologists (in the process of helping others to change, they can also change) and private investigators, or in other lines of work that involve delving into secrets.

Scorpio North Node people have innate gifts of thoroughness and determination, which can build lasting results. When they use these past-life gifts as a means for creating stability in crisis situations, their dependability creates an environment that feels comfortable and safe to all concerned. However, if they involve themselves in professions that are status quo oriented, that require maintenance without growth, they may soon become stagnant, bogged down, and lacking in vitality. They are better off in professions that are crisis oriented or involve constant change and growth, as this brings excitement and the potential for personal evolution.

HEALING AFFIRMATIONS SPECIFIC
TO SCORPIO NORTH NODE

- "Embracing change will lead to vitality."
- "When I choose energizing change, I win; when I choose the status quo, I lose."
- "The alternative to change is stagnation."
- "As I empower others, they recognize my worth."
- "When I look deeply into others' values and motives, I know whom to trust."

PERSONALITY

PAST LIVES

RIGID, LIMITING VALUES

Scorpio North Node people came into this incarnation with rigid past-life ideas about what they have to do to feel good about themselves—which is a very heavy burden for them.

Most babies are born naked, but not these folks! It's as if Scorpio North Node people were born wearing ten shirts, fourteen sweatshirts, twelve pairs of pants, and a half-dozen overcoats. They bring all their past-life burdens with them, and this makes walking through life a lot more difficult than it needs to be. Their primary challenge in this lifetime is to let go. Otherwise, too many material possessions, unreasonable attachment to past-life values ("the way things ought to be"), and reluctance to relate with others may cause these folks to stagnate.

They need to be open to life's energy and listen to others' ideas. When someone says: "Look—that overcoat isn't attractive. It would be much better to take it off and wear the one underneath," their first instinct is to hold on to what they've got. But if they listen and discard that overcoat (the old value), they feel much lighter. If they look at a value and their energy level starts going down, *that* is a value they need to release.

For example, if these folks hold a value requiring that every morning they get up, light a candle, and touch each corner of the bedroom before starting their day, the ritual can bog them down. Their past-life ideas of how things should be may keep them "stuck." But they are learning to recognize that these values are no longer accurate and are actually draining their energy.

They can do two things to help themselves let go: First, they need to re-evaluate the values and ideals that are holding them back—values regarding work, religion, relationships, self-worth, ethics, creativity, family, goals, and so on—about what people have to do in order to be "okay." When they think: "I need to do *this* to be okay," if they feel a sense of heaviness around it, they know they can release that idea and feel lighter. Second, they need to become more interested in other people's values. They need to truly listen to what *others* think is important, since other people can offer valuable perspectives that energize the Scorpio North Node person and lighten his or her load.

Scorpio North Node people also benefit by helping others attain their goals, because this process shows what the other person thinks is important about *them*. In this lifetime, others often have a clearer sense of these folks' value than do Scorpio North Node people themselves. This is because Scorpio North Nodes' job is to help others build tangible results, and others know what they need from the Scorpio North Node person in order to do that.

As they empower other people and help them manifest their dreams, others reciprocate by feeding these folks the energy that lets them change and grow. They need to allow other people and other people's values to help them expand beyond the confines of their limited world into the vitality of the present.

Scorpio North Node people can even become attached to spiritual values in a way that leads to contraction rather than expansion. For example, let's say the native values honesty, integrity, and loyalty. These values are always correct when practiced in the here and now. But if Scorpio North Node people remain in a job for twenty years when, after five years, it severely suppresses their life force, they are not being loyal to themselves. Even their spiritual values need to be translated into the moment. What is loyalty? Loyalty means being true to the deepest part of oneself, and that may change as life progresses.

TUNNEL VISION

It will also be useful for these folks not to become single-minded and overly focused. Once they define their goal, they need to deliberately approach the project or task by expanding their view. When they allow other people and other creative styles to participate, the endeavor is more fascinating and fun. Then the *purpose* becomes enjoying the close relationships of bonding with others to reach a common goal. This helps Scorpio North Node people put the emphasis on the people involved, rather than the task.

If they don't deliberately experiment with keeping their mind expanded, they may get so locked into seeing only "one way" of doing things that they create a compulsive energy around having things go a certain way. They suffer more than anyone, as it leads to immense amounts of overwork on their part.

The key is to become aware of their "tunnel vision" mode. Once they realize what they are doing, they can stop, take a deep breath, expand their thinking, and see that maybe getting their way isn't so important after all.

To gain mastery over this "tunnel vision" tendency takes a great deal of effort on their part. It really is difficult for them to move out of that emotional space—trying to prove that their way is right—to a space where they can listen. It's a new habit; but once they begin really focusing on the other person's motives, needs, and desires, they have more talent than any other nodal group in combining with the other to create more power and vitality for both.

SENSUALITY

Scorpio North Node people have had many past-life experiences of comfort and pleasure; they are no strangers to the sensual side of life. Actually, this past-life tendency can lead to overindulgence in food, drink, and accumulation. Because of their instinctive attunement to the sensual, they think that if something feels good it will keep feeling good as long as they repeat it. But in this incarnation, that idea doesn't work. For these folks, repetition of pleasure leads to the burden of accumulation—whether possessions, pounds of flesh, work habits, or stagnation.

For example, if they like soft-shelled crabs, they can eat them without limit. Or if it's a good wine or bourbon, they could drink it forever. Ultimately, the only way to rein in their senses is to eliminate excess and recognize that the long-term consequences are not worth the momentary joy. There's no middle ground for these folks—it's a matter of totally giving up things that hold them back and not indulging anymore. Their sensual and physical pleasures need to be mitigated by self-discipline in order for them to attain self-empowerment.

Sometimes it takes an external crisis to prompt them to change excessive habits. For example, if they have a health scare involving their heart, they may instantly switch gears to a healthy diet. Then they are in a new rut—but one that is beneficial.

These folks derive a lot of genuine pleasure from all their physical senses: touching, tasting, smelling—they were born with an attunement to Mother Nature, and the physical realms yield a great deal of nurturing for them. That's why they often enjoy gardening: They like working with their hands and gain satisfaction from relating to the earth. They gain a sense of calmness and joy when they are in touch with the energy of nature rather than their mental pictures of how things *ought* to be growing. When they become aware of what each plant needs in order to thrive, and provide it, it teaches them the value of tuning in to an energy outside themselves to determine individual needs.

"My Way: The Hard Way"

SELF-RELIANT

Scorpio North Node people were hard workers in past lives: farmers, landholders, and builders. These were lifetimes where survival depended on their self-sufficiency—forging their own way and building what they thought was valuable. They earned their way through their own efforts; possessions and accumulation of wealth were the prizes that validated their worth.

These folks were master builders. Thus, in this life they approach everything with the mindset of a builder—slow and steady, not skipping any steps. They have an attachment to pride in their work, to thoroughness and doing things "their way, the hard way" to be sure the results are exactly what they want. Although this approach worked well in past lives, in this lifetime it bogs them down and slows their progress to the extent that they often give up—the task becomes too much for them.

In past lives, wealth, possessions, a full larder, and material comfort were the goals. To concentrate on meeting their families' material needs, they had to tune out their sensitivity to psychological needs. They developed the habit of considering only the task at hand.

Their sense of self-worth was based on what they did, not on who they were as individuals. The irony is that in this life, real material success is denied them until they link with a partner. In past lives they built what *they* thought was important, but now they have to build what is useful to society. To achieve this, they need to link with others. They are not allowed to do it "on their own" any longer, as that would only increase their sense of isolation, powerlessness, and stagnation.

Although in past lives these folks did not notice the value of the people around them, now their challenge is to recognize the strengths and talents of others and join with them for mutual empowerment. In this incarnation, they are scheduled to let go of resistance to partnering and sharing resources. They are learning how to merge their power with others, re-energizing their life and making their path easier. They can regain their power through supporting—and being supported by—those who have power in their own right, and through gleaning material and spiritual benefits from the mutual energies exchanged.

TASK ORIENTED

Scorpio North Node people are attached to thoroughness: "my way, the hard way." In this lifetime, other people are supposed to give them fresh ideas, materials, money, and so on to help them. But they don't want help. Even in simple things like mowing the lawn, they have their own way of doing it. They make life much more difficult than it needs to be; at the time they may think "there's no other way," but in the end they feel exhausted.

Although they are generally unaware of it, their extreme task orientation can be defeating for those around them. They are learning to delegate in a way that is empowering for others and enlists the other person's creativity. For example, if they are teaching their daughter to make a cake, and they allow her to do it her own way, it gives the child the opportunity to develop her skills, apply her creativity, and gain confidence in her own ability.

Creativity is energy. For a person to want to put energy into something, she must feel she's being creative and can do it her own way. This idea is new for Scorpio North Node people. Rather than thinking of the child's creativity, they would normally focus on: "We have this *job* to do, to make a cake, and of course you always follow the recipe, and of course you always use the right utensils, etc." Their focus is on the task rather than the person. Now they are learning to refocus on the person and how to support him or her in developing confidence to do the task at hand. The rewards of shifting focus *from* the task *to* the person are enormous.

ACCEPTING HELP

These natives have had so many lifetimes where survival was physically difficult that in this incarnation they may feel "comfortable" with life being one long, hard process after another because, subconsciously, they are accustomed to it. This is not correct, even though it feels like it is. Scorpio North Node people need to trade "being comfortable" for the excitement and vitality of doing things with others.

Also, these folks' resistance to receiving help from others is based on a feeling that they already "know it all"—so they don't want to listen. They insist on doing everything their way to validate themselves through their own efforts. Unfortunately, it's a bottomless pit. In this incarnation, they can never sufficiently build up their sense of self-worth—on their own—to feel good about themselves.

Recognizing this pattern is the first step in escaping it. But when they are going down a "tunnel" of preprogrammed actions from past-life experiences, it can be very tough to listen to others, even though the answers that worked in a past situation usually don't fit the current problem. By being open to others' input—the way *their* energy and psychology alters the situation—the native can see how to adapt what was learned in the past to the current problem, and his or her efforts become more effective.

Scorpio North Node people have such good and simple hearts, others want to help them if they'll only accept it. This takes the humility to let others in and the willingness to release sole ownership. The ability to do this comes through appreciating the goodness of the other person. As they begin to value others, they naturally open to accept the help that others offer them.

They are tired of all the hard work of past incarnations—and the hard work in this lifetime—but they equate change with more effort, and thus resist it. Actually, change is the key to their revitalization, freedom, and joy! So a willingness to take risks and go through changes—even if it means a loss of control and comfort—is the right path.

Their lives can become hard because they're trying to do everything on their own and they don't want to have to deal with one more idea. Actually, they don't even hear what the other person says (they don't *want* to hear it) because it feels like "one more thing" to make their load heavier. They think people are going to require more energy of them, but if they open to the input of others, others feed them the energy they need. In fact, they need the knowledge of others to get out of their ruts and be freed from their monumental tasks.

RESISTANCE

STUBBORNNESS

To some extent, Scorpio North Node people have an innate resistance to other people being "right," which works to their detriment. Without realizing it, they can turn away those who are seeking to add to their energy and resources.

They have a tendency to be extremely stubborn, and they are victimized as much by this trait as those around them. In past lives, they had to muster absolute determination and single-minded intention to reach their goals; through overuse, their determination has become irrational stubbornness. Now this blocks them from accepting the ideas that they need to revitalize their energy and free themselves from obstructions.

Stubbornness can be a major roadblock for these folks. If someone tells them to do something, they may deliberately not do it; if someone says "Don't do it!" they may do it anyway simply because they don't want to be told what to do. These folks are so stubborn because they look at things as "my way versus your way," which turns everything into a win/lose situation. Instead, when someone tells them to do something, their best bet is to *investigate* and ask the other person: "Why are you telling me to do that? What is your goal and your intention?" There's an energy in stubbornness that repels the other person. But when the native investigates: "What are you trying to accomplish by doing it this way?" the feelings of competition and stubbornness disappear.

Once they understand the other person's purpose, Scorpio North Node people are more willing to support him. By asking the other person what his motive is and what he is trying to achieve, it opens these folks to thinking: "Wait a minute, maybe this *is* something we could do together and create a win/win situation."

Often, when these folks get stubborn, it's a matter of timing. They tend to proceed slowly, step by step, thinking this is the best way to reach their goal. Then, when other people offer suggestions that could help them achieve their goal more quickly, they may feel frightened of speeding up their timing. They fear going too fast, missing a step, and losing control. Then the results may not be 100 percent "their own," and they are so attached to ownership that the thought of sharing it makes them insecure.

And in some ways they may be right. If they *indiscriminately* trust all input from others, they take a chance that some of it may lead them in a different direction rather than streamline their process. So they need to attune to the motivations of others, temporarily allowing themselves to join with the other person's force field to see if they feel more empowered and energized by combining. If the answer is yes, then it behooves them to relinquish sole ownership, blend with the other person's timing, and join in creating a mutually empowering partnership.

When they are going slowly, they feel reassured and comfortable because they can see that, step by step, they will reach their goal in a predictable manner. When people with faster timing enter the picture, they're afraid of speeding up lest they encounter instability and failure. What they are over-looking is the power of the other person.

For example, they may not want to risk missing the train from New York to Delaware because the next train doesn't leave until tomorrow, even though the partner who has come along owns a private jet! They need to consider that people with faster timing may have talents and resources that can help them reach their goals more quickly by a more direct route—with exciting adventures along the way. Although they may miss the ponderous feeling of ownership, they will gain the vitality of achieving mutual goals much more quickly and easily, and the process itself will be far more enjoy-able.

CHANGE, GROWTH, AND RENEWAL

As long as these folks think they know everything, they limit their field of experience. This is how they get stuck in ruts. Also, they think they know everything because they know it from their side. They know their needs, so they think they know what's going to work for them *and* the other person, and they are surprised when the other person doesn't automatically agree. When they forget to investigate things from the other person's point of view—the other's values and needs—they may be shocked when their plans are resisted. The secret is in taking the extra step of investigating where the other person is coming from *before* assuming they know how to proceed.

Scorpio North Node people do have special knowledge about building things (a relationship, a business, etc.); they can build things in a way that will last forever. However, they can become so locked into making things tangible and solid that they miss the excitement of change—of appreciating the joy and intense energy from expanding beyond old boundaries into new dimensions that evoke freedom, love, power, and self-confidence.

There are two kinds of security: the security of owning so many material possessions that one is insulated from change, and the security of having grown beyond personal limitations to gain a sense of power. From that position, personal security is also ensured—because regardless of what changes occur, one is secure, confident, and powerful inside oneself. And for that to occur, Scorpio North Node people need the expertise of others and the personal humility to appreciate that others may be bringing them a knowledge that could be more valuable than anything they had in the past.

NEEDS

RELEASING ATTACHMENT

As long as Scorpio North Node people focus on material needs, their needs seem endless. The irony is that when they stop feeding the inner mechanism that urges them to possess, they begin releasing what they own and feel much better. A new energy enters their lives. The peace and contentment they seek come in a new and unexpected way: a spiritual way. In this lifetime they are scheduled to give up trying to fill the emptiness inside through material things and instead pursue pathways that will lead to fulfillment of their spiritual needs. Acknowledging the intangible, spiritual part of themselves will bring them a sense of self-worth. Any step they take in the direction of gaining insight—by keeping a journal, undergoing psychotherapy, or learning self-mastery through taking risks and having transformational experiences—will reap immediate rewards.

MONEY ISSUES

These folks often seem to have money at the forefront of their concerns. There is a feeling of crisis around money, and always the desire to accrue more. There can also be a lack of logic around money, either holding on to it too tightly or spending it too freely. Often they feel they are constantly struggling—working incredibly long hours "just to get by."

They have serious "money karma" and a lot of ideas about money that are not accurate; by allowing other people to advise them about money, they would experience a lot less stress. But they are stubborn and want to do things their way—the hard way. Every time they do that, they lose. For example, someone might say to them: "Well, all you have to do is get rid of this electric heater and your electric bill will go down by $50 a month." The Scorpio North Node person will say: "No, no! I have to keep this electric heater because my daughter used it in college, etc., etc." Such attachments keep them poor. To gain prosperity and ease, they have to let go.

The secret to accumulation is proper distribution. If they want to be wealthy, these folks must learn to be stewards of money rather than hoarders of money. They think the key to having money is holding on to it, whereas in fact the opposite is true. Money loves to circulate and is attracted to people who will keep it in motion. If they don't allow money to flow to others *through* them, only a certain amount can come back to them because they are not a clear channel.

They are beginning to learn that as they release money with love—gladly using it to increase the wealth of others—more money comes to them. It is an attitude about money, as well as appropriate action. They need to love both parts of the process of money—the receiving and the giving—in order for money to be easily attracted to them. However, these folks often have a difficult time letting go of anything—and money most of all!

There are many things Scorpio North Node people can do to foster the habit of releasing money with love. When they pay their bills, they can consciously feel love around the process (they have to spend the money anyway; they might as well feel loving about it!). When they write the rent or mortgage check, they can consciously send love and wishes for prosperity to the person or bank. If they add the ingredient of gratitude ("Thank heavens I have enough money to be able to pay my bills") rather than begrudge their expenses, they become receptive to more money coming in to meet their expenses and thereby strengthen the energy of good financial karma coming into their life.

Another key to increasing their capacity as money magnets is to consciously praise the universe for the financial bounty currently operating in their life. Even if it's only a little, the idea is to appreciate and feel grateful for what is there rather than desiring more—which, on an energy level, translates into fear and anxiety about not having enough. Gratitude for what they have releases anxiety so they no longer block the flow of money and material things. If they let money and possessions pass through them in love, more will always be there.

ACCUMULATION AND OWNERSHIP

These folks are so used to accumulation from past lives that they think solutions have to do with more accumulation. They think that if they can describe their problem they will own it. They know themselves—all their functional and dysfunctional areas—so they think there's nothing else to know.

If they share a problem with a friend, even if the friend offers a solution that could lift the problem from them, when they leave they take the problem rather than the solution. They don't want solutions. They want the feeling of accumulation, and that means holding on to their problematic patterns. They don't realize that through the process of accumulation and ownership they are accepting limitation after limitation, until soon their life is boring and stagnant. For Scorpio North Node people, gain is equivalent to letting go of limiting ideas. In this incarnation they are learning to value the input of others and to gratefully allow the solutions coming through others to lift their self-imposed limitations. Then they become free and begin enjoying life's vitality.

The theme of accumulation was a primary focus in past lives for these folks, and it carries over on every level in this incarnation. In this life they tend to save everything long beyond the point of usefulness or need. They are learning that too many possessions are an encumbrance, slowing down their mobility and the vitality of change. Having excess possessions is like weighing an extra 40 pounds—it's tiring!

In the Bible, the old wine had to be poured out before there was room to receive the new. If Scorpio North Node people want new activity in their lives, they must get rid of excess. For example, they have clothes in their closets they haven't worn in fifteen years—maybe even of a different size— yet they think they "may need them in the future." The best thing they can do is go through their closets and pack up stuff for Goodwill or other charitable organizations. The idea is to have more trust in life: If they have a need, the universe will fill it. They don't need to hang on to things to protect themselves from lack.

They will be amazed at how this re-energizes their lives. Once they have decided to give something away—or walk away from something—they must not look back. These folks have such strong accumulation karma that if they look back at a relationship they've left, or think about a possession they've decided to part with, they're goners. They'll bring it back into the house again.

Scorpio North Node people make their lives a lot easier when they release attachment to ownership on all levels. They are even reluctant to allow the input of others because they want total ownership over ideas as well as material things. They don't want to say "It was his idea" because they want the ownership and the credit. Also, they want to be part of the deal—they're afraid that if it isn't completely "their thing," they might be left out. In fact, as long as they are a source of power for a project, others won't want to leave them out because they depend on these folks.

REVITALIZATION

To regenerate their lives, make money, and gain a sense of power, Scorpio North Node people need the help of others. That requires the humility to say: "Look—you've got an energy I need. What do I have to do to get an interaction going?" They need to experiment to find out what is going to get the energy they need coming back to them on a practical level, since identifying and feeling that kind of energy in the physical world is new for them. They are not familiar with it because they are not used to looking to others to get their needs met. But the energy they need can only come from other people—who will only give it to them when these folks are giving the other person exactly what that person needs. Scorpio North Node people need to tune in to what others are telling them and support them in exactly those ways. If they feel bogged down in any way, they can team up with another person who is willing to invest time, energy, or money with them—and suddenly that area of their lives will be bursting with vitality.

SELF-DISCIPLINE

Scorpio North Node people may think they have self-discipline, but actually it's a character trait they need to develop in this lifetime. These people tend to excess and often don't set healthy limits in their lives. In fact, they have no choice but to accept discipline imposed from without because they don't have it within themselves. Sometimes they mistake "being driven" for self-discipline, but their compulsive overdoing is really a sign of excess. Self-discipline involves leading the self in a balanced, self-aware way to a predetermined goal—the ability to conceive and execute a plan.

Once these folks do decide to discipline themselves, they go for it! They postpone for a long time with halfhearted efforts, and then suddenly they just do it—they don't give themselves any alternatives. It's easy for them to stray; when they do, they often slide back into excess and feel terrible about themselves afterwards. Eventually, they learn that they experience more self-esteem when they maintain their self-discipline.

For these folks, self-discipline also means directing themselves in ways that are in their best interest. They need to begin treating themselves in the way they are learning to treat others: being kinder, more sensitive, and less driven. They need to periodically ask themselves: "In this situation, what is going to give me a sense of power and a feeling of freedom and vitality?" Rather than going from task to task, they should notice their own needs for rest and recuperation and then to do those things that re-energize them. The idea is to be open to forces *outside of themselves*—whether people or nature—to redirect them in ways that make their tasks and their lives easier.

So-called obstructions can actually be helpful ways of breaking their stubborn and debilitating single-mindedness. For instance, if it's a rainy day and they can't fix the shed, maybe it's the universe's way of saying that they need to slow down and rest. When other people appear to be "opposing" them, the universe may be saying: "You're working too hard. Here's some outside intervention to make you take a breather!" If they look at it that way, they will relax their overfocused energy and accept others' input.

Sometimes Scorpio North Node people hear advice from others and know it's something they "should" do, but they have an inner resistance to doing what is in their own best interest. When they focus on their immediate needs for gratification, those needs become magnified and their feelings go totally out of control. To prevent this, the key is to stay mentally focused on only what they really want. This will give them the power to rise above the trap of needing immediate gratification, and they will automatically have the self-discipline to reach their goals.

Often Scorpio North Node people have to be pressured from the outside to make a change. When they have a crisis, it stimulates them to action. But rather than wait for a serious crisis (a health problem, bankruptcy, etc.), they are better off accepting change sooner. By "planning" a crisis (giving themselves a deadline of three months to prepare their house and put it on the market, a month to figure out a new dietary plan, etc.), they access the energy they need to change without having to face a situation that threatens their well-being. But either way, they have to make the decision and the commitment to go through a temporary period of hard work and discomfort in order to get out of their rut. And it helps when they let others help them, rather than doing it their way—the hard way.

VALUES

Scorpio North Node people need their whole value system to be reborn because the old is wearing them down. One way the universe helps them let go is by bringing them into contact with people whose beliefs and values are contrary to the specific things that these natives need to change. If they need to let go of believing that they should wait three seconds after the traffic light changes to green before they proceed, because that belief is limiting them, they will attract a person who believes that "Time is of the essence;

when the signal turns green, it's the universe's way of prompting us into immediate action."

As soon as the new value or belief is presented, Scorpio North Nodes' opposing value will rise to the surface. Right then and there, these folks start feeling tense: What should they do? Which way should they follow? If they "tune in" and feel that the new value is actually more useful and accurate, they need to immediately drop the old value, embrace the new, act on it, and not look back. This is how they change. It takes integrity, courage, self-discipline, and action. When they choose change, they win; when they choose the old way of doing things, they lose.

These folks are learning to be more open in terms of what will work for them—they can be too rigid about their past-life value systems. The principles they are attached to are often correct; but if they become fixated on the form in which those principles are supposed to manifest, they lose the spirit and are bound by the behavior. For example, they may value beauty (a spiritual attribute) and then become attached to everything in their environment being in "perfect order." They may value devotion in marriage and then become attached to a specific form of devotion. They tend to not take into account other people's ideas about form, which, if combined with their own ideas, could actually promote a heightened experience of the value they seek.

For example, rather than being compulsive about "Perfect order in the home equals beauty," they could say to their housemates: "I place a high value on beauty. Do you have any ideas for how we could bring more beauty into our home?" This could lead to an expanded idea of beauty beyond what Scorpio North Node considered. They need to remember that in this lifetime, their source of nourishment will come not from the value or task but from synergistically combining with other people.

Scorpio North Node people are also learning how to meet their needs without going to extremes. For example, if they value beauty and order, putting energy into creating those things is energizing for them—up to a certain point. But then comes the law of diminishing returns: They tend to continue past that point and feel enslaved to what they've created. Or they may expect others to continue their efforts (*their* way) so things can be beautiful and orderly. And that keeps them invested in the task at the expense of other people.

On the other hand, if these folks feed that same energy to a person they want to support, the other person will eventually start feeding them energy back—which will empower the native to feed him even more. Scorpio North Node people think they don't know how to feed that essential energy to another person, but actually it's simple. Other people know their own needs, so all these folks have to do is have the humility to *ask* the others what they need, listen to what they say, and give it to them.

PARTNERSHIP

BLENDING AND VALIDATION

Scorpio North Node people are learning to let go of old patterns. To do this, they need a partner—or partners—with whom to build a relationship and empower one another. Often these folks are fine in group situations but are fearful of one-on-one connections, because they have not asked themselves: "What does the other person need? What would support him? What would empower him?" When they take the focus off themselves and truly tune in to what the other person needs, it establishes a feeling of rapport.

To do this, they must overcome the fear that they won't be liked or that people will be angry with them. In fact, these responses from others only happen when Scorpio North Nodes are not exercising their innate talents for mutual empowerment. If their motive is to support the other person regardless of the response, they won't get hurt. In the process of sincerely exploring what will work for the other person, these natives open up—and that's when they connect with the reciprocal, rejuvenating energy they need.

Scorpio North Node people may come across as nice, humble, salt-of-the-earth individuals, but true modesty involves being receptive to the input of others and does not seek to dominate the situation. Underneath, these natives have an arrogance and stubbornness—an ego encrustation from past incarnations—that needs to be released. They are learning to relax their tight grip on controlling outcomes and let go of the rigid past-life values that oppress them.

Scorpio North Node people need the validation of others, as this is what allows them to open and change. The energy of other people recognizing and valuing their worth is nurturing for them and is an accurate barometer of whether they are on the right path. This is another reason why they work so hard—they think if they follow a hard work ethic, others will notice and value them. So they put out tremendous time and effort to reach a goal, yet others don't give them the positive feedback they're looking for. The problem is their *method* for gaining validation. If they try to get it by being passive so as not to displease others, they start boiling inside; and it's not empowering for either person. The task itself can't give back energy to them; and if they do it their way, without integrating the needs and contributions of the others, they won't get the validation they seek. The resolution involves taking time to ask: "What does this person need? What is important to him in this situation?" If they take the other person into account, when they make their contribution they *will* be appreciated.

In this lifetime, Scorpio North Node people do not have to be "right" or prove that their way of doing things is best. They've already done that. A higher value involves learning how to combine with others to build a greater success than either person could have accomplished alone. This requires being receptive to others' ideas and truly supporting the others' spirit. Scorpio North Nodes must be careful not to superimpose their values on the other person, but to do what they can to enhance and help that person's values to work more powerfully. This will create the synergy these folks need for completion.

SELF-WORTH

Scorpio North Node people think they have a solid sense of their own self-worth—and in some ways they do—but at times they exaggerate their worth and at other times they undervalue themselves. Because they are accustomed to doing things on their own, they seem very independent. They are confident in that they know they can rely on themselves to pull through any situation. They are aware of their talents, abilities, and willingness to work hard, and they value their own resourcefulness.

The problem is that they only value themselves from their *own* perspective and tend to underestimate their value to others. This is one reason why they may have money problems. They inadvertently limit themselves because, by the other person's standards, they are often worth a lot more than they realize. Thus, it behooves them to take the time to learn what the other person values about them, and then to strengthen those qualities.

Underneath, Scorpio North Node people have deep feelings of unworthiness. However, these feelings only surface when Scorpio North Nodes begin comparing themselves to others (in terms of talent, beauty, money, ability, popularity, etc.). Whenever they compare themselves to others, they feel inadequate. However, when they focus on the gifts and talents that others have, enhancing those gifts by making others aware of their abilities, suddenly these folks become aware of their own value. In the process of helping others to manifest their dreams in practical ways, they shine. They know they've played a part in making the other person successful; and if the other person's values are similar to their own, then what *they* consider important also becomes actualized.

But these natives need to guard against being so focused on the task that the people become secondary. They may not even realize that is the message they are projecting. Their self-worth is largely based on what they do, not who they are; so to feel good about themselves, they think they have to constantly prove their abilities. In this lifetime they are readjusting their definition of self-worth—learning that it has to do with who they are as a person, the qualities they possess, and how they relate to other people.

CREATIVE TRANSFORMATION

In this incarnation, Scorpio North Node people are destined for major changes. Only through complete transformation can they escape the ruts they so easily fall into and regain the vitality and sense of aliveness they desire. For them, transformation has to do with other people: getting in touch with what others consider important and pursuing new directions that trigger excitement.

These folks need highly creative energy to rouse them out of their comfortable routines. Crisis situations stimulate them in a positive way to disengage from the steady, reliable pace that has become oppressive. They change, grow, and gain excitement in their lives when they're rising to the occasion and taking risks that require reaching into the unknown. This type of creative stimulation and "living on the edge" needs to be expressed on a regular basis if they are to enjoy life.

Scorpio North Node people were once master builders. However, in this incarnation, in order to build they first must clear the ground for fresh, new structures. They can't expect to build one skyscraper on top of another. It's time to let go of everything that oppresses them: the past, excessive material possessions, anything that has outlived its usefulness in the present.

But these folks are afraid to let go of things lest they'll forget the past. And the fact is, they will. That's good; that's part of transformation. When misunderstandings are transformed, they dissolve—much as the caterpillar turns into the butterfly. Why should the butterfly look back to its caterpillar days? It needs to fly away and enjoy its newfound beauty and freedom! Likewise, Scorpio North Node people need to let go of the past in order to better enjoy what they have become.

TAKING RISKS

It's important for Scorpio North Node people to discriminate in their risk taking. There is a difference between taking inappropriate risks that bring a sense of carelessness and appropriate risks that bring a sense of growth. If Scorpio North Nodes are in doubt, their best bet is to ask others to appraise the situation.

For example, I had a client with this nodal position who found a house she fell in love with. Everything about it was right, but on some level she didn't feel comfortable with it. So she asked her father-in-law for his opinion, and he said he didn't like it because of the woods in back of the house. It made him nervous, as she had two small children and spent a lot of time at home. So she drove by again on her own and let the energy of the house impact her, and she didn't get a happy feeling. Then she investigated the schools in the area and heard things about the curriculum that made her uncomfortable. As she investigated, the feedback she got did not stimulate a sense of vitality for her, but rather a sense of fear. However, since her desire for accumulation was strong, she had an engineering report done. It indicated structural problems with the house. So she finally let others' input help her make her decision, and in spite of her desire for ownership she did not take the risk. This is a perfect example of how these folks can combine their highly attuned sense of "comfort" in a constructive way with input from the outside.

But there's a difference between comfort on a psychic level and comfort on a physical level. When these natives make choices based on what's physically comfortable (that is, what is easy and predictable), it is usually not the road that will stimulate change and make them happy. When they link up with a person or project outside themselves and they feel psychically happy and energetic, that is a signal they can trust. In pursuing that, happiness awaits them.

SPIRITUALITY

In this incarnation, Scorpio North Node people have strong spiritual needs that must be honored: quiet, relaxing time for reflection, creativity, and renewal. They are so tired from the hard work of past incarnations that in this lifetime they need to rest. The problem is, they are not accustomed to resting! They are so used to being responsible for keeping their material world in order that they are still preoccupied with survival.

These folks need to recognize that in this incarnation, their spiritual and psychological needs are as important as their physical needs. In fact, their spiritual needs are *more* important. They've already mastered the material realm; now it's time to explore the spiritual realm, involving themselves in experiences that promote personal transformation: psychology, consciousness-expanding seminars, or self-help classes. They need to be involved in pursuits that will free them from the bondage of the material realm.

As long as they base their sense of self-worth on material outcomes, they depend on the external world to maintain their sense of well-being. This leaves them with a deep feeling of powerlessness, as it is impossible to prevent change—change is the one absolute that underlies all material existence. A primary lesson for Scorpio North Node people is to embrace change, because trying to hold on to anything material is hopeless: Everything material is born, matures, disintegrates, and dies.

But *spirit* never dies, and these natives are learning to align themselves with the spiritual side of life. Rather than saying: "I want things to go my way," they are discovering the spiritual power of saying: "I want it to be exactly the way it is." And then they win—they see what actions to take and their lives become magical! They are learning to attach themselves to universal energy and trust the natural unfolding of life.

Scorpio North Node people are finding out that "When one door closes, another door opens." As they allow things to pass out of their lives without the emotional attachment that is so draining, they gain an independence, strength, and freedom they have never before experienced. Their load is lightened enormously, and they can experience life without being "sucked in" by changing material circumstances. When they align themselves with spirit and take chances that are in alignment with the universal plan, they are "on path."

In the material realm their needs are endless, and they never accumulate enough or do enough to feel complete. The only thing that will give these folks the feeling of satisfaction they seek is the spiritual realm. So the key is to stop making more material commitments and begin making commitments that will increase their spiritual awareness. If they can pursue spiritual matters in the company of other people, the participation of others will give them the energy they need to change.

RELATIONSHIPS

LACK OF AWARENESS

Scorpio North Node people approach relationships in the same way they do everything else—from the perspective of the master builder. From past incarnations, they are accustomed to the seasons and the natural progression of time and effort leading to predictable, lasting results. In relationships they are willing to take their time with the other person, hold hands, talk, and discover what they like to do together. Each thing becomes a building block, and the relationship either grows or doesn't, based on their enjoyment of each stage and the extent to which they respect each other as individuals.

Yet at the same time Scorpio North Nodes can be largely unaware of others and not really address the other person's needs. For example, I had a Scorpio North Node client who was a workaholic. He was driven to make money to provide a good lifestyle for his family and send his four children to the best colleges. His wife, whom he deeply loved, kept telling him that she didn't need the luxury houses; what she needed was for him to spend more time with her. He couldn't understand why she didn't value his spending so much time making money—after all, he had to pay for the children's college; that was the main thing.

So he postponed spending more time with his wife, thinking that when the children had graduated from college they would begin enjoying their lives together—which he greatly anticipated. Before his fourth child had completed college, his wife died. Needless to say, he felt a lot of remorse. Perhaps subconsciously his wife was in touch with how little time she had. Her need to spend time with him may have been based on an awareness that he had no way of understanding—except by valuing what was important to her.

Sometimes these folks get so focused that they become brusque without realizing it. One client with this nodal position, a grandmother, was so task oriented and efficient that one of her grandchildren grew completely silent around her. She had so much to take care of in shepherding everyone around, her voice sounded impatient: "Come on, come on! We have to get going!"—and her grandson would clam up. After a week with the kids, she noticed what she was doing and said: "You all need to understand that when Grandma gets in that frenzied state, it doesn't have anything to do with you. Sometimes I feel so worried about getting everything done that I don't notice how I'm talking to you and what my voice sounds like." Right away her grandson started talking again.

Scorpio North Node people are recognizing that when they become overly focused on the goal, they affect other people negatively. They don't mean to; it's something they don't even recognize until they begin paying attention. But when they communicate to those around them about what's going on, others don't take it personally.

OTHERS' VALUES

These folks are comfortable with a certain way of doing things and a certain set of values. They don't want to be challenged by other people's value systems. If they discover that someone they respect lives according to values different from their own, their first instinct is to react personally and be disappointed, rather than expanding to allow for a fuller understanding of the other person.

They are learning that other people's values are not a threat to their own. Values are a reflection of inherent personal needs and tastes. For example, a person who is very thin and gets cold easily may value bulky winter coats, whereas another person may prefer a different type of coat more suited to her own body. One person may value refined elegance, whereas another feels more at home in a sporty environment. One person may place a high value on physical affection in relationships, whereas another may place more emphasis on mental rapport.

There is no "right" or "wrong" about any of these values. The more these natives are open to learning about another's values, the more they can understand and appreciate the other person and his or her reality. Then they can more easily accept what others are offering without thinking they have to change them—or themselves—in order for constructive interaction to take place.

Scorpio North Node people have great business karma, since, in the business world, they tend to be more open and accepting of new ideas. In business, people share a common goal: making money. When it comes to making money, very little conflicts with Scorpio North Nodes' value system because they are able to focus on the larger goal. Someone could approach them with a business idea based on ideals very different from their own, but they would still listen because the end result would be something they value. And that is the key. In any area of their life, these natives need to focus on shared values and be willing to adapt their process to work with the other person.

If their values in any area are too limited or narrow, they are in constant conflict with others to maintain their ground. For example, if their religion is limited to only one belief system, they must be on constant alert to repel all contrary beliefs. However, if they search for a deeper value (for example, the *purpose* of religion being to promote universal values of love, forgiveness, harmony, self-understanding, ethics, etc.), then they can accept different pathways for reaching those larger goals, which could be enriching.

INVOLVEMENT WITH OTHERS

In relationships, Scorpio North Node people tend to take over the decision making for the team. Their partners may say: "Why can't you just be in partnership with me? You always go off on your own and do it the way *you* want to do it." Scorpio North Node people don't realize that when they leave their partners out of the decision-making process, they inadvertently invalidate the others' worth.

These folks have a tendency to "push against" the other person, to use the other's energy as motivation to do things their own way. They can use the energy of the partnership to fuel their own direction, without recognizing that it is the partnership that is empowering them. They need to be aware of and have the humility to acknowledge the difference in their own personal power that their partner has made. Once they realize how much the other person has contributed, it will be easier for them to include their partner in the decision-making process. Sometimes Scorpio North Node people just want to go off on their own and not have to consider others, but they will have better quality time alone when they include their partner in their plans, because then the other person will support them.

If they have a problem, their first instinct is to keep it to themselves rather than invite the perspectives of others, and they tend to project that other people are also that way. They assume that others want them to stay out of their business, when in fact the opposite may be true. When these folks attune themselves to the other person to see how they can truly help, others welcome their ideas, perspectives, and suggestions—the Scorpio North Node person feels validated, and everyone wins! And just as they have the power to help others, others have the power to help them when they have the humility to receive.

In becoming involved in other people's business, motive is the key factor. If Scorpio North Nodes' motive is to make a judgment or try to "fix" the other person so he'll do something their way, the other will sense it and become resentful. Or if the silent message is: "You should have done more," the other person will sense it, become discouraged, and rebuff the Scorpio North Node person. But if the motive is truly to become lovingly involved with the other person, he'll feel *that* and respond with appreciation.

These folks are in charge of their underlying motive. If they are in doubt about whether to approach another person and ask about his or her affairs, they can first ask themselves: "What is my *motive* for asking?" If the motive is to change the other person, their best bet is to back away because they will lose. If the motive is to gain a better understanding of the other person, they can trust that their interest will be welcomed. They are natural therapists who heal people by listening and sharing their deep understanding.

When Scorpio North Node people "tune in" to the other person, with the motive of truly wanting to lighten the other person's load, they always see what they can do to help. Sometimes it involves taking a small part of the load on their own shoulders: offering to do the other person's laundry, fill out a form, or run an errand. They may be "off path" if they offer advice about how the other person should do it: "If you would just do your wash the same day each week, you wouldn't run into this kind of time crunch!" If the other person responds with irritation, the native will know her suggestion wasn't helpful. If she says: "Look, I have a few extra minutes, would it help if I put in a load of wash for you?" and the other person responds with appreciation, she will know that was the help the other needed.

When their motive is to be supportive, Scorpio North Node people can see what is easy for them but would be a tremendous relief for the other person. When they offer to do it, the appreciation that comes back is enormous. If they are unsure of what to do, they can always ask: "What can I do to support you?" And the other person will tell them—it's very simple and practical. Through such interaction they will forge a loving bond with the other person that will bring rewards far beyond their expectations.

It's a new habit for these folks to approach people in this way; but the more they do it, the easier it will become. Their lives will gain a new dimension of fullness and love, as they experience the unique satisfaction of being deeply connected with other people.

MERGING

ATTUNING TO OTHERS

To increase their power, Scorpio North Node people are learning to validate the worth of others so that they can be open to successful merging. However, sometimes they reverse the process and tear others down—their importance, value, and good qualities—in order to demonstrate their own worth. It's as though they subconsciously feel that to devalue someone else will make them more valuable. But it never does; it just leaves them feeling isolated and drained.

At work, for example, if someone says the head of the accounting department is doing an excellent job, a person from this nodal group may say:
"Well, I knew the head of another accounting department who could run
rings around this fellow." When an employee does a good job, instead of
complimenting her on her success and good points, Scorpio North Nodes
may make light of the accomplishment while faulting her in another area.
Something in other people's performance is always wrong or "less than" it
could be, according to these folks' appraisal. As a result, those around them
become discouraged—they feel their light has been diminished and their
value discounted. Scorpio North Node people truly do not realize how
much damage they do to those around them or how they lose points in the
eyes of those they would like to impress. It would be in their best interest to
become aware of and release the habit of downgrading others.

One experiment that can help them break this habit is to begin noticing
one good thing about each person every day. Perhaps the secretary has a
pleasant voice or a way of putting customers at ease when they are waiting
for appointments. Perhaps the accountant goes out of her way to have the
figures the decision makers need so they can act quickly and make the most
of good opportunities. The idea is to consciously appreciate one good thing
about each person each day. This will be a great help in reprogramming
their past-life tendency to diminish others, and in enhancing their innate
ability to appreciate them.

Scorpio North Node people need the validation of others in order to feel
good about themselves in this lifetime. Partnerships work for them—they
need the energy—and they are learning to have the humility to recognize
this. Being essentially practical people, they can say to themselves: "Okay,
the truth is that I need the validation of others to be happy. Now, what do I
have to do to get it? I'd better find out what's important to them and give it
to them. And, if I include them in my process and make *them* feel important, they will make me feel important." This approach will work for Scorpio North Nodes as they remember to openly notice, appreciate, and
validate others—their good qualities and the work they have done. Scorpio
North Nodes neglect this crucial step when they forget that they need
others' validation to feel good themselves.

In every area of their lives, it works best when these folks have a powerful
partner whose strengths they admire and talents they recognize. As they

learn to consciously appreciate the unique talents, knowledge, and perspectives of others, Scorpio North Nodes see how to combine their own resources and talents with another's to create something different than either would have thought of on their own. This is synergy. Through combining, both people will be able to use and display their unique talents in ways that demonstrate how "The whole is greater than the sum of its parts." Scorpio North Node people are scheduled for magic in this lifetime—synergy, empowerment, and the exciting vitality of ongoing creativity!

LISTENING

Scorpio North Node people think they already know everything, so they're not open to others giving them insights that would make their path easier. This means they are constantly missing opportunities to break free from their limitations.

Sometimes these folks are "stuck" because of underlying feelings of inadequacy. For example, I had a Scorpio North Node client who became a voice teacher. At first she had many clients; she was well qualified by education and experience. However, after a time her clients began dropping away and no one would tell her why. In fact, people were coming to her to improve their singing—but she was giving them weeks of breathing exercises to expand their *capacity* to sing. She wasn't giving them what they wanted, and she had all kinds of justifications for it. But underneath, she felt inadequate in her ability to play the piano and feared she wouldn't be able to play the pieces her students brought to sing. Once she voiced her concerns, others provided many ideas. She ultimately hired a music student to accompany her clients while she concentrated on their singing.

When these folks finally acknowledge their feelings of inadequacy, others are able to help; but when they think they know everything, they're not open to learning and may stay trapped. When others approach them with new ideas that conflict with one of their values, even if they are excited about the input, they tend to squelch it immediately. This is one of their greatest errors. Eventually others cease to offer suggestions that could resolve the problems because they know these folks aren't receptive.

The resolutions they will accept for their problems can be so limited that their obstacles become unresolvable. For example, they may want to sell their car, but they feel attached to it so they establish unreasonable conditions for the sale: The buyer must have blond hair, at least two years of college, and be a nonsmoker. Naturally they're never going to sell the car!

Scorpio North Node people can be "stuck" in these problematic situations far longer than those in other nodal groups. To break free, they need to *hear* an entirely different view based on a value system different from their own. Then they can bounce their concerns off the other person: "What about my attachment to the car? What if the car becomes abused?" After they hear how the other person would resolve those concerns according to the other's value system, they can rethink their position. Sometimes it's easier for them to take the advice of a stranger than to listen to their partner. They may have prejudged their partner and discount his or her input, yet usually it is the people closest to them who can give the most accurate feedback and best recognize their strengths. So it behooves them to really listen to those who know them best, and allow themselves to be influenced if they feel truth and energy in what they hear.

When they think they already know everything, their relationships revolve around filling their basic, physical needs. But once those needs are filled, they still feel flat and lifeless. They need to go beyond their own physical needs to experience vitality, empowerment, personal growth, and transformation. That is the happiness they seek, and nothing less will satisfy them.

DISCRIMINATION

Scorpio North Node people have an inner fear that others' ideas may be right and they themselves may have to change. There is always fear and/or excitement that accompanies great change; it's natural. And on the deepest level, these folks want change. They want to cast off the oppressive burdens that make their lives so difficult; they know they need to be open to the flow of suggestions and knowledge from others. They are learning to see other people *not* as invaders but as rescuing helpers.

Once they decide to be open, the issue becomes one of discrimination. Their success often depends on a careful choice of whom they partner with. Not everyone is a "rescuing helper," so they need to discriminate regarding whom to allow to deeply affect and change them. The key is to tune in to the other person's energy field. If they tune in to the motives of the other person and feel degraded, that person probably has harmful intentions toward them or is appeasing them for personal gain.

The right partner will spark new ideas that stimulate their own energy, creativity, and excitement. There are people with whom they connect very powerfully; when they become energized about a certain person, they are finally willing to relinquish outmoded values. Now they are dealing with a force that is more powerful than their values, and when they follow it, the relationship works. (If finances are involved, they can be motivated to take the risk by reminding themselves that they will make more money when they team up with the financial energy of another.)

Bonding

Scorpio North Node people are destined to experience a total bonding with another on a one-to-one basis. The problem is that although bonding is what they most long for, at the same time they are terrified of it. They fear that if they let go of what they know, there will be nothing for them to hold on to. The irony is that when they begin experimenting with new ideas, they feel less need for control because the excitement is so satisfying.

These natives have an amazing capacity for bonding, owing to their ability to make others feel understood. When they listen deeply and understand the other person, their attentive listening makes the other feel loved and accepted. Their talent for listening also allows them to connect with the psychic energy of another and to bond with that person if they choose. It is this deep bonding with others that is their passport to renewal and release from stagnation.

Psychic Sensitivity

Scorpio North Node people have the ability to "tune in" to the hidden thoughts of others. When they stand near someone, if they open up to receive that person's energy they will know his or her character and motives. When they misjudge someone's character, it's because they are projecting their own values on the other person. When they do this, they can be fooled. However, they are never fooled when they genuinely "tune in" and trust what they sense about the other person.

When these folks feel the inner turmoil of others, they want to help—but they don't know how without feedback. When someone they care about is upset and feeling helpless, their best response is: "What can I do to support you?" The other person may respond with something that sounds like total idiocy: "I need you to call me at 9:00 A.M. every morning and remind me to get up and make my bed." Yet by supporting the other person in exactly that way they empower the other, who will subsequently validate their worth. This will create success in their relationships.

If problems arise, it's because Scorpio North Nodes want to "fix" the other person—*their way*! They have many ideas about how to alleviate the other's pain and better the situation. They project what *they* would do in the situation and neglect taking the other person's needs into account. Instead, they must be receptive to what the other person is telling them.

However, this doesn't mean that Scorpio North Node people must sacrifice themselves. If the other person says he needs to get married in order to feel secure in the relationship, it doesn't mean the Scorpio North Node should marry him if it's not something she wants to do. Rather than try to talk the person out of feeling a need for marriage, or tell him what he ought to do to successfully pursue marriage, her best bet is to directly ask him what he needs for support: "Look, I can feel your turmoil and I want to help. I would like to continue with our relationship, but I don't want to get married at this point in my life. So how can I best support you? Do you want me to encourage you to find someone else who is ready for marriage, or do you want me to support you in getting past the fears that you think will be resolved through marriage?"

Scorpio North Node people need to let the other person tell them what will ease his or her inner conflict and answer his or her needs. They will know if they are "on track" by the other person's response: Others will enthusiastically validate their support when it has really been helpful.

ANXIETY

When Scorpio North Node people feel anxious, they may be reluctant to reveal their true feelings. They don't want to get into a conflict, so they bury their emotions and communication stops. Instead, they are learning to move past the block by discussing it with the other person. They need to get beyond their assumptions about the other person by risking a confrontation—by being willing to be uncomfortable for the sake of forming a closer bond through honest communication. If their motive is to gain more understanding of the other's values and needs, it can be very productive. This is how to build a relationship with the other person, rather than trying to do the whole thing on their own.

When these folks feel anxious because they don't know how to relate, it's a signal from the universe saying: "You need to go *further* into the person's psyche." Habitually, when Scorpio North Node people feel that fear, they pull back, which is the *opposite* of what will work. They need to investigate at a deeper level to understand the other person's desires, motives, and values. *That* will resolve their anxiety.

For example, when someone counters what they're saying, they automatically feel a need to defend their point of view. At that moment, if they deliberately turn it around and investigate the other person's perspective, simply changing the focus takes the pressure off. They could say: "Look— I'm not sure I understand where you're coming from. I'd like to know more about what you're thinking." Their automatic response is always on themselves, but they need to refocus on the other person.

SOUL MATES

For Scorpio North Node people, this is a partnership lifetime. Whether a spouse and/or a business partner, they need a partner to feed them the energy that keeps them stimulated and free from stagnation. This is a soul mate lifetime, so life will bring them opportunity after opportunity to experience a soul mate relationship. A soul mate relationship is really a combining—on an energetic level—with someone with whom they have the right "chemistry"; who gives them a sense of excitement. As they empower their partner, the partner responds by validating and taking care of them. The mutual energy revitalizes those parts of the Scorpio North Node person that became stagnant during past incarnations.

Soul mate relationships are not limited to sexual relationships. If two people share a common goal—such as writing a book, running a restaurant, starting a business—it can be a soul mate relationship. Both people become one on an energetic or psychic level to more powerfully produce their project. Each person has to be willing to let go of personal issues to allow both partners' energies to integrate. These folks need to be willing to understand the other person, what he or she is offering, and what his or her resources are in order to combine and achieve maximum mutual gain. That is where they shine!

It's the same principle in romantic/personal relationships. If Scorpio North Node people focus on "my values versus your values," they will lose. On the other hand, if they are clear about the higher goal they want to *experience* with the other person, and that's agreed on, then these folks are willing to adjust their methodology to work with the other person and gain the experience.

This could be as basic as deciding the kind of relationship they want to create, and then supporting each other in reaching the ideal. When couples are younger, they may have the goal of raising children. Later it might be the goal of living together according to certain spiritual ideals, growing together through self-help or transformational experiences, supporting each other in reaching shared health goals, and so on.

The best approach to creating personal relationships is to get to know the other person and see if that person's values, desires, and motives are compatible. Having shared values is very important, and Scorpio North Nodes may be fooled. If there's too much instinctive projection of their own values, they won't get an accurate picture. But if they are really open to the other person's sharing, they will be able to feel if they are energized by the other person's values. These may be values that Scorpio North Nodes have not even thought of—the next step on their path!

Owing to past lives of being very attuned to the physical senses, Scorpio North Node people are generally quite interested in sex and physical demonstrations of affection. They are aware of their bodies and know how to enjoy them. However, they can be so aware of sensual enjoyment that they miss the transformation that is possible through sexual interaction on an energy level.

If they tune in to the psychic energies of their partner (that is, consciously appreciate the resources and energy of the other person), then, when they combine sexually, the experience far exceeds anything they could have imagined. Scorpio North Node people have latent talents in this regard, as soon as they become aware of the value of psychic/spiritual attunement and bonding in combination with the physical. Through their openness to their partner's energies they can share an enjoyment beyond sensual pleasure, expanding into the dimension of spiritual alchemy and empowerment.

GOALS

RECIPROCITY

Because Scorpio North Node people tend to think in extremes ("my way or your way"), sometimes, in an attempt to combine with others, they completely let go of their values. They become "people pleasers," which doesn't work. In this lifetime they want to stop relating to others from a "me/you" position and start relating from a position of "what's best for us." Then they can share the power of appreciation and respect from the motive of *mutual* empowerment and reciprocity.

They have a talent for offering encouragement, enthusiasm, and support to the other person, which heals the other person and makes his or her life easier. The other person senses a soul mate and a source of strength in the Scorpio North Node person, and responds with love, appreciation, and gratitude.

However, when others reciprocate by asking Scorpio North Node people what *they* need, they may close down and act as if "everything's under control." But they need to allow others to see *their* situation and suggest ways to make their lives easier. It's reciprocal. As these folks see how others accept support and are empowered by it, they can learn to begin graciously accepting support themselves.

They only know how to see themselves as givers or receivers. They are totally unaware of the reciprocal process of how to receive through giving— how they get back an energy that enriches them and helps them grow. For example, if they volunteer to head a charity event, in their mind it is simply a matter of giving their time and energy to make the event successful. They may miss the reality of what they are getting out of it.

ACCEPTING LEGACIES

For Scorpio North Node people, this is a lifetime of receiving legacies from others. Inheritance is healthy for them. People are supposed to give them money, energy, ideas, and so on. Their job is to release what they're holding—to empty themselves—and be open to receive the benefits of others' energies. This applies to every area of their lives.

It works for them to run problems by someone else for feedback. If another person offers a suggestion that they "know is right" but have resistance to implementing, it may be time to practice self-discipline—reining in their need for immediate gratification in order to accomplish their goal. If in doubt, they can always experiment with trying the suggestion to see if it works on a practical level (for example, not making demands on a boyfriend for one week to see if he stops being so distant).

When these folks ask for advice from people who are successful at what *they* want to learn, they really enjoy hearing others' ideas and perspectives and they become more powerful. This has to do with the practicality of looking at what works and adopting that style—whether they thought of it themselves or it came from someone else. It also has to do with gaining the benefit of other people's experience and not always having to learn on their own, the hard way. Other people are supposed to help them along with fresh ideas and energy.

HUMILITY AND RECEPTIVITY

Scorpio North Node people often seem focused on themselves. When they are not tuned in to others, their words reflect it. To establish comfort with another, these folks need to genuinely seek to connect with them from a motive of establishing deeper understanding—then they will naturally use words that prompt the other to trust them.

These folks actually feel very frustrated when they focus on themselves, because from that position they can't really understand what's happening. They can understand *only* by relinquishing their own position and submerging themselves in the other person's position—without judgment.

One thing these folks are learning in this lifetime is the humility to see that they do need others and that it is empowering to connect with the vibrational fields of other people. It is important that they discriminate between which people boost their energy field and which ones don't. Then they need to have the humility to validate the worth of those people.

Scorpio North Node's job is to connect with another person who has a goal that stimulates her energy, and ask herself, "How can I feed the other person the power to reach his goal?" When Scorpio North Node's entire focus is on empowering the other person, she automatically knows what to say and do that will give the other person confidence in his ability to succeed.

As Scorpio North Node people help others achieve, they feel that they have achieved something themselves and gain self-confidence. Because they have linked their creativity and power with others, the energy and joy of success skyrocket! Others know they couldn't have done it without the energy and support of these folks, so they naturally want to give back. This is the key to Scorpio North Node people enhancing their sense of self-worth in a way that energizes them and makes them free.

Sadly, Scorpio North Node people often don't value the gifts that could lead to freedom from their self-imposed bondage. If they don't value and respect these gifts, they can't really use them. In this way, their egos cut them off from recognizing the opportunities—and benefiting from the gifts—that life brings them through other people. These folks are learning to appreciate not only what they have earned through their own efforts but also the gifts that others bring them.

If they only value what is obtained through their own hard work, they are not open to grace. In the end, only grace can take them beyond their own rigidity. Their job is to have the humility to let go and let grace—through other people—operate in their lives.

SUCCESSFUL PARTNERING

Scorpio North Node people are better off when they apply their talents to other people's projects or join a project based on someone else's idea. The exception is if their idea has an intangible or spiritual source. They are better off pursuing projects and pathways that emanate from a presence outside of their rigid, conditioned value system.

EMPOWERING OTHERS

Because Scorpio North Node people have spent many past lives building a sense of self-worth, they are astonished when others around them do not recognize *their* own value. They don't understand it when others don't appreciate their own natural abilities and do what's needed on a practical level to use their talents and feel good about themselves. Scorpio North Nodes' greatest challenge lies in successfully empowering their partners or those in other close personal relationships.

It's easy for them to have a positive spirit about their partner. They can "talk up" the other person's talents and encourage that person. The problem is that the romantic partners these folks attract don't seem to have the will to take the action needed to accomplish results. They are often not motivated to achieve practical, self-empowering goals and/or lack the qualities that would allow them to do this.

If their partner is not motivated from within, these folks don't understand and don't know how to get the partner going. So they turn to their own resources and use the energy of the partnership to fire their own ability to create solid results. Unfortunately, this is the same old "I have to do everything myself" scenario, which makes the partner feel powerless and left out of the creative process.

If Scorpio North Node people find themselves in this situation, they need to take the time to get more deeply in touch with their partner. If they approach the partner with a genuine interest in his or her motivations, they can begin to discover the other person's desires and needs. People have the enthusiasm to initiate action only when they are motivated by something they want. Because Scorpio North Node people are inherently motivated by money and comfort, they assume everyone else is fired by those desires; but this is not true. They need to help their partners get in touch with what motivates them.

For example, the other person may want to break free from inhibiting fears of success. Such a person would be motivated to take action for the sake of breaking through his or her feelings of limitation, and Scorpio North Nodes can remind the person that by going after a new job, he or she will be taking a step toward overcoming those fears. Perhaps what motivates the other is making a contribution to society, or a desire to be in the limelight and get attention from others. Scorpio North Node people are experts at uncovering the hidden desires and drives of others, and they can put their partners in touch with their own inner motivation. This in itself is an empowerment. When the partner is supported by the Scorpio North Node's talent, he or she will go into action and the result will include financial rewards. This is what these folks wanted—to build self-esteem in their partner, and to achieve security and comfort for both of them!

From past lives, Scorpio North Node people already have confidence in their ability to get the task done. Now they are teaching others to value themselves. By valuing others enough to help them, they automatically empower the other person.

The only glitch occurs when these folks try to tell others how to do things. This never works because they *don't know* the other person's talents and powers; they only know their own. For example, if the Scorpio North Node person decides to run a 50-yard race, he knows exactly how long his stride needs to be relative to his height, leg length, and amount of speed needed to win. Now, the person he's empowering may be much shorter and have very short legs. If *she* tried to use the same stride as the Scorpio North Node person, it wouldn't be correct relative to her body and she would never win the race.

Thus, these folks need to avoid the temptation to always tell the other person what works for *them,* and then conclude that the other person's way isn't right. Such self-centeredness is tough for them to control. But their job in this lifetime is to adapt what they know to the *other* person's value system to help him or her win.

For example, if the shorter person wants to run the race, she might say: "I want to figure out what my stride needs to be in proportion to my height and my leg length." The Scorpio North Node person knows how he figured it out for himself, so he can apply the same formula to the other person, taking into account her body size, temperament, weaknesses, and strengths. These folks can help others come up with a plan they feel good about that will work for them—rather than doing it Scorpio North Nodes' way.

DEVELOPING PSYCHOLOGICAL AWARENESS

Scorpio North Node people make excellent psychologists. They are naturally attuned to the worries and longing of others. This is a special talent that they haven't had in past lives. When they free their minds of the prejudice of their own values, they have an incredible ability to enter the mindset of another person and understand the other's motives, needs, and values.

These folks know how to create success. They are learning that to help others create success, they have to take the other person's psychology into account. Sometimes people take advantage of Scorpio North Nodes' giving nature without their being aware of it until after the fact. They can avoid this by not accepting others' proposals until they have had time to think about it and tune in to the others' motives: "Gosh—that sounds great! Let me think about it and I'll get back to you." They tend to respond too quickly; they are better off taking some time to tune in psychically to the other person and the situation. If they feel energized, they can go for it. However, if they get a bad feeling or begin to lose energy, it's a warning.

It's important for these folks to pay attention to people's motives. This seldom occurs to them, so they sometimes get disappointed and feel let down. They project that others operate from the same values and are always being honest. But when they take the time to study people's motives, they can tell what people pretend to be and what they really are.

The idea is to really investigate potential partners—Scorpio North Nodes are the *best* detectives! For them, it's a partnership lifetime, one-on-one, so it behooves them to examine the other person's ideas, motives, purposes, and values on a deep level.

SYNTHESIS

These folks have a difficult time changing directions. They set a goal, figure out how to get there, and their energy becomes so focused that it's almost impossible to turn around—even if they discover halfway down the road that they're on the wrong path.

I had a Scorpio North Node client, a teacher, who was on the "Building Leadership Team" at a high school. The team was working on making some changes. She came to the meeting with a precise plan already worked out in her mind. When someone suggested a different plan, she became very impatient. She tried to convince the other that her way was the right way, and either that the other's idea was insignificant, or that it wouldn't work, or that the group didn't have time to think about it. She had the exact plan in her mind of "the only way to do it," and anything else represented a threat to her.

Synthesis can be difficult for these folks, since it is hard for them to let go of their position long enough to actually take in what the other person is saying. They need to deliberately train themselves to focus on the shared objective—the result—and to think in terms of how their ideas and the other person's could combine to bring about maximum success.

They are learning the art of synergy. The first step is to remember that the people involved must always be more important than the goal. It behooves Scorpio North Nodes to constantly remind themselves of this. In the example at the high school, my client should have focused on the people as most important. Then when others brought up their ideas, she would have listened to their perspectives and discovered what creative gifts they were bringing to the project.

Seeing the people as more important is tough for Scorpio North Nodes, and it takes practice. Usually they are in the middle of a situation before they realize they've trampled on someone. However, at that point they can stop and apologize: "I just realized that I got so focused on *my* idea that I didn't hear your suggestion clearly. I apologize if I've hurt your feelings." Then they can make a deliberate attempt to hear the other person's idea.

Avoiding Stagnation

The Energy of Change

Scorpio North Node people have a great deal of difficulty breaking out of their stagnant ruts—they get "stuck" in situations that are not satisfying for them. These folks have to be really excited to break out of their routine. And when they are presented with something that excites them, they must have the self-discipline to follow through and stay on the path that feeds them energy. They have to be willing to let go of factors that are holding them back.

In a way, Scorpio North Node people like to be in a rut, because it's comfortable and familiar. On the other hand, they know they're not getting enough out of life or having the experiences they want. But there has to be a certain level of dissatisfaction for them to want to do things differently. Discomfort and dissatisfaction prod them to change and broaden their horizons.

For example, a Scorpio North Node person may want to move because he is no longer comfortable in his current situation. Moving takes a lot of energy: sorting through possessions, fixing up the house to sell, and so on. He has to be willing to exert himself, and it takes self-discipline to do the work required to make the change. But if he does, the energy of "crisis" will feed him excitement and spur him on—especially if he is going through it with a partner and is willing to *not* do everything "his way, the hard way." Thoroughness is an asset in the process of building but can be a hindrance in making changes.

The energy of change is different from the energy of building. The energy of building requires a thorough, step-by-step process. However, the energy of change requires rapid, intense motion. Scorpio North Node people must discard the old, go in a new direction, get rid of things that are holding them back, and choose quick results over perfection. If they move too slowly, they'll lose the momentum needed to make the change. Change itself will feed them the adrenaline they need to get out of their rut, but they have to keep moving!

It's like a surfer in the ocean—if you deliberate too long, you miss the wave. Scorpio North Node people have to catch the wave of change; even though they may lose control temporarily and feel fearful, if they stay on that wave it will take them to shore. To make the change, they have to stay in touch with the new energy they are feeling. In walking away from the old, it is better for them to discard too much rather than too little. Hindsight will show that making the change was a far wiser and more satisfying path than anything they may have discarded along the way.

RELEASING LIMITATIONS

Scorpio North Node people don't have an innate sense of balance in their lives. They head in one direction, and their consciousness becomes so tuned in to that direction that they can't see anything else—they just keep on going.

They become bound to the physical world, manipulating matter and forgetting spirit. That's why their lives are so difficult—they are too materially oriented and there's too much density around them. For their own sake, they need to lighten up so they can travel more easily through life. These folks are better off pulling back from their material situation and reflecting on what they actually want to *experience* in this lifetime. How can they put their material affairs in order in a way that will give them the freedom to explore the horizons that excite them? Since the input of others is helpful in this lifetime, a monthly counseling session or a power meeting with a friend for clarifying where they are going would definitely be wise.

It's best for these folks not to allow themselves to pursue lines of action or thinking that bog them down. They are learning to be less attached to worldly things so that they can be free to soar in spiritual realms and enjoy their psychological/astral connections with others. This is a whole new realm of pleasure beyond the strictly physical enjoyment they are accustomed to from past lives, and it requires releasing attachment to the material plane. By allowing their energy to combine with others, they detach themselves from bondage to the strictly physical.

For example, if they buy a home and are faced with the project of redecorating it, their first instinct is to do it *their* way so they can be attached to every part of it, because it reflects their style. This approach leads to a perpetuation of bondage to past-life values and the material realm; it equals "how to lose" for Scorpio North Node people.

If instead they bring in a decorator—or a friend with artistic talents—and allow the other person to add expertise, remaining open to doing it the other person's way, then Scorpio North Nodes will have a beautiful environment that they are not attached to. Then they can live in comfort, supported by their environment without being limited by it. This leaves them free to expand into the psychological and astral worlds that are so invigorating for them.

HEALING THEME SONG *

Because of the compelling way that music can emotionally support us in taking risks, I have written a healing song for each nodal group to help shift its energy in a positive direction.

GREET THE NEW

The healing message of this song can arouse Scorpio North Nodes' recognition of the energy available to them through accepting change and successfully combining with others to create mutual empowerment and reciprocity. Through welcoming the new opportunities life brings, the tendency to "get stuck" can be effortlessly bypassed.

Selected lyrics:

> *What's the point in hanging on?*
> *Your dream is true, but not the form*
> *What brings you joy in life today*
> *May come true a different way!*
>
> *Reach your arms up to the sky—*
> *Greet the new that's in your life today*
> *Life sent it just to you,*
> *'Cause you're ready for something new*
> *But you've got to let go of what's already gone*
> *You've got to let go, it's time to move on . . .*

---

* These lyrics are set to music and sung in their entirety on the CD and cassette tape "Unfolding As It Should."

North Node in Sagittarius

and North Node in the 9th House

OVERVIEW

Attributes to Develop

Work in these areas can help uncover hidden gifts and talents

- Reliance on intuition, prophetic abilities, and invisible guidance
- Speaking from Higher Consciousness
- Spontaneity—developing a sense of freedom and adventure
- Direct communication free from censorship
- Trusting oneself
- Spending time alone and in nature
- Patience
- Intuitive listening—hearing the meaning behind the words

Tendencies to Leave Behind

Working to reduce the influence of these tendencies can help make life easier and more enjoyable

- Second-guessing what others are thinking
- Indecisiveness
- Perpetually seeking more information
- Saying what others want to hear
- Invalidating intuitive knowing with logic
- Gossiping
- Impatience—wanting immediate answers
- Trusting others' perceptions instead of one's own—including others' perceptions about oneself

ACHILLES' HEEL/TRAP TO AVOID/THE BOTTOM LINE

Sagittarius North Node people's Achilles' heel is mental security ("If I can figure out what other people are thinking and then say the right thing so they'll agree with my ideas, I will always feel secure"). This can lead them into the trap of an unending search for information ("If I can just get enough facts, I'll be able to find the 'truth,' and then I will know what to do"). But it's a bottomless pit: They can never read people's minds well enough to assure themselves that they will say the right thing. They need to let go of control and heed their own intuition. Trusting and acting from their *own* truth brings out their integrity, which will draw the right people to them to help them gain the security and peace of mind they seek.

The bottom line is that they will never have enough information to *know* what the "truth" is. At some point Sagittarius North Node people simply have to go beyond logic to their intuition, and demonstrate what their higher truth is telling them. Ironically, when they have faith in their spiritual guidance, they will also gain a correct perception of what is occurring around them.

What These People Really Want

What these people really want is to feel connected with others while confidently being themselves. They want the total agreement of everyone around them—for everyone to understand their point of view, to accept and support them, and to recognize their positive motivations. To achieve this, they try to manipulate people into thinking their way. Using their talent for understanding others, Sagittarius North Node people think they can say exactly the right words to make others change their minds and agree with them. But it doesn't work; in order to reach their goals, they need to refocus their attention on their own truth.

When Sagittarius North Node people speak the words they intuitively feel, situations in which they find themselves come into harmony. When they live and speak from their higher self, companions who are not suitable withdraw and new people appear who are compatible. As Sagittarius North Node people act in accordance with their higher truth, others who are similarly attuned innately understand them and prove the most trustworthy of friends, as they share the same spiritual values.

Talents/Profession

These people are highly intuitive and excel in the psychic fields, channeling and "reading" for others from their intuitive awareness. They can also be highly successful in situations involving interactions with foreign countries. These folks are the happiest, as well as the most financially successful, when they use their talents to find solutions. Good choices include: lawyer, religious or spiritual leader, professor, publisher, or a role in advertising—any way they can be involved in distributing ideas on a mass level or promoting a cause they believe in.

Sagittarius North Node people have inherent gifts for understanding the mindsets of others, so they often foresee probable outcomes—the "writing on the wall." When they verbalize the truths they see through their intuitive process, their natural communication skills create a win/win situation. However, if they work in professions where understanding and reporting how others think is the goal, they may not fare as well. Teaching mundane subjects, or writing projects that deal with fact rather than inspiration, can promote their uneasiness and fears of being hurt unexpectedly. They are better off when they use their innate writing/speaking abilities as a means of communicating and implementing higher truths.

HEALING AFFIRMATIONS SPECIFIC TO SAGITTARIUS NORTH NODE

- "When I follow my own sense of truth, I win."
- "My intuition will show me the right road, spontaneously, as events occur."
- "When I let others be themselves, I am free."
- "When I trust my intuition and verbally communicate what occurs to me in the moment, I win."

PERSONALITY

PAST LIVES

Sagittarius North Node people have spent many past lives in positions where it was essential for them to understand how others think: as teachers, writers, orators, and salespeople. Teachers aren't successful unless they understand their pupil's thought process and impart information in a way the pupil can accept.

Sagittarius North Node people came into this incarnation with the talent of seeing everyone else's point of view, but in the process they have lost touch with their own truth. Now they need to connect with their spirituality—and rediscover themselves.

The gift of understanding also means that these folks can talk to anyone about anything—they have the gift of gab. They can see into the mindset of the other person and keep small talk going for hours, making the other person feel comfortable through an easy exchange of friendly conversation and acceptance.

But they are so aware of the mindsets of other people that they often overtranslate the others' ideas. They think they need to speak the other person's words to be understood, and soon they get lost and forget what they really wanted to say. Thus, when they "get something" from their intuition, they should say it directly without trying to edit or "translate" it.

INDECISIVENESS

Sagittarius North Node people have a tough time making decisions. They are accustomed to seeing both sides, so even when they *know* what to do they also see the alternative viewpoint and get confused. For example, if they ask themselves: "Should I go to the party or stay home and rest?" they have an instinctive "knowing" or "feeling" that tells them which choice will make them happy. But then they question their knowing: "Yes, it would make me happy to stay home and I need to rest, but if I don't go to the party, maybe I'll miss something. . . . On the other hand, I really need the rest—I've been out three nights in a row. . . . And yet *this* party might be attended by some very interesting folks . . ." and on and on. Pretty soon they can't make a decision. To avoid this problem, they must not allow themselves to question their first feeling of "knowing." Their intuition is almost 100 percent accurate. They are learning to recognize it, rely on it, and allow it to lead them. Additionally, they need to trust that they won't "miss" anything or anyone that is truly destined for them. When they follow their spontaneous inner knowing, they will always be "on track."

These folks are indecisive because they think of so many reasons for going in any direction. It's never just between yes and no—it's "yes, because of such-and-such" and "no, because of something else"—until it becomes so convoluted that they can't decide at all.

SECOND-GUESSING

Sagittarius North Node people go through a lengthy and nerve-wracking process of second-guessing themselves (and others) owing to insecurity. They don't trust their intuition. In past incarnations, they were so accustomed to being part of other people's lives and ideas that they lost touch with their own identity. All their past lives of identifying with society have taught them reliance on others. But now they need to rely on themselves—without trying to "explain" their intuition. When they apply logic to intuition, they become even more confused.

This process is very painful for them. They become so internally conflicted that they feel they have no stable base. These people can see the pros and cons of any decision, and by the time they've thought through all the possible ramifications it feels like a "no win" situation. The entire process is associated with loss: What do they stand to lose with each of the different options? By focusing on this negative aspect, they become more and more insecure.

Yet what these folks really want is to *win* something. They have to stay focused on their goal, and when they consider others, it should be in terms of who can assist them in getting what they want. The irony is that the minute they make a firm decision, the universe supports them and everything works smoothly and beautifully!

However, before they reach this point, they drive the people around them crazy because they want to check each decision with everyone they know. Their good friends can hear what these folks really are seeking behind their frantic, "logical" points of view and lovingly point them back to their original, intuitive knowing. Sagittarius North Node people need a lot more help to make their dreams come true than they realize. They need spiritual help—straight from the universe itself—to reach their goals, and it is available to them in this lifetime if they are open to it.

They are learning that to take the next step toward their dreams, it is necessary to let go of the step below. Loss is always part of a greater gain. To gain the benefits of an independent lifestyle, they must let go of dependency on their parents; to gain the benefits of a promotion, they must let go of their former job. They need to stay focused on gain—the new growth, environment, and people that surround them as they work toward their goals and follow their spontaneous inner prompting.

Sagittarius North Node people need to switch their sense of responsibility from *evoking* a desired response to *being an accurate channel* for their gift of inner guidance. Instead of being the caretaker, in this lifetime they are to be the initiator. It's so simple if they let it be! The minute they make the decision: "I'm choosing this," or "I'm taking that road," they reach a new level. They don't have to go through the painful intermediate process of second-guessing themselves. All they have to do is to trust what they intuitively feel to be right, decide to follow their intuitive path, and use their logic to figure out the best way to make it happen.

When they're trying to figure out how others will react, what they are seeing is how others would react *before* they make their decision. But when Sagittarius North Node people *make* the decision, it actually changes the other person's reaction. Thus, Sagittarius North Nodes cannot logically predict how others will respond to them. All their experience with decision making brings them back to the same point: In this lifetime, it works when they trust their intuition and follow their own path.

REASONING AND LOGIC

Owing to past lives of being enmeshed in society and dependent on others, these folks have learned how to "get along" with just about anyone. And in past incarnations they used deductive reasoning to reach their goals. They came to a conclusion based on the information they gathered, together with their awareness of the desires of those around them. Their decisions were based on a complex system of weighing all the factors, which led them to the "right answer" for their situation. The process worked well for them in past lives; however, in this lifetime deductive reasoning is not scheduled to work for them. What is scheduled to work now is inductive reasoning. This process is based on intuitively knowing the "right answer" and using logic to figure out how to make it happen on the practical level. It involves seeing the solution first and then working backwards to determine how best to implement it.

Sagittarius North Node people have permission to be illogical in this lifetime. In past lives they overused logic, and now they will see everything as "somewhat right" because they can see the truth in any point of view. Therefore, logic cannot bring them to any accurate conclusion.

Overthinking causes other problems for these folks, too. They have a tough time saying "no," chiefly because they hate the possibility of missing a potential opportunity for anything. Also, they don't want to alienate anyone's goodwill. But when they communicate a decision they have made, it's perfectly fine for them not to give all their logical reasons. They should just be honest about it: "Thank you for offering me the opportunity. It sounds wonderful, but I feel I should go in another direction right now." They will be surprised at how easily people accept their decisions without the need for justification. If pressed, they can always say: "It's just a feeling; I really don't have an explanation for it." It's much better than doing things they don't really want to do simply because they can't think of a good excuse to decline. It's also better than lying: In this incarnation, lies tend to confuse their identity.

Thinking or speaking in terms of options is counterproductive for Sagittarius North Node people, and it doesn't work for them to give others options, either. They need to be direct: "This is what I want and when I want it." If the other person doesn't like it he or she will leave, making room for someone of greater affinity. If the other person *does* like it, he or she will support and respect the Sagittarius North Node person and the relationship will become closer.

Facts are also not helpful to these folks, unless they are using them as a springboard to launch their intuitive process. If they are seeking more and more facts for the purpose of finally making a decision, it's an endless process. They can never get enough information to feel certain about their decisions. When a decision is based only on information, they change their mind when new information becomes available.

But truth doesn't change; so when they are making decisions based on an inner feeling or intuitive knowing, they have the power to stay with it. For example, I had a client with this nodal position who was having digestive problems. She read a myriad of books but was unable to heal herself. She would start down one path, read new information, change her mind, and go in another direction. Then one day she started a program that put her in touch with her own truth: She fasted for three days and then gradually began to reintroduce foods in a prescribed order, noting how her body reacted to each one. She then concluded—from her own personal, internal experience—which foods caused her problems. She is now committed with 100 percent certainty (rare for these folks!) to staying within her dietary guidelines because the decision is based on her own personal experience.

If these folks have really lost touch with their intuitive knowing, they could make a list of pros and cons regarding the matter ("Should I buy a new car?" "Should I apply for this job?"). They should write down *all* the pros ("A new car would boost my spirits, give me more self-confidence, provide reliable transportation, etc.") as well as *all* the cons ("I would have to come up with extra money each month; my mother will say I'm being extravagant; I'll have to sell my current car; etc."), leaving nothing out. This helps empty their minds of all concerns and considerations. Then, once everything is written down, they can stand back and assess the situation objectively. The process releases them to see the "bigger picture" and puts them back in touch with their intuitive truth.

MISUSE OF MIND

EXPLANATIONS

Too much "explanation" generally does not work for Sagittarius North Node people. For example, if someone says something that they interpret as "against" their goal, they insist on a full explanation of what the other person meant. They will go over it again and again, trying to use logic to talk the other person out of his or her perspective. By hashing it out this way, they are actually doing what they fear most: bringing negative ideas into powerful focus and injecting negativity into the relationship. They are better off letting the "small stuff" slide, unless their motive for questioning the other person is actually to listen and learn more about the other. If their motive is to talk someone out of his or her point of view, they will generally lose in the interaction.

DEBATES

Debates do not work for Sagittarius North Node people. They have too great a need for others to see life from their point of view. For them, a debate is not a stimulating interchange between two people meant to give both parties a broader view—these folks want their point of view validated, so debates are about control. Others sense this and tend to pull away.

When Sagittarius North Node people are trying to force their idea of truth on others, they do very little listening. They focus on manipulating the other person's mind into alignment with what they want. This approach can temporarily overpower the other person, but the battle will continue!

These folks sometimes enter a debate inadvertently. If they haven't made a decision in their own minds, they may try to involve another person in their intense logical process of wrestling it out. The other person often gets angry and feels manipulated or forced to come to a prearranged conclusion. Sagittarius North Node doesn't understand why the other person gets angry, but the other person thinks Sagittarius North Node is trying to force acceptance of a personally inappropriate opinion—the other person feels in a battle to maintain his or her own integrity.

These folks are much better off staying away from debates altogether. Whenever they try to win a point by getting their "logic" involved, they are treading on thin ice. In such moments of temptation, they should pull back to a peaceful place inside themselves.

MANIPULATION

If Sagittarius North Node people use their capacity for understanding others to deceive others, they can get themselves in trouble. Sometimes they get away with it for a while, but eventually it backfires.

They may see a situation unfolding that—when they look at the logical, linear progression of events—seems likely to leave them with the short end of the stick. They panic and try to figure out how to secure their position. They look at different ways the situation could play itself out, then they go about influencing others' thinking so the results will turn out in their own favor.

However, when these folks get what they want by manipulating others, they can only hold on to it through unending manipulation. And it's exhausting!

Their destiny in this lifetime is to channel healing truth, optimism, and faith into the world. If they violate their destiny by resorting to trickery to get their way, they inadvertently attract an opponent stronger than themselves. All the opponent has to do to win is be honest. If they refuse to align themselves as a channel of honesty, they attract a situation where the truth will defeat them.

Sagittarius North Node people often panic when they view life only from a logical base. For all of us, there are times when things don't go our way and the possible scenarios look pretty scary. This is the time to remember faith. Logic does not include goodwill or the fact that in the big picture, everything is working to our advantage. If these folks look back over their lives, they will see that every change has meant increase and improvement for them. There are a thousand ways that a situation can unfold as people add their own unexpected ingredients. If one has faith in an ultimately positive outcome, the positive path will reveal itself.

WHITE LIES

Because Sagittarius North Node people are so friendly and want to get along with others, they can slip into the habit of telling white lies. Sometimes they seem to get away with it, but they are filled with uneasiness because they know they are not standing on solid ground. They have to stay alert to keep the lie going, and this creates tension. Misrepresentation is not good karma for them, and it inevitably backfires in unpleasant ways.

If they indulge in only a "little white lie"—hoping the other person will forget the original agreement or will go along with a "slight" lack of integrity on their part—they might as well forget it. The discrepancy they sought to "cover" will inevitably come to light in a way that is most embarrassing for them. But once they are aware of the repercussions, these folks are too intelligent to waste their mental energy on "covering up."

Using manipulation to deal with others also severely limits Sagittarius North Node people on a personal level—it is painful and unnecessarily restrictive of their freedom in ways they may not even recognize. These folks fear that if they can't manipulate the other person, they will have to go along with the other person's will. Aside from artful manipulation, they feel they don't have any power. But quite the contrary is true. Their strength in this incarnation—their special gift—is truth. When they honestly and directly reveal their own point of view, others respect what they say. Other people will yield to them or respond in a straightforward way that leads to greater understanding and trust.

POSITIVE ATTRIBUTES

Winning is very important to Sagittarius North Node people, which is another reason they carefully consider all their options before making a decision. The desire to move forward is so strong for these folks that every decision becomes monumental—they don't want to make a mistake. Yet, if they look back over their lives, they will see that when they followed their intuition they never made the mistakes they feared they would. When they follow their inner prompting, they don't have regrets. The bottom line for these folks is their desire to win and reach the next level—the desire to win is correct and healthy for them.

In this lifetime, they want to escape the maelstrom of other people's thoughts; they want vitality on a new level. Thus, to base their decisions on thinking from the old level will not help them win; it will keep them "stuck" in the same place. They need to trust whatever gives them a sense of energy and vitality, and that's the "win" they're seeking. The "win" is a feeling for them—it's growth and the desire to move forward and up. So when an idea occurs to them and they intuitively feel: "Yes, I should do that," accompanied by exciting, vital energy, *that* is an energy they can trust and a path that will lead to the new level they seek.

The opposite is also true for Sagittarius North Node people. Whatever seems oppressive and makes them anxious is not an appropriate choice. It's better for them to say "no," because something about the situation will not turn out to their advantage. However, their overactive mind will try to intervene and say: "It's a good thing and you have to do it, etc., etc."

But when they give themselves permission to follow their intuition, they can respond authentically. However, they must wait until they have decided where they stand before responding. When these folks are clear within themselves, they automatically present their decision in a loving way the other person can accept.

INTUITION

The logic developed in past lives allows Sagittarius North Node people to realize that it is self-defeating to view life from a negative perspective. How we view our lives and circumstances determines our emotional state. To augment the positive makes us happy and confident.

Unfortunately, from so much past-life reliance on logic and mental agility, these folks lost touch with the power of truth. They tend to ignore the warning signals of their keen intuition and continue to think positively, only to see important situations fall apart. Then they feel totally unprepared—they didn't see it coming.

To prevent this from happening again, they develop a "logical" structure of fear to "protect" them from future pain. The following scenario unfolds: Using logic, they think positively about a situation and feel happy. Then, remembering past disappointments that occurred when they felt confident, fear sets in. To avoid disappointment, they think of all the possible negative outcomes and become afraid and unhappy. The result of these mental gym-

nastics is a basic distrust of life, of other people, and of themselves. Therefore, in this lifetime, they need to learn to trust their *intuition* in order to
avoid pain.

Their logic tells Sagittarius North Node people that no person or situation merits total trust. People change, situations shift, unexpected events
occur, and we ourselves make mistakes. Who is to be trusted? If they look
back over their lives, the one thing that has always accurately shown them
the outcome of a situation is the clear voice of their intuition. That is the
factor they can trust.

As an illustration of how their gift of intuition works, recall old horror
movies. A familiar theme would repeat itself: The haunted house would be
on an isolated hill, way out of town. A carload of teenagers would be
driving by, laughing, carefree. As they passed by the haunted house, the
camera would zoom in on one of the tires, and suddenly it would go flat.
From the camera work and the scary music, the audience would think:
"Don't go in that house!" The camera would show a close-up of the face of
one of the teenagers, and intuitively he knew it, too! If they went into that
house, terrible things would happen. But his friends were careless and confident, so he discounted his inner prompting and followed them into the
house—and, in fact, terrible things did happen.

This is a perfect story for Sagittarius North Node people. They always
know what's going to happen beforehand. When they discount their intuition and walk into a situation because of "logic" or out of concern for what
others will think, they always lose—and sometimes terrible things happen.
When they listen to their inner prompting and follow their intuition, they
always win. Their lives become magical; they avoid pitfalls and keep experiencing successes.

CHEERFULNESS

Sagittarius North Node people are positive, cheerful, and outgoing. They
have happy, lighthearted connections with others, and they have a helpful
disposition. They are attuned to insight from their Guides and Angels, and
are open to higher inspiration. These folks have a natural optimism and are
willing to work hard to get the results they feel are awaiting them.

Even if their thoughts are giving them negative messages, these folks still act from their positive expectations for the future. They may talk about their fears, but in their behavior they follow their optimism. They know good things will happen for them if they do their part.

Sagittarius North Node people have a feeling they're going to make it—and that's what supports their cheerful disposition. They see all the things that could go wrong, but they go forward and do it anyway—no matter how much it costs. When they become negative, it's because they're thinking too much. Their minds have been very overactive in past lives, so their best bet now is to turn things over to their higher self and ask their Guides to lead them in the right direction. As they relax their minds, their natural faith in positive outcomes will be able to re-establish itself.

One of the greatest gifts Sagittarius North Node people can share with others is their unique ability to help people overcome negative thoughts and to show them how to take a positive point of view. When their writing or speaking takes that slant—directing people's minds toward faith in positive outcomes—their message is welcomed by all who are exposed to it. Also, when they help others focus on the bright side, these natives become brighter in their own thinking.

NEEDS

SOLITUDE

SHARING VERSUS PERSONAL INTEGRATION

Although in past lives these folks were accustomed to surrounding themselves with people, in this lifetime it's essential for them to spend a significant amount of time alone. When they get *away* from people they gain clarity, connect with their truth, and establish a sense of peace and well-being. Sometimes they are better off when they don't communicate and share their ideas. They may get an insight and, because they were teachers in past lives, their first instinct is to generously share their knowledge with everyone else. But as they share, the power of their insight begins to dissipate.

First, if people disagree with Sagittarius North Nodes' truth, they immediately try to see it from the other's point of view. Even if the other person doesn't overtly disagree, Sagittarius North Node people are so sensitive to the others' reactions that they can feel any objection at all; then they become insecure and the energy dissipates. Instead, they should keep a new insight or revelation to themselves until they have been nourished by it, integrated it, and begun to demonstrate its effects in their own life.

For example, if these folks think that facing fear head-on turns it into laughter, they should work on translating that insight into action in their daily lives. In this way they become a personal demonstration of this truth.

NATURAL LIVING: THE "BIG PICTURE"

It's very healthy for Sagittarius North Node people to retreat from society: to spend time outdoors and get back in touch with what is natural. It reminds them about being themselves and strengthens their confidence in the power of their authenticity. Nature's cycles give them peace of mind and help them remember that there is a plan unfolding that is larger than the manipulation of people's minds. The minutiae that tend to obsess them lose importance. Spending time in the country gives these folks an expanded view. Without that perspective, they can short-circuit: Their minds are so active that they become overstimulated when they spend too much time around people and the city.

Spending time with animals also helps Sagittarius North Node people relax and gain clarity. When there is another living being in their environment that is basic, simple, and real, they can center on a calmer frequency. These people really benefit from seeing the world through the eyes of a creature that is less complex than a human. They need to keep their perception focused on simple things.

Likewise, foreign travel is good for these folks. With a foreign language and an unfamiliar mindset, they are forced to see the people around them in an uncomplicated, basic way. They become aware of the simplicity and beauty of their fellow beings: their customs and manners, and how they dress and interact with one another. Sagittarius North Node people may think that what they are enjoying is a simpler culture, but what they are actually enjoying is their own capacity to view people and events in a simpler way.

These folks are hungering for simplicity. And for them, the path to simplicity involves taking people at face value and trusting their own intuition. As they learn to simplify and remain honest with themselves, they automatically begin to view others in the same way. As they begin to operate from a place of authenticity within themselves, they will be able to imagine others also operating without deceptions or ulterior motives. As their minds relax in this way, their lives become more joyful.

On all levels, Sagittarius North Node people must get back in touch with what is natural. For example, I had a client with this nodal position who had a new puppy. One day while I was visiting her she became agitated, repeatedly looking at her watch because it was time to take the puppy for a walk. But the puppy was sleeping! According to her "how to raise a puppy" book, it was time for a walk—and all she could see were the rules.

This client was out of touch with what was actually occurring. The puppy was sleeping, so, let her sleep! These folks need to get back in touch with the miracle of life's natural, peaceful unfolding—and to trust the natural rhythms of people, relationships, and events.

UNDERSTANDING AND ACCEPTANCE

For Sagittarius North Node people the key to being understood and accepted—not on a temporary basis, but on a deep, permanent level—lies in being themselves. Although these folks can often predict how those around them will respond, sometimes they can be surprised. For example, I had a Sagittarius North Node client who had written a play about her early years and the people in her family. She was terrified for certain family members to see it because she thought it might be hurtful to them. While writing it, she was second-guessing herself and trying to predict their responses to every line.

She was particularly concerned about how her mother would react to the play. Ultimately, the play was performed off-Broadway and several of her relatives attended the opening night, including her mother. Much to her surprise, they *loved* it! Her mother was beaming with pride at her daughter's success. The relief my client felt was incredible. Communicating her truth the way she saw it created a win/win situation for everyone involved. Also, because the play was honest (she told the story from *her* point of view, not from everyone else's) it was a success with the general audience as well.

When the motive behind direct communication is to express themselves—without intending to hurt or manipulate anyone else—it always turns out well for these folks. It can even work for Sagittarius North Node people to get a little bit righteous. They have too great a tendency to go along with others' ideas—fitting into the nooks and crannies of other people's lives, allowing themselves to be taken advantage of. But when they say: "Hey—you can't do that to me! I don't deserve that kind of treatment!" and stand up for themselves, it works!

SELF-DEFINITION

Sagittarius North Node people are so desperately seeking a point of view that will give them peace of mind that they can become attached to the philosophy of another person. For a while, this system may work for them. They may even accept the parameters of that belief system as "the only truth" and be reluctant to step beyond those boundaries.

This can cause problems in meaningful communication, as these folks tend to insist that others conform to their vocabulary and basic precepts before relating to them on a deep level. But they are using logic to find Truth, and logic can only work when certain assumptions are mutually agreed on. The philosophy they espouse has given them comfort, and they don't trust themselves to find Truth on their own, beyond the limits of a structured definition. They may try to use rationality and logic, instead of immersing themselves in the energy of Truth itself.

It is fine for Sagittarius North Node people to temporarily adopt the philosophy of another as a springboard to boost them toward Truth; but once they have connected with the energy of Truth, their best bet is to let go of the words that got them there.

These folks have much to learn from others to find the fullness of the truth they are seeking. But they must listen and allow life to teach them, rather than relying on books or outer authority figures. Input from other people can help them see flaws in their thinking, as well as offer alternative perceptions that enable them to achieve practical success.

They are learning that any set belief system blocks them from a living, vital connection with the wholeness of Truth. Truth is beyond any point of view. It is an energy, not a concept. It is eminently practical—it works! Truth is also moving (fluid), and Sagittarius North Nodes are learning to allow Truth to lead them.

SELF-ACCEPTANCE

Sagittarius North Node people have been teachers in past lives, and they continue trying to teach others now. Acceptance of their ideas—their truth—by others is important to them. However, in this lifetime acceptance of their ideas is not a barometer of whether they are on track. Instead, they should focus on becoming an example of their truth—applying Truth in their own behavior so it is self-evident.

These folks feel a tremendous spiritual void: They think they lack something that is needed to give them strength and self-confidence. Indeed, what is being overlooked is their own self. They have had so many incarnations enmeshed in society that they have lost touch with the silence and presence of their spiritual connection. Thus, they have a deep need to reattune themselves to their spirituality. Taking up the spiritual quest as a primary aim in this incarnation is altogether appropriate for Sagittarius North Node people.

On one level, this need can be satisfied by reading spiritual books and spending time by themselves in prayer or meditation. On a "daily life" level, they can strengthen the connection with their spirituality by acknowledging their desires. They tend to hold back in communicating what they want for fear that their desires will not be accepted by others. Yet desires are a prompting from the internal, spiritual part of ourselves, urging us to go in a certain direction so we can experience our own completion. Thus, when these folks accept their desires and communicate them to others, they take a step toward accepting themselves.

The irony is that as they begin to practice self-acceptance, they find themselves feeling less desperate about being accepted by others. They have been honest, true to themselves, and had the courage to reveal their own desires. As a result, they feel a tremendous satisfaction, fulfillment, and peace—a sense of completion within.

DIRECT COMMUNICATION

An important goal for Sagittarius North Node people is to practice the art of direct communication. This can be intimidating, because in past lives they were manipulative and indirect. In this lifetime they dislike those qualities in others but can inadvertently participate in such behavior themselves.

These folks have the gift of words from past lives. They can frame their communication so that others will agree; and they referee arguments between groups or individuals who don't understand each other, not just by being diplomatic but by manipulating both sides. They don't like confrontations. If they can make others agree with their point of view, they won't have to risk being direct because the other person will already see things the way they see them. But in that process everyone loses, because the interaction is not based on directness and truth. And then these folks feel awful. They have betrayed themselves and betrayed the truth, and some part of them knows it.

It's better for Sagittarius North Node people to look at the truth behind the situation and simply communicate what they see, without logically "figuring out" what would be to their best advantage. By trusting this, the power of Truth itself paves the way for their success. The good feeling they will have is confirmation that they are on the right path. It takes remembering and practicing, but as they experience positive results, they will learn to trust it more.

NEED FOR ACCEPTANCE

These folks tend to mitigate what they have to say by first considering how the other person will accept their words. This results in an indirect communication, which means they're sharing only whatever they think will lead the other person to accept their point of view. They fear losing the acceptance and support of others, and they seek to keep the conversation on a light-hearted, social level.

However, when Sagittarius North Node people communicate *directly,* a happy exchange of mental energy can resume after the issue has been openly addressed. If they see every "obstacle" (that is, the other person having a different point of view) as the next step in creating greater rapport, trusting that the universe is providing things that will bring them closer to others, then each obstruction becomes simply the next area of focus that will take them to their goal.

Owing to past conditioning, these folks have a tendency to "pull their punches," fearing they'll get in trouble if they speak up. But habits that worked in past lives are not scheduled for success in this incarnation: When they don't speak up is when they get in trouble! If they don't tell others where they stand or what they want, they are overlooked or ignored—which they really dislike.

Sagittarius North Node people have to be very direct. If they compromise their words they'll forget their point and lose their energy. It can be scary for them to be themselves, but they can do it if they see themselves as being a channel for the truth within.

DEFINING THEIR POSITION

It's better when these folks make up their minds about where they stand and what they want before discussing their decision with others. For example, I had a client with this nodal position who was an actress. A well-established New York producer offered her the opportunity to audition for a part that called for a dancer and singer. My client was a strong singer, but not so strong a dancer. Her spontaneous response was: "Oh, no. This is going nowhere. Do I really have to go through the ordeal of this audition?" Then came the "logical" second-guessing of her original "knowing": "What will the producer say if I decline? Maybe he'll take it personally and not invite me to audition for his next play. What if this is an opportunity leading to something really big and I just don't see it?"

Finally, she called the producer and explained that she didn't feel she was right for the part because her strength was singing, not dancing. After reconsidering, he agreed that it probably wasn't the right opportunity for her. The interaction ended on a positive note.

My client knew—in advance of the call—where she stood. The conversation was a matter of communicating her point of view. She had reached her decision *before* talking to the producer, so she could communicate directly and tactfully. The challenge for Sagittarius North Nodes is to figure out where they stand. Once they do this they automatically communicate their decision in a way that allows others to be accepting and cooperative.

FEAR OF MISUNDERSTANDING

Sagittarius North Node people have a tremendous fear of being misunderstood. To a large extent, they base their security and peace of mind on having established feelings of rapport with others. Yet for them to feel a solid sense of acceptance, this rapport must be based on revealing their own truth.

These folks often get a sense of "right and wrong" as soon as something is presented to them. Yet when they share what they sense, others may think they're "off the wall." Time usually proves their first impression to be right—so it's okay for them to speak up and remind others that their past intuitions have been correct. Because of their desire for acceptance, they don't want others to think of them as "arrogant," so they often downplay this ability. But in fact, these perceptions aren't their own ideas; they simply "see" them intuitively. By pointing this out, they can make other people aware of the advantage of connecting with their own intuitive process.

Sagittarius North Node people are learning to trust the accuracy of their first inner feeling and not second-guess themselves later on. Often when they interact with someone who is important to them, they have an "all is well" feeling afterwards. Later, something they said during the conversation comes to mind: "I wonder if he knew what I meant by that? Oh, *no*! He probably thinks that I think that . . ." and they have an anxiety attack! The entire conversation replays within their mind. They dissect it, noting all the places where miscommunication might have occurred. Soon they are convinced that there is a huge misunderstanding between themselves and the other person.

They may think about calling the other person to explain everything. But this generally confuses the situation—and the other person may begin to doubt Sagittarius North Nodes' sincerity. These folks sense this, and then feel embarrassed and even more insecure than before. In questioning the interaction they put negative mental energy into the relationship, which harms their connection with the other person. This entire process works against them.

Sagittarius North Node people need an accurate barometer of what occurred in the original conversation. They have to learn to trust their inner knowing: the feeling they have about the conversation *immediately* afterwards. If they have an uneasy sense that something was "not quite right," their intuition is most likely correct. Either the person wasn't "being straight" with them, or there was a misunderstanding. If their first feeling is that things went well, they need to trust that feeling and not rehash the conversation, using logic to tear it apart. For these people, intuition is much more accurate than logic.

Sagittarius North Node people also have an incredible gift of silent communication through the atmosphere. If they feel uneasy about any relationship, they should go within themselves and send love to the other person. That alone can be enough to stimulate a healing.

PEACE OF MIND

One of the greatest challenges Sagittarius North Node people face is achieving peace of mind. One viewpoint that could help is: "Hey, this is all just an adventure! It's an experiment, a discovery!" The word "adventure" is magical for them: It means fun, expansion, and learning.

While on the adventure they'll discover more about other paths, different from the one they've known. That requires a leap of faith into the unknown; yet when they do it, everything turns to their advantage and they feel vital and alive. Others see them as enormously brave, but when they view their situation as an adventure, they feel free to take chances and explore.

When they go with their own instincts, magic happens. And the positive response in their energy field will feed them the encouragement and enthusiasm they need to keep going.

PATIENCE

Sagittarius North Node people are learning about patience. They often want to rush results. What they see with their minds, they want to have happen immediately. They are so identified with their mental processes, and their mind works so fast, that they end up traveling faster than the "natural flow." When things don't seem to be going right, or seem out of order, these folks need to deliberately slow themselves down and have patience.

They need to wait and see what is going to unfold next in the natural sequence of events.

But these folks often have the feeling that time is running out, and their nervous energy can be very taxing to their bodies, their nervous systems, and their general health. Sometimes a health warning can jolt them into slowing down and becoming more observant. They are learning to be more receptive to life—not trying to control it. Slowing down allows them to get in touch with the truth within the moment.

Sagittarius North Node people can also practice patience with themselves. If they feel that something is "off" about an opportunity, but something about it also makes a lot of sense, it may be that the timing is not right. Their intuition is simply telling them: "It is not right for you to proceed at this time." Later on the internal message may change, when the outer environment has come into a more positive alignment.

RELAXATION

Because of their tendency to become mentally overstimulated, it can be tough for these folks to relax. Their minds are going constantly, revving up their nervous systems, and they may have difficulty sleeping from time to time. One challenge is to find ways to relax. Many things can increase their sense of peacefulness. Meditation is a great remedy: It calms the nervous system and recharges them with peace. Hot baths and swimming are soothing, as well. In fact, all kinds of interactions with water have a calming effect—even a fish tank, a water view, or a tape of water sounds.

Regular exercise helps balance Sagittarius North Node people, bringing their minds in tune with their bodies. Sports or outdoor activities are great for them: jogging, biking, hiking, walking, rock climbing, or camping. For deeper relaxation involving the mind, they will be amazed at the wonderful results they can reap from studying philosophy and spiritual or religious practices.

RELATIONSHIPS

Personal Relationships

Friendship

These folks have had a lot of people lifetimes: fitting in with others, being interested in their daily routines, getting to know the inner workings of their lives. Consequently, especially in the early years, there's always a lot of social activity with people calling, "hanging out" with friends, and attending social events. Yet in this incarnation, socializing doesn't fulfill their deepest needs. In fact, being with people too much drains their energy and makes them overly sensitive and insecure. They feel clearer when they spend time alone.

If Sagittarius North Node people become more direct in their communication and lessen their involvement in conversations that don't really interest them, they find that people with whom they have little in common begin to leave their circle of friends. Yet their good friends appreciate their directness, so being direct helps them discriminate between people who belong around them and those without any deep connection.

These folks can be great advisors. They readily listen to everyone's stories and try to help them; because they understand how others think, everyone feels comfortable with them. But it's to their advantage when the quantity of people around them diminishes, as they can spend more time with like-minded friends who nurture them in return.

Sagittarius North Node people sometimes remain in superficial relationships because they have an insatiable need for attention. They will do anything for it: make up stories, pretend to be curious about people when they are not really interested, and even create unnecessary problems in their lives so they can be the center of attention. Underneath this need is a sense of restlessness and a fear of boredom. They are so terrified of boredom that every time they come up against it, they run the other way and try to distract themselves.

In their friendships, these folks need to be careful about indulging in gossip. Other people seem to get away with it, but whenever these folks participate in gossip, life really lets them have it. It's just one of those things they are not allowed to do in this lifetime.

ROMANCE

Sagittarius North Node people are learning that if they manipulate their partner, they end up being trapped themselves. In romantic relationships, they seek control by forming a close bond with their mate. They keep the lines of communication open all the time—at least superficially—so they can share their partner's "mind space" and keep the situation under control. These folks stay connected with their partners through constant phone calls and the like, and they are very sensitive to any pulling back on the other person's part.

Unfortunately, this communication is happening on a superficial, "chatty" level, and it never addresses the underlying, significant issues in the relationship. But these folks feel very insecure without the constant checking-in; they're afraid they'll lose control and the other person will leave. They can spend the whole day "chatting": discussing this and that, bringing the partner up to date on the latest news, and sharing their thoughts.

Over the years, Sagittarius North Node people grow weary of the constant mental interaction they think they need just to maintain control. They may become bored and think about leaving the relationship, especially if they haven't been able to manipulate the other person into doing what they want. Yet by that time, they have not only trapped the other person into dependency—they have also trapped themselves. And they become increasingly confused and mentally weak the longer the co-dependency continues. Often they try to break the bond they have forged, becoming angry with the partner to create mental distance and regain a sense of freedom and independence. Sometimes they devise a "plan of escape," taking the partner totally by surprise when they leave.

There is nothing wrong with having preferences regarding a mate's behavior; however, these folks would save time and energy by taking a more direct approach in the beginning of a relationship. They have the idea that after marriage, through cheerful manipulation of the other person, they will slowly change the partner's behavior. But this technique is not scheduled to work for them in this lifetime.

Once mutual attraction has been established, Sagittarius North Node people should reveal their ideas about creating a life filled with a sense of adventure and fun. When they have openly shared their fantasies of their future, they will see whether or not the other person resonates with their dreams. If they meet resistance, no amount of mental manipulation over a thirty-year marriage will change the other person. If they meet with enthusiasm and support, the potential is there for a good relationship.

These folks occasionally get so caught up in their mental processes that they lose touch with their bodies and their sexuality. They almost seem to get lost in their minds! To come down to earth, they might try a camping trip or an outdoor adventure. Being in natural environments calms their high-frequency nervous system and allows them to re-establish their natural sensuality and bodily rhythms. Also, when they view sex as fun or an unexpected adventure, they reconnect.

Sometimes these people think they don't attract the right romantic candidates. But this happens because they are not being themselves; they're being a chameleon in order to be accepted. They use logic to pick a romantic partner, then they use their ability to understand how the person thinks to create artificial harmony. But when they constantly alter their ideas so the other person will accept them, they dilute their own sense of who they are and what they want.

Relationships based on truth maintain themselves naturally. Just by being oneself, the other person stays happy and giving. Relationships based on manipulation must be maintained by manipulation. When these folks respond naturally and directly, those who are attracted by their true nature will draw closer. Sagittarius North Node people need to be with a mate who can resonate with *their* truth! And they can only find such a person by being themselves and speaking directly.

LOYALTY AND COMMITMENT

Sagittarius North Node people are learning that loyalty is not based on pitting one person against another. This is temporary loyalty that breaks down under stress. Loyalty really means consistently supporting loved ones in reaching goals and doing what they say they are going to do. Until these folks learn to keep their word—simply because they have *given* their word—loyalty from others will elude them.

INTEGRITY VERSUS TRICKERY

In close relationships, these folks face the temptation of using their mental agility to trick the other person into changing. They are trying to be tactful, but it is really manipulation—and the other person will resist. For example, the native may say to herself: "He's perfect, but *he has to change in this one area*. If I make him see life differently, he'll change." But this tactic doesn't work over the long haul. It results in resentment, anger, and wasted time.

A direct approach works much better. For example, Sagittarius North Node could say: "Look, I love everything about you. However, the right man for me will *also* have this one certain quality. Are you willing to develop that quality within yourself?" These folks have natural tact. They don't need to worry about saying the wrong thing. Their challenge is to take a stand and then see how the other person responds.

Being direct does not mean being angry with the other person. Being direct simply means they have to tell the truth. They should be assertive but not aggressive. Assertiveness involves stating things as they are; aggressiveness involves having anger as a motivation. Aggressiveness is aimed at the other person, but Sagittarius North Nodes need to aim for their own truth.

Sometimes when these folks speak directly, they become very emotional. They feel vulnerable, and their feelings are very intense because they've been bottled up for so long. Initially, when these folks begin to speak, these emotions may flow out with their words. But that's fine—it will work to their advantage.

MORALITY AND ETHICS

Sagittarius North Node people see everything from so many points of view that they have a tough time holding any belief or perception as "sacred." Because of this, they may mislead others about their motives or intentions. For them, it can be a matter of deciding what they have to say to get what they want. They may even put others down for being honest: "Why did he say that? That was stupid! Now he won't get what he wants. He *should* have just said what they wanted to hear." These folks often don't recognize the inherent value of telling the truth. They lack faith in the goodness of life and the benefits of following natural law. They think everything depends on their ability to outmaneuver others. But they are discovering the strength, calm, and confidence that emerge when one's words are a true reflection of one's inner being. There is nothing to hide, no reason to be "on guard," and no need to use mental energy "covering their tracks." They are also learning to trust in positive outcomes—if they are honest, the "right things" will happen.

When they are not operating with integrity, they often project this onto others and become suspicious about what people are "up to." This leads to paranoia, mistrust, and anguish, since they assume that others are also trying to trick and outmaneuver *them*.

Honesty—Truth—Freedom . . . these three energies are interdependent. Without Honesty, Sagittarius North Node people will never see Truth and obtain Freedom. The habit of dishonesty leads to confusion, and when we confuse others, we end up being victimized by confusion in our own lives. Sagittarius North Node people are learning that their greatest protection against ambush or trickery from others is to be straightforward themselves.

PRODUCTIVE COMMUNICATION

LISTENING

In spite of the fact that these folks have a strong ability to understand others, they often do not truly listen to what the other person is saying. They get so distracted by sharing their own predetermined point of view, or by what they want the other person to think of them, that there is no true communication or mutual growth.

Sagittarius North Node people need to develop more peacefulness in their conversations—a stronger desire to find Truth through a mutual sharing of ideas. In this process they will retain their own truth at the same time that they heed their intuition regarding others' words being accurate and relevant. They have had so many past lives as teachers and interpreters that they tend to listen too "exactly" to the words people use. In this lifetime, rather than listening to the words with both ears, they are better off listening with one ear and attuning their other ear to their own intuition. When they listen with their intuition rather than with their logic, they will truly understand what is being said and will be able to create a nurturing rapport with others.

HEARING OTHERS' TRUTH

Because these folks have a tough time defining their own personal truth, they assume that others have the same problem. But this is not the case. They are learning to accept that what others say about their (the others') motives, desires, interests, and values generally *is* true. True communication requires a willingness to go beyond logic to the truth the other person is offering. The tendency of Sagittarius North Node people to reduce conversation to a sharing of predictable words, rather than allowing it to be a vehicle through which a higher truth emerges, can lead to misunderstanding in relationships.

Motive is everything. If the native's motive is to listen and grow closer to Truth through the interchange of words, he will win and so will the other person. When his motive is to appear intelligent and show mental superiority, his spontaneity leads to carelessness, painful misunderstandings, and missed opportunities.

FINDING RESOLUTION

Sagittarius North Node people need to see their interactions with others as opportunities to find "higher solutions" to their problems, *not* as times to tap into an endless stream of information. Questions and curiosity do not work for these folks. They already see too many options. They need to let go of their desire to question and simply be open to what their intuitive process shows them. On the intuitive level, they are brilliant.

Even in the closest friendships, misunderstandings arise. If the Sagittarius North Node person doesn't honestly, directly, and immediately communicate his hurts and fears, negative thoughts will "simmer." Over time, these "withholds" accumulate and the relationship dissipates. In this way, Sagittarius North Node loses friendships that could have brought nurturing rewards over a lifetime. But if the Sagittarius North Node person directly communicates what he is feeling and thinking, his friend has a chance to accept him, understand him better, and be more supportive. The obstacle becomes a way for a deeper alliance to be formed.

These folks are learning that the best resolutions come out of a blending of two people's ideas—a higher perception than either one could have attained on his or her own. Truth is an energy, not a personal opinion; it cannot be reached with two concepts struggling against each other to be "right." The energy of Truth is accessed through two people who are being open to each other's ideas and wanting to find Truth together.

SOCIAL SITUATIONS

MANNERS

Owing to so many past incarnations spent in the midst of society, Sagittarius North Node people have become overly sensitized to others' opinions and overly attached to doing things in a way that is socially acceptable. They place too much emphasis on "good manners" and are constantly mindful of the social graces, including tact, courtesy, and discretion. Thus, they do not understand when others behave with rudeness, crudeness, or just a general lack of etiquette.

Each of us has our own karmic history, and only the Sagittarius North Node people have an overabundance of past lives spent learning about the rules of society. Rather than condemn people for not embodying the social graces, these folks can help others learn how to interact in a way that is supportive to society as a whole. This is a gift they have to share.

For instance, these folks don't want to put anyone in a situation of having to say "no"—they want to be gracious and keep the interchange friendly. They are aware of how others think and have a keen sense of when the timing is right to present an idea. Therefore, they do not understand when people put *them* in the often awkward position of having to say "no." When others put them in this position, these natives think it is purposeful and unfair. In fact, other people *don't realize* they are putting anyone in a difficult situation.

Sagittarius North Node people are so aware of others' thoughts that they can tell when something they said or did hurt the other person, and they feel badly. They are kindly people and don't want to hurt others. However, it is also important to take their own feelings into account. When they hold back and don't speak directly, *they* get hurt. But when they have been direct (not in a hurtful way, but in a forthright way), they have taken responsibility for themselves. Only then are they in a position to help others.

WHAT OTHERS THINK

Sagittarius North Node people can be insecure in social situations. Primarily, this is because they are oversensitive to what other people think about them. They may start out feeling inwardly calm and happy from having spent time alone. Then, after an evening of interaction, they return home besieged with thoughts about what others said, what they meant, how they treated the native—and all the possible hidden meanings. In defense, they form harsh judgments about how they think others were viewing them, and then they shut down, pull back, and resolve never to go out again. Social interactions can be hurtful for these folks when they allow their minds to become overstimulated.

For example, I had a Sagittarius North Node client who told me about something that was a consistent source of upset for her. Every day she would go to a coffee shop near her office, order a large cup of hot water, and pay five cents for the cup. Because her digestive system was sensitive, she preferred to drink only hot water. Each day, the same young girl at the counter gave my client a look that she interpreted to be degrading. Finally, my client said: "Do you have a problem with my order? I have the impression that it bothers you, and I want you to know that I can't drink anything but hot water, so that's all I can order." The girl broke into a big smile and said: "I don't have any problem with that!" And my client felt at ease again.

When Sagittarius North Node people finally communicate in these situations, they almost always find that what they took personally is actually just a reflection of the other person's mood and a lack of awareness of how they are affecting others. Rather than pretending that the other person isn't affecting them, or running away from people because of their sensitivity, Sagittarius North Node people should take a direct approach that allows them to maintain their own integrity. In the process of acknowledging their vulnerability, they become *invulnerable* to victimization by others' thoughts.

GAINING PERSPECTIVE

Sagittarius North Node people are proud of being able to see things from everyone else's point of view—but doing it drives them nuts. They are so aware of how others are viewing them moment to moment that they close down because they feel too vulnerable. Although they appear friendly and open, many times they are actually "closed" out of fear of being judged by others.

These folks need to step back from the situation and become aware of the overall picture. Once they gain perspective, they can use their power with words to say something that will make the other person feel better. For example, stepping back and recognizing how much pressure the young girl at the coffee shop was under, my client could have said: "I guess things get pretty busy around here at lunchtime," which would have validated the waitress's situation and established the rapport she was seeking.

There is no one better equipped than these folks to project mental lightness, ease, and a feeling of acceptance. And when they do that in the moment, with that one other person, it benefits not only themselves but the whole planet. They have used their past-life powers of communication to help their neighbor. This is not a lifetime where they should limit the scope of their interests to those in their immediate environment. They are here to restore a positive mental attitude to whoever comes across their path.

WORDS VERSUS MEANING

These folks often *think* they have a hard time with words and communication. In fact, they communicate very well; but they often feel they're struggling. Because they are so accurate with words and are so aware of the mindset of the other person, they are hoping to find the exact word that will speak in the other person's language as well as convey precisely what they mean. Obviously, going through such mental gymnastics in the process of a simple conversation can be a struggle.

Sagittarius North Node people don't realize that most people communicate with less precision. Others are less preoccupied with words—and perhaps more careless—more intent on simply expressing what's inside of them. But the issue of words is important to Sagittarius North Nodes. They have a tendency to listen too closely to others' words and miss the meaning.

They may even keep interrupting and correcting the other person, which misses the point entirely—and makes the other person frustrated! These folks are not trying to antagonize the other person by changing his or her words; they're *trying* to communicate.

Sometimes, Sagittarius North Node people will pick out one word the other person has used and go off on a tangent: "What is this person talking about—'real' . . ." and they go on and on about what "real" means to *them*. When a word "stops" them, they need to ask the other person what it means to him or her. That helps the Sagittarius North Node person attune to the other person and loosens the attachment to specific words. Even though these people are often highly intelligent, their attachment to words can impede their intellect and "bog down" the conversation for others. They must see beyond the words to the meaning of what is being said.

GOALS

CREATING A BALANCED LIFE

TRUST AND DISCERNMENT

Sagittarius North Node people are learning to trust themselves and their inner knowledge of what is "true." Theirs is an irrational kind of knowing—an intuitive feeling about the truth of a situation. Because it's irrational, they often question their conclusions, and their ability to make decisions becomes paralyzed. But when they trust logic as an accurate barometer of the situation, they generally lose. As long as they trust their inner knowledge, they generally win.

Sagittarius North Node people worry about others' responses to every move they make. They jump past their intuitive knowing to what they "should" do to please everyone else. Their challenge in this lifetime is to stick with what they feel and take action appropriate to that initial knowing. Once they have made a decision, other people come into alignment with them and give them support and strength—it's simple! They have such complex minds that it can be a challenge to defy their logic and, instead, trust the simplicity of their intuition.

These folks are strongly motivated to help others. But they need to recognize that the best help they can be in this lifetime is to share with others what they're *intuitively* given, allowing themselves to be a channel for their gifts and keeping their ego (and their second-guessing) out of the way. As long as their motive is pure, Sagittarius North Node people can trust their inner knowing in any situation.

Discerning the other person's motive will help Sagittarius North Node people know when to be open to another person's point of view and when to be cautious. What are the needs and desires of the other person? What does the other person consider important in life?

For example, if the other person considers social image important (having more money or possessions than her neighbors, or the approval of her peers), then all her ideas will reflect her perception of how to succeed in the material world. If the Sagittarius North Node person's values are different, he might not get much out of the other person's ideas of "truth."

Sagittarius North Node must also ask: What is the specific motive of the other person toward me? Does she want to be helpful and supportive, or is she just seeking a sounding board for her own opinions? When Sagittarius North Node listens to his intuition, he can feel the other person's motive: If it is to help and support, then it is to the native's advantage to allow the other person's truth to reach him.

INTEGRITY

The absolute necessity of living a life of integrity can be a difficult lesson for Sagittarius North Node people. They are so accustomed to justifying their position by seeing all points of view that it is very easy for them to overlook the integrity of aligning oneself with the truth of one's own being and acting from that center regardless of the consequences. This can be tough, because these folks so often get their way through being "nice," using tact and saying what people want to hear.

However, for their lives to become strong, these folks must commit to living by the principle of morality. Just as one cannot violate the law of gravity without falling, these folks cannot violate spiritual laws without suffering painful consequences. Thus, it is to their advantage to acquaint themselves with the spiritual laws operating on this earthly plane and cooperate with them rather than resist them.

Sagittarius North Node people are also learning that the outcome of lying is always destructive. Lies may seem to succeed temporarily—or lull a difficult situation into status quo—but this only postpones facing an outcome based on truth. The postponement may even cause a deteriorating situation to go beyond the point of no return. The underlying truth in any circumstance is always the key to change, renewed growth, and greater aliveness; and it is the only way to discern natural compatibility.

Sagittarius North Node people are discovering that even on the most mundane level, lies in all forms represent a breaking of a higher, universal law. Ultimately, lying results in lack of clarity about one's own nature, distrust of others, isolation, and anxiety. The "temporary fix" that lies provide holds no true resolution, but instead leads to more lies, more confusion, and decreased personal power. On the other hand, speaking with love, honesty, and caring creates receptivity in the other person, empowering both people to be themselves in a way that leads them to even greater intimacy.

Being of service wherever they can is a quality of love in this nodal group. They are capable of handling lots of information and doing lots of things at once, so they become a cog in the wheel that makes things run smoothly for everyone else. Their desire to help needs to be focused on being true to the voice within themselves, rather than all the other voices they hear. Once again, they need to release worry about what everyone is thinking and just do what they know is right. By setting an example, they more deeply serve others through their own expression of a Higher Power. The infusion of truth into daily life is a key lesson Sagittarius North Node people are learning; and as they learn, they teach.

Through direct communication of what they *sense* to be true, they are acting in alignment with a larger picture that they may not understand but *feel* is correct. Experience has shown them that others didn't respond as expected once they took their stand. So they might as well align themselves with the power and protection of speaking their truth—being a mouthpiece for what they feel to be correct—and see how the drama around them unfolds. They will find that taking the leap of faith adds more adventure to their lives!

THE SPIRITUAL PATH

These folks have spent so many lifetimes seeing things from so many different points of view that they are often naïve and shortsighted, not looking far enough ahead to realize the consequences of their actions. They feel vacant spiritually: bereft of the joy, faith, and substance others seem to have. In this incarnation, Sagittarius North Node people have the job of connecting with their spirituality and walking the spiritual path.

To restore their spiritual connection, they must work to maintain integrity, morality, and commitment—putting their allegiance to Truth instead of falling to the temptations of manipulation and trickery. When they walk the spiritual path and trust and follow principles of Truth and honesty in their daily lives, the whole world yields to them and they attract those things that truly make them happy.

CONSCIENCE

Sagittarius North Node people see everything as a point of view and thus tend to discount integrity as an absolute. If they are tempted to do something for personal gain at someone else's expense, their conscience will admonish them: "No—don't do that. That's not right." But then they may use logic to rationalize their way out of it: "It doesn't feel like that's the right thing to do. But if I *don't* do it, this thing or that thing could happen. And it isn't really such a bad thing." By considering the situation from so many different points of view, they lose sight of the *truthful* view and end up justifying a decision based on self-interest.

Truth is not a point of view; if Sagittarius North Node people act against the voice of their conscience, they always lose. They lose the connection with their own spirituality—because their bad decision closes the door to the sense of well-being they seek. They also expose themselves to unexpected material loss, since the situation may well backfire further down the line. They cannot expect to gain the benefits of spiritual peace if they are not living truthfully in their daily lives.

These folks rob themselves of divine protection when they rob others by disobeying their conscience. When they turn their back on the Light by not choosing Right Action, they open themselves to manifestations of negative energy. Negative things, seemingly unrelated to things they have done, begin to affect their lives. They may suffer unexpected financial losses, betrayals, even public disgraces; emergency and crisis follow one after another. Other repercussions of ignoring their conscience include general unrest and anxiety—a sense that "all is not well."

Their only redemption lies in turning back to their spiritual path and promising—on the deepest level—to follow the voice of their conscience and intuition. For these folks, loyalty to Truth is vital in order to disconnect from the realm of superficiality and reclaim their moral and spiritual strength. They know that when they consistently practice the principles of Truth and Integrity in their own personal lives, they gain the peace of mind they seek. When they choose Right Action over desired results, they make themselves worthy of receiving the greatest gifts life has to offer.

COMMITMENT

Sagittarius North Node people have had so many past lives making decisions that benefited them temporarily that they are accustomed to a shortsighted view. Yet commitment—keeping their word, no matter what—builds moral strength that will lead to peace and joy. These folks can easily talk themselves out of keeping their word by seeing an alternate perspective that justifies their behavior.

Commitment doesn't mean staying with something (a job, a relationship, etc.) if it becomes destructive or devitalizing. Commitment means being direct about one's intentions and, if the situation changes, communicating honestly with the other person. Essentially, it is commitment to follow one's own integrity—it is a commitment to Truth.

Sagittarius North Node people are learning to keep their word. If they promise to do something or to be somewhere at a certain time, they should keep the appointment as if their life depended on it. In a way, it does. When they keep their word 100 percent, their word gains strength. Any breach of integrity causes their word to lose power and the universe to pull back its support. If they always support their commitments (or communicate in advance when they cannot), others will come into alignment with them to support the things Sagittarius North Node people seek. They are learning the power of loyalty. It's simple: Their joy and peace lie in walking the straight and narrow path.

Tuning In to Guidance

Spontaneity Versus Impulsiveness

Sagittarius North Node people are most successful when they listen to their internal responses. For example, when the outside environment gives them something to make a decision about, their inner knowing will immediately say "yes" or "no." They don't always realize they're being directed, but these folks have a special connection with their Guides—their personalized sense of Higher Power—that clearly shows them which direction to follow. Sometimes they feel the guidance is unavailable, but actually they're just blocking it. It's always there for them when they quiet their minds, tune in, and listen for an answer.

Along the way on their adventure, spiritual truths and insights will occur to them, and they will need to begin applying them in their daily lives. Their pathway may not display much logic, and they may occasionally feel foolish following their guidance without any preplanned route. Sometimes this guidance may cause them to go in an unexpected direction and have an adventure they can't predict—yet when they follow it, they win.

These folks are learning to discriminate between impulsiveness and spontaneity. When they act impulsively, they lose. For them, impulsiveness can be an obsession. When they allow their minds to go into overdrive, especially relative to their fears of how a situation may turn out, they feel compelled to do something to regain their peace of mind. But here, motive determines the result. When Sagittarius North Node tries to change the other person's point of view so he (Sagittarius North Node) can get what he wants, then impulsive action results in less security for him.

On the other hand, spontaneity is the absence of obsession—it means being free to act without thinking. Spontaneity is in alignment with Truth; there's no manipulation behind it. Spontaneous people are sharing their truth in the moment, with no fear, ego involvement, or conscious motive driving them. When these folks respond to a situation in this way, they always take the right action or say words that are in their best interest. Also, they gain peace of mind because they know the action was not driven by any hidden agenda. Owing to the purity of their motive, they can trust that the long-term results will be in the best interests of everyone involved.

THE SPIRITUAL CONNECTION

In past lives, Sagittarius North Node people became reliant on the "social mind"—the part of their thinking that tells them how to survive in the context of society. Through many past incarnations of losing themselves in the mindsets of others, they came into this incarnation without knowing what their own ideas are. In a way, this is beneficial. They have no preconceived beliefs and are therefore open to ideas from their higher—or intuitive—mind. Yet they are totally unaccustomed to trusting this gift of spiritual guidance.

In this life, they have such wonderful psychic and intuitive gifts that they can help others, even professionally, if they want to. They are natural channels of Truth. They can be unparalleled in reading Tarot cards. The "feeling" messages of the pictures, combined with Sagittarius North Nodes' natural mental fluidity, can boost them and others to new, creative ways of viewing life.

These folks also have the gift of direct access to their spiritual Guides. When Sagittarius North Node says: "Okay—this is what I want" and starts following her defined aim, then she is "on path." Her job is to allow her inner guidance to lead her directly to her goal. For example, she may decide she wants an active social life and a happy romantic relationship, and then a friend says: "Would you like to go to a party Saturday night?" If her energy soars, that's her Guides' way of telling her that going to the party will further her goal.

But then Sagittarius North Node starts second-guessing herself: "Well, the people who invited me will invite other people who are not likely romantic candidates anyway. And my other friend invited me to see a movie Saturday night. And I don't have the perfect outfit, so even if I did meet someone, it probably wouldn't work out because I wouldn't look good." After these complex mental gymnastics, she doesn't go to the party. Later she complains: "I never get what I want!" Second-guessing equals "how to lose" for these folks!

When her spirit spontaneously soars, her job is to follow that soaring feeling, that intuitive *"Yes!"*—regardless of what her mind says. It's an adventure to see where that path will lead if she follows that happy feeling. In this way, she allows her Guides to help her realize her dreams.

These folks are surrounded by Guides and Angels. It is not a "do-it-yourself" lifetime for them. This higher information and guidance translate through the intuitive process, so it's perfectly fine for them to be illogical in this lifetime—relying on "feelings" rather than the conscious mind.

Sagittarius North Node people spend so much time thinking about what *others* think, they should worry about their poor Guides and how *they* feel! Their Guides' job is to direct them toward what will make them happy—and these folks keep invalidating the guidance. The Guides can see a lot farther than they can, so the Guides go to great lengths to get everything set up just right—but then the Sagittarius North Node person starts following logic instead of the happy feeling his Guides give him! If Sagittarius North Node people don't follow their intuitions, their Guides can't help give them what they want. But it could be so easy: All they have to do is to follow their sense of adventure and their intuitive knowing—and joy will find *them*.

HEALING THEME SONG*

Music has a unique power to emotionally support us in taking risks, so I have written a healing song for each nodal group to help shift its energy in a positive way.

TRUSTING

The lyrics of this song impart a message meant to bolster confidence and encourage Sagittarius North Nodes' subconscious to take the leap of faith necessary to follow their inner knowing, instead of their mental process. Once they learn to trust in the positive spiritual forces surrounding them, they reconnect with the peace of mind they have been seeking.

Selected lyrics:

> So now I'm here, and it wasn't so hard at all
> To become what I saw, 'cause I believed it in my heart
> And it's so much more than words—but I had to do my part
> Looking back I can recall, that the hardest part of all
> Was a risk to my whole Being
> It took so much trusting . . .

---

* These lyrics are set to music and sung in their entirety on the CD and cassette tape "Unfolding As It Should."

North Node in Capricorn

and North Node in the 10th House

OVERVIEW

Attributes to Develop

Work in these areas can help uncover hidden gifts and talents

- Self-control
- Approaching life from an adult position
- Self-respect
- Staying goal oriented
- Sensible approaches to problem solving
- Keeping commitments and promises
- Letting go of the past
- Self-care
- Accepting responsibility for success

Tendencies to Leave Behind

Working to reduce the influence of these tendencies can help make life easier and more enjoyable

- Dependence
- Moodiness
- Insecurity leading to inaction
- Limiting self through fear
- Using the past to avoid the present
- Isolation—spending too much time at home
- Lack of self-respect
- Avoidance of personal risk
- Controlling others through emotional overreactions

ACHILLES' HEEL/TRAP TO AVOID/THE BOTTOM LINE

The Achilles' heel Capricorn North Node people need to be aware of is dependence. The desire to be taken care of ("If there's no one to take care of me, I won't survive") can lead them into the trap of an unending search for security ("If I can just get a strong enough foundation under me, I'll have the energy I need to take charge of my life"). They develop emotional dependencies on others, which force people into becoming a basis for their security. But it's a bottomless pit: They can never get enough reassurance to feel safe, so they never gain the security they think they need to be capable adults and take charge of their lives.

The bottom line is that at some point they simply have to be willing to run the risk, take charge, and assume full responsibility for the consequences. When Capricorn North Node people recognize a goal that's truly important to them and live by it, they gain the self-respect and assurance they need to live responsibly. The irony is that once they take charge, they feel secure and in control of their own destiny.

What These People Really Want

What these people really want is an environment in which to feel safe, protected, cared for, and doted on—a place where they feel they truly belong. To achieve this, they must be willing to let go of the idea that one special person—or group of people—is going to provide it just because they think they need it. Instead, Capricorn North Nodes must take charge of creating what they need for themselves. By pursuing a goal that energizes them, or by finding an ideal or set of principles that builds their self-respect, they will develop feelings of belonging in whatever circumstances they find themselves.

Capricorn North Node people need to find a focus beyond their scattered emotional needs and those of people around them. When they bring themselves into alignment with a higher principle or spiritual belief, they feel protected and nurtured.

Talents/Profession

These people excel at being the "boss," so management, public speaking, politics, and entrepreneurship are good choices for them. Others are willing to cooperate with their goals, since they approach people under their authority with sensitivity. To achieve success in any area, these folks need to be "in charge" of their own piece of the puzzle.

Additionally, Capricorn North Node people have finely honed instincts for empathy. They are always aware of the feelings of others, and when they use this ability in a management situation their sensitivity encourages people to assist them with goodwill and enthusiasm. However, if they involve themselves in professions that stress nurturing as the end result, they often become enmeshed in feelings of helplessness, unable to get "on top" of the situation. They are better off in goal-oriented professions or positions that enable them to use their sensitivity to lovingly organize others to work toward a specific goal.

HEALING AFFIRMATIONS SPECIFIC
TO CAPRICORN NORTH NODE

- "I cannot control others, but I *can* control myself."
- "In releasing the past, I deal more effectively with the present."
- "When I take charge, I win."
- "When I feel self-respect, I'm on the right path."
- "I don't need to depend on anyone else to take care of me."
- "I can take charge in this situation."
- "I am in charge of my inner state of being."

PERSONALITY

PAST LIVES

Capricorn North Node people have spent many lifetimes as householders: As central figures in the home and on the farm, they were thoroughly identified with their family or clan. Through these incarnations, they developed a natural understanding of how families work and the emotional attunement to others that is characteristic of this nodal group. But they have not had a lot of past-life experience being out on their own. And although in this lifetime their greatest joy will come from being out in the world, the problem is getting them out there! By giving up worldly experience to be in the home, they sacrificed their sense of competence and self-respect. In this incarnation, they are learning to be in charge of their own destinies.

In past lives the home was everything to these folks, and all their needs were taken care of by the family: They were fed, clothed, given shelter, and protected. So they came into this lifetime with tremendous dependence needs and now look to others to help them "get their life together." When things don't go as they want, they overreact emotionally, subconsciously hoping that others will see how upset they are and change their behavior. But other people perceive this as a means of controlling and are unwilling to modify their behavior just to appease these natives.

Capricorn North Node people are learning that in order for their lives to work, they must approach situations from a position of being "in charge."

They must discard all tendencies to manipulate people through emotional outbursts, and instead approach others from a position of authority—with quiet self-respect that is removed from emotional reactions. It is a byproduct of taking charge of themselves and having their own life goals. From a take-charge position, they can relate as equals without depending on others' goals for security.

FAMILY KARMA

These folks have difficult family karma. Too often, they are born into a situation where immediate family members have many emotional problems, and the Capricorn North Nodes spend a lot of time being sensitive and empathetic. However, they are drained by the incessant demands of those around them because they take on others' problems but don't feel capable of helping them change.

From past lives, Capricorn North Node people are so used to nurturing family members that they have lost a sense of their own direction. Thus, in this lifetime they tend to have difficulty when they get too close to members of their immediate family. Actually, the problem isn't the closeness but rather their subconscious intent: "If only I can get this person on track, then finally I can have my own life, pursue my own goals, and be a person in my own right!"

Because of this subconscious motive, their "support" of family members has an unpleasant emotional intensity. They want to "get it over with" so they can live their own life. The problem is twofold: (1) trying to get the other person on track is a way to postpone making the commitment to taking care of their own lives; and (2) trying to help someone else achieve success is premature when they have not yet learned how to do it themselves.

The first job for these folks is to decide to distance themselves from total emotional involvement with their family. Once they let go, they are in a position to proceed with their own life. It is fine for them to be in touch with family members when they can objectively understand others' emotional needs from a detached position. When their happiness is no longer dependent on resolving the problems of everyone in the family, they are actually quite good at managing the family in a way that brings productive results for all concerned.

If Capricorn North Node people were to manage their families the way they run businesses, their family life would be extremely successful. In fact, they are *expert* managers because they have a natural understanding of people and can gently align others to cooperate in reaching the goal in ways that don't hurt anyone's feelings. They need to approach family members in the same way: from a position of authority, not of need. To do this, they need to discover what the other person's goal is and objectively support him or her in reaching it. Alternatively, they need to have specific goals in terms of how to run the family, assume the role of manager, and facilitate family members in reaching the goals that promote everyone's best interests.

EMOTIONAL SENSITIVITY

These folks are extremely sensitive to their own emotions and those of others. Because of this innate awareness, they understand why people become upset and can't do things. They are so aware of the reasons people fail that they often become too accepting of their own lack of accomplishment. When they are having a "bad day" or don't feel like being disciplined enough to work toward their goal, they apply that same understanding and sympathy to themselves as an excuse to postpone direct action—and it becomes a self-defeating escape hatch!

Capricorn North Node people are also very tuned in to the realm of emotional connectedness and understand how people's feelings can affect others. This is both an asset and a detriment. On the plus side, it enables them to negotiate life more smoothly. The liability is that they sometimes feel for other people more than others are feeling for themselves—and this can be debilitating. They can't handle negative energy, so they mitigate their own behavior—their plans and their own personal direction—in order to accommodate others. In this way they don't have to deal with others' emotional distress—but they can easily end up being controlled by the feelings of everyone around them.

These folks take personal responsibility for other people's moods; they want to make the other person happy so that *they* can feel better! They can't separate themselves from the generalized mood of people in their immediate environment. And the other people may resent not being allowed to express their true feelings because it upsets the Capricorn North Node person.

For example, if a family member invites Capricorn North Node for dinner and she really doesn't want to go, she will generally go anyway to avoid bad feelings. These natives live in avoidance of anything that might stir up emotions—in themselves or in others. This is one more technique to avoid responsibility: They don't want to make decisions because they're afraid that any decision might cause negative feelings in someone else.

Capricorn North Node people are learning to stop controlling other people's moods and simply allow those around them to feel what they feel. Sometimes people have to experience negative feelings in order to resolve important issues; when these folks try to block that experience, they rob the other person of the opportunity to grow. If someone puts his hand on a hot stove and gets burned, *that's* part of learning not to put his hand on stoves. The same holds true on the emotional plane. To a large extent, these folks operate from their emotions, and this equals "how to lose" for them in this lifetime. Their unique challenge is to take charge of their emotions rather than being victimized by them, and to allow others to take responsibility for their own feelings, and to grow and mature as a result.

DEALING WITH EMOTIONAL ENERGY

Capricorn North Node people are very emotional. They cry at movies and at sad stories; their feelings are very present and available to them. These folks can be so overrun by their emotions that they can't think, they can't function, and they don't know why. This can happen when they are faced with personal loss or in professional situations involving confrontation or performance; they can't seem to control it—it simply escalates.

One thing that helps when their emotions take over is to concentrate on slowing down their breathing. They need to relax, focus on letting go of the thoughts that are making them nervous, and visualize memories that have made them feel happy and peaceful: a beautiful mountain, a time by the seashore, and the like. Then they will calm down and be able to function again.

When these folks face circumstances requiring them to take charge, they may think the situation is beyond their ability to control, and they panic. They think of the possible negative consequences, their fears and insecurities arise, and all the muscles in their body tighten up. Thus, when emotions start to overwhelm them, they need to deliberately breathe, relax, and *expand* beyond the emotions. They can visualize themselves becoming bigger than the emotions and regaining their serenity.

Ultimately, they should not allow themselves to get into this kind of frenzy to begin with. To that end, they can notice that whenever they allow something to become excessively important to them, they become anxious. Recognizing this can make a significant difference in maintaining their peace of mind.

FEAR OF REJECTION

Capricorn North Node people hate the possibility of rejection—in fact, even the thought of being rejected is crippling for them. If someone rejects them, not only do they feel bad about themselves but they also think it was their fault. These folks are so insecure and so terrified of rejection that they enter situations very cautiously.

Part of this fear of rejection stems from their past lives, when they were shielded from the world by stronger family members. They harbor a perception that they aren't worth much by themselves; and when they are rejected, it proves to them that they're not worth much. This response is irrational, but it reinforces their inner fear, and when they think someone has rejected them, they can't sleep all night! Understandably, then, these folks hate rejecting others. They tend to take responsibility for other people's feelings and spend a long time going over all the reasons why they were justified if they have to reject someone. But they know how it feels, and thoughts of how others are feeling can upset them for hours.

Making a decision to take charge will empower Capricorn North Node people to rise above their anxieties and take steps to resolve difficult situations in a responsible way. In a personal relationship where a misunderstanding has occurred, they can take the initiative and call the other person: "I'm concerned we may have a misunderstanding, and I want you to know I would never do anything to intentionally hurt your feelings." Or: "I think we may have had a misunderstanding, and I don't want you to feel rejected."

If they come from the position of taking charge to create mutual harmony, they will know what to say to promote that harmony. If they are temporarily too upset to make the call, their best bet is to wait until they've calmed down. They can say to themselves: "There's nothing I can do about this right now. So I'm going to call tomorrow and resolve the issue in a caring way."

Hanging On

Capricorn North Node people are so open to their feelings that they also tend to keep open a door to feelings from the past. They don't want to close off any of the happy times, because they don't know what's going to happen in the future. They usually avoid thinking about the future at all costs. But until they begin to consciously visualize a positive future, their only reality is the past and the present. When the present does not make them happy, they drift back into thinking about the past. This process is not healthy because it distracts them from taking constructive action in the present.

When they look back at the past, these folks are seeking to regain memories and feelings of joy and love. But they also become aware of things they didn't do and wish they had, which makes them feel remorseful. This diminishes their power to take charge in the present. They need to remember that their past oversights occurred simply because they didn't have the Light at the time to know what they should do. But what they know *now* can empower them to reach their goals if they remain focused in the present and look to the future. The past is only beneficial when they use it to take note of which behaviors were self-defeating and which behaviors led to self-respect and strength.

Capricorn North Node people have a difficult time letting go. They are very sentimental, and they don't want to hurt anyone's feelings. When they start to leave a situation, even if it's clearly not working, they get depressed—so they tend to "hang in there" until they realize, deep down, that there's no hope. They do all they can to make the relationship, the job, or the situation work. When their survival is threatened, they will leave; but they would be much better off letting go *before* the situation escalates to that point.

Their difficulty in letting go occurs when they lack goals for the future. Then they dwell on the past, which makes leaving an old situation far more difficult. For these folks, the best way to let go of the past (or a difficult situation in the present) is to focus on a specific goal that gives them a sense of purpose and direction. For example, if they have left a romantic relationship and miss the intimacy, their first tendency is to feel nostalgic and dwell on the closeness they no longer have. A better resolution would be to focus their energy on establishing a new relationship by joining a dating service, going dancing, or participating in other enjoyable social activities. The past must be released in order to experience the empowerment of acting in the present.

One of the most difficult things for Capricorn North Node people to let go of is their drive to control. They always want to make situations work out *their* way. They think that if they are in control, they are realizing their potential—but they need to recognize the difference between control and management. Trying to *control* other people so that their own emotions remain undisturbed means that Capricorn North Nodes are operating from an emotional plane with a self-centered view.

However, when their intent is to *manage* a situation, they organize things according to a bigger picture—they have already determined what will work for everyone. Now they are coming from a place of mental process *(not emotions)* and goal orientation. But to reach that place, they must first release the desire to control others.

THE PERENNIAL CHILD

Capricorn North Node people always want more—more attention, more time, more nurturing—in order to feel good. Their whole world revolves around their family, and they expect the dynamics to be reciprocal. But more nurturing from family members usually isn't forthcoming—it's just not set up that way in this lifetime.

Moreover, these folks avoid taking action by always thinking they need more help, more advice, more confidence—more of "something" first! They think that the "more" they are seeking will come from other people. Actually, the "more" that will truly fulfill them involves focusing on goals that will expand them personally—and then taking consistent, daily action to reach those goals.

As parents, Capricorn North Node people often seem like "one of the kids," because they approach children as equals rather than as parents. They are reluctant to assume the responsibilities of parenthood; they question their capability to take care of others when they are not even sure they can take care of themselves.

NEED FOR ATTENTION

Especially when they are young, these folks do anything for attention. Often when they act moody or snap at another person, it's an attempt to gain attention. This attribute sometimes keeps them from exercising their achievement "muscles"—they think they should be given attention for who they are, not for what they do. They may even create crisis in their lives so other people will become interested in them. However, it's a double-edged sword because they often sense this problem in themselves (the fact that they are "manic" for attention), so they feel guilty and berate themselves when they think they are getting too much attention.

When they are holding back and not reaching for their goals, they feel they don't deserve attention and thereby keep themselves from receiving the very thing they crave the most. The irony is that when they set a goal and go for it, others *do* notice and willingly give them attention and respect in a healthy, satisfying way. In addition, when Capricorn North Nodes are taking chances with their lives and working toward their goals, they feel worthy and become open to noticing and receiving the attention they need from others.

It would also help these folks to begin paying attention to themselves; to give themselves credit for making improvements in various areas of their lives. When they show care and concern for themselves it mellows them; they begin to feel better about themselves and less dependent on others.

AVOIDING RESPONSIBILITY

These folks hesitate to take full responsibility for themselves—it goes against their grain. They would have to "leave the womb" and go out into the world! Sometimes it takes a sledgehammer to wake them up and get them to take charge. They often *appear* to be taking responsibility, and with the "small stuff" they usually do: paying the bills, buying groceries, listening to family problems, and so on. But they continue to avoid larger issues. For example, when they try to figure out what to do with their lives, they just sit around and consider an endless stream of ideas. When they finally become motivated, they ask themselves: "Do I really want to do this?" Then they give up again!

Capricorn North Node people have a thousand excuses emanating from their subconscious, urging them to postpone working toward what they are here to do in this lifetime—what would truly make them fulfilled. If they finally say to themselves: "This is *ridiculous*! I'm just going to *do* it!" the commitment is made and they begin taking steps toward the goal.

Because these folks are very loving, their habit of yielding to others tends to interfere with their life. They may allow sympathy to cloud their vision because they don't want to evoke an emotional response from others. They let others have their way, rather than holding to their own principles.

They need to re-examine their values in relation to how they show love. One value should be keeping commitments, which creates a basis of inner strength. Capricorn North Node people need to let others know what the rules and limits are, and then stick to them unflinchingly. If they say to their teenage son: "You may go out, but be back by 10 P.M. or you can't go out for the next three nights," they need to stand by that statement. If the teenager returns at 10:30 P.M., they must be willing to endure his temper tantrums over the next three nights to stand by what they said.

Of course, if they have done this consistently, the teenager will already understand that if he breaks the rules, his parents will stand by the punishment. But if the parents become "sympathetic" and let their son go out, he will cease to respect them, and they will cease to respect themselves. These folks must learn to stand behind their word. Their commitment must be stronger than their fear of upsetting the other person.

Capricorn North Node people are learning to become responsible for themselves in this lifetime: figuring out "what they want to be when they 'grow up'" and clarifying their goals. Being responsible for themselves includes supporting themselves financially and finding other levels on which they have never taken charge before. That's exciting and challenging—and it will give them a chance to grow!

LEARNING ADULT APPROACHES

Capricorn North Node people are learning to be adults in this lifetime and to discard their tendency to have childish reactions. To be adults requires them to actually make a commitment to a goal. When they do this, that area of their life becomes absolutely magical. Suddenly everything works to their advantage, they are filled with vitality and confidence, and they walk the pathway to success easily and with great joy. They need to use the technique of making commitments in areas of their life that are not yet yielding the results they want. Being willing to face the fear and develop the habit of making commitments is their key to self-respect and success.

These folks often have a "hyper" quality—they want to "get to the next thing." This emotional restlessness prevents them from understanding what is important to them and following through. As soon as they focus on a specific personal goal, the restless emotional energy is channeled in a productive direction. Until then, they will only be working toward *others'* goals, and will never notice the opportunities that are being presented to themselves.

Also, Capricorn North Node people sometimes doubt their own competence to take advantage of opportunities for themselves. In a childlike way, they think they're supposed to know things that they truly don't know, and they try to hide their lack of experience by pretending the information isn't important to them. The adult perspective is to understand that everyone needs information from others to reach their goals—no one reaches a goal without input from others who are more experienced.

These people may also be too ready to obey outer authorities rather than listen to their own inner truth. They may blindly follow another's expertise—especially if they're paying a lot of money—even if, in their hearts, they know that something else works better. However, they are learning to trust themselves and remember that no one knows what will work for them as well as they do.

These folks have a tough time being the ultimate authority. They can take charge, instruct others, be the boss, and supervise lots of employees—under the auspices of someone else. It's easier for them to work toward someone else's goal. They don't care about getting the credit, and they certainly don't want the ultimate responsibility.

The irony is that Capricorn North Node people, more than any other nodal group, are gifted in their ability to be "the boss." They are so emotionally sensitive to others that when they take charge, they do it in a way that does not diminish others. They are not blocked in reaching their goal because they haven't alienated anyone along the way. As a result, however high their goal, everyone will support them in reaching it. In fact, they are scheduled for easy professional success this lifetime, once they've made the commitment to create it.

Often these folks think they are not good communicators, but they only have difficulty in this area when they become emotional. When they allow themselves to get lost in their emotions, they can't think straight; then, when they speak, it's just a jumble of emotion! However, if they pull back from their emotions and speak from the "in charge" part of themselves, they find the perfect words to evoke respect and cooperation from others. The difference is the part of themselves they access: the emotional part, or the adult part. If they become emotional, they can regain inner equilibrium by asking themselves: "What can I do to take charge of this situation from an adult point of view?"

For Capricorn North Node people, strength increases with age. This applies to every aspect of their life, but especially to their professional life or other areas of goal fulfillment. The passing years also help these folks to take things less personally. When things go "wrong" they understand that they are not personally at fault—different things come together to create a difficult situation. As Capricorn North Node people begin to expand and take a larger, more compassionate view, they also ease up on themselves. When they stop blaming themselves for everything, they also stop blaming others.

NEEDS

SECURITY

Capricorn North Node people have an insatiable need to feel secure. From past lives they are accustomed to being nurtured and protected, and although in this lifetime *they* are the ones scheduled to provide for others, they remain content to just breathe their way through life—to just get through it with as little exertion as possible! They like the safety of routines: waking up at a certain time, eating at a certain time, coming home, watching television or reading, going to bed at a certain time. Ultimately, however, they will have to leave their routines behind to find the greater security of self-confidence: knowing they can take risks and succeed.

BELONGING

These folks have a deep need to "belong." In past lives, they strongly identified with their families and took comfort in being part of a group. Now they must learn to be discriminating and choose to spend time with people who give them that feeling of belonging—to satisfy their need in a responsible way. Home and property are also important in giving them a sense of security. (However, unless there are other factors in the birth chart indicating otherwise, these natives do not have very good "real estate karma" in terms of making money.)

Because of the focus on home, they may spend too much time there. When they do, the home can keep them from expanding and taking charge of their life. If these natives run their own business, it is generally a good idea for them *not* to run it from their home, but to rent a space—even if it has to be in someone else's home. They need to get out into the world on a regular basis to keep their energy in motion. Excessive time at home can make them too comfortable and life can become a routine they use to avoid interacting with the outside world. Then the opportunity for true vitality, growth, and progress is aborted.

Capricorn North Node people are afraid that they don't belong—and they don't know how to behave in order to be accepted. So they look around to see what behaviors are approved of by "the group" and then emulate those behaviors. They crave intimacy, and the only way they can think to get it is by yielding to the group. However, going along when they don't really want to can be a source of deep disappointment for them. The group generally doesn't reciprocate by yielding to them.

These folks can also get derailed when they become part of a "clan" or "clique" because they apply their "adopted" principles to *other* groups, which leaves them feeling alienated. And they don't understand why! The problem with trying to meet their need to belong by becoming part of a clique is that it implies exclusion of other groups—they think they only belong with a limited number of people. Although it *does work* to pledge themselves to a cause that is greater than their personal life, problems arise when they forget to discriminate. For example, if they have fervor about Republican politics when they're in a group of Republicans, that group will make them feel as if they belong. But the same fervor will make them feel alienated in a room full of Democrats. If they want to feel accepted, they should focus on whatever principles they have in common with the people they're speaking to.

FEAR OF FAILURE VERSUS SELF-RESPECT

Capricorn North Node people have such an exaggerated fear of failure that it cripples them, stopping them from making the changes that could lead to success. As long as they are afraid they are going to fail, they think they can "get away with" depending on others. They think they "aren't quite ready" to be adults and seek opportunities for success. However, sooner or later they recognize that no one else is going to take care of them—it's just not set up that way in this lifetime.

Sometimes these folks use any excuse whatsoever—even their age—to avoid facing their fears and going out in the world. After years of wrestling with themselves and finally deciding they won't be fulfilled until they accomplish their "mission," they may decide that their age will interfere with attaining the goal. Fear of aging can—for these folks—be a reflection of the part of them that doesn't want to grow up.

However, Capricorn North Nodes are the very people who should embrace age: "Thank goodness I've finally reached maturity!" What they'll be embracing is a willingness to start working toward a goal that will make life meaningful, bring them fulfillment, and give them self-respect. With these folks, it is illogical to think that age could work against them professionally: The roles they seek are usually enhanced by age, as it gives them more power, credibility, and authority. While they can also achieve their goals early on, often it is in the second half of life that Capricorn North Nodes finally take a stand. Thus, when they feel pressured by age considerations, it's really their psyche saying: "It's time!"

These people recognize that they will be much more unhappy if they never try to attain their goal than if they try and fail—as long as they give it 100 percent of their effort. The voice that keeps saying: "What if you fail?" is part of the past-life mechanism that doesn't want them to be out in the world. It's really saying: "Don't grow up . . . Don't go out," and this is self-defeating. If they listen to that voice, they will never gain self-respect.

In a past life the Capricorn North Node may have had a husband who didn't allow her to go out, or an overly protective parent whose voice she has internalized. But it finally boils down to saying: "Okay—that's it," and taking charge of her situation. In that instant, her position in life makes a complete turnaround. When these natives are willing to take full responsibility, they begin to exercise control over their lives and gain a sense of self-respect, which is what they need more than anything else.

In fact, when Capricorn North Node people are in doubt about whether a specific action is correct, they can use the barometer of self-respect to determine if they are "on path." For example, if they are anxious about making a phone call, they can ask themselves: "Regardless of the outcome, will making this call give me a sense of self-respect?" If the answer is yes, they will "win" by making the call. If the answer is no, they should re-think their position.

Capricorn North Nodes like to float along in an emotional haze, which automatically puts them in a "one down" position. But when they approach life from a "take charge" position, everything shifts and they feel empowered. Yet there's a lot of fear around doing this because they're not accustomed to it, and they're afraid of not being perfect or not being competent. But regardless of how long they postpone, sooner or later in this lifetime they will have to stand up and take charge. The sooner they make this shift in attitude, the sooner they'll start enjoying themselves.

For example, I had a Capricorn North Node client who wanted to be a teacher. Many educators go right into teaching after college, but he post-poned it until he had earned *three* college degrees—and even then he didn't feel ready to be in a position where he would be expected to "take charge." Ultimately, he just did it—and that's what it takes for these folks. Once they take the plunge and "just do it," their success validates their abilities.

Once these natives are in charge, they are in control of their emotional needs and can be sure they are taken care of. No longer at the mercy of other people, they finally feel self-sufficient and secure.

MAINTAINING A POSITIVE FOCUS

Capricorn North Node people are good at encouraging others to pursue their dreams by offering motivation, enthusiasm, and supportive energy. Now they are learning how to encourage themselves. Although these folks are subject to dark moods, they are very resilient. They don't "get down and stay down"; when they're pushed down, they get back up. They just have to remember that if things don't turn out exactly as they want, that's okay. Their challenge is to go out and give it their best shot.

These folks have an unparalleled connection with their emotions. When they say: "I'll bet you can do it!" with feeling, it reassures others and themselves that they can indeed accomplish their goals. Because they have such a strong mind-feeling connection, they also are good healers. However, to truly be a source of encouragement for themselves and their loved ones, they need to overcome the habit of dwelling on the potentially negative consequences of every situation. They think they're "protecting" the other person from being hurt down the line, but actually they're creating road-blocks in that person's path. They need to focus only on achieving *positive* results. These natives are not normally courageous and do not take the chances that those in other nodal signs might be inclined to take. Thus, when people they care about are excited to take a chance in life, these folks need to consciously show a positive attitude.

The best bet for Capricorn North Node people is to overcome their fear by concentrating on creating success. For these folks, looking at the negative side only drains energy from the focus they need to win. They must remind themselves of past successes and concentrate on the nuts and bolts of how to attain specific goals. When they learn to focus on the positive, their emotions will support them in creating the results they want and in encouraging others to succeed as well.

TAKING CHARGE

These folks often come from a framework of limited goals. From past lives of spending all their time in family environments, these natives are new at being in the world, and they lack the confidence that comes from experience. But in this lifetime, it's set up for them to win every time they take charge and accept the opportunities presented to them. Through positive experiences they will gain confidence in their own abilities. They need to recognize that since their goals are often "safe" and not based on taking risks, it will benefit them to be open to other people's input. This input can help them expand to new levels they wouldn't have thought of on their own.

FACING ISSUES

Capricorn North Node people may think they're very open, but actually they have a lot of trouble sharing how they feel. They can appear shallow to others, since they don't see very far beyond their immediate situation. They may understand things easily—they are often very intelligent—but putting their ideas into practice is tough for them. They have so many negative thoughts that it's difficult for them to accomplish things or to face issues in a positive way.

They avoid issues partly because they imagine so many reasons why the other person responded in a certain way—without asking the other person what is really going on. They get "feelings" and "hunches" about why the person rejected them, or said what he said, and so on. However, their instincts are nearly always wrong. If they look back over previous experiences, they notice that what they suspected was behind other people's behavior *was often inaccurate.* Thus, their best bet is to directly ask the other person why he responded in the way he did, and then *listen to what he says.*

It helps if these folks have a specific goal in mind before trying to resolve an issue with another person: wanting to create unity, wanting to end the relationship, wanting feedback so they can modify their behavior to get better results, and so on. If they have a defined goal—separate from the feelings of the people involved—it helps them remain objective. For example, if they have to fire an employee, focusing on the goal—firing the employee—is the only thing that keeps them from being lost in the intensity of the ensuing feelings.

In resolving a misunderstanding in a friendship, their best bet is to have a goal in mind and let the other person know their intention: "Look, there's something I want to share with you, and I want you to know that my intention is to create greater closeness between us." When Capricorn North Nodes take charge and let the other person know their feelings have been hurt, they often find that the other person didn't realize how they were affected.

INTEGRITY

These folks are learning to be forthright and have integrity about what they do and do not know. Because they tend to feel incompetent when they don't have all the answers, they often do nothing in situations that seem overwhelming—or else they respond with a behavior pattern from their past. They are learning to acknowledge when they do not have the answers—by speaking directly to the other person—and to get more feedback about what the other person needs. For example, I had a client with this nodal position who taught high school students how to play all the band instruments. He was proficient on the drums and knew the other instruments only superficially. One day a student approached him with a question about the trumpet: "How do you play an F note?"

My client was worried: "What if I tell him the wrong thing? I'll look stupid!" But he knew there were different ways he could respond. He could intimidate the student: "What do you mean? You don't *know*?"—which would deny the student the help he needed. Or he could say: "Listen, I don't know right now, but I'll check on it and get back to you." When these folks say "I don't know," it makes them equal with others and promotes the feeling of intimacy they seek. When they follow through and find the information, they generate respect and appreciation.

The first step is to have the humility to admit "I don't know." Then they can seek more information. When they take the other route (intimidating the person with an overly emotional response), they distance themselves, and mistrust and defensiveness result instead of the intimacy they desire.

FREEDOM FROM EMOTIONAL BONDAGE

RELEASING THE PAST

Capricorn North Node people often dislike, and feel alienated from, one or both of their parents. They may not overtly express this, but deep down it is true. They may think their parents didn't give them the support they needed to successfully go out into the world. Or they may think their parents tried to make them into someone other than the person they were destined to be. These thoughts can cause them to achieve less than what their innate capabilities would allow. In a subconscious attempt to punish their parents for this injustice, they may keep themselves from reaching their goals. For example, if a parent once told the Capricorn North Node she was a failure or made her feel that she was "not good enough," she may sabotage herself in order to punish her parent for the mistreatment: "See—I'm *not* a success, and it's all your fault!"

To be successful, these folks have to be willing to put their own best interests and self-respect ahead of the desire to cast their parents or others as wrong. They have to be willing to say: "Yes, you are right. I *am* capable of more than what I was achieving before." This requires maturity. It also requires a conscious effort not to dwell on the past, and to stay focused on what makes their lives strong in the present—*doing* things that bring them self-respect.

MASTERING THE EMOTIONS

Capricorn North Node people are so sensitive that they are aware of all levels of communication, including others' words, feelings, and body language—and all the discrepancies and uncertainties that accompany them! When someone communicates a decision to them, they are immediately aware of all the contradictory feelings underneath. For example, if they are invited to someone's home for dinner and they say "No thank you," even if the person says "Fine, another time," these folks will stew for hours about how, underneath, the person had many other feelings—which may or may not be true! These folks need to remember that the friend, taking into account his or her feelings of disappointment, sadness, understanding, and caring, decided to respond by saying: "Fine, another time." They are learning to attune to others' actual responses—not to the feelings they imagine are underneath.

These people always do better if they have time to think things through, because an unexpected event or new information can cause their emotions to boil over and confuse their thinking. Sometimes, if they can't find a solution or make a decision immediately, they react with frustration. They can't get a handle on how to respond because there is so much emotional interference. But taking a stand involves making a decision, and there are contradictory feelings about nearly every decision one makes. The idea is to focus on the decision and not on the possible repercussions. Handling negative repercussions is simply an opportunity to grow and become stronger.

These natives also need a defined goal to keep from being lost in their emotions. If you place a handful of crabs in a barrel, the crabs will remain on the bottom of the barrel even if the lid is off and they have the opportunity to climb up to freedom. Occasionally, one crab may start climbing up the side of the barrel, and all the other crabs will pull him back down to the bottom again. For Capricorn North Node people, their emotions are like fearful and possessive crabs: They always pull these natives back down until they simply make up their minds to go for the freedom and let nothing hold them back!

Sometimes these folks need to suffer an incident that wakes them up to the necessity of facing their emotions—then life becomes much easier. Up to that point, they are victimized by their emotions—totally overwhelmed by their feelings on a regular basis. Until they learn to put their feelings in perspective, their emotions represent something scary and "out of control" that they want to avoid. When these natives indulge in negativity, the negative feelings overwhelm them and they even begin to experience negative *physical* reactions.

One of their greatest challenges in this lifetime is discriminating between positive feelings and debilitating, negative emotions. There are four primary emotions that, when indulged, are a Pandora's box for Capricorn North

Node people: Fear, Anger, Guilt, and Insecurity. They absolutely cannot afford to indulge in any of these four emotions, because they don't know when to stop! Once they get into Guilt, for example, they can never feel guilty "enough"—they keep piling it on and it lasts for a lifetime.

These folks are so conditioned to indulging the negative feelings that they don't even know they're doing it. The first step is to notice when they are experiencing one of the four emotions and to be aware of the consequences. For example, when they allow themselves to become angry, for a brief period they may actually be "mad" (that is, insane). They say and do things they wouldn't say or do if they were thinking clearly. They need to notice the consequences of acting on any of those four emotions, and they will see the disintegrating effect. Then they can learn to stop, just as they wouldn't keep their hand on a hot stove once they see that it's getting burned.

Other nodal groups know where to draw the line and can use these emotions as a "wake-up call" to change their behavior. But Capricorn North Node people are addicted to their emotions and absolutely cannot allow themselves to indulge in any of the "big four"—just as alcoholics cannot allow themselves to take even one drink. Fear, Anger, Guilt, and Insecurity are not only mentally debilitating but physically dangerous as well. On the other hand, Joy, Love, and Appreciation are pleasurable and healthy. In fact, any other emotions—aside from the "big four"—are fine for these folks, because they don't lead to uncontrolled excess.

RELATIONSHIPS

DEALING WITH EMOTIONS

Everyone wins when Capricorn North Node people learn to pull back and don't allow themselves to be caught up in others' emotions. Other people win because they can express how they feel without the native reacting inappropriately. Capricorn North Node people win because they don't have to appease others for fear of their emotional response. They can just watch the other person objectively and say to themselves: "Well, that's Joe having a temper tantrum," or "That's Mary being Mary." They can allow other people to be themselves without being swept up in the negative energy. To acquire the habit of a healthy emotional distance, they can silently remind themselves: "When I let others be themselves, I am free."

DEPENDENCE

In past lives, these folks got used to other people rushing to their rescue whenever they became upset, which led to reliance on others for emotional stability. However, the price was high: This behavior robbed them of the strength of knowing that they are capable of solving their own problems and being in charge of their own emotional states.

Too much support from others actually became a liability for them, creating a deep insecurity that they might not be able to "get it together" on their own. Thus, in this lifetime they are no longer allowed emotional dependence. When they get truly upset and "fall apart," it doesn't work for them—it's not set up in their charts that way. Whenever they become overly emotional, they might as well know that rather than taking care of them, others will walk away. This is life's way of curbing self-defeating emotional dependence.

Capricorn North Node people's emotional upsets are a bottomless pit. They want attention: They want someone to enter their emotional state and resolve it for them. But when they act on this they don't feel good about themselves after the emotional frenzy and are left hoping the other person doesn't think less of them. This is why consciously behaving in ways that gain respect from others—and, more important, increase their own self-respect—is so important for them. It is a compass that keeps them on track and leads them through the mire of shifting moods.

These folks are often especially susceptible to developing an overdependence on family—a feeling of "us against the world." This is why they tend to be patriotic—it's an extension of the "us against them" principle. Often they go out of their way to pay full taxes, feeling obligated to do their share to support the expanded "family unit" of their country. Subconsciously, they still feel dependent on family for survival. In past lives, if the family rejected them, they were banished to fend for themselves and their survival was in jeopardy.

Capricorn North Node people think they need to rely on others. They want to know that someone else is there, and they tend to create a habit of dependence: giving people rides, buying things for them, and so on. Their entire life revolves around the other person.

When they feel someone is there to back them up, they can summon the courage to successfully enter the world. Yet should that person suddenly leave, these folks fall apart professionally as well as personally. Suddenly they're terrified that they can't achieve their goals, even if they have been successful for years.

Actually, these folks are the ones with the power. When they misunderstand that and give their partners the power, it spells disaster for the relationship. When they let others be in charge and make all the decisions, they aren't being adults and they ultimately lose the respect and love of their partners. However, at any point they can turn the situation around and say to themselves: "Okay—now I'm going to take back my power and start being an adult in this relationship," and change their behavior.

Sometimes the "child pattern" is triggered when the Capricorn North Node gets married. As soon as he has that secure "family" feeling, he starts giving the other person all the responsibility. As long as he does this, he'll never have a happy marriage. Whenever the overly emotional child part of these natives emerges, the situation goes downhill. But all they have to do is consciously access the adult part of themselves and start practicing right where they are! Once they take responsibility for their own success, others never let them down. Capricorn North Nodes are in charge, and their lives become magical.

CONTROL

Capricorn North Node people have problems being assertive because they don't want to upset others. If they hurt the other person, they know they will feel bad, so they tend to go along when they really don't want to. If someone close wants to do something and they don't want to, they are likely to go along and be miserable rather than make the other person unhappy. To take charge in that kind of situation, their best bet is to say "I don't want to do it," explain how it would be counterproductive, state what they would rather do, and stick to it. This builds self-respect. When they do it without an emotional charge, the other person is generally fine with it, so both people are happy.

Because Capricorn North Node people feel controlled by the emotional reactions of others, they try and control others through their own emotional outbursts. When they get upset, their emotions fill their words and their energy field, and others often acquiesce simply because it's not worth dealing with the intense emotions that emerge when Capricorn North Nodes don't get their way.

It is their *style* in asserting themselves that determines the result. For example, if they are going to be working late, they tend to make excuses: "Well, I think I can get this done in 30 minutes and then I'll hurry and come down and get dinner . . . and what would you like to eat . . . oh my God, oh my God." That's not being an adult; that's a child trying to please. An adult would say something like: "I'm going to be working until 9:00 tonight, so you might want to go out and get your own dinner because I won't have time to make it."

Alternatively, if another person wants them to do something and they say: "I don't want to do it!" with an emotional charge, the person will back off. But this doesn't promote closeness. The idea is for these folks to establish a sensible, in-charge-of-self position: "I don't want to go with you this weekend because I have to get up early for work on Monday and I need to catch up on my rest." They need to let the other person know *why* they have decided it is not in their best interest to "go along," and then *stick to it.*

If they want some time to think it through, they should say: "It sounds like a great idea. Let me think about it and I'll get back to you." They are learning to stand up for themselves in a rational way instead of allowing themselves to be influenced by other people's emotional intensity or seeking to control the situation through their own emotions.

DENIAL

Capricorn North Node people sometimes overlook problems because they don't want to deal with anything that is emotionally unpleasant. They fear they may somehow create a crisis by facing things directly. If no one else brings it up, they let it pass and hope it will go away.

The problem is that they don't speak up about things that hurt their own feelings. They overcompensate by taking on too many of the little responsibilities in a relationship because they're afraid of losing their partner. They think: "Well, if I really love her, I'll just accept it." They avoid direct communication and instead get angry and quiet with the other person— and then the relationship ends anyway!

Another technique of denial is using a lack of understanding as a way to postpone taking responsibility: "I don't understand it enough to take charge yet." Capricorn North Node people also use the word "understand" when they actually mean "accept." They may *say:* "I don't understand why you are doing this to me! I don't understand why you are so upset!" But they are just putting the attention back on themselves; they're *really* saying: "I don't accept that you are doing this to me! I don't accept that you are so upset!" They use denial as a means of avoiding responsibility for finding a resolution.

Owing to their sensitivity to emotions, these folks are acutely aware when problems exist in their relationships. Denying the discontent may work for a while, but the problems don't "go away." Capricorn North Nodes never want to bring up unresolved issues because part of them fears they may not be able to handle the conflict. Actually, a festering issue becomes more difficult to resolve over time—a difference of opinion can lead to a divorce. Facing it right away and exposing the underlying feelings are the keys to talking it out and restoring good feelings on both sides. When the partner says "I'm upset—I have a problem in this relationship," going into denial is absolutely "how to lose."

For Capricorn North Node people, exposing the problems they see is the key to keeping the relationships that are important to them, but everything depends on the approach. If they approach the other person from a position of taking responsibility for guiding the relationship to a predetermined goal (a happy marriage; a long-lasting, permanent friendship; a long-term business partnership, etc.), they can expose the problem in the context of seeking a mutually satisfying solution. For example: "There is an issue in our relationship that is upsetting for me, and I want to discuss it and learn more about how we both feel, what we need, and how we can handle it in a way that works for both of us." They should identify the problem, explain how they feel, and solicit information about how the other person feels, keeping the positive goal in mind.

Once they have initiated an exchange of information and viewpoints, they open the way to a higher level of emotional well-being for both people.

In a marriage where a situation has been unresolved for a long time, taking charge may mean going to a marriage counselor to make sure that each person understands the other. After all, the relationship exists because at one time both people wanted it; with proper communication, the original enthusiasm can be restored and perhaps even enriched.

ROLES

ATTRACTING THE RIGHT MATE

Owing to past lifetimes of dependence, Capricorn North Node people think they need a strong partner for protection and support. Sometimes they attract the wrong person to partner with—someone who wants to take care of them and keep them in the home. But if this happens, their inner self begins to rebel after a time, and they end up repelling the very person they were attracted to. In this lifetime, something inside them wants to prove their capacity to take care of themselves. What they really need is a partner who can support them in developing their own professional and personal authority.

When these folks come from a position of neediness, their relationships break down. However, when they enter a relationship with the resolution to take responsibility for their own happiness, the relationship can assume its proper importance. But the fulfillment they seek can never come primarily from a relationship; it will come from actively pursuing their mission and participating in life from a take-charge position that builds self-respect.

Even in close relationships, these natives are better off maintaining a sense of their own authority—not compromising themselves to appease their partner. For example, I had a client with this nodal position who had tremendous creative energy and a real talent for writing—she was published nationally while still in college. When she married she stopped writing, putting all her energy into emotionally supporting her husband and children. She "didn't want to upstage [her] husband and undermine his confidence."

Twenty years passed. When her children left home she was filled with resentment toward her husband, blaming him because she hadn't pursued her writing career. Her husband had actually encouraged her writing, but she projected that her success would have upset him emotionally even though he encouraged her verbally. I had occasion to speak with her husband, and he truly *did* want her to pursue her career! It even would have helped out the family financially. This particular story does not have a happy ending: The wife chose to continue blaming others for her sense of failure, which prevented her from actively taking charge of her own life.

This is what happens when the Capricorn North Node uses others' feelings as an excuse for not living her own life. In fact, she is responsible for using her time in ways that build self-respect. The first person who needs to understand where she wants to go and what she wants to do is Capricorn North Node herself. Then, when she lets her partner know what's important to her, the relationship begins to accommodate her!

Once these folks are actively pursuing their own goals, acting out of integrity and being themselves, they can see whether the people who are attracted to them will be an asset or a liability. They can be objective, because they don't *need* the other person for their survival. In fact, the right person will be attracted to them when they have found a goal, made the commitment, and are actively on their own path. Then they emit an energy that is aligned with their spiritual self, and people who can support that energy will be attracted to them. If they are already married, taking charge will give their partners an opportunity to support them in a new way.

THE NURTURING MOTHER

Capricorn North Node people too easily take on an exaggerated "mother" role in personal relationships. This absolutely does not work for them—or their loved ones. They often become lost in the role of nurturing mother, subject to the constantly changing emotional force fields of others. When they find their lives swallowed up in catering to other people, they feel victimized. In fact, no one requires the amount of "presence" that these folks tend to provide.

Their motive in playing the role of the nurturing mother is to keep the moods of those around them happy. But others perceive it as interference, and Capricorn North Nodes experience an energy drain, so both people lose. Also, oversensitivity to others' moods can cause these folks to be manipulated. Others become dependent on them to supply physical things to keep them in a good mood. It is a form of constant nurturing, and these natives generally feel good providing it. But they should protect themselves from those who approach them in hopes that they will play the "caretaker" role all the time.

Philosophically, Capricorn North Node people think that all people should help each other and, if everyone did so, the world would be a better place. So they usually try to help if they can, and they do it without an ulterior motive. But although they instinctively take care of people, it's often without knowing what will really help. They consider others' physical needs but not the deeper issues. They would like to be able to take care of others' spiritual needs, but they don't know how.

Instead of playing the nurturing mother role in this lifetime, they need to put more emphasis on the "father" role—taking responsibility to help others achieve constructive goals. This means *listening* to accurately discern the intentions of the other person, and then consciously deciding to help. Sometimes they take on a mothering role in the hope that it will evoke a "take-charge" attitude in the other person. Ultimately, for their relationships to work, these folks must become conscious of how others are really feeling and then take charge. If they need help in making a decision, they should call on an invisible father figure—their Higher Power—to enable them to assume the father role in difficult situations.

INTIMACY

Capricorn North Node people value intimacy: being able to talk freely, bare their souls, and be close without fear of judgment. They don't understand when this intimacy doesn't happen. When they find someone they want to be close to, they usually work hard to create intimacy; but sometimes no matter what they do they ultimately feel shut out. One of their lessons is learning not to take things personally: Some people *don't want* intimacy. Not everyone holds the same values as they do. They are learning not to waste their time trying to create intimacy with those who don't want it. If it isn't working, their best bet is to let it go. They need to allow other people to *choose* whether or not to be intimate, and respect their choice.

On the other hand, some people may indeed want to be intimate with the Capricorn North Node, but she may not value closeness with them. The person might be a business associate whom she sees regularly; but when they establish intimacy, the Capricorn North Node ends up feeling drained or depressed. Perhaps underneath she doesn't really respect the other person's principles. Once again, discrimination is the key. It may be that there are some people with whom it is not appropriate for the Capricorn North Node to be intimate, even if the other person desires closeness. The native can tell by monitoring her energy level. If she feels happy and invigorated, then creating intimacy with that person is appropriate.

COMMUNICATION

A primary factor in the problems experienced by Capricorn North Node people in relationships and intimacy is their disinclination to listen. They can be practically impossible to talk to, unless the other person is willing to do all the listening. They are so thrilled when the attention is on them or when someone asks their opinion that they lose touch with what the other person wants. They mean to be helpful, but since they don't really listen they can't see where the other person is headed or the answer he is looking for—so they just go on and on without any focus. Their minds jump in a lateral direction. It reflects a lack of discipline on their part.

To truly hear the other person, listening has to be very deliberate for these folks. Often they don't listen because they don't think they have anything to gain. Unless it directly involves them, they don't take the trouble to come out of themselves and connect with others, empathize, and actively participate—it requires too much effort. They tend to think only in terms of: "How does this affect *me*?" When something larger is presented, they don't always understand its importance. Indulgence in this tendency keeps them from establishing the intimacy they long for, since they aren't really connecting with others.

If what the other person is saying doesn't immediately affect them, they start thinking about something else, so their response may be inappropriate and invite rejection or misunderstanding. However, they gain more from their interactions when they *do* take an interest in the other person. When they deliberately pay attention and try to hear the other person, their responses are much different. Both people feel more at ease in the interaction, and Capricorn North Nodes realize that putting energy into hearing the other person is worthwhile. They will gain more satisfaction and a better understanding of both themselves and others.

Capricorn North Node people also tend to project their own needs onto others, rather than hearing the other person's needs. They may even say: "Tell me what you want, and I'll see if I can do it"—but then they don't hear what the other person says. They hear the words but don't understand the meaning, so they can't act on it. Especially if the relationship has emotional or personal overtones, the other person's communication may seem threatening. This is because deep down, they think they are incapable of filling other people's nonphysical needs. They're afraid that even if they understand, they won't be able to do anything about it—and then the other person will be disappointed and they will feel incompetent.

To make their relationships work, Capricorn North Nodes must deliberately concentrate on listening. Even if it's something that they fear may upset them, they must be open to hearing it in order to gain accurate knowledge of what is happening. Their minds work quickly, but unless it's a poignant or pragmatic matter they know they can't process the information instantly, so they don't even want to allow the information in. It is perfectly understandable that these folks don't process information as quickly as those in other nodal groups because their emotions are connected with their minds. It takes them awhile to separate their mental process from their feelings, and they need private time to reflect on the overall picture. Being willing to think about it later gives them the space to listen without feeling they have to respond on the spot.

Sometimes in conversation Capricorn North Node people become flustered because the other person asks for feedback or advice. They're surprised that the other person would respect their judgment. But when they haven't listened, they haven't taken responsibility for wanting to help the other person and aren't *able* to respond. When they are focused on helping others, they can bypass their emotional response and connect with their ability to see the larger picture.

Another block to communication occurs when these folks think they already know everything. And they do know how everything operates in the context of their own world. They know how to maintain the status quo in their family unit, and they're comfortable in their "womb." They fight to maintain the principles of *their* world rather than recognizing that there are other "worlds" from which they could benefit as well. *They will grow and gain from what they don't know, not from what they already know.* If they become more solution oriented—open to ideas beyond what they already know—they will no longer fear not having "the answer."

Not listening also causes them to miss opportunities because they are concerned only with their immediate affairs and not the larger view. In order to stop missing these opportunities, they can consciously say to themselves: "What opportunity is this person bringing me? What is the opportunity in this situation?" By focusing on opportunities that are being presented, Capricorn North Nodes' capacity to listen will shift to a focused, take-charge mode.

SELF-CENTEREDNESS

Capricorn North Node people often are self-centered, and that is one of the reasons they don't use their gift of empathy: They don't want to exert themselves. They regard themselves as very practical people. If they don't think there's something they can do about a problem, they don't want to "waste" the energy. They may think they're being sympathetic with someone, but it's not true caring because it doesn't contribute to the other person's well-being.

Empathy involves being with someone. It's an active process: "getting into" the other person's situation and feeling what the other person feels. What can help these folks make the transition from sympathy to empathy is realizing the shortcomings of sympathy: Sympathy doesn't solve problems.

No other nodal group has such tremendous capacity for empathy, yet Capricorn North Nodes may be afraid to actively empathize with someone. They sense how the other person is feeling, and they fear that if they allow themselves to experience it, they'll get hurt too and *still* not be able to help. When they do step out of themselves and empathize with the other person, suddenly the answers come to them and they are able to constructively improve the situation.

For example, I had a Capricorn North Node client whose father recently passed away. The day before his father died, my client entered the hospital room and his father—who was in an oxygen tent—stretched out his arms and said: "I'm having a hard time breathing." My client didn't know what to do to help. So he stayed for a few minutes longer, made an excuse, and left. When he reflected on the incident later and empathized with his father, he realized that he should have simply stayed and held his father's hand.

These folks have beautiful and loving ways of helping—when they take a few moments to empathize, they know exactly what to do. When they clearly distinguish between sympathy and empathy, they want to be empathetic. They realize it is good to exert themselves and contribute in some way so they feel connected and can establish the intimacy they seek.

GOALS

GOAL ORIENTATION

The salvation for Capricorn North Node people lies in becoming more objective and goal oriented in all areas of life. Without a goal, they drift in a sea of emotions and are pulled under by their own moods and feelings— and those of the people around them. There's no way out of the fluctuating emotional morass other than to attach themselves to a goal that is larger than their personal life. By holding to that goal, they can pull themselves out of the emotional force field.

In any area of life where they feel bogged down by emotions and needs, they must set a specific goal. For example, if they find themselves bogged down by their children, they could set a goal for ways of dealing with the children (for example, to concentrate on breathing, to maintain a state of serenity). Actually, they may want to establish a specific goal in relation to each child (to support Johnny in being more lighthearted, to help Cindy gain confidence, etc.). By focusing on the goal rather than the child's current emotional state, they will be able to maintain their own emotional balance and be more effective as parents.

Commitment is key for these folks: making the decision to achieve a role with dignity, self-respect, and the integrity of actualizing their potential. In working toward their chosen goal, considerable character development takes place. Reaching a goal is extremely fulfilling for these folks; it validates their power, expertise, and competence in a way that nothing else can. In the end, the self-assurance and self-respect that has been gained from the process is their true reward.

SETTING GOALS

Having a defined goal is an absolute necessity for Capricorn North Node people. In the process of working toward a goal, their whole life takes on power and vitality. Thus, finding a goal that they feel is appropriate, and then going about attaining it, is the real key to enjoying their life. Once they define a goal, their access to emotional power helps them get there; this is a highly positive use of their emotions.

In any area of life, when they exercise self-control it's healthy for them. If they take control of their diet and pay close attention to their eating habits, it's positive and nurturing and they feel great about themselves. If they schedule a regular exercise routine, it gives them the self-respect of applying discipline to reach a goal.

Capricorn North Node people have a desire to demonstrate that they can handle their life and prove their competence. They're not afraid to work, but they don't have much confidence—and the only thing that will *give* them confidence is the success of accomplishment itself. No matter how intelligent they are, if they don't put anything into practice they will fall short of realizing their full potential.

For these folks, part of being able to achieve goals involves being realistic in terms of what they can do. Once they see the bigger picture, they can set smaller goals to get there systematically. When they set goals they know they can achieve, meeting each one gives them confidence to go on to the next.

For example, they may want to lose 50 pounds. Rather than setting one ultimate goal of losing 50 pounds, they are better off saying: "I want to lose 2 pounds in a month." Then, if they lose *more* than 2 pounds in the first month, they can expand the goal to 4 pounds in the second month. If the result is too difficult to attain, then the next month the idea is to set their expectations lower. It's important that they be flexible and not pressure themselves—they can readjust the goal according to the results they achieve. If they have a smaller goal and attain it, it makes them feel good. They validate what they accomplished, and they have more confidence to proceed to the next goal.

I once had a Capricorn North Node client who wanted to exercise by swimming. At first he swam one lane at super speed and was exhausted. He wanted to be able to swim back and forth, and he could see people 70 years old who were going back and forth—how did they do that? So he talked to them and he practiced, and after a while he was able to swim back and forth. His next goal was to be able to swim a mile, and after that he set a goal of swimming his mile in 45 minutes. Then he got it down to 32 minutes—and after that he felt like he was training for the Olympics! This is how these folks become experts at accomplishment: They set attainable goals and then expand them. They are learning how to accomplish goals by staying focused and not getting frustrated. Then the entire process is exhilarating!

SENSIBLE APPROACHES TO REACHING GOALS

A primary purpose of this incarnation for Capricorn North Node people is to learn the art of goal achievement, and they are destined for great success once they learn how. Ultimately, it is their destiny to learn how to take care of themselves. By postponing the time when they take charge, they waste the resources of vitality and youth—after all, it takes energy to build a financial base or a business that will support them. The sooner they take control of their life and start to plan ahead, the better their chances for success. Their best bet is to identify a long-range goal they can begin working toward energetically and get right to it!

These folks often worry that by pursuing a larger goal, their personal life will suffer. So they become immersed in their daily pleasures and problems, ignoring the fact that they're not taking sensible steps to ensure their future. They don't take opportunities because all they think about is what they *don't* want to do, rather than focusing on the larger picture of what they *do* want to do—and then going for it. They don't want to disrupt the status quo to build for their future, when in fact putting their attention on planning for the future ensures their happiness in the present.

Because no one else is going to take responsibility for Capricorn North Nodes' happiness and security, there is no escaping their destiny. The sooner they take charge, the easier it will be and the more nurtured they will feel. For example, I had a Capricorn North Node client whose money from her divorce settlement was almost gone. She had an opportunity to buy a successful pet grooming business with nothing down and an affordable payment schedule. She was good with animals and loved them, and she had the artistic ability to do the grooming. This opportunity was truly a gift of circumstance.

Immediately, rather than seeing the fortuitous nature of the opportunity, this client began creating emotionally charged concerns. Was it truly the "destiny" she was born for? Was it what she wanted to do with the rest of her life? Was it going to interfere with her community theater activities and her favorite morning class at the gym? She approached me with the question of whether she should accept this opportunity or, instead, sell her mortgage-free house to buy more time before deciding how to earn a living.

Once again, Capricorn North Node people are learning to focus on the reality of the future in a sensible way. Selling the house would only postpone a decision and leave this woman in a worse position. And because she would have to pay rent somewhere else, she would need even more income. However, if she rose to the occasion and accepted this business opportunity, she could easily provide for her future. It would require pouring her full concentration and energy into the business for the first year or two, but once it was established and operating smoothly, she could hire people to take over (and she could use her native talent to manage others). After two or three years, she would have more free time and the security of still living in a mortgage-free home, supporting herself with earnings from her own business.

SEEING THE LARGER PICTURE

When Capricorn North Node people focus on the goal they want to attain, they can easily create success. Thus, it is crucial for them to see the big picture—truly understand the larger goal—so they have confidence in playing their part. If they don't understand exactly how their part affects the total picture, they lose confidence.

A HIGHER POWER

To transform their needs for dependence into strength, these folks would do well to align themselves with a spiritual presence or Higher Power that they can depend on to take care of them. This will help them focus beyond their scattered emotional needs and retain a sense of being in control without being controlling. If these folks feel they aren't in control of a situation, they go nuts. For example, if they're driving and the traffic is slowing them down, they often overreact. Actually, it is valid for them to want to feel in control of their lives. However, as in the example, this is not always possible; they need to understand that they are ultimately in control of *themselves,* regardless of outer circumstances.

One way of doing this is by recognizing that a Higher Power is always in control and, thus, whatever is happening will ultimately work to their bene- fit. In the example, being delayed in traffic might mean they won't meet someone they would rather avoid! When they keep their eye on the bigger picture, it prevents them from feeling helpless. Then, when they are in a position in which they have no apparent control, they can say: "There's a reason for this," and just let it go.

Capricorn North Node people have a feeling that there is a job they were born to do, a "higher mission" that is part of their destiny. If they don't realize this life purpose, part of them feels deeply unfulfilled and guilty. That destiny is different for each of these folks, but inwardly they know which direction to take. It will always involve achieving a position of au- thority, accepting responsibility, representing an ideal, or demonstrating a truth that is more important than their personal lives.

They will know their mission because it is the natural pathway that opens before them. They may even pursue it for a while, feel wonderful about themselves and achieve remarkable success, and then abandon the path for one reason or another. Until they go back, pick up the pieces, and follow that sense of mission, they will feel restless. The issue of success or failure is far less important than making the commitment and actively pursuing the goal. These folks must rise above the temptation to get so bogged down and distracted that they accomplish nothing beyond meeting personal needs. When they exert themselves and put a social good above their personal desire to remain comfortable, they are filled with a sense of love and the feeling that "this is right." Then they know they are performing their mission.

ROLE MODELS

Capricorn North Node people love role models—they want to be like their ideal of someone else who has a good wit, "presence," a command of the language, or success in achieving a goal they admire. This can be positive for Capricorn North Nodes. When they have a role model to emulate, it helps them grow and everyone wins!

It works for these folks to emulate successful people. They can take courage from how the role model does things and learn how to succeed themselves, if they really pay attention. In past lives, they invalidated the authoritative part of themselves that took responsibility for guiding the ship. In the process of allowing others to be in charge lifetime after lifetime, their own capacity to take charge became weakened. But in this incarnation it is *their* job to direct the ship; like it or not, others are depending on them to do so. Every time they take responsibility, others appreciate and support them and all of life supports them as well. It's up to them to fill the role for which they were destined and, in the process, become a role model for others.

Capricorn North Node people tend to let others take credit for their work. Secretly, a part of them doesn't want to be publicly acknowledged as being responsible for the outcome—even if the outcome is successful. They're happy just to see their mission fulfilled; they aren't particularly motivated to get the credit. On a practical level, however, it's in their best interest to be willing to accept credit when they've earned it.

For one thing, public recognition is a healthy energy for them—it validates their self-esteem and acts as a barometer to show when they are on track and fulfilling a public need. Someone has to take credit for the success, and it might as well be these folks because the energy of acknowledgment is not an ego trip for them and does feed an area in their psyche that lacks energy.

Moreover, accepting recognition gives them more credibility as individuals who can create success in the projects they undertake. For example, if they organize co-workers to make a change that is good for the company, and accept recognition as the one who headed the project, their managerial talents will be validated and they may be promoted to positions where they can better use their abilities. Recognition is a key to opening up more opportunities to exercise their sense of public responsibility.

THE MANAGER

This is a lifetime in which the universe supports Capricorn North Node people taking public positions and pursuing professional goals. They do especially well when they are in charge, because they are excellent managers. They are most confident when they approach a situation from a position of authority; this applies to both their personal and professional lives.

Also, in the process of managing others, these folks learn how to better manage themselves. For that to occur, they need to manifest integrity and an absolute commitment to keeping their word. In order to stay in touch with their power, Capricorn North Node people must be on time, do what they say they are going to do, be honest with others, and always behave in a way that promotes self-respect. This will make their lives strong. They are not allowed to "get away with" childish or irresponsible behavior.

From past lives, these natives developed tremendous emotional sensitivity. When they take a moment to "tune in" to the emotional states of others, they accurately understand other people's needs and concerns and can speak to them in a way that rallies the necessary mental *and* emotional support to reach the goal. They do this automatically, although it is a gift that most other people do not possess. In this lifetime, they also have the gift of seeing the bigger picture and being aware of the correct path to follow in order to achieve goals. This is a new gift (not from past lives), which they must begin to exercise in order to recognize that they have it. These gifts make them highly successful as managers because they're managing and motivating with an awareness of how others are feeling and directing them with understanding.

Capricorn North Node people become upset when those in higher positions do not manage them—or others—well. Something within them deeply resents mismanagement from lack of knowledge and/or insensitivity, because they instinctively know how to manage in a way that inspires willing support without diminishing others. They can become very unhappy and critical. They tend to hover around taking responsibility, and they're filled with opinions about how things should be run. They come close to "stepping over the line" when someone else is in charge because they think they should "run the show"—and indeed they should! They are often afraid to take charge, and at the last minute they say: "Oh, no—*you* do it, and I'll help you." When they hold back, they never really know if their ideas would work.

Because these folks do have a talent for humane and wise management, they have the responsibility to try to shift the way any mismanagement is handled when a lot of people are being affected. They need to apply for a promotion or otherwise do what they can to bring good management to the situation by sharing their knowledge in appropriate ways. For instance, if their feelings are hurt owing to insensitive management, they could communicate it in a responsible way: "You may not be aware of it, but it hurt me very much when . . ." and then let the manager know what can be done to make it right. "When you changed my title it hurt me very much. I respond better when I have a title that gives me a feeling of importance." By helping others to learn better management, they validate their own knowledge and satisfy their sense of mission.

SEIZING OPPORTUNITIES

Capricorn North Node people don't usually see the vision of what can be. They are generally good at whatever they are doing, they like the safety of it, and they're hard workers; but they are not accustomed to recognizing opportunities. It's important for them to seize opportunities in order to avoid regrets later in life.

When these folks allow themselves to become too limited in their own worlds, they can't envision possibilities for the future. They see other people taking risks and admire them for it, but they are reluctant to do the same because they are afraid of losing what they have. They must recognize that safety can lead to stagnation.

This is a lifetime for learning to take advantage of opportunities. They need to focus on one goal and then make a 100 percent commitment to reach it. The instant they make the commitment, they have the power to do it—and suddenly opportunities stream across their path. As they take each opportunity and complete it, they have taken one more step toward accomplishing their final goal. Each time they complete a step, the energy of success feeds them power and confidence to seize the next opportunity. They gain so much strength and competence from the path itself that by the time they reach their goal they are fully qualified—and centered inwardly—to be in that position.

RECOGNIZING OPPORTUNITIES

Owing to so many past lifetimes spent in family environments, it's natural that Capricorn North Node people think in a supportive way rather than an opportunistic way. They have a natural desire to help people, and this is why they attract people who need help. But they need to be open to the possibility that they could help the other person and help themselves at the same time, creating a win/win situation. In this incarnation they are learning to utilize the opportunities life brings to further their own position, prove their own competence, and personally get "on top."

For example, I had a Capricorn North Node friend who sold life insurance. One of his clients died. My friend was working with the widow, who now had a large business and didn't know what to do with it. Wanting to help out, my friend connected this woman with a business broker, and she received a lot of money and some very valuable stock from the deal. The broker asked my friend: "What do you want out of this?" He answered: "Well, I just want her to come out all right." He should have made a commission and gotten some stock, but these folks often miss opportunities that fall in their laps in just this way, and then regret it later.

They must be alert for unexpected opportunities, which are gifts life wants to bring them. If they miss the opportunity by virtue of their naïveté, someone else will point it out to them as the business broker did. Owing to their lack of past-life experience, Capricorn North Node people can't expect to always spot opportunities on their own—but they can listen to others. When someone asks them a question regarding personal gain for themselves, their best bet is to say: "Gosh, let me think about it, and I'll get back to you." They need to slow down and give themselves time to think it over.

Life and other people know, on a deep level, that these folks are not used to being in the world. So it's perfectly fine for them to check out what is fair by asking others who are already successful in the world. Better yet, they could say to the person who is pointing out the opportunity: "What do *you* think would be fair in this case? What would *you* do if you were in my position?"

Capricorn North Node people are highly active and tend to act without thinking. But restless, nondirected motion is counterproductive for them. They become so involved in doing that they don't stop to think about where their energy is—or is not—taking them, what the end result will be, or how it will affect other people. They must be more aware of the possible consequences of their actions and deliberately channel their energy in ways that will help them get on top of things. Since they are responsible for the results, it behooves them to take charge of the process to ensure that the results are in alignment with what they want.

For example, I had a client whose father was a Capricorn North Node person. She came from a very close family, and over the years her uncles and other relatives had given her father many opportunities to become wealthy. They brought him real estate deals, business partnerships, and investments. But her father stood firm: "No, I'm a working man; I don't invest." So he never bought his own home or invested for his future or the future of his family. He took care of day-to-day responsibilities, working long hours six days a week, but never took the initiative to be responsible in a future-oriented, sensible way.

Today my client's uncles and cousins are all wealthy, but her father is running out of money in his retirement and doesn't understand how he got into this situation. He just kept putting one foot in front of the other, going along in his comfort zone. Subconsciously, he was thinking that someone else would take responsibility, which equals "how to lose" for Capricorn North Node people.

These folks often get "stuck" in a conservative position as a way to avoid "upsetting the apple cart" or risking emotional responses from others. Also, by supporting the established way of doing things, they are less likely to have to take a stand. Until they understand that this is a lifetime of accepting opportunities, they don't want to take risks. They are afraid of losing the day-to-day security of their stable life and of taking responsibility for change.

I had a client with this nodal position who ran a small franchise business and rented an office in a large building. He was approached by the owner of the building with the opportunity to purchase it for a good price. My client didn't take it because he didn't have the money. He might have found a way to do it, but he didn't see the opportunity. His first thought was: "Why would I want the burden of owning an office when I can rent it?" The property later sold for such a high price that my client would rather not even have known about it!

In becoming goal oriented, these folks are learning how to use every "obstacle" to their advantage, so that everything becomes a stepping-stone for reaching their goal. As factors they didn't anticipate arise to distract them, they are learning to see the larger picture and regard everything as an opportunity they can use to their advantage, rather than becoming emotionally overwhelmed.

For example, if the Capricorn North Node is training for a marathon and strains a calf muscle so he can't run for a few weeks, he should use the time to develop his upper-body strength. If success is in his mind, he can accept everything that happens and use it to his advantage. The sense of self-sufficiency gained through this process will be enormous, as these natives recognize that all along they had the qualities they needed to manifest their dreams.

CONVERTING EMOTIONAL ENERGY INTO POWER

Owing to many past incarnations immersed in family life and focused on feelings, in this lifetime Capricorn North Node people are born with direct access to raw emotion. The only problem is that they're stuck in the middle of it! Emotion is an incredible power, and they are learning how to direct it in a positive way.

The irony is that these folks always seem to think they lack the positive qualities inherent in the negative emotion they are holding. For example, those who have a lot of pent-up anger generally feel lacking in assertiveness, initiative, courage, and independence—aspects of the positive side of the raw emotional energy whose negative expression is anger. By consciously directing this energy into a take-charge attitude, it will naturally be discharged in a constructive direction—working for them rather than against them.

Interestingly, in astrology the same planet that rules initiative, courage, assertiveness, and independence—Mars—also rules anger. To get the angry energy out in a positive form, Capricorn North Node people must take charge, assert themselves, and take the initiative in all areas of their lives.

For example, I had a client with this nodal position who went out of her way to take a friend to a big clothing sale. They arranged to go at 1:00 in the afternoon. My client was free until 6:30, when she had another appointment. However, her friend arrived late, took an inordinate amount of time at the sale, and insisted on "primping" in the bathroom before going home. My client became more and more angry as she watched the time slipping away. She mentioned to her friend that she had a 6:30 appointment, but the friend didn't seem to care. In the end, my client was late for her appointment and felt angry and frustrated throughout the rest of the evening.

How could she have converted the angry energy into initiative? She could have taken charge at the very beginning and said: "We have to be done shopping by 5:00." By stating the goal at the very beginning, these folks can bypass getting angry when they don't get their way. When their motive is pure—they want to help—they need to let others know in advance what the parameters are: "I'll help you with this, and I need to be done at this time. Does that work for you?" There will be awareness and agreement about what is going on—and they will have converted anger into executive energy.

HEALING THEME SONG *

As music is an empowering medium for emotionally supporting us in taking risks, I have written a healing song for each nodal group to help shift its energy in a positive way.

GOING HOME

The message of this song is meant to effortlessly shift Capricorn North Nodes' consciousness into a more courageous mode, encouraging them to leave the confining safety of the home they know and reach for a new home of splendid accomplishment!

Selected lyrics:

> *Have you ever felt like I do*
> *Knowing you must walk on ahead*
> *And take the next step into something new?*
> *You can't see beyond the level you're on*
> *Afraid to let go because inside you know*
> *There's no returning—back to where you've been?*
>
> *The level you're on isn't working*
> *Let go of the past and keep walking*
> *Think you're leaving home?*
> *No, no! You're going, you're going, you're going Home!*

---

* These lyrics are set to music and sung in their entirety on the CD and cassette tape "Unfolding As It Should."

North Node in Aquarius

and North Node in the 11th House

OVERVIEW

Attributes to Develop

Work in these areas can help uncover hidden gifts and talents

- Objectivity (seeing the "total picture")
- Desire for friendship
- Making decisions for the group's best interest
- Willingness to share unconventional ideas
- Willingness to champion humanitarian causes
- Active participation in groups
- Awareness of equality
- Relating to others as individuals, apart from their specific roles (gardener, doctor, lover, etc.)
- Creating win/win situations
- Recognizing how others are special

Tendencies to Leave Behind

Working to reduce the influence of these tendencies can help make life easier and more enjoyable

- Insistence on getting one's way
- Making changes just to exercise authority
- Attachment to taking risks (romance or gambling)
- Willfulness and stubbornness
- Attachment to the need for approval
- Melodramatic tendencies
- Doing what's expected instead of following one's heart
- Unbridled passion—going to extremes
- Unawareness of others' importance
- Prideful responses based on fear

ACHILLES' HEEL/TRAP TO AVOID/THE BOTTOM LINE

The Achilles' heel Aquarius North Node people need to be aware of is their need for others' approval ("My survival depends on others giving me approval") and thinking that if they have others' approval their life is on the right track. But it's a bottomless pit: Aquarius North Node people can never get enough approval to feel satisfied or to feel free to be themselves. Actually, for them the approval of others is a false barometer. They must risk *disapproval* and be true to their own unorthodox ideas in order to develop the deeper and more satisfying feeling of *self-approval.*

The trap that Aquarius North Node people fall into is an unending search for risk taking—especially in romance ("If I can just have a happy love life, then I will feel complete and can begin to do my part to help the planet"). However, if they don't balance this romantic energy with a daily commitment to some type of humanitarian cause, it becomes too intense and they inadvertently destroy the very relationship they want so badly.

The bottom line is that they'll never feel free to dedicate themselves to humanitarian concerns unless they can forget their personal desires. When they add their considerable talents to making universal causes successful, their efforts are energizing and rewarding for everyone concerned. The irony is that when Aquarius North Node people dedicate themselves to a larger cause, they find that the universe will fulfill them on the personal level as well. They need only be mindful of the old adage: "Be careful what you ask for, because you just might get it"!

WHAT THESE PEOPLE REALLY WANT

What these people really want is to be in love: to be adored and share "center stage" with someone who returns their passion. To reach this goal they must learn to go with the flow—to tell the universe what they want and let life (with its perfect timing) bring others who will recognize and adore them. They need to learn to receive love naturally—to be alert to the window of opportunity and respond to those who come into their lives to love them. Spending time with like-minded people, openly expressing their unorthodox ideas and visions of the future, attracts lovers who can also be friends and give them the support they need. When they focus on enacting their altruistic dreams, life will send them special people to charge their dreams with romantic energy.

TALENTS/PROFESSION

These people are effective with groups, as they can see how to promote open, harmonious cooperation. Their interests are nonpartisan, so they are capable of doing what's best for the group as a whole. They are successful at furthering idealistic causes or humanitarian goals in which they believe. Aquarius North Node people are good in positions that require objectivity; they succeed as scientists, astrologers, electricians, technicians, computer experts, or in any occupation where the ability to see the future and bring it into the present is an asset. They are successful and happy in work that brings innovative ideas to the public. These natives produce positive results through their own properly applied creative energy, and they are able to see things through to completion. Broadcast work in radio or television is another field in which they have innate talents.

Additionally, Aquarius North Node people are extremely creative and ready to bring enthusiasm, passion, and raw energy to get any job done. When they use their determination to carry through in ways that empower the group or further a higher cause, they energize others. However, if they willfully enter professions that spotlight themselves rather than a higher principle (for example, movie star, corporate head, military or political figurehead), it leaves them hardened and unable to relate to others with equality. They are better off in fields where they can use their skills to further important universal causes.

HEALING AFFIRMATIONS SPECIFIC TO AQUARIUS NORTH NODE

- "When I release willfulness, I win."
- "I don't know what 'ought' to be."
- "When I do what's best for everyone involved, I win."
- "Once I decide what I want, the universe will bring it to me."
- "I don't have to dominate others to feel okay about myself."

PERSONALITY

PAST LIVES

Aquarius North Node people were kings and queens in past lives, or entertainers—people accustomed to being "special." Receiving all that applause and admiration formed an ego encrustation that now keeps them from feeling equal with others—they came into this incarnation still feeling "special."

To regain a sense of equality and belonging, these folks need to give others all the excess energy of fame that was given to them, and they can do it by using their tremendous strength to further humanitarian causes. They are here to help bring in the New Age. Their destiny is to come down from their isolated thrones and re-establish themselves as part of the collective.

When something unfortunate happens, they tend to respond with: "To *me*? It's happening to *me*?" They don't believe they are deserving of bad luck. One of the lessons they're learning is that "life" happens to everyone. But from past incarnations of privilege, these folks are outraged when they are treated like everyone else—they're naïve and spoiled.

In other past-life positions of rulership—as chiefs, kings, dictators, or heads of household—they were Very Important People (VIPs) and accustomed to getting their way. Thus, they tend to be demanding and take it as an affront when others don't heed their wishes, although they do have good hearts. They have so much emotional energy that they often bulldoze others without even realizing it. They are experts at pushing the energy of the id to obtain the results they want, and in this incarnation they are here to share the power of their will with others. They need to consciously focus on the people they interact with and encourage them to get in touch with their own needs and to manifest their own dreams!

CONFIDENCE AND WILLPOWER

Because Aquarius North Node people overdeveloped their will in past lives, in this incarnation it is sometimes out of control—trying to change things, even against their best interests, just for the sake of change. They may be having a nice time in the most pleasant circumstance, when suddenly their will flares up and demands to have its way. This can be very disconcerting. Aquarius North Nodes' best bet to re-establish equality when this happens is to acknowledge what's going on: "Sorry—that was my will getting out of hand again. What did you say your idea was?"

These folks were also well-known artists and other highly creative people in past lives. This caused them to develop an attachment to pride, arrogantly promoting their vision above all others. Their powerful will works to their advantage when they apply it to reach a goal, as it gives them the strength and determination to see difficult projects through to completion; but it's a negative influence when it spreads indiscriminately into other areas of their life. They have spent so many lifetimes building ego, determination, and personal will that they lost their group awareness. Thus, in this incarnation they need to intentionally expand their thinking to include the individual needs of others.

Their will must be focused on promoting the general good in order to be supported by others. Problems arise when Aquarius North Nodes try to control every step of how their dreams are manifested. If they try to control the process, frustration results. *What* they want is valid; but they are learning to release attachment to *how* it comes about. The universe wants to meet their needs, and as they learn to bypass their ego, all they require will come to them.

Aquarius North Node people do have an innate confidence in their power to overcome life's obstacles. Perhaps this is why they have such tremendous resilience and are able to bounce back from catastrophes with a happy heart and a spirit that is willing to go on to the next adventure. They accurately appraise their talents and needs, and then set about creating positive solutions. They don't seek security through conventional means—they depend on their own wits to ensure their destiny.

In past lives these folks did everything on their own, and this is one reason they are so willful. They push until the desired objective is obtained or until the resistance is so great that they simply have to give up. When they finally do let go of something that isn't working, they see a higher answer for why the situation didn't work out as they wanted. And they have lots of help: The Angels and their own intuition will show them the larger picture, and they can count on help from friends who share the same ideals. This is not a "do it yourself" lifetime for Aquarius North Node people; when they allow others to help them reach their goals, it creates a lot of positive, reciprocal energy.

TAKING RISKS

Aquarius North Node people hate to lose when they take risks. Even in playing a simple card game or gambling with low stakes, when money is involved these folks are not "good sports." They take it very seriously and forget that it's a game. They were gamblers in past lives, so now they're not afraid to take risks. Yet owing to a lack of objectivity, they are generally not good gamblers in this lifetime.

These folks never stop to think about the potentially disastrous consequences of whatever risk they are taking—consequences that would cause those in other nodal groups to shudder! They think they are invincible. Often they don't slow down long enough to evaluate the odds, weigh the situation, and make a practical appraisal that takes into account the wishes of others. They feel an incredible surge of emotional energy, and they take the leap.

Consider love affairs. When Aquarius North Node's passion is ignited she wants to jump in and invest 100 percent of her devotion—and her mind will create whatever fantasy is necessary to keep the fervor going. She only sees positive qualities in the other person and puts him on a pedestal, making the relationship bigger than life—which creates the emotional charge to which she is addicted.

She is so completely and quickly invested that the stakes of winning or losing the love object become exaggerated. This blurs her vision, and she often finds herself in the middle of a drama where she is the only player. It's the same in business deals. If she thinks she's going to make a "killing" following her gambling instincts, she sets herself up for loss. It is important that she take her time and not gamble with more resources than she can afford to lose, whether it's her money or her heart!

When Aquarius North Node people blindly follow passion (the "high" that accompanies what appears to be an "easy win"), they always lose, whether the situation is a love affair or a financial gamble. When passion is aroused, their best bet is to force themselves to slow down and evaluate the risk. Then they will have the clarity to make a wise decision. They lose when their only goal is self-gratification. When higher, altruistic "stakes" are involved—an objective awareness of the other person's situation—it gives them the "edge"—the expanded vision they need to strategize success- fully.

OVERDEVELOPED EGO

Aquarius North Node people have spent so many past lives developing the ego that the superego was neglected. (Here, "id" refers to primal needs and desires, "ego" to the aspect of self that mediates those wants with the outside world, and "superego" to an awareness of other people's needs, society's mores, etc.)

All the past lives spent building the ego have given these folks the power to get what they want. However, sometimes they become so involved in getting what they want that they don't stop to make sure it answers a true need (id). Or they may not get what they want because they discount the superego and forget to ask themselves whether what they want is going to diminish or benefit the other people involved. In this incarnation Aquarius North Nodes need to develop their connection to the superego: The stronger this connection, the more effective their use of personal ego in this lifetime will be.

Aquarius North Node people's primary lesson is to transform their over-active ego into a vehicle for furthering the evolution of humankind. To rein in the ego requires a spiritual connection and strong self-discipline. They simply must not allow themselves to indulge in petty, negative emotional states. Those patterns of thinking feed their egos and hurt their hearts. Others may "get away with it," but these natives don't. They have an overabundance of highly charged creative emotional energy, and whatever they focus on expands and assumes a life of its own. They must turn their backs on thoughts that promote envy, arrogance, and pride—it is dangerous for them to indulge in *any* negativity.

They are well equipped to use their powerful will in this lifetime—to keep the ego from feeding them counterproductive thoughts. For example, when things don't go their way these folks tend to blame themselves or others for the outcome and become very frustrated. This is the time to stop the bombardment of negative thoughts and remind themselves: "I don't know what ought to be." That thought, summoned at key moments, stops their runaway will and brings them peace.

Affirmations are excellent in helping them break free from negative thoughts: "I am filled with loving kindness. Love permeates my being." By deliberately repeating this type of thought during the day, they can recon-nect with their true nature.

Aquarius North Nodes can also work to free themselves from ego entrap-ment by ceasing to judge and compare themselves with other people. "Well, she's better off than I am. She's got more public recognition, more money, more property . . ." Such comparisons make them angry and envious. They may look at someone else and think: "She has a less prestigious job, she makes less money, she doesn't have a good relationship . . ." and then begin to feel superior. They always lose when they judge in this way, be-cause it precludes any true connection or mutual support. And if they resent someone who is close to them, they do not feel good about themselves.

To avoid falling into this trap, they need to recognize when it's happening and immediately substitute other thoughts: what to buy for dinner, what to do at work, and so on. They also need to recognize that whether a person is striving to become president of the United States, earn a college degree, or make enough money to feed the family, the struggle is the same. If Aquarius North Node people look beyond external appearances and realize that we all share the same struggle, they will relax and feel equal with others again.

These natives were kings and queens in past lives, and they were not petty. They must use their innately regal qualities of dignity, benevolence, and determination to rise above petty emotional reactions unbefitting the temperament of royalty.

ARROGANCE

Arrogance is inherent in Aquarius North Node people, as they have spent many past lives in positions "above" others. The energy of arrogance can result in isolation, preventing them from getting and keeping those things in life that are most important. However, arrogance can also be translated into a force that empowers them to do their part to bring about evolutionary change and help initiate the New Age for their generation.

These folks think: "My way is best. If I ruled the universe, things would be a lot better." When they say "my way is best," the energy of arrogance is driving them to solve problems and contribute to what is happening on the planet. Nonetheless, it must be coupled with humility: "My vision is best, but maybe I don't always know the best way to *implement* it—the vision may be coming about in a way I didn't anticipate."

When the idea that "my way is best" is strongly based in a perception of what's going on in the larger picture, then Aquarius North Nodes' way generally *is* best—if everyone involved is taken into account. But if it's: "I want my way regardless of what others want," then the approach doesn't work. These folks need to be willing to be flexible—not so attached to a certain sequence of events that they miss the opportunity being presented.

Suspending Judgment

Because of past lives of privilege, Aquarius North Node people expect things to work to their advantage. If an unfortunate event occurs, their first response is often indignation: "I don't deserve it!"—which implies that there might be other people who deserve misfortune more than they do. When they think in those terms, they lose touch with their innate generosity and start feeling more special than others—and that's when others take a stand against them. (It's the "Marie Antoinette syndrome": Their pompous behavior provokes others to bring them down.) But these folks are operating from a basic naïveté; even when they provoke others, they don't realize they are doing it.

These folks *are* operating from an inner framework of goodness and kindness, are basically well disposed toward others, and believe in the goodness of life. Because of these attributes, they generally seem to have "good luck." However, when things don't go their way, the spoiled child within often emerges and they feel outraged at the universe and at life itself. Their anger compounds the problem because they block their receptivity to good and get emotionally lost in the bad luck—which creates *more* bad luck!

If they allow themselves to sink deeper into negative comparisons, their attitude toward people becomes either resentment or disdain. This makes them unpopular—the people they disdain want to bring them down, and those they perceive as "better off" are not inclined to help them because they can sense Aquarius North Nodes' resentment.

Aquarius North Node people are learning to suspend judgment and take the time to get to know others more deeply: to investigate *why* others think the way they do and to find out what they may have in common. They cut themselves off from many happy interactions because they are so quick to judge superficial appearances. The only way out of this self-destructive pattern is for Aquarius North Nodes to consciously evoke their inherent generosity. Through many past incarnations of being "special" to others and protected by the universe, these folks have become generous and usually give back from their good fortune. When these natives bless the efforts of others and rejoice in others' victories, they open the floodgates to their own good fortune.

PRACTICING APPRECIATION

Another strategy that will keep open the gates to good fortune is for Aquarius North Node people to consciously appreciate the good things that are already coming their way. It's important that they come from a place of appreciation rather than arrogance. For example, if they are invited to an exclusive party and inwardly respond with arrogance ("Well, it's about time they invited me!"), they may feel happy temporarily, but this attitude often attracts misfortune. If for some reason the invitation is withdrawn, their arrogance may cause them to react with: "How dare he do that! I deserve to go to that party! Life is against me!"

Unfortunately, since they have enormous creative energy, focusing on the negative becomes a constant battle. But if they believe in—and are receptive to—life's goodness, when opportunities are presented they recognize them and naturally move in the direction of success.

For example, I had a client with this nodal position who had an accident and broke her pelvis. As she was carried out on a stretcher, she said to herself: "Life loves me [all Aquarius North Node people know this!] and something good will come out of this." Indeed, during the time she was bedridden she wrote a proposal for a new project that propelled her business to the national level. A relationship that had ended came back into her life to help her, and as of this writing the two are still happily together. Her whole life was redirected and changed because her receptivity to good allowed her to use this seemingly negative event to her advantage.

On the other hand, I had a friend with this nodal position whom I agreed to meet at a popular New York spot before going to the theater. I couldn't find her inside, so I went outside and found her waiting in line with about thirty other people—and there was a very handsome man standing right behind her in line. She was furious with me for being late and spent the entire time walking to the theater "making me wrong." What she was *really* upset about was the fact that she hadn't been allowed inside, which she interpreted as a personal insult. (These folks can be as sweet as honey when they are being treated with deference, but heaven help those around them if they are treated as equal with others—as "commoners"!) She didn't get her way, so she made everyone around her miserable (including herself) and missed the generous opportunity that life had brought her: the chance to meet the handsome man who was behind her in the line!

These people are learning to trust the Flow. They are very generous, and life responds to them with generosity. If they don't get their way—or if someone says "no" to them—they need to expand their vision to see what other opportunity life is bringing. They must let go of their limited picture of what will make them happy and be open to life's bounty—then a wealth of new experiences will bring them unexpected pleasure.

NEED FOR APPROVAL

APPLAUSE AND ACCLAIM

Aquarius North Node people have had too many lifetimes of being the center-stage star and having constant public attention, so in this incarnation part of them resists being in that position. Fear of not playing their role correctly and inviting disapproval is a great emotional risk, and now they are generally not rewarded when they take the "star" position.

In this lifetime the enthusiastic applause of others does not nurture these folks. But they are great audience members, supporting others in taking center stage. Their natural enthusiasm evokes excitement from the rest of the audience. In this way, they give back the energy of approval to others and remain free to be themselves.

If they can't avoid being the center of attention, their best bet is to shift the focus to something outside themselves. For example, if Aquarius North Node is a public speaker, he could focus the audience's attention on the topic. If he wins approval for his principles or projects rather than seeking it only for himself, his enthusiasm becomes boundless and he has tremendous creative power. Approval is like food for Aquarius North Node people. Conversely, their fear of disapproval may be so enormous that they avoid sharing their true opinions or feelings.

In past lives, Aquarius North Node people were VIPs who had to spout the conventional line—that was part of their job. However, in this incarnation they are here to share unconventional knowledge, and they may not always get approval because they are voicing something new. People seldom accept new knowledge easily because it takes time to see its value, come into alignment with it, and integrate it. These folks need to be willing to risk disapproval in voicing their innovative ideas. They must allow themselves to feel the empowerment of their own self-approval.

When they see themselves as channels for knowledge to flow through, it frees them enormously because they don't have to be "right." It also frees them from the vulnerability of needing approval from others. When they realize that they're just "picking up" free-floating ideas and bringing them through, then whether other people approve or not isn't a factor.

When these folks are in group situations, very often they have excellent ideas that others accept with enthusiasm. An idea comes to fruition and no one remembers that it was Aquarius North Node's idea. These folks may have delusions of grandeur, but when they keep a low profile they reach their greatest potential and have the most success.

Not waiting for applause keeps them unencumbered to go on to the next great thing. When they receive a lot of attention, it blocks their access to new ideas. Thus, their fate is to work behind the scenes and with others to make things happen. Then, if fame should come to them, they can accept it in a balanced way and not take it personally.

PERSONAL VALIDATION

These folks want everyone to like them—it's the motive behind much of what they do. If they do something and *don't* get validation, they have a hard time dealing with it. Because of past-life experiences, they subconsciously use approval from others as a barometer of whether they are on track and doing a good job. On one level, Aquarius North Node people are still burdened by thinking they have to "live up to" an image. Although in this lifetime they rebel against that restriction, they are so accustomed to sacrificing their real selves to perform a "role" and earn approval that they all too easily behave in ways they feel are expected—contrary to their own hearts.

Their desire for approval often causes them tremendous inner conflict. They are so aware of others' responses to them that they often manipulate their image in the others' eyes. They don't respond naturally to the flow of events because they want to say exactly the "right thing" to win approval.

But by focusing so much on themselves, they inadvertently deplete their natural self-confidence. If they continually worry about how they appear to others and need a certain amount of approval to be happy, the balance is very fragile. They are under constant pressure to present an image they think is required for the positive feedback they think they need.

These folks are much better off when they respond authentically from who they really are—and then see how the *other* person responds and whether or not they approve of the other person. When they interact honestly with another person, the other's response will show them whether they want to spend time with that person. This is a stronger, healthier position for the Aquarius North Node person.

NEEDS

BALANCING THE EGO

Before Aquarius North Node people can gain the self-confidence needed to successfully pursue their goals, the hindrance of excessive personal ego must be discarded. The ego has been so built up that in this incarnation they practically have to starve it to regain inner balance. Their hunger for prestige can be a bottomless pit, causing them to live beyond their means, adopt a superior attitude, and always want "more, more, more." Others are allowed to enhance and expand the ego, but Aquarius North Nodes are not. Their desire for acclaim can too easily become an ego trip with an arrogant attitude that summons disaster. So the universe often keeps success from them until they learn to respond in a balanced and gracious way.

Life gives them lots of chances. Because they are inherently confident, energetic, and willing to take risks, their spirit of enterprise rightfully puts them in a position to be victorious. And then life watches to see how they handle each success: If they become pompous, life removes some of the spoils. However, if they handle small victories graciously, life brings an abundance of what they seek—as long as they avoid pride and arrogance and continue to receive with thankful humility.

Aquarius North Node people have a mechanism in the psyche that reflects on self-glory and inflates the ego—then the power goes out of their lives and they attract defeat. Whenever they notice the mechanism activating, their best bet is to immediately disengage it. They must stop thinking how glorious they are and consciously remind themselves: "Okay, I don't know if I'm going to win or lose, but I think maybe I could help others have a positive experience." This will allow them to re-establish a balanced perspective.

Another approach to circumvent the problem of overdeveloped ego is to deliberately use the ego to benefit other people or humanitarian causes. These people were royalty in past lives; now, by focusing on benefiting "the people" instead of enhancing their own reflection, they will win.

DELUSIONS OF GRANDEUR

Aquarius North Node people have vivid imaginations and often entertain themselves with fantasies of grandeur. For instance, if they become bored in their professional life, they may imagine they're going to write a best-selling book and appear on all the talk shows. It doesn't matter if the fantasy is unrealistic; it's pleasant and becomes satisfying in its own right. Unfortunately, such fantasies take the "edge" off, giving Aquarius North Nodes a certain level of satisfaction that blocks creative action.

The irony is that these folks have all the creative power they need to make their fantasies come true—but their *motive* determines the outcome. In the example, if the motive for writing the book is fame and glory, success will elude them because, in this incarnation, it's set up for the ego to defeat them whenever they try to feed it. However, if the motive is to help other people, there's no limit to the heights they can attain! The humanitarian side of their nature must be developed.

Another problem with fantasizing is that it moves reality into the future, which makes Aquarius North Node people much less effective in handling the present. For example, if they focus on fantasies of fame as authors of best-selling books, they may pass up opportunities to write articles for a local magazine. They miss the stepping-stones that would lead to their dreams actually coming true.

The same tendency undermines their relationships. If they are romantically attracted to someone, they begin fantasizing and make the person the ideal future mate of their fantasy. They begin living so much in the future that they start relating to their partner as that ideal person and miss the steps in the present that could, over time, bring about what they want. Thus, their challenge is to stop fantasizing and, instead, respond to the opportunities unfolding in the here and now. When there is not a fantasy attached to their present circumstances, they always know what to do to succeed. Luckily Aquarius North Node people have plenty of will and mental discipline, because it takes every ounce of both to keep their minds from wandering into the dimension of fantasy and delusions of grandeur that block action in the here and now.

To ensure success, these folks always have to be aware of their intent. When they allow the motive of self-aggrandizement to take the upper hand, it immediately drains the energy they need to succeed. For example, if they want to help people by starting a meditation group, they need to stay focused on their altruistic motives. In this way they will have the energy, clarity, and joy required to manifest the idea. The way to make their dreams happen will occur to them as they move ahead, and doors will magically open to make the path easier.

However, sometimes they allow themselves to think of personal gain or loss: "Gosh, maybe I'll become a guru and people will begin following me," or "I wonder what my professional peers will think if they find out I'm into meditation." Either way, as soon as they allow themselves to think of personal gain or loss, all the energy for accomplishment begins to dissipate and they end up doing nothing.

Also, involvement with ego interferes with their vision to such an extent that they may overlook what people actually need from them. This limits their success. But when their conscious motive is 100 percent altruistic, they will tune in to the specific help needed on the planet at a given time in a given situation. Once they truly see an existing need and respond to it from a place of nonego, they reap success and fame.

HUMILITY

These folks are better off when they choose a more humble path, walking away from the spotlight and acclaim. They instinctively seek credit and fame; but when they get it, it inflates their ego and they lose their sense of graciousness and equality. When Aquarius North Node people adopt an attitude of humility, their lives become magical and everything works to their advantage. They finally see clear, practical outlets for their gifts. But if they maintain a prideful position, their talents may not find expression so easily.

For example, I had a client with this nodal position who wrote a book containing many New Age ideas. Right away she swelled with pride, considering which major publisher she wanted to handle her book. It didn't occur to her that because she had no pre-established reputation in the field, she might also want to approach a smaller publishing house. The large publishing houses turned her down, she turned up her nose at starting smaller, and she ultimately abandoned the project. Everyone lost, including the people who would have benefited from her ideas if she had been willing to begin more modestly.

Arrogance can also be a problem when the universe sends others to help bring Aquarius North Nodes' ideas to completion. Often these natives don't want to share the credit or the money, and they don't want to lose control. They fear that if they work with others they may have to give up some of what they want. "Their way" and "their ideas" become paramount; they become less interested in solutions that will actually help other people—the humanitarian attitude they need to develop in this lifetime.

An example is my client whose husband, a North Node in Aquarius, was a therapist. He was writing an advice column to teenagers and showed his wife a response he was writing to a girl. The wife (my client) disagreed with his approach, and in this case her ideas were actually much better. Her husband was missing something, and he felt it too, yet he went ahead with his own ideas and never again showed her any other responses. If he had the humility to put the goal of helping first—regardless of whose idea it was—he would have been objective and open to her input.

These folks have their own vision and know exactly how they want it to turn out. They want to do it their way. However, if two people come together with a shared altruistic ideal or vision, that will become more important than either one's idea of how to get there. This is what actually happens when Aquarius North Node people are humble enough to work with others.

An Impersonal Perspective

Altruism

In this incarnation, Aquarius North Node people need to make a choice: personal, ego-centered life versus impersonal dedication to humanity. When they choose to focus on personal life, they lose; when they choose impersonal dedication to humanitarian causes, they win—and the personal life they always longed for is magically added!

To fulfill their need for appreciation, they need to get past the limitations of personal ego and give back to humankind as a whole—to find some humanitarian service or cause they can support. Dedicating their lives to something bigger than ego gives them a purity of purpose that enables them to invest themselves without taking the results personally. In fact, altruism helps them develop their tremendous capacity for self-confidence.

Otherwise there are times when they don't trust their motives. Especially during their youth, these folks may wonder if anyone really does things from pure altruism. But if their conscious intention is to help, their concentration will automatically be on the alert for whatever will work to get people what they need.

Aquarius North Nodes have such a generous nature that they often are devastated when others do not accept their gifts or respond with applause. They can prevent this problem by actively seeking information about what others want and need, and what they are doing that is keeping them from getting the response they want. These folks may have a tough time hearing feedback in a constructive way, but they are learning to see the larger view.

For example, if they write children's stories, they first find out which publishers are interested in that kind of story. If they receive a rejection slip, they should find out what the publisher needs and then tailor their creative product to fit, or write another story that better meets the publisher's needs.

Moreover, they are recognizing that they can't take credit for their ideas anyway, because none of them are truly "theirs"! New Age, innovative ideas are floating in the air, and Aquarius North Nodes' gift is that their "antennae" are tuned to the right frequency to pick them up. Recognizing this can release their fears of both success and failure, because their ideas really have nothing to do with them personally. Their job is simply to "pick up" the ideas and transmit them to others.

These folks have access to knowledge that helps free people. Thus, when their intention is to empower others, the motive is so clear that the necessary ideas just "come through"—intuitively, or from other people. The only way they can know which information is truly helpful in a particular situation is by paying attention to others' responses. Ideas that are useful will be well received. If Aquarius North Nodes share knowledge with others that is *not* accepted, it simply means they need to proceed to the next idea and see if that one is useful. Others will pull the knowledge they need from these folks—it's a very impersonal thing.

For example, if Aquarius North Node writes a book on philosophy and the publishers turn it down, perhaps that philosophy is not the vehicle people need in order to hear the message. However, if he presents the same message in a novel, perhaps there will be an instant demand. Aquarius North Node can tell by others' response which format is correct.

If Aquarius North Node people believe that by putting effort into helping their fellow beings something positive will come back to them, then they have endless energy to keep trying until they discover which of their talents others respond to in a positive way. Life is like a boomerang: When they use their creative energy to help others, whatever they need comes back to help them. There is great power for these folks in altruism. When the ego is not involved and they are not personally invested in the results, it's easy for them to become creatively involved. Self-gain will be a natural by-product. The universe keeps filling them up because they're passing on the benefits of their creative energy to others.

GAINING OBJECTIVITY

Aquarius North Node people need impersonal feedback to gain perspective, because they are so identified with themselves that they can't see themselves clearly. Input from someone they trust can be helpful—they want to see the larger view so they can cooperate and get what they desire! For example, in a romantic relationship they are usually blissfully ignorant of what is going on. Then, because of factors in the larger picture that they didn't see, they get hurt. To avoid emotional pain, they need an objective guidance system for their personal life.

These folks need to modify the ego and bring themselves into alignment with the Flow. The Esoteric Sciences (Astrology, Numerology, Tarot, Handwriting Analysis, etc.) can provide the objectivity to restrategize. These resources increase Aquarius North Nodes' powers of correct observation and modify their tendency to automatically react to situations in an ego-centered way. The I Ching is an excellent tool for this; it gives the "inside scoop" on what is troubling them, and it empowers them to come into alignment with what is actually happening.

Astrology is also an excellent tool for fostering objectivity: It allows them to see themselves and others impartially, releasing them from the frustration of trying to evoke things in the other person that are not there, and providing otherwise hidden knowledge of who they really are. It helps them lovingly accept themselves and others, and value others' individuality.

Aquarius North Node people are very talented in these sciences and could easily enter one of these fields professionally. They have an ability to "read the map" of the astrology chart, or the Tarot—any divination base that is an objective "launching pad" from which to direct their antennae toward the innovative knowledge that can help free themselves and others.

Another resource is their friends. They have great friendship karma. Honest feedback from friends can help them understand where ego is blocking their happiness. Gaining knowledge is their key to freedom, showing them how to avoid defeating patterns of ego expression. In this way, they gain a measure of control over their destiny.

When they step back and deliberately look at situations from the other person's perspective (what the other person wants and needs), then they can make choices in alignment with what will work for everyone—including themselves—in each situation. But ultimately, to gain the full measure of freedom and love they so fervently seek requires these folks to not only objectively view others but also objectively view themselves. They need to watch themselves brushing their teeth, walking down the street, interacting with others, and so on. As they begin to observe themselves in action, watching without judging, they gain the perspective to authentically be themselves without fear.

ALIGNING WITH THE FLOW

Aquarius North Node people are learning to recognize that if they can't make progress on a current project, the universe is trying to send them in a different direction. They should allow the flow of natural events to show them where to put their time and energy, rather than trying to dictate those decisions from their own point of view. If something doesn't turn out the way they want it, perhaps the outcome is destined to be something they aren't yet aware of.

They can free themselves of the negative and obsessive energy of: "I'm not getting my way; it's not turning out the way I envisioned" by allowing themselves to be distracted in a direction where they can constructively express their creative energies. They need to notice where the universe has opened the doors and be willing to walk through!

Rather than putting out so much personal effort, they need to relax and remain open to the Flow—then they will travel with true power behind them. For example, even though it's the job of Aquarius North Node to bring in the New Age, if they don't allow the Angels to help them, they will become too attached to their own personal effort and won't have the power they need to accomplish this goal. If they rest in the Flow, they will find themselves using minimal effort to accomplish maximum results.

RELEASING EXPECTATIONS

These folks sometimes inadvertently defeat their own happiness through simple misunderstanding. In past lives, others gave them what they wanted and they were happy. But in this lifetime, when others give them what they want, they don't feel as happy as they thought they would. This is because being so attached to a *specific idea* of what they need to be happy limits the bounty they can attract. In this lifetime their job is simply to be receptive, to see what life brings; they will discover that *this* will actually make them happy.

Aquarius North Node people are learning to release their expectations of what they *think* will bring them happiness and believe that life wants them to be happy. Then they can just accept the next thing along the road that brings them a feeling of joy. When they fight for something, they generally don't get it simply because the intensity of trying to grab it pushes it further away. In this lifetime they are learning to *receive* love. If they push with their will and get it, generally they aren't happy with it. They are learning that if life brings it *to* them, it is right for them at that time and they can enjoy it. Their greatest pleasure comes from experiencing with awe and gratitude the bounty of the Flow.

Many of their expectations come from the fact that they have already played out a situation in their head and given everyone their proper lines—so when they are actually with those people, they subconsciously force them into the role of their fantasy. This leads to two problems. First, when the other person doesn't go along with the script, Aquarius North Node is confused and angry; her expectations are disappointed. Second, when she's focused on the "script" she can't see what is happening in the present, so she loses touch with her ability to change the situation to her advantage.

Aquarius North Node people are learning that when they try to remind everyone else of their lines and expected behavior, they forget to play their own authentic part. They need to stand back and observe others objectively. Over time, the other person's qualities will become clear. The native won't be disappointed because she is simply observing who the other person is without any expectations. Then she can tune in to how the other person's behavior affects her. Rather than trying to change people, she can decide who she feels good spending time with.

A further advantage of this approach is that by allowing the other person to be himself, it gives Aquarius North Node space to be herself as well. Then, keeping her goal in mind, she can spontaneously express her reactions in ways that are appropriate to the situation as it unfolds.

CREATING WIN/WIN SITUATIONS

When Aquarius North Node people become indignant that others are getting something they are *not* getting, they may indulge in an overly dramatic reaction that alienates those around them and undermines their own position. This can be anything from a careless "attitude" on their part to a serious misunderstanding that eventually results in disaster. These folks are often too quick to resist the wills of others. When someone else asserts his or her will, these natives tend to automatically respond with resistance. It's like a reflex. Even if the other person's action or comment is based on wisdom, the natives' reaction will still be to try and get their way, which will be exactly the opposite of what the other person wants. This can cause others to lose interest in them.

When these folks use willfulness to achieve their goals, without considering the people involved, they alienate others. They tend to move too quickly; they see the goal and want to get there immediately. This short-circuits the entire process of cooperative partnership—for others as well as for themselves—and no one wins. Often the process is filled with a series of false starts and confusion—all because Aquarius North Nodes did not wait for the logical, successful pathway to reveal itself. They are learning to stand back and watch the situation: to observe what is occurring instead of always being so intensely involved. Then they will find themselves less threatened by others' assertiveness and less reactive in ways they later regret.

Aquarius North Node people can be so willful, and so intent on what they want, that they sometimes blatantly disregard whether or not something is fair for the other people involved. When they get a little "puffed up" with their own importance, it can lead to carelessness in their relationships with others. Although other people have helped them reach success, they may think they should have the lion's share of the rewards and forget to consider what is fair. When others become aware of their lack of concern, they may question these folks' good intentions and whether they can be trusted with leadership. Others become uneasy about how far Aquarius North Nodes would go to get their way. They need to let others see how they (the others) are also going to win, and then those people will be more supportive of the natives' plans.

These people are learning a very important lesson: Life has to be a win/win situation! Others won't want to play unless their own needs will be met. If Aquarius North Node people consider what is fair for others, it will help them relax about getting their way and create situations that are in everyone's best interests. Then others will welcome their enthusiastic participation. Also, they will gain a clearer perspective of the motives of the people around them. They may find that a person they have seen as an enemy is actually someone who truly wants to support them. By deliberately cultivating a humanitarian attitude and staying aware of the larger picture, their innate generosity is freed and their energy infuses a group bonding that empowers everyone.

RELATIONSHIPS

EQUALITY

In past lives others put Aquarius North Node people on a pedestal, and over many lifetimes they lost their awareness of how to be part of the "human collective." But this led to isolation and loneliness, and now they are re-establishing identity with humankind and gaining a sense of equality. When they focus on what they can do to enhance others, they begin to recognize that their happiness is not a by-product of getting their own way. Rather, it comes from the happiness of the "collective"—be it their partner, their family group, or the whole world.

RECOGNIZING OTHERS AS SPECIAL

One way these folks can break through the isolation of having been special in past lives is to begin recognizing the specialness in others. When they deliberately acknowledge and encourage the unique, creative life force in others, they feel energized, equal, and part of humankind again. They have a tremendous ability to put another person at "center stage." If they are ever in a situation where they lack confidence, all they have to do is put the spotlight on someone else. Then they will automatically feel more secure and at ease with themselves.

Aquarius North Node people have an incredible gift for friendship when they access it. Once they come down from their thrones and take an interest in others, they are joyously included. For this to happen, they need to develop a genuine curiosity about others: their lives and struggles. These folks are so charged with the creative energy of success that their confidence is infectious and encourages others to rise above their problems. Then every-one wins, because the Aquarius North Node finally feels loved and included for who he is as a person, rather than for the role he plays.

Their innate confidence, combined with their childlike trust, enables Aquarius North Node people to reach out freely to others, and they make friends easily when they want to. These folks have great friendship karma; if they relate to others from a position of friendship first, they have their best chance at a successful relationship—whether it be with a child, lover, spouse, parent, or co-worker. Cultivating friendship as the basis for all their relationships is the key for their success.

Friendship is an equal relationship in which both people objectively consider what is best for the other, supporting the other person in what will make him or her happy. For example, if a friend has a once-in-a-lifetime opportunity to accept a job offer 1,000 miles away, these natives will, without hesitation, encourage the friend to accept the job regardless of the fact that they will miss the friend.

Unselfishness in supporting the other person leads to wonderful friendships for Aquarius North Node people. Trust is built, because the other person sees that the native is truly thinking of what is best for the friend, without any ulterior motive. And these folks give great advice! Their friends are loyal because they feel the natives' enthusiasm and good intentions.

In romantic relationships, Aquarius North Nodes' tendency to feel "more special" than others sometimes defeats them. They do not usually initiate romantic situations, so it is often completely unexpected when someone is attracted to them. But if the feeling is mutual, their powerful passions are instantly aroused. The other person usually makes them feel very important. They are put on a pedestal, and past-life memories of being admired begin to stir.

If they don't recognize that the other person needs to admire them in order to fall in love, they lose perspective, begin to take their own importance seriously, and inadvertently start dominating the partner. This attitude can cause the partner to "turn off," and the Aquarius North Node is left with another romantic disappointment. The lesson is to remember that romance involves admiring the specialness *in each other*.

WORKING WITH OTHERS

Owing to their past-life experience, Aquarius North Node people instinctively approach a project with the idea of doing it by themselves, their way. But when they do, not a lot of energy comes back. They are better off uniting with peers who have similar ideals. This is why they have such excellent friendship karma: When they do things with others, they are filled with creative energy.

Anything they approach on their own becomes bogged down and difficult for them in this lifetime. They want to make all the decisions, but when others are involved, they're forced to stay open, so they naturally expand and become more innovative and creative. And much to their surprise, when they do link with others it's much more fun (even though they don't like sharing the control).

In choosing projects, their best bet is to follow the energy that attracts them. Once involved, if their energy soars, they are "on path." They should do what they can to creatively further the project. Every group has a need, and because their antennae are so sensitive, these natives can see innovative solutions that will create successful results for everyone. The more they give credit to just "seeing ideas" rather than personally "having ideas," the more ideas will come to them.

If they get feedback: "Your idea is great, but it needs more development," perhaps it's time to link with others to modify and develop it. Their motive is to help, and the universe will open the path to successful manifestation.

Sometimes Aquarius North Node people notice the talent and creativity of others and become envious. They don't want to admit that someone might be "better" than they are. Yet it is only when they access their natural generosity of spirit and stay focused from the perspective of equality that they become open to being successful themselves. Furthermore, it's important for them to generously acknowledge and appreciate others' talents, because their greatest individual power is expressed when uniting with others to reach a common goal. Moreover, just as others benefit when these folks point out ways they are special, Aquarius North Nodes also benefit by being open to what others consider special about *them*. The aspects that others value in them are the qualities they need to accentuate, the strengths they need to build to gain the influence they seek.

Another important factor is carefully choosing whom to work with. They do better with like-minded people who are not controlling and are open to new ways of doing things. Aquarius North Node people are kids at heart— they don't want any "adult" telling them what to do! They need to work with people who are generous, who respect them, and who value their ideas. When they involve others, their creative process becomes energized and the successes generated by the shared energy are far greater.

These folks have tremendous powers of persuasion. If their focus is on the "greater good" and their way of getting there is indeed a better way, they will have no problem persuading others. Indeed, others welcome their creative, innovative ideas. When they focus—and keep others focused—on the higher purpose that is being served, all self-defeating limitations of ego depart. The natives become objective and are able to access their power.

Aquarius North Node people are talented and have much to contribute, but they seldom achieve their highest goals when they resist sharing the credit and the glory. This is a group-oriented lifetime. It takes a lot of people to bring in a New Age, and when these folks unite with others to manifest new values and ideas, success comes easily and everyone has a lot more fun!

ROMANCE

Aquarius North Node people love being in love, but they need to apply the same unselfishness and objectivity in their love affairs as in their friendships. By taking the time to build a friendship before allowing romance to fully ignite, their willingness to "be there" for the other person comes through. This leads to trust, and the relationship has a chance at success.

These folks require equality in every area of their lives, especially romance and marriage. They need to meet their match: someone who is as strong as they are so they don't overshadow the other person. Both partners should feel complete in their own right. They need to make sure that their basic needs are being met through some vehicle other than the romantic partner. Then they can be a little more objective—not so desperate to get what they want—and they will be more successful with their relationships.

In romance, as soon as they are given special attention it activates past-life memories of when—to keep the attention and adulation going—they performed and gave the audience what it wanted. Now, in relationships, they inadvertently begin to "perform"—to be what they think the other person wants. They can become "people pleasers," which causes the other person to lose interest, and once again they experience romantic disappointment. They need to stay in touch with their own dreams and actively pursue their goals aside from the relationship.

Aquarius North Node people have an incredible capacity to give love; when they channel all that love into only one person, the receptacle isn't big enough to contain the energy. They need something bigger. That's why it is crucial not to focus exclusively on the object of their passion. If they want a romantic relationship to work, they must consciously divert some of their intense energy to other friendships and toward humanitarian causes.

PASSION

Passion is an intense configuration of vital life energy. When that level of energy is ignited between two people, an instinctive desire for union and bonding arises. However, the process of successful bonding takes time, and Aquarius North Node people don't want to wait. An addiction to romantic passion is a primary area of challenge for this nodal group.

Generally, the other person begins showing romantic interest in the native. At first, these folks don't "get it," but if the other person continues to pursue them, and some physical bonding takes place, then forget it! When passion hits (that is, a combination of physical "chemistry" and a person who meets their romantic ideals), they dedicate their lives to following that feeling and the person who activates it. Because they are so desperate for romantic passion, when it's activated it's like getting a summons. They want to live life without regrets of not having experienced the high points.

Past-life feelings of loyalty and allegiance emerge, and these folks become devoted to their romantic ideal. Suddenly these cheerful, friendly, and emotionally self-sufficient natives become totally influenced by the actions of the other person. If the relationship is going well, they float through the day in a state of bliss; but if their beloved isn't responding, they become insecure and depressed.

When they are apart from the beloved, Aquarius North Nodes' imaginations go wild. They use their enormous power of creative visualization to imagine all the possibilities of the relationship and to idealize the other person. Throwing caution to the wind, they immerse themselves in a blissful romantic fog. It doesn't matter how old they are; when passion hits they become like teenagers in love, which can cause problems in settling down to a committed relationship.

However, these folks usually don't get a chance to settle down with someone they are truly "in love" with—someone who fully activates their passion—because once passion takes over, they lose clarity. They may exaggerate the glory and attractiveness of the other person, put him or her on a pedestal, and feel "lesser" in comparison. They stop being themselves and try to "act out" the part they feel will make the other person love them. Then they can't see what's really going on, and they make foolish mistakes that sabotage the relationship. They pour too much intensity into the relationship too soon and inadvertently destroy it.

Sometimes they become so involved in the romance of their own inner drama that they lose touch with the partner: They don't hear what the other person is trying to communicate. The partner begins to feel that the Aquarius North Node is only interested in a love object, and the partner loses interest in the relationship. Then these folks' hearts are broken and they don't understand what happened.

They think they are giving, but how can they give when they are not even hearing what the other person needs? The first step is to disengage from their passions and take the time to become interested in the other person as an individual. They need to find out who the other person really is—his wants, problems, thoughts, and needs. They must establish a foundation of mutual trust, understanding, acceptance, and caring, upon which romantic passion can thrive.

Owing to their passionate instincts, Aquarius North Node people have a strong need to be in a relationship. But they tend to lose the relationships in which they feel profound mutual passion and often end up marrying people they care less deeply about. When they are with someone they enjoy but who doesn't arouse their passion, they can establish the distance to be themselves and make appropriate decisions. Their basic qualities of friendliness and support shine through, and the other person feels safe and desires a closer union with them.

Sometimes these relationships work out well. Having a marriage partner that is essentially a friend gives them the independence they need to focus their unlimited creative energy on humanitarian projects. As mates, these people are loyal and very committed to monogamy. However, if they are not getting the feeling of romance they need at home, they may become vulnerable to encounters outside marriage. Owing to their innate sense of loyalty, there's confusion when primary relationships become stale. But further down the road, if they meet someone who *does* inspire that romantic passion, they may throw their entire life aside to pursue it.

ACCEPTANCE AND TIMING

Aquarius North Node people are learning to accept love with thankfulness and humility, rather than overreaction. Underneath their need for approval, these folks carry the seed of: "I am not worthy of being loved." That is why they put out so much effort: They are trying to earn the right to be loved.

However, when someone genuinely falls in love with them (for themselves—not the "role" they are playing), at first they don't feel anything. Then, when they do "get it," if they feel a reciprocal attraction they overreact and send out signals that repel the other person. Subconsciously they push the other person away because they don't feel worthy of being loved.

Often these folks act very superior when someone falls in love with them. This is another type of overreaction. Someone wants to share the experience of romance with them—that's all—but they take it as though they are really something special! Then, while they are busy being "puffed up," the other person loses interest, never knowing that the native was deeply interested in return.

Aquarius North Node people need to recognize that within each of us is love itself, worthy of being recognized. When someone is attracted to them, it simply means that the frequency of love in that person is recognizing the frequency of love in the native. We all want to share the experience of love with someone with whom we resonate. Aquarius North Nodes are discovering how to graciously accept and flow with the experience of being loved.

Another lesson these folks are learning is the element of timing. They see what they want and they want it right away—and end up destroying it because they don't allow the timing to unfold naturally. This is especially a problem in intimate relationships. These natives are learning that what is meant to be theirs will come to them through its own perfect timing.

They love romance, the vitality of being totally involved in a situation that is in the midst of being created. It feels like gambling; but owing to their lack of objectivity, their timing is off. A successful gambler recognizes when it is appropriate to press forward and when to pull back.

But Aquarius North Node people think they can only move in fast-forward! They need to recognize that it takes time and cultivation to integrate individual energies and allow romance to develop successfully. Time is needed for each person to influence the other. There are times of coming together and times of pulling back to integrate and adapt to the other: to reflect on what's been said and come to understand the other person's mindset, values, character, dreams, and goals. These natives need to see how open they are to expanding to include the other's values. Then they can come together harmoniously, and the relationship will be based on reality (the true identities of both partners) instead of fantasy. In determining when to advance or retreat, their best bet is to be aware of the other person's energy. If the other person invites an advance, they can continue without fear, but if the other's energy is closed, they need to rein in their will and wait for a more receptive opportunity.

In this lifetime, these folks are learning that whenever passion crosses their path the best bet is to pull back and let the other person give to them. Their job now is to receive love—to allow others to give at their own pace and in their own way. It is the natives' job to graciously receive love from others without trying to rush it or change it. Their challenge in romance is to discipline their passions long enough to establish a solid bond of friendship with those who truly activate their heartstrings.

HONESTY

CHILDREN AT HEART

Aquarius North Node people have a basically happy, carefree nature. Their willfulness and determination, which can appear to others as arrogance and selfishness, are really a result of their naïve lack of awareness of their own equality. At birth, they automatically started ordering everyone around— including their parents! They assume that other people will give them what they want simply because *they* want it! They are confident that they can have anything and be anything they want. Like teenagers, they are willful yet dependent on the approval of peers, and filled with new ideas not accepted by the established generations.

They want immediate gratification and become desperate if they don't get it. Like a child in a candy store, they think if they can't have the candy right then, when it's in front of them, they'll never be able to have it. Also like children, they think the present will last forever. If they are in a "dry" period romantically—or not feeling happy—they think it's always going to be that way. They are learning that in reality, sometimes the tide is out and sometimes it's in—life is changing all the time.

Aquarius North Node people need to be honest with others about their own nature. They believe what others tell them and are deeply hurt when "adults" (that is, all others!) break their word. They behave in a straightforward way and don't understand when others treat them unkindly or play "games" with them. Their only defense against the more sophisticated thinking of others is to honestly be themselves. People will not be threatened if these folks reveal the reasons behind their actions. They need to let others know what they're thinking, fearing, and so on. When others recognize their simple sincerity, they will treat these natives like the vulnerable, creative, kindhearted "children" they are.

They may make mistakes, they may be naïve, and they may be bossy and willful, but there is a basic goodness in their nature. They are aware of this goodness, which gives them enormous confidence. These natives are innately generous and truly care about uplifting those around them. They go out of their way to buy a card or gift for a friend, or to listen with support and encouragement to others' problems. They genuinely want to make those around them happy and inspire them to be the best they can.

Even though this is the true heart of their nature, occasionally they lose sight of their inherent generosity and begin to feel envious of another person's position. This only happens because these folks are so naïve that they don't stop to honestly think about what it took for the other person to get there: They overlook the hard work, intelligent strategy, and method that created the result. They may tell themselves it was just "the luck of the draw"—but every good poker player knows that victory is really determined by how you play the game. In this lifetime, if the native feels envious about something, it may mean that he's supposed to have it, too. The next step is for him to make an honest appraisal of how to bring about those same results in his own life: to discern the proper strategy, summon the self-discipline, and begin the hard work involved in gaining the prize.

Their best bet is not to focus attention on whether the other person's circumstances are better or worse, but on what they can do to help the other person attain a greater victory. In this way they re-establish a sense of their own equality. When they start thinking in terms of helping others and working to bring in the New Age, lots of magical good luck comes their way. Because they're giving to others, the universe gives to them.

RELEASING SCRIPTS AND ROLES

Aquarius North Node people have had extensive past-life experience being at center stage—knowing how the script was written and what their lines were in the play. So they came into this lifetime with a mental picture of how their life is supposed to unfold—and fortunately for them, it isn't unfolding as they expect. Otherwise their lives would be devoid of the surprises and vital experiences that bring out the playfulness of their child-like nature. They are learning to release their mental picture of the way relationships, projects, events, and the like are supposed to unfold, and pay more attention to the opportunities that do arise.

These folks are learning to approach relationships from a position of friendship and experience the excitement of the unknown. If they have scripted expectations, but the other person doesn't follow the script, they are upset and disappointed. If they are reading their "script" when the "love of their life" walks in, Aquarius North Nodes may think the other person has to look or act a certain way in order to fulfill the script. This person may in fact be exactly what they need and want, but other aspects of the person may blind them to this fact. These folks should not try to fit the other person into their concept of the perfect partner. It causes them to discount who the person is and what he or she really has to offer.

However, if they have no expectations, the other person's unique style of giving love may bring all sorts of happy surprises! At the very least, Aquarius North Nodes will see the other person objectively and know whether he wants to pursue the relationship. There is a larger timing of events going on beyond Aquarius North Nodes' script. Everyone has the right to be them-selves and go at their own speed. Sometimes these folks will need to with-draw and say: "Well, this person isn't ready for me" and let it go, without being angry or judging the other person as inferior. If they can completely let go in this way, then—if the relationship is meant to be—it will come back to them.

However, these folks are so hungry for approval that it's hard to let go;

they may be willing to play any role necessary to win the approval and love they want. But they won't have a good sense of what role to play (what is actually desired by the loved one) if they haven't objectively observed the other's fantasies. Since they lack the objective perception to play the game well, it is much better for them not to play at all. Instead, they need to relax, go with the flow, and tell the truth about who they are and how they feel as the situation unfolds. Then the other person will either resonate or not, so the romantic relationship can be based on the same honesty as a friendship.

The irony is that Aquarius North Node people are coming from a place of such goodness and love that when they allow others to see their inherent innocence by releasing willfulness and revealing their honest responses, the other person most often responds with love.

GOALS

BRINGING IN THE NEW AGE

Aquarius North Node people are here to help bring in a New Age. They are taking the power accrued from past lives and giving it back by building a bridge between the future and the present. They are talented in applying humanitarian ideals to current circumstances. They clearly see what is for the good of humankind, are excellent networkers, and—when working to translate their vision into reality—are extremely happy. Also, because they are doing what they are uniquely equipped to do, life supports them and their projects succeed.

As they contribute to humanitarian goals, using their power and energy as a channel for unconventional ideas, their past-life pride dissipates and self-confidence returns. They are natural doers—they know how to get results. Their job is to act without identifying with the results of their actions; then they are truly free to experiment and be themselves.

These folks do have a natural attunement to the future; however, this can be confusing in a number of ways. On a personal level, they may see that their future contains a particular outcome and then feel frustrated when the outcome is withheld from them in the present. For example, they may see themselves running their own company, feel completely comfortable with that idea, and not understand why they are still working for someone else with no opportunity to go out on their own. But it may just be a matter of timing: They may need to do their current job in order to learn skills that will be required for success later.

In fact, they are nearly always "ahead of their time." They may love a particular shade of violet ten years before it's the rage, or be attracted to music that doesn't become popular until eight or nine years later. Recognizing that they have an attunement to the future can help them feel more comfortable with being a bit unorthodox.

Aquarius North Node people see the next step that humankind needs to take for its own growth. They are messengers from the future, and by sharing their innovative ideas they empower humankind to evolve in consciousness. So it is important for them not to hold back because of their desire for approval.

A LARGER PURPOSE

These folks have a larger purpose than simply fulfilling the interests of their personal life. They are here to take an active role in furthering human evolution—both through the personal transformation necessary to set an example, and through contributing their energy to humanitarian causes that help others gain a more universal view.

The sooner Aquarius North Node people begin playing their part to further the idealistic causes they are drawn to support, the sooner they will feel more of a sense of wholeness. Their action might take the form of group efforts to protect the environment, recycle, save animals, build playgrounds for inner-city kids, end world hunger, and the like; or they might donate monies to humanitarian causes. They might begin their own project, using their creative talents (writing, painting, music, photography, etc.).

If they are actively doing their part and someone else "discovers" something that had also occurred to them, they are able to respond with generosity: "Oh, good, that's taken care of. Now I can move on to the next thing." They don't have to worry—there's plenty of New Age work to go around! And when they are adding creative energy to the movement, they are part of the larger group effort. Thus, when others are successful in working toward the mutual goal, it is Aquarius North Nodes' victory as well.

However, it is important that these folks do what they have been individually called to do, because they can't count on others to handle it. There may be five people scheduled to introduce a law that protects the environment, but the other four may drop out. So the native must be sure to do his or her part.

GROUP KARMA

Aquarius North Node people have wonderful group karma (three or more people constitute a group). Their best qualities emerge to support, solidify, and inspire the groups of which they are a part. They are great networkers—they love connecting with others and are talented at finding a common bond among people. However, when they work in group situations they like to be the undisputed head of their own area. They like their role to be defined and prefer to do it in their own way.

Often, Aquarius North Node people access innovative ideas that can greatly assist the group, but owing to past-life needs for approval they refrain from sharing these ideas—or their spontaneous reactions to others' ideas—for fear of disapproval. If they keep their truth locked within, they end up feeling isolated. However, openly sharing their ideas and personal reactions makes them feel connected and often turns out to be exactly what was needed to move the group forward in a cohesive way.

They think their reaction is personal, but usually their antennae are picking up the group's reaction and combining it with their own New Age insight. For example, if someone proposes a measure and Aquarius North Node feels uncomfortable, she might say: "For some reason, I don't feel comfortable with this." The idea is to be honest about whatever her antennae pick up at the time—and often she discovers that it was exactly what others were feeling as well.

As these natives work to further the humanitarian goals that stimulate them (that they feel they were born to be a part of), they will meet others who were born to work toward the same goals. Joining with these people in group situations actually facilitates the manifestation of those goals.

FOCUSING CREATIVITY

Aquarius North Node people must release their abundant creative energy toward directed goals in order to feel happy and balanced. If not directed, the excess fiery energy causes bad moods, resentment of others' good luck, and the tendency to make mountains out of molehills. Unless these folks are "creating," dissatisfaction undermines other areas of their life.

Their creativity can be released through a business, an art form, the furthering of humanitarian causes, or acceleration of their spiritual growth. Whether they are re-creating themselves through spiritual disciplines or initiating projects in the tangible world, it is in their best interest to be conscious of what they want to create and use their passion to actively pursue it.

PASSION AND CREATIVE ENERGY

These folks have a tremendous amount of passion and creative energy. They are happiest being involved in projects that allow them to express this in their own way. They love to contribute, but they need to be free to be innovative and creative. They don't want to follow someone else's directions—it limits them and lowers their "frequency." If they try to slow down their high-frequency, intense energy, it makes them crazy. When they ignore their own creative impulses and do what they *think* they should do, their energy plummets.

Aquarius North Node people were such powerful creators in past lives that in this incarnation they are able to manifest anything they want—they know how to do it. They can "source" things, confidently creating something out of nothing. They are innovators, not imitators. They can start businesses and creative projects on their own and bring them to completion.

However, to achieve success they need to remember that there are two parts to the creative process: observation and action. Observation consists of research: What does the public need? What does the other person want? This part of the creative dance moves ahead in a measured way that objectively considers prevailing circumstances and allows others to adjust to cooperate with the vision.

Action requires will and determination to manifest a result and capture the prize. Creative action requires ego; observation requires nonego objectivity. If these folks experience a rebuff, their best bet is to pull out of ego and move back into nonego observation mode so they can objectively evaluate what has occurred. Then, when the path ahead is clear, they can re-connect with ego and press for results.

As long as they are not seeking self-aggrandizement, Aquarius North Node people have the ability to intuit what will help people and what will actually work for the good of the group. All the power of the universe will support them because they're contributing to a higher cause—and this gives them access to incredible power.

People may respond by putting the natives on a pedestal, but it will be out of a sense of thankfulness because they have really helped. They have helped from a position of equality, rather than from a position of being "above" others—from being who they really are rather than from playing a role.

These folks can create anything they decide they want. By having the humility to enlist knowledge and help from others and the openness to allow the natural timing of events to unfold, they can easily manifest all their dreams that are in alignment with the larger purpose of their life.

RELEASING INTENSITY AND DRAMA

Aquarius North Node people have a tremendous amount of creative passion; when they use it to produce a work of art or a product, their focused intensity can be to their advantage. However, when they apply the same intense passion to negotiating in the world, they encounter problems. They tend to overfocus their highly charismatic energy, and that's one reason things "blow up" around them! Their intensity actually repels what they're trying to attract.

When their creative process isn't going the way they want, it's usually an indication that they need to gain more knowledge before moving ahead. They may need a deeper understanding; in fact, it often helps to use a friend as a sounding board. When they aren't quite sure what to do next, the best bet is to do nothing and wait for more information. If they charge ahead anyway, they generally end up causing bigger problems.

These folks tend to react to external stimuli in an overly dramatic way that intimidates others. Before considering what the other person is saying, they may respond in a way that circumvents further communication. They may try to force their will by having a temper tantrum: becoming enraged at the other person, crying, or being otherwise dramatic to get the other person to live up to their expectations. But willfulness and pride block the energy of the relationship.

They may also respond with impatience: "Why doesn't he take control of his life? Why doesn't he do this for himself?" But in fact others are doing what is right for them at the time. There's no point in these folks judging the other person for not living up to *their* script!

When Aquarius North Node people get melodramatic, it's because they are magnifying reality and are afraid they won't get their way. They take any incident (a slight, a rejection, etc.) and magnify it out of emotional proportion. However, whenever they allow themselves to have excessive emotional reactions, that area of their life will not work out. If they react dramatically to changes in financial status, money will continue to be a source of difficulty. If they get overly excited about a love affair, their intensity may push the other person away.

Another "glitch" that occurs when their passion is aroused (whether a romantic relationship or a goal that is extremely important) is their tendency to take things too seriously. They often become weighed down with the importance of their quest and lose the lighthearted mental agility that would show them the way to success.

These folks can even become "drama queens," because the intensity and intrigue of their life resemble a soap opera. The problem is that although the action continues, the fun begins going out of the play. Shakespearean drama always has a tragic ending. When passion is involved, Aquarius North Nodes lose all perspective and inadvertently set into motion unbalanced energies that cause emotionally tragic consequences.

To maintain perspective, Aquarius North Node people need to think of life as a comedy instead of a drama. There are many people they are destined to meet, experiences they are meant to have, and knowledge they are supposed to share with others. Rather than overreacting, they are better off using their creativity to see the "higher reason" and cooperate with the Flow.

SEEING THE LARGER PICTURE

In past incarnations, these folks developed ego at the expense of superego, thereby weakening their sense of morality as dictated by society, family, and religion—and their awareness of humanitarian ideals. For balance, they now need to develop an awareness of the larger picture. Then they can assert their will in alignment with the best interests of everyone around them.

By accessing an expanded level of consciousness, they will find a goal that allows them to rise above ego. For example, I had an Aquarius North Node client who was a photographer. Her work was extremely creative; emitted a very loving, spiritual feeling; and was altogether in alignment with doing her part to bring in the New Age. However, because her motive was a strong ego desire for acknowledgment and fame, she couldn't see clearly how to get her photography out into the world. She kept pursuing conventional methods (private showings, etc.), none of which produced adequate results.

Finally she began to make her primary goal that of simply exposing her art to the general public. She began to place her work wherever she felt it would be seen (in bagel shops, bookstores, etc.)—and overnight, her photographs began to sell! This took humility, as my client's work had been exhibited in museums and leading universities. But she found the path to success when she acted on the bigger picture, even if it didn't feed her ego.

TRUSTING THE FLOW

Aquarius North Node people are accustomed to getting their way, and they often become very upset when events don't unfold according to *their* timetable. Instead of allowing themselves to be redirected, they become outraged at the obstruction. Rather than recognizing that the tide has changed, and that perhaps life itself has a larger plan that requires present events to unfold exactly as they are, these folks resist. In this way they make the path a lot more difficult than it has to be.

These folks need to be on the lookout for their own willfulness. The personal will was so indulged in past lives that they came into this incarnation and, as young children, said: "I want this!"—and were truly shocked when their parents said "no." As adults, they are still shocked when the universe says "no." They are learning to transform personal will into a willingness to go with the flow and lovingly accept the gifts that life brings.

When they try to force a result, they become strong, determined, and obstinate. Their will can be a positive force when used as a warrior's strength for good, but negative when translated into a tantrum. Part of the work of transforming an overdeveloped will into a willingness to cooperate is to recognize good and bad timing. For example, if Aquarius North Nodes' will has become fixed on going to the beach on Saturday, they will want to go even if it's snowing! It's difficult for them to objectively factor in changing conditions and modify their course accordingly. Thus, they miss opportunities to advance by adapting to the larger picture, which is always for the greater good—including their own.

Life doesn't want to hurt them, but they ultimately hurt themselves by resisting the timing of the universe. They are learning to accept whatever happens in their lives as appropriate in order to take the next step.

These folks are learning that when one door closes, another opens. For example, they may have the opportunity to experience the joy of a wonderful love affair. Someone new comes along and sweeps them off their feet. But they have a serious career objective in mind, try to postpone the love affair, and lose the opportunity to experience love. Ironically, the career move they were seeking may not materialize until six months later, which would have given them plenty of time to experience the joy of the relationship. They often cheat themselves of the gifts life brings, thinking they "know better," and then they feel regret.

Life may be bringing an opportunity for an entirely new career endeavor that will give them more joy than anything they did before. In subconscious readiness for the change, they begin to tire of the old job but have no intention of leaving because of the good benefits, income, and so on. Suddenly, events at work force them to leave, and they become indignant and resistant: "Why is the universe doing this to me?" Their anger may prevent them from seeing the new window of opportunity; they are too distracted by what they "don't want" to see what is opening up for them.

Once again, self-discipline is the key: to keep from always "having their way" by staying objective and focused on the larger picture. This is not an instinctual response, so it requires conscious intention. For example, if they are raising a daughter and their goal is for her to grow up to be a strong woman, keeping that goal in mind will help them rein in their ego and allow the child to have her own way some of the time in order to support her strength. Or if the goal is for their children to grow up in a harmonious atmosphere, this may keep their ego from having to argue about how to load the dishwasher. To discipline the ego, they have to consciously have a larger goal that is personally meaningful to them.

Aquarius North Node people are learning to trust that there is a bigger picture and that the Flow is always bringing opportunities for their greatest good and happiness. They are learning to embrace humility and graciously accept the gifts that life brings *when* those gifts are presented—according to the timing of the universe rather than through their own will.

ANGELIC HELP

In this lifetime, others are automatically drawn to Aquarius North Node people to support them in altruistic projects. Also, they are surrounded by Angels and spiritual Guides. It's almost as though before incarnating they were part of a larger group, and now they are here on earth while other members of the group are in the invisible realm to guide and help them.

Because these natives are incarnated in a physical body, they can't always see ahead clearly. Because they are accustomed to being self-sufficient, they bluster ahead and often get hurt—but they don't have to do this. All they need to do is tune their antennae and listen to their guidance, and the path will be much easier to follow. This is not a "do it yourself" lifetime; their Guides are part of their destiny and want to help them succeed, but it's up to them to keep the connection open.

In this incarnation, Aquarius North Node people are instruments for higher forces. Thus, when they have an idea that is truly in alignment with what is needed on the planet, the universe will set it up so that they connect with the right people to help manifest the idea. These folks are eclectic, combining the best of the associations they are involved in under the auspices of their larger life path and inner knowledge about the New Age. In this lifetime, the idea is for them to *transfer* some of their strong loyalty to the Infinite, to their own spirituality, and to cooperating with the larger Flow. In this way their incredible creative will from past lives can click in and their path to success will become magical. As long as they give credit to "good luck," the Angels, or the universe itself for the ideas they put out, they are totally free to succeed. Nothing holds them back because they are not interpreting success in a way that overinflates their ego.

HEALING THEME SONG *

Music has a unique power to emotionally support us in taking risks, so I have written a healing song for each nodal group to help shift its energy in a positive way.

THE SUN COMES UP

The message of this song is meant to gently shift Aquarius North Nodes' focus to an awareness of the bigger picture—the natural order and timing of life—thus empowering them to relax their resistance. Then they can become aware of and "tap into" the natural Flow, proceeding in a direct path to making their dreams come true.

Selected lyrics:

> *Why do we prevent our own happiness*
> *By resisting the timing of life*
> *Trying to decide what's wrong and what's right*
> *With our foolish human minds!*
>
> *And the sun comes up each morning*
> *And it goes down every night.*
> *And in the night, it's the moon that comes*
> *It never is the sun.*
> *There is system and order here*
> *And it's reflected all around*
> *Why not trust in the laws of life*
> *They never let us down!*

---

* These lyrics are set to music and sung in their entirety on the CD and cassette tape "Unfolding As It Should."

North Node in Pisces

and North Node in the 12th House

OVERVIEW

Attributes to Develop

Work in these areas can help uncover hidden gifts and talents

- Being nonjudgmental
- Compassion
- Surrendering anxiety to a Higher Power
- Freeing the mind through meditation and self-reflection
- Focusing on the spiritual pathway
- Trusting in positive outcomes
- Acknowledging connection with the universe
- Welcoming change

Tendencies to Leave Behind

Working to reduce the influence of these tendencies can help make
life easier and more enjoyable

- Hyperanxiety reactions
- Overanalysis
- Obsessive worry
- Exaggerating the importance of details
- Critical first reactions
- Fault finding—making others wrong
- Excessive anxiety over making mistakes
- Being Mr. or Ms. Perfect
- Staying in unpleasant situations
- Inflexibility

ACHILLES' HEEL/TRAP TO AVOID/THE BOTTOM LINE

The Achilles' heel Pisces North Node people need to be aware of is their
compulsive need for order ("My survival depends on everything being in
order according to my view of how life ought to be and how others ought to
behave"), and it can lead them into the trap of an unending search for
perfection ("If only the people around me were more perfect, I could relax
and trust"). But it's a bottomless pit: Since life and other people are never in
a static state of perfect order long enough for Pisces North Nodes to feel
secure, their expectations can lead to continual tension and anxiety. Because
life—and others—are never ideal enough for them to let go of control, they
continually postpone trust and joy.

The bottom line involves accepting that the universe's plan is better than
theirs and that things *are* unfolding properly, regardless of how it seems.
The only place they can create "perfect order" is within themselves, by
surrendering to a Higher Power and trusting that everything is indeed in
order. The irony is that when Pisces North Node people blindly trust the

Infinite and accept that everything contributes to their greater happiness, they suddenly become aware of the larger picture and begin to sense how things are working to their advantage. Then they can let go of control and be happy.

What These People Really Want

What these people really want is to be right all the time and to be perfect in the sense that they—and everyone else—are following "the plan" 100 percent of the time. But they want everyone to be in total, perfect alignment with "the plan" that *they* think is right. First they need to accept that they do not know what "the plan" is. They need to turn away from rigid physical and material planning and refocus on the larger, spiritual vision. Through trusting and surrendering to the wisdom of the Higher Power, they can watch life's circumstances with the conviction that what is unfolding is indeed part of "the plan." Then the way becomes clear. They are filled with calm and feel in alignment with "the plan" because the spiritual vision is the energy of perfection they are seeking.

Pisces rules enlightened states of consciousness, the oceanic feeling of oneness with all life. At times Pisces North Node people have slipped into an enlightenment state—a state of total connection with the universe. Their life purpose is to nurture that state and make it part of their daily experience.

Talents/Profession

These people need to have their own private office or space. They work very well alone and enjoy projects that involve discovering and carrying out a vision where the work is done in private (such as research, library work, or computer work). Pisces North Node people succeed in any profession that involves the individual pursuit of spiritual Truth, including working and living in monasteries or convents. They can be fantastic artists, craftspeople, performers, or musicians—bringing their private dream to others. They are also great promoters, because they are so good at "behind the scenes" activities. Even if they work in a regular job, they need to allow themselves ample time for solitude and reflection.

Pisces North Node people also have inherent gifts for noticing pertinent details and analyzing the significance of information. When they use these past-life gifts as a backdrop for manifesting their dreams, their innate practicality will help them. However, if they involve themselves in professions that stress attention to detail, in-depth analysis, perfection, or accuracy (such as bookkeeping or systems analysis), they are likely to experience anxiety and restlessness. These folks are better off when their profession focuses on manifesting a vision, empowering them to use their practical skills to bring it into reality.

HEALING AFFIRMATIONS SPECIFIC TO PISCES NORTH NODE

- "All is well and everything is unfolding as it should."
- "God's spiritual government can never fall out of place."
- "When I 'Let Go and Let God'—I win."
- "My survival is not threatened by disorder."
- "This isn't my job—it's God's job."

PERSONALITY

PAST LIVES

Pisces North Node people spent many past lifetimes as physical healers and helpers: They were the surgeons, doctors, and nurses in many different cultures. These were critical positions where they had to focus and "do it right," because a person's life depended on it. Thus, there's a lot of attachment to and a sense of urgency about doing things perfectly in this lifetime. When things go according to plan, Pisces North Nodes feel confident and strong; everything's under control and the "operation" is proceeding successfully. But when the unexpected occurs, they panic. Subconsciously, they think when something has gone "wrong," someone's going to die.

As medical personnel they had set rules and procedures—there could be no mistakes. Thus, in this incarnation they carry an overattachment to doing things in an exacting, flawless way. They not only burden themselves with this expectation of impeccable behavior, but they tend to apply the same rigid standards to those around them, especially in the workplace. Perhaps because of their past lives in the medical field, they are often very health-conscious, have a fear of contamination, and feel a need to keep their environment spotlessly clean.

Additionally, Pisces North Node people have had past incarnations representing spiritual truth by being of practical service in the world through perfect, "by the book" behavior—as monks, nuns, and "Mother Teresa"-type people. They were role models; others looked to them to learn how spiritual people should behave. Because their behavior resulted in admiration and rewards, they have a subconscious association between being "perfect" and having things in the material world go their way. However, in those past lives they got "stuck" on the perfection of form and lost touch with the essence of their healing power. This is understandable because they had to perform rituals and always dress and act in a certain way. Thus, in this lifetime they want to release attachment to form and get back in touch with essence. It's time for them to claim the rewards of peace and inner contentment for their past-life service.

ANALYTICAL TENDENCIES

In past lives, Pisces North Nodes' analytical processes were overused and overdeveloped, so now they are born with a propensity to analyze everything. They are constantly pulling things apart to see how they work, and they tend to be dissatisfied until they understand. Their mental processes are in high gear all the time, often analyzing things that should be left alone. Like peeling an onion, they take off layer after layer until there's nothing left—and then they end up feeling empty and anxious. This lifetime, it's not set up for them to find the answers they are seeking through analysis.

These folks analyze problems from every possible direction with an intensity that drives the other nodal types crazy! They think of all the things that could go wrong—things they can't control. Once they decide there's something to worry about, it puts them in an intense, frantic state that, when activated, is very hard to disengage. It isn't the present that worries them so much as what might happen in the future. The overwhelming majority of their worries never materialize, but that doesn't stop these folks from living in a continual state of anxiety.

There are several reasons why their projected "worse-case scenarios" are unlikely to happen: (1) They don't consider new insights or actions that can circumvent the feared outcome; (2) they don't allow for outside intervention; and (3) most important, they don't allow their intuition to provide an accurate "sense" of the future—whether there is actually something to be concerned about. They have to *stop thinking* in order to tune in and "feel" the future.

Many problems arise for Pisces North Node people because of their tendency to overanalyze. For example, they have a vision and then try to force it into manifestation without allowing the universe to unfold it in its own way. They do see a path, but it's not necessarily the whole road; it may be just a narrow trail. Perhaps one person can go that way, but when there are others involved it requires a larger vision.

These folks are so accustomed to implementing that they become too narrowly focused on the task at hand and don't take other circumstances into account. Their best bet—when things stop working according to their plan—is to step back. Rather than panic, they need to remind themselves that a higher plan may be unfolding of which they are unaware.

HAVING THE ANSWERS

Owing to past lives spent creating order in situations of chaos, these folks are born with the feeling that they are always supposed to have the answers. So they constantly seek ways to create healing and restore order—both for themselves and others. When they are faced with a problem, they begin to tense up and try to figure out the answer—then the situation worsens and so does their anxiety. It can take days to get over their feelings of inadequacy at not being able to find the "right answer."

The irony is that these people *do* have access to the answers, but only when they first acknowledge that, all on their own, they *don't* have the answers. They must surrender the problem to a Higher Power and be open to insights that come through their intuitive process, not their analytical process. Then the "right" answers do come, either in the form of an insight or through a general sense of well-being in the situation.

For example, I had a Pisces North Node client who, after years of study in Europe, was highly schooled in traditional techniques for teaching people how to sing. But when she applied these techniques to her students, the results were frustrating and time-consuming. Only when she began to relax and allow their individual vocal dysfunctions to permeate her being, releasing "the problem" to a Higher Power, was she able to intuitively see how to communicate the exact perspective that each person needed to unblock his or her voice. Ironically, by not feeling pressured to immediately know "the answer," she found that part of her subconscious did know the answer and that she did have a true gift for developing her students' voices.

SELF-CONCEPT

Pisces North Node people are always trying to figure out where they "belong": where their slot is, what their job is, how they fit in with everyone else. This pressing urge is based on an inner feeling that they have no value apart from their job or duty; and the idea of not being defined is terrifying for them.

What they are looking for (the ultimate security) is where they "fit" within themselves. Until they recognize this, they spend time and energy in a futile search, because in this incarnation they are not scheduled to fit in a tangible position. To feel their "fit," they must access the spiritual dimension of life; this is where meditation, relaxation techniques, yoga, and spiritual pursuits are so valuable. These practices focus attention on the intangible context within which all tangible, material things exist.

Focusing on the spiritual atmosphere behind what is happening in the material world gives Pisces North Node people a comfortable and secure sense of being connected with others and helps them expand their vision to include a larger awareness—a sense of the wholeness of everything that transpires. As they experience wholeness and serenity within themselves, they will grow more aware of the atmosphere they create. By learning to identify with their own energy field, they will be able to "fit into" the *atmosphere* surrounding them wherever they go.

PERFECTIONISM

Pisces North Node people have had so many lifetimes of needing to be "perfect" that they came into this incarnation with a "be perfect" script embedded in their subconscious. They think they have to be "Mr. or Ms. Perfect" all the time. The good news is that in this lifetime, it's fine for them to make mistakes. In fact, they are not *allowed* to be perfect—a "glitch" always arises at the last minute to upset their "perfect" image. This is the universe reminding them that in this lifetime it's okay to make mistakes, to be human, and to be themselves.

PLANNING

These folks are really into planning. They focus on where they want to go and structure *exactly* how they will get there. Then, because in past lives they were so accustomed to keeping their eye on details, they become fixated on the plan and lose sight of the vision! The slightest alteration of their plan makes them "go ballistic," because they think they're not going to get what they want.

They think that if they do everything "just right" they can keep their world under control. They are shocked when, in spite of their attention to detail, their world starts to fall apart (the wife leaves, the business fails, a child begins acting out, etc.). Just when they get their plans all "set," life sends in something from left field to shake everything up. This is the universe's way of letting them know that when they get too rigidly attached to their *method* for reaching their goal, it won't work—because they're excluding themselves from the fun and adventure of unexpected things happening along the way. When they have their mind set on *exactly* what they want, the best that can happen is limited by their own preconceived ideas.

For example, a Pisces North Node person and a friend may want to go from New York to Los Angeles. Pisces North Node will probably plan out the entire route in a specific way that is direct and practical. When they start out, the friend looks ahead, sees that a blizzard is predicted to cross their route, and suggests taking a route that will bypass the storm. Pisces North Node is likely to become upset: She is totally attached to her plan and fears that if they don't follow that precise route they may never reach Los Angeles.

These folks also have a tendency to overplan, pressing themselves to get a lot done in a short period of time. However, the solution does not lie in structuring their time to accommodate all their activities, but in totally unstructuring it—just observing themselves in action. This approach will create a natural, proper distribution of time that brings ease and balance to their lives.

One thing Pisces North Node people can do to encourage this process is to consciously do *less:* Plan less, schedule less, and allow for more spontaneity. In this way they can best stay in touch with their vision, which will lead to a more productive use of their time. They need a stronger sense of purpose and a more relaxed idea of how to get there. If they allow everything to flow, it leads them to an inner certainty, a *knowing* that things will go well for them.

CRITICISM

Pisces North Node people tend to be excessively judgmental. They are harder on themselves than anyone else, and this constant judging of "right or wrong" results in tension and guilt. They feel responsible for anything that goes "wrong" in their environment, including what happens to the people they are close to. They feel they personally caused the problems because their behavior wasn't perfect. This can lead to paralysis in making constructive changes in their lives, for fear of causing problems for others.

These folks have a tendency to blame themselves for little things that don't meet their self-imposed image. They hate to be wrong, and when they make a mistake they are hard on themselves. They want to analyze it, rationalize why they did it, and explain themselves. It can be very difficult for them to say: "I'm sorry, I made a mistake." Owing to their past-life perfectionism, they carry a subconscious fear of behaving in a way that reflects badly on the ideal they represent. Thus, in this life "being right" almost feels like a sacred obligation.

The irony is that when they admit they've made a mistake, they gain the position of strength because they are standing in Truth. Then they can just say: "I've made a mistake, and where do we go from here?" When these folks beat themselves up in their effort to be perfect, they lose and everyone around them loses. They must give up all judgments in order to gain the peace they seek.

Whenever they hear themselves say: "I caused that because I didn't do a good job," they know they are plugging in to their past-life Achilles' heel. Whenever they start judging themselves—or someone else—against an ideal, they're off path. The universe is teaching them humility by putting them in situations where they "goof up," so that they can let go of the need to be perfect and get over the idea that "something is wrong." Nothing is wrong; everything is just "happening." When they realize this and go with the Flow of life, they are on the right path. Then they are in a position to heal through their own confidence in the natural unfolding of events.

"FIXING"

Pisces North Node people are extremely serious because they're always focused on what is wrong so they can fix it. They are so hyper-aware that when there's any deviation from "smooth, uninterrupted flow," they panic and their critical, anxious mood upsets and disrupts everyone around them.

Their past-life work gave them a very narrow focus, and in this life they also tend to become focused in a narrow way. Part of the problem has to do with *where* they *put* their attention: on the details of what is happening on the tangible level. Many times, Pisces North Node people become fixated on a problem because they are so close to it they can't see anything else. They're like a child with his face pressed against the glass. When they get "stuck" in the middle of a problem in this way, feeling frustrated and ineffective because they are unable to restore order, they can easily become obsessed with some detail that seems to be "out of place." This can lead to a state of tension and worry that is difficult to shake—like trying to separate a dog from his bone!

Ironically, the way out of this dilemma is also found in their ability to focus: They need to shift focus from the mechanics of the problem, to releasing the situation to a Higher Power. In this incarnation, when they get attached to results in the physical world, they are overcome with nervous irritability that affects their relationships and everything they do. They get so tense that it almost turns their stomach into a knot. When they feel that tightening in the stomach, it's a signal to step back from the situation and let it go.

Sometimes the best way to detach themselves is to say the affirmation: "All is well, and everything is unfolding as it should." They may need to say it several times in order to cease overanalyzing the situation and to get the psychological distance they need. Then they can pause and see what comes to them. They don't have to figure anything out; they just need to see what comes. By surrendering the problem to a Higher Power and just being in the situation, the healing energy emerges and the proper resolution is revealed to everyone involved.

For example, I had a Pisces North Node client whose mother-in-law was quite abusive. She became defensive and took it personally if my client didn't come to visit. She had a problem with alcohol and generally made those around her feel badly about wanting to lead their own lives. For many years my client tried to help this woman to feel better, but she got nowhere. Then suddenly, when she stopped helping, her mother-in-law told her that she had begun seeing a therapist and would like it if each family member would go with her as part of her treatment. My client was thrilled and totally supported her mother-in-law. Her biggest surprise was that it didn't happen until she accepted the situation as it was, stopped trying to help, and released it: "I didn't do a *thing*!" she said.

Magical results happen when these people truly release a problem and get out of the way. They think the world depends on their participation and are surprised when they don't participate and things get done anyway. When things *do* fall into place without their intervention, they may take it personally: "You mean they can get along *without* me?"

Obsessiveness

Pisces North Node people often have a problem with obsessions—compulsive mental patterns that are not in their best interest. Or their minds can have an obsessive quality that causes them to continue to analyze a situation but fail to come up with a resolution that brings peace of mind. Sometimes, out of the blue, the problem or the addiction will be lifted. Their best bet is to not analyze why, but to simply recognize that the problem is gone and to consciously express feelings of appreciation and gratitude. They need to accept the gift, not analyze it.

When they obsess on "why," they are actually driven by fear that the problem might return. But in the process of analyzing it, they often reattract the problem. Their best bet is to simply allow negative conditions to disappear from their lives without having to understand "why." They are learning to appreciate the wonder of life, to recognize how everything flows together and to feel a sense of awe at the solutions that life itself brings to them.

SUPERIORITY: THE ROLE MODEL

In past lives these folks developed an ego encrustation that revolved around being "right" all the time. Doctors and surgeons are like gods: Everyone reveres them, and it's easy for them to buy into their own publicity. Then the process of serving other people becomes an ego trip.

So Pisces North Node people often come into this incarnation with a superiority complex. They feel they have to be a role model (teacher, minister, firefighter, police officer, etc.) because, in one way or another, they represent an archetype that needs to bring a certain value to the human stream of experience. As a role model they feel they have to be impeccable. Yet to do things perfectly implies superiority, and this is the beginning of the end for these folks. This is true both in terms of being trapped by the role they are playing *and* in terms of abusing power in ways that result in others taking a stand against them.

These folks identify strongly with the work or service they perform. They may become immersed in work and be unable to separate themselves from it. What begins as noticing "one more detail" before leaving their job soon becomes the workaholic syndrome. Although their job enslaves them, they may not see themselves as being obsessive—they're "just doing what has to be done." They must let go of identifying with their work; then they can do a good job without losing so much of themselves. Even if they are not spending lots of hours on the job, they may spend a lot of time worrying about work. Either way, work is a central, all-pervasive issue in their lives.

They also have a tough time with employees or co-workers. It's hard for them to let go of wanting to control others' behavior—they're not sure others can do the job. Pisces North Node people are learning that their idea of the "right way" to do a job might be different from the other person's idea, yet both ways might produce good results. They need to give people the latitude to have different styles. They also need to recognize that others may be learning "how to get the job done"—they can't expect everyone to already know the best way.

These folks feel they have to stay apart from others because they have a certain duty to perform on the earth. They are afraid that if they let themselves be equal and become emotionally involved they might forget their job, and that would strip away their self-definition. To play out their role they have to keep the mask on, because to let go of the mask and yield to their emotions would make them part of the collective whole, rather than a role model.

In fact, when they *do* act out a role, they attract others to them who actually expect them to play that role. When someone says: "Be this for me," it feeds their ego but then they're trapped in that role. The irony is that they *are* bringing a higher energy onto the planet, but they are ineffective as long as they try to do it on an ego level. They are learning that instead of *doing* something, they simply have to *be* who they really are.

DUTY AND GUILT

Pisces North Node people are attached to a sense of duty for the purpose of creating order. They think they must play a particular role or enact a particular ritual or routine, and that it's their responsibility to perform this duty or service. To them, becoming part of the Flow would mean agreeing to be nobody. Yet agreeing to be nobody makes them think they're not doing their job—and that brings up guilt. "If I don't fulfill my duty, I'm doing something wrong." It's a self-perpetuating cycle that is entirely in their minds. It's based on the idea that they are superior to others and thus have a lofty mission.

Something has to "jolt" them in order to release them from this cycle and force them to accept their own humanity. They may find themselves embroiled in a situation that is truly out of their control. Humility and acceptance are the only way out, the only way they can let go of the vicious perfection/duty/guilt cycle. At some point, letting go would mean saying: "Well, I guess I can't do a perfect job. I guess I'll just have to give it to God." That is when their consciousness shifts and they are able to see a much larger vision.

NEEDS

RELEASING DEFINITIONS AND STRUCTURE

Pisces North Node people notice the details of everything and seek to categorize everything. They do this partly because moving into a situation that isn't defined makes them very uncomfortable. They think they need a rigid definition of who they are—their role, their job, the service they provide, their routine, their rules and regulations—to feel stable. But in truth, the fewer self-definitions they have, the better off they are, as it is easier for them to move through life *more* in touch with themselves and *less* connected to the ups and downs of their environment.

These folks need to recognize the difference between knowing where they want to go and having a rigid definition of how they will get there. To have a defined sense of purpose, a goal, or a vision is healthy for them and gives them the stability they need. However, their ideas regarding the means for reaching the goal needs to remain fluid—who knows what they will need or how it's going to happen? They need to release preconceived ideas of what it's going to take and just keep focused on the goal. They are learning to let experience precede definition, rather than allowing their rigid definitions to limit their experience.

Their inborn tendency to define everything can be to their advantage when it's kept fluid. They can loosely define present circumstances to see how they best fit with their private dreams. But it should be a temporary definition, left open for future adjustments as they receive more information. If the motive behind their defining a situation is to see where they "fit," they will lose, because the definition becomes a limitation. If the motive is to see how they can best relate the situation to their vision, they will win, because they are able to receive new input.

ACCEPTING CHANGE

Pisces North Node people are comfortable with predictability and routine and have an innate resistance to any kind of change. Even a promotion, if it's unexpected, is likely to be met with resistance! They are attached to their systems, which give them a feeling of security. Unfortunately, this can evoke a rigidity that prohibits them from freely experiencing life's blessings.

In this incarnation, these folks are learning to release their grip on "the known" and greet change willingly. They can do this only when they have consciously thought through their relationship with "the unknown." If they fear the unknown, they will try to hold on to their routines, even against their own best interest. When they are unhappy in a situation or their circumstances begin to change, they need to open their arms in acceptance. After all, maybe the current situation is breaking down because something better is awaiting them. If they can acknowledge that they are facing the unknown, they may recognize what is emerging around them as a possible next step to a greater level of satisfaction.

In reality, these folks get bored very easily—they need change to keep them vital and alive. Their nervous systems are so sensitive that if they try to resist change or control their environment, they go on overload and something starts breaking down, physically or psychologically. Thus, the sooner they can relax and open themselves to accepting change, the happier and more peaceful they will be. Their challenge is to allow the changes that flow through their lives to reposition them and smooth out the rough edges. Rather than being in a power boat trying to go upriver, they need to take a canoe and follow the flow of the stream. They can still steer, but they don't need to fight the current.

For example, I had a client with this nodal position who decided to make his morning exercise walk more enjoyable by taking his child along. In only a few blocks they came to some standing water. The son wanted to stop and look, but my client wanted to go ahead with his walk. His child got a little misty-eyed and said: "Well, I'm tired. I don't want to walk." My client, frustrated because things weren't going as he had planned, threatened to take his son back to the house and never take him on a walk again. Upset, the boy sat down and looked at the water. Finally my client accepted that he wasn't going to be able to continue his walk until they looked at the water. It turned out to be a beautiful walk! They stopped to look at ants and pieces of glass and rocks—and they did end up walking a couple of miles (he ran up and down some hills along the way to get his heart pumping). He didn't get his medium-impact exercise walk as planned, but he spent time with his son and saw sights he had passed a hundred times before and never noticed because he was too focused on walking. Life doesn't always go according to plan, but if these folks just cooperate with the way it's *already* going, the joy they thought they would get from the plan is multiplied by what actually happens.

UNIVERSAL FLOW AND TIMING

Pisces North Node people are always rushing around. Despite their incredible ability to focus, their timing is a bit jagged since they are usually trying to do too many things in too few hours. This is why they can have a problem being on time—although generally they are punctual because it's one of the "social rules." Nonetheless, they frequently feel there are not enough hours in the day.

The resolution for this dilemma is in slowing down until they match the rate of the Flow—the timing of life's natural unfolding. The universal Flow has its own timing, frequency, and speed; when one is in alignment with it, there is a natural ease to life. Events seem to occur simultaneously with the time one is prepared to handle them, and there are fewer "rough edges" when one walks in the rhythm of its heartbeat.

Thus, by slowing down and doing less, Pisces North Node people accomplish more. When the frequency they are emitting doesn't match the frequency of the Flow because they are operating at such a frantic pace, things around them start "glitching." These folks actually "overshoot" the situation; they suddenly come to a brick wall and wonder: "Why can't I get things done?"

When they meet this type of resistance, the best thing is to slow down. This allows other people or new ideas to come in to help them. By slowing down, they come into sync with the other parts of their universe; their frequency aligns with what's going on around them and they become part of the Flow.

FINDING PEACE

SELF-PURIFICATION

Pisces North Node people feel a need for self-purification before opening themselves up to an energy that can truly transform their consciousness. But this can be an unending process. These folks never think they are pure enough or their behavior perfect enough to open up to higher energies.

Moreover, their approach to self-purification is based on rigid rules regarding behavior. These folks try to live up to their own expectations, pushing through obstructions in the name of "duty" in order to "purify" themselves. But in reality, the purification they need is to let go of self-limiting definitions. They are learning to disengage their identity from their function: Their job does not define them; their duty doesn't make them human.

To attain the higher realms of consciousness they yearn for, they must release all self-definition of being any particular kind of person playing any particular role.

Pisces North Node people have already developed worldly competence; in this incarnation they primarily need to relax and find inner peace. But owing to constant mental activity (trying to analyze everything around them and "fix" what—or who—they perceive to be less than "perfect"), they are often in a perpetual state of stress and tension. As they try to implement these changes they think they need in order to find inner peace, they are constantly tense.

These folks need to spend time alone, to resolve their worries by going inside themselves. They have to pull the issue they are concerned with inside and think about it, feel it, and go through an inner process to release it. They need time to process the anxiety pulsing through their system. Pisces North Node people need this private process of inner purification, and they can only do it when they have solitude.

Once they are able to detach from being so involved in everything, they can begin to objectively *watch* themselves respond to each situation as it comes along. Through this process, the attachments that held them in bondage to the material plane will begin to dissipate. Everything within them that is resisting the natural flow of events will begin to drop away, and this is the only self-purification they really need.

If they try to interact with their environment without taking the time to resolve their tension, they will continue to be plagued by anxiety-producing thoughts and worries. Their need for solitude and meditation must be understood and honored by them and by those close to them. They must systematically spend time in some type of meditative activity to release tension and allow their inner happiness to grow.

SURRENDER

As soon as things in the outer world start to "go wrong" and they begin to feel tense, the best thing Pisces North Node people can do is to take it as an "omen" that it's time to pull back and take a second look from a distance. To their amazement, they often find that less is better. When they apply *more* energy they become more enmeshed, feel more anxious, and make more mistakes. As the outer problem seems to get worse instead of better, they finally become so frustrated that they throw their hands up and surrender.

It would be much better if these folks surrendered right at the beginning. One of their greatest tools is their capacity to open to their own spirituality through the process of surrender. No matter what may be occurring in their lives, they need to trust that the Infinite is on their side and that something better is unfolding for them. As they give the resolution of the situation at hand over to the Infinite, they expand into a higher place in their own consciousness that empowers them to recognize how events could resolve in ways that are more to their advantage.

For example, I had a client with this nodal position who owned a small nursing home. She became increasingly involved in all the details of the business until she had no time for anything else: for play, for family, for fun. Unexpectedly, three violations were filed against her home in rapid succession, leading to the possibility that her facility would be closed. All three incidents were unrelated and "out of the blue." She panicked for fear of losing her only source of income. She prayed unceasingly for the outcome to go "her way" so she could keep her business. Then, at some point, she simply relaxed. She realized that if she negotiated with the board, rather than close her down they would send an administrator to run her business for a trial period. And although she would have to pay the administrator, she could see what an advantage it would be for her to pull back and let someone else run the business. Then she could focus her energies on promoting her home and filling the empty beds, which would yield enough money to cover the salary of the administrator and actually increase her income. Most important, she would have her life back again.

Pisces North Node people are learning that the universe's plan for their happiness is generally a lot better than their own!

RECHARGING

HIGHER CONSCIOUSNESS

Pisces North Node people have had so many incarnations of service that in this lifetime they are ready to rest and recharge their souls. This is why they become physically exhausted when they spend too much time in the outer world; they need to retreat into an inner world of peace to heal. This is correct for them; there needs to be time in their lives to escape from daily routines.

These folks occasionally slip into higher states of consciousness without even trying. Once they have experienced this they always want to reclaim it. They may spend hours in meditation, practicing every technique they can think of, and may even become completely isolated in order to regain that state. But when they try to push for it, they push it away. The idea is for them to relax and accept that they are surrounded by it, as a fish is surrounded by water.

When they are in that state, they are happy just to enjoy life. But they have so many ideas about the roles they should play (the teacher bringing others to the Light, etc.) that their mental activity pushes away that natural state of bliss. If they simply relax—without a myriad of activities scheduled for the day—they will find the energy they seek naturally flowing around them. Pisces rules enlightened states of consciousness—the oceanic feeling of oneness with all life. Pisces North Nodes' life purpose is to do whatever increases that higher state of consciousness—to make it part of their daily life—which will automatically help those around them.

These folks' ability to create organization and definition is a tremendous asset, but not when it's applied to the material world. When they are in tune with the larger picture (keeping their peripheral vision open and simply moving through life with an expanded awareness of what's going on), they can make sense of the chaos and see the Flow. Then they will know what to do to align with the Flow in a practical way that accomplishes their dreams.

Pisces North Node people want to surrender to the Infinite, to a Higher Power. If they cannot do this on their own, they sometimes become addicted to drugs, alcohol, or other means of escape. They are trying to silence the anxiety from their overly analytical processes. They may unconsciously turn to substance abuse as a pathway to get them into Alcoholics Anonymous, Narcotics Anonymous, Overeaters Anonymous, or other groups that focus on surrender to a Higher Power. Interestingly enough, the sign of Pisces rules drugs, alcohol, excessive sleep, self-destructive behaviors—all forms of escapism—but also rules meditation, the highest forms of spirituality, and unconditional love and bliss.

To prevent problems, these folks need a place of solitude, even in the workplace. Work can be a major source of stress for them because it stimulates their tendency to "fix things." At work, they are much better off with their own space: a private office or a corner where they have a sense of privacy. If they work with a group of people, it helps to turn their desks away from other people and face the wall. They are much happier and more productive when they have a "space" with no one else's energy around them. It helps them remain calm and see situations from an expanded point of view.

MEANINGFUL WORK

The one thing Pisces North Node people can commit to on a lifelong basis is learning and growing. Often a need to understand and accept the people around them will point to exciting directions for research and study.

These folks excel at any type of work that is inspirational, spiritual, or promotional. They have brilliant imaginations; when they focus on ideas that help manifest a vision, they are on track. Their job is to stay in touch with the vision and impart to others how to take care of the details. They are great at charging others with enthusiasm when they share their ideas from the vantage point of the vision, reminding others of what everyone is aiming for.

Pisces North Node people are able to apply this mindset, whatever their job or position. As bank tellers, they could have the larger view of wanting to serve people compassionately through their understanding that many people have financial worries and come to the bank feeling upset. As salespeople, they could keep in mind the larger view of wanting the store to do well, working to keep the customers happy by relating to them from a position of love and service, and being conscious of not making judgments about the salesperson next to them.

Unfortunately, for many of these folks, the worst confrontations seem to occur in the workplace. They love to be the ones who keep the project moving forward. However, their egos can get a bit puffed up if they lose sight of the larger vision. They need to stay focused on: "This is the work that needs to be done." It's easy to get caught up in: "*I'm* the one getting the work done. I'm organizing it, I'm getting this person to do this . . . I'm getting that person to take care of that detail . . . And where's my coffee, Mac?" They will only have enough energy to keep the project on track if they are humble and stay connected to the vision. Otherwise people resist them, and then they don't know what to do. They become disconnected from their power.

Another issue in the workplace is that Pisces North Node people are subject to mood swings: They go along happily, but all of a sudden their energy drops and they become anxious. Others around them are greatly affected by their mood changes—they have the power to create an atmosphere that everyone responds to. When they are happy and peaceful, they bring the mood up and everyone around them feels better. But when they're down or anxious, everyone feels that as well. This is an awesome power, and they may not even be aware of it.

When these folks become anxious, others feel anxiety and begin to perform less efficiently. When they feel calm and confident, others feel it and naturally become more productive. Thus, Pisces North Nodes can correct the behavior of others simply by filling the atmosphere with positive, confident thoughts and energies.

What precedes their affecting the atmosphere in a negative way is a reversal in their own mood. Their mind may become too involved and critical about details. They get upset when things aren't working the way they think they "should" or when another person isn't doing the job in a way they think it ought to be done. Or if something unexpected happens they may think the universe isn't supporting them and get absorbed in a whirlwind of tension and anxiety. So Pisces North Node people need to recognize that they *really don't know* how life "ought to be" unfolding. Maybe the other person has to make a certain mistake because that will facilitate seeing a far *bigger* problem that has been overlooked.

If their suggestions meet with resistance, people may be rejecting their negative energy rather than their ideas. Focusing on success will help to create success; when they communicate, it will be with a positive attitude. When they focus on the vision, the mundane details will take care of themselves.

What doesn't work for these folks is letting go of the vision and trying to become one of the workers. It is *not* their job to take care of all the details and organize success on that level—their job is to keep everyone focused on the overall positive vision. That's where their genius and natural leadership abilities shine.

RELATIONSHIPS

ROMANCE

In relationships, Pisces North Node people have everything backwards. They should be detached from external results and reliant on the flow of a Higher Power, which enables them to be very personable with other people. However, when they adhere to their role and feel attached to controlling external results, they appear impersonal to others. They put all their energy into their role, and other people cannot see the real person underneath.

When they release the role, they become more human again, allowing their personal power to shine through. In the role, they stay within their definition of how their "character" is supposed to act. But when they become themselves, they react openly to what's going on around them, responding naturally in ways that lead to mutual respect and appreciation in their relationships.

FEAR OF EMOTIONS

Pisces North Node people tend to be very earthy and enjoy the sensual side of life. However, they may feel awkward in joining fully with another person in true intimacy—combining both the physical and the emotional. Thus, although they are physically very responsive, emotionally they tend to remain withdrawn and unavailable. They may even go to great lengths to create workaholic schedules to avoid deep emotional connections with others. They're uncomfortable relating with others on an equal level and allowing themselves to be vulnerable.

They are so accustomed to living their lives according to an analytical process that to allow themselves to be emotionally open is unfamiliar territory. Part of them wants to be pulled into a new way of experiencing the other person, but they often get caught in their fear of the unknown. Emotions can be a barrage of undefined energy, causing experiences to go in unpredictable directions. Emotions don't make sense, and yielding to those waves of emotion would take them beyond the realm of logical explanation.

They prefer to operate without spontaneous feelings. They know their role: They perform certain duties, act a certain way, and have defined reactions and feelings in specific situations. To step into the natural flow of emotions dissolves their known structures and requires them to be vulnerable. Surrendering to the flow of emotion terrifies them—it feels like death itself! What they are sensing is actually a death of the part of their ego that keeps them from feeling emotional and spiritual connectedness with others. Truly, in this incarnation Pisces North Node people are promised the gift of bliss that unites them with all people. But for this to occur, they must be willing to release their hold on structure and surrender to the unknown. This is the key to their salvation and completion.

One thing that will help in their intimate relationships is to take the time to create a specific atmosphere with their sexual partner. Dinner out once a week, music that promotes a romantic atmosphere, candles, flowers, or whatever else puts them in a romantic mood can go a long way in freeing them from their rigid roles and adding emotional depth to their relationships. The joy and pleasure such rituals will bring are well worth the extra time and effort. Relationships are work, and one of the things these folks are learning is the importance of doing their part. Rather than assuming certain things are going to happen, they need to put forth the effort to consciously create a positive situation with their partner.

For Pisces North Node people, the challenge is to focus on love, to allow it to create every possible vision—the ultimate pleasure and bliss—by accepting love without trying to dictate what direction it should take. If they put their total faith in the love that exists and just let it be, the results will amaze them.

Of course, the love may only be apparent in moments. The idea is to enjoy it while it's there; when it's not there, Pisces North Nodes need to recognize that it was real. Rather than thinking in terms of giving or receiving, simply accepting the other person—with no barriers and no judgments—will allow them to access unconditional love.

RELATING TO OTHERS

Because Pisces North Node people were focused in past lives on their own concerns, they often forget to take other people into account when they make plans. Life is going on for everybody, not just for them. We all have dreams to be manifested, mistakes to make, and lessons to be learned, but these folks seem to be innocently unaware of this total picture.

It is not that they do not want other people to manifest their dreams. They are oriented to service and sincerely want to help, but their focus is so narrow they often fail to take others' visions into account. And when others feel their dreams and agendas are not being considered, they often become adversarial. Then Pisces North Nodes' tendency is to blindly resist the initiative of the other person. Every time the other person tries to assert his or her plan, the Pisces North Node person reacts with frantic resistance—all they can see is that it goes against their plan. The result is a standoff where neither party wins and communication shuts down.

These folks have had too many past lives when they weren't allowed to make a mistake, so in this lifetime there's a chip in their mental computer that says they absolutely cannot be "wrong." This causes them to become defensive and unable to hear the other person's point of view, which is the basis of most of their misunderstandings. To establish a channel of communication, the first thing the other person needs to do is to relax Pisces North Nodes' "be right" mechanism by validating their idea. "You are absolutely *right*. And . . . from *my* point of view, it looks like this: . . ." The operative word is "right."

Pisces North Node people are as victimized by that mechanism in their brain as are those around them. The need to be "right" propels much of their anxiety. When they start thinking too much, it helps to reassure themselves: "I did the right thing. I did the best I could with the Light that I had in that situation." Then they will feel more peaceful.

These folks are very sensitive to shifts in energy. When they tune in to the material world, they respond to other people's energy all the time. By contrast, if they work to develop a more spiritual focus—through watching themselves objectively and detaching from the material world—they can chart their course from their own vision instead of allowing others to influence them. It's an entirely different reality. They will find themselves responding to a spiritual energy field rather than the emotional energy fields of other people. Turning their powerful concentration away from the material world and toward the intangible world requires conscious focus. When they objectively observe themselves and the way their bodies respond in different situations, they are able to make choices that are not influenced by the force fields of those around them.

EXPECTATIONS

Expectations—for themselves and others—are the biggest source of disappointment for Pisces North Node people in this lifetime. These folks need to stay in touch with their vision in order to really shine—it brings out the best in them. Thus, in a relationship, if they have a vision or a larger goal of what they want to experience (to consistently put positive energy into the relationship, to keep the flow of unconditional love going, etc.), it will work beautifully. They will know what to do at every step of the way. If, however, they are looking at what's going wrong and the ways in which the other person isn't meeting their expectations, everything starts going downhill. They need a higher cause—loftier than their daily activities—to give spiritual significance to whatever they are doing.

CRITICISM AND JUDGMENT

Pisces North Node people fear criticism more than any other nodal type. They can't bear the thought of anyone (especially themselves!) thinking they aren't perfect. So they're caught in a cycle in which they have to perform perfectly in order to avoid the criticism that would make them feel badly. They can lead their entire life around the attempt to avoid criticism—deep down, they fear it would be a tremendous embarrassment or even a public disgrace to make a mistake.

Owing to past lives when their behavior had to be perfect to save people physically or spiritually, they have a critical eye and easily see others' flaws.

In the desire to correct and heal, they constantly judge the people around them. They may not verbalize their judgments, but others feel the weight of their critical eye and analytical mind. In the workplace, they can be so critical that they alienate co-workers. And their criticism can cause their children to become insecure.

These folks think that if only the other person would fix the flaw that *they* are so aware of, they could both find love and peace of mind. But it's not set up to work that way. Subconsciously, others know that it is the native's job to learn unconditional love in this lifetime. Sometimes, the other person feels victimized by an unwanted habit that is actually—on a subconscious level—being held in place by the Pisces North Node's refusal to accept the other completely. The native feels victimized because the other person isn't changing the behavior that the native thinks would bring peace of mind. Both people lose.

To turn this into a win/win situation, these folks need to alter the silent, critical thoughts in their own minds. Rather than focusing on "the flaw" and viewing it as intentional, they need to shift the way they see the person. As they view the other person in terms of his or her helplessness and unconscious habits, their hearts will be filled with love and compassion and their minds will be filled with peace. Then both people win: The other person feels supported and has the freedom to change his or her behavior (or not!); the native is already feeling peace, whether or not the behavior of the other person changes.

COMPULSION TO "FIX"

Pisces North Node people are always on the lookout for a problem; they think it's their personal responsibility to see that everything is working smoothly. Because of this constant anxiety, they end up tampering with things inappropriately, which can frustrate and annoy those around them. When their desire to help emanates from their compulsive desire to fix things, people are likely to reject their input. In this lifetime it's their job to accept things as they are and to offer people a broader view of what's going on that gives them confidence. Their job is to provide comfort, support, and compassion rather than criticism—no matter how "constructive" it might be.

Also, instead of focusing on the other person's problem, Pisces North Nodes should look at themselves to see if something they are doing is a problem. Rather than saying: "Gosh, there's no way to get along with this other person—they're just too difficult," they can look inward and change themselves to evoke a different response from the other person.

In all their relationships, these folks need to surrender to the Infinite. Indeed, the natural unfolding of events may show them that their partner is not compatible. The partner may have deep-seated psychological problems that result in negative behaviors, and Pisces North Nodes' Achilles' heel is thinking that they can "fix" the partner. They've been doctors and nurses in many past lifetimes, and they think they can put other people together again in a healthy way. But the fact is that if the other person doesn't want to change, he or she is not "fixable."

Pisces North Node people need to discriminate between those who are asking to be fixed and those who are not. Many people don't want to be fixed; they think they're fine just the way they are. In that case, the natives must fix those parts of *themselves* that have allowed them to become involved with someone who is engaged in such destructive behavior. When they allow negative energy to injure them, it hurts not only them but the people around them as well. It robs their energy, prevents them from helping others, and sets a bad example for their children and others.

Another problem arises from Pisces North Nodes' preoccupation with "fixing people": They naturally attract someone who needs fixing! This can be a subconscious ego trip for them. They have been in the position of "fixing" so many times that they view themselves as better than others. It's always an ego trip if they think they can help someone who doesn't want to be helped. In this lifetime, to release a situation with the acknowledgment "I can't fix this one" can be an act of true humility and the correct path.

ENTRAPMENT

Pisces North Node people sometimes become trapped in relationships out of an extreme sense of responsibility to the other person. They are driven by their sense of duty. If they don't live up to their self-imposed ideal of perfect behavior, they feel tremendous guilt—and this can be a major factor in remaining in a situation long after it has ceased to be of any benefit to them.

These folks can't say "no" to loved ones or those they feel responsible for, and this can trigger situations where they are taken advantage of. If they are giving because of rules and regulations, they will expect others to give back to them and the exchange will lack the blessed ingredient of love. To bring love into their interactions, they must trust themselves and not give past their personal boundaries. Actually, others are not nearly as needy and dependent as these folks think, and that is why others don't give back. They don't really require the amount of sacrifice and service the Pisces North Node person is enacting.

Part of what propels Pisces North Nodes' sense of duty is a feeling of inadequacy. They think: "All I have to give is me." They compensate by giving and giving, and they never feel that it's "enough."

Sometimes Pisces North Node people will release this pattern because it gets so hard they grow tired of it. They finally realize that if they spend their entire life being of service to other people, they have nothing left for themselves. Once they realize that others are taking their service for granted, without appreciating what the sacrifice is costing them, then they change.

A major step in resolving the dilemma is to put themselves first—not their idea of themselves or their "role," but their humanness. They need to ask themselves: "If I do this, is it going to benefit me, or is it just for others?" They love to help others, but if they violate the voice within—their own humanity—then they're performing an empty service and no one wins.

The only way these folks actually know if they're helping another person or doing damage ("enabling" them or usurping their responsibility and power) is by how *they* feel about it. If they are doing a service for someone and they feel good and enjoy it, then it's accurate. But if they feel badly about themselves or unhappy in that environment, it isn't really a service.

The answer lies in developing a sense of duty to self rather than to everyone else. When Pisces North Node people include duty to self as part of the picture, things begin to come into balance. Their lesson in this lifetime has less to do with how they relate to other people and more to do with how they relate to themselves. Their only barometer is their own inner state of being—their sense of peace and contentment. They need to trust that the self is spiritual, their intentions are good, and when the inner self says "no," it's a correct response to outer circumstances.

ENERGETIC SLAVERY

Pisces North Node people seldom partner with those who primarily evoke feelings of love and inner peace. They marry someone with whom they can remain secure in their self-imposed role. Then they may discover, as the other person begins to take Pisces North Nodes' service-oriented behavior for granted, that the attraction and structure that felt so comfortable at first have become a jail from which they want to break free. But by that time there may be other responsibilities (children, shared resources, business connections) that keep them bound to the situation through a sense of personal duty—they feel they must live up to their image.

They also connect to the partner on an energy level, and once committed, they think they can't leave until that energy has been worked out. The other person has to release them from the bond before they feel they have fulfilled their duty and are free to go.

Their sense of duty and the need for perfect behavior can keep these folks in the very worst of marriages, and sometimes they even provoke abuse through their subservient attitude. When they are responding to the other person from their role, rather than from the truth of how they really feel, they are of endless, long-suffering service regardless of how the other person treats them. But if their natural, human response is honest, it tells others where their boundaries are and engenders mutual awareness, respect, and appreciation. It is the key ingredient. It cannot be sidestepped if they want happy, nurturing relationships.

Pisces North Node people are extremely sensitive to energy currents around them. They think they must constructively participate with those currents for their lives to work in a magical way. This is another reason why they stay in relationships—no matter how painful, stressful, or unhappy—until the energetic connection is somehow dissolved. They feel the karmic pull, the magnetism, and think there is something to "work out" before they can move on—their partner isn't through with them yet. So they keep serving the other person, hoping to complete the karma. However, those attachments *can* be released on one level by a recognition that the Pisces North Node has been not only unappreciated but used by that other person.

Pisces North Node people think they're doing their partner a favor by sacrificing themselves, but they're not helping anyone. They are giving the message: "You can be abusive to others and not appreciate them, and they will stay with you anyway. It's okay to get your way at another's expense." And that is not the truth. When they subconsciously attract a spouse that needs "fixing" and the spouse becomes abusive, they must recognize that in the perfect scheme of things, perhaps their partner's next lesson is that it's impossible to abuse people and get away with it.

LETTING GO

It can be difficult for Pisces North Node people to leave abusive marriages for several reasons. First, they have a tough time admitting that they made a poor choice. Also, when Pisces North Node people marry, they are relieved to find they have a companion with whom they can share all their anxieties—and they do! The spouse is likely to hear all the problems and injustices that occur every day at work, and may begin to feel like a sounding board for all the anxieties and fears of the Pisces North Node. To the outside world, these folks may seem to be on top of things, but their partner comes to know the frantic child underneath the exterior.

Although these folks tell their partners all their problems, anxieties, and fears, they rarely listen for answers. If the other person offers suggestions, he or she is usually pushed away because the Pisces North Node is looking for a "higher resolution" on a spiritual level. No practical ideas or human empathy will help. However, Pisces North Nodes do come to depend on the spouse as a sounding board, and that is another reason they tend to stay in one relationship. They don't think anyone else will be able to accept their anxieties, so they cling to the spouse they have.

On another level, these folks feel guilty because they realize their own behavior has not been "perfect"; they allow the partner a wide berth of imperfection that even extends to tyranny. The abuse that they endure can be terribly damaging to their self-worth; they may lose confidence in their ability to ever leave the situation and begin again on their own. But they must be willing to leave relationships that are destructive to their mental and spiritual peace. No analyzing or making judgments—simply leaving the proximity of those who are disruptive to their well-being. This means trusting the inner feeling of spiritual peace to lead them to new situations that are right.

There is a story that several decades ago in Japan, an argument arose among the followers of three of the martial arts: Karate (mastery of offense); Judo (mastery of self-defense); and Aikido (mastery of dodging). The top master in each discipline was summoned to see which martial art was most effective. After the competition, it was the Aikido master who was left standing. Aikido is the art of dodging: You just step out of the way. You never strike a blow or raise your arms in self-defense; you simply move out of the way and the force of your opponent's attack will cause him to fall over. Pisces North Node people would do well to learn from this story: When there is negativity, their best bet is to not interact but to simply move out of the way.

LIVING CONSCIOUSLY

Pisces North Node people need to be conscious of where they are (not their fantasy) and truthful with themselves about their feelings. Often they really aren't happy but refuse to admit it. They may be in denial about their sense of entrapment in the roles they play. They feel guilty and think they "shouldn't" feel that way or they should play out their role regardless of how they feel.

Unconsciously, they are overly optimistic—trusting everyone and everything and constantly being influenced by other people's energy fields. They are more concerned with what is happening moment by moment in the relationship, rather than with their vision. But when they stay in touch with the larger picture, they are able to follow their intuition and don't run into things blindly.

There are no shortcuts for Pisces North Node people, but fortunately they are accustomed to hard work. In this lifetime, the hard work required is to not let themselves be controlled by their circumstances. Then they can establish situations that are more in accord with who they really are. If they want to be happy, they must give up the role and start relating from the authenticity and strength of their true nature.

GOALS

Facing the Unknown

On a deep level, Pisces North Node people know they are headed into the unknown—that is their destiny! Yet they dig their heels in. They are used to organization and form; any new experience is frightening and is met with initial resistance. They don't know what role to play or what is expected of them. There are certain definitions in their role, and when they move into the unknown, there are no definitions. They fear being swept away.

Another reason they dread the unknown is that they have had negative experiences where something unexpected "blindsided" them. Thus, they are afraid of what they cannot yet see. They focus on analyzing the details, hoping to keep their world under control. Unfortunately, this is exactly the opposite of what will work for them. By being so focused on the details, they lose touch with the larger vision and don't notice what's happening on the periphery. Then unexpected things actually *can* surprise them. (It's like a driver being so focused on not hitting the car in front of him that he misses the fact that the car on his right is weaving over the line.) These folks need to step back from the here and now so they can gain a broader view of life unfolding around them.

Pisces North Node people may think they have to purify their personality as much as possible before it's safe to bring in energy that can truly transform and open their consciousness. They think that any blocks in their consciousness will stop the flow of energy, depriving them of the strength to deal with the unknown. Indeed, on their own they don't have the energy to handle it with clarity and focus, which is why they need to align themselves with a Higher Power. Once they move into the unknown, the clarity and focus they seek will emerge.

Chaos

These folks hate disorder and chaos. It evokes tremendous fear of getting lost and not knowing where they belong. They need to be willing to trust that a positive Higher Power is in charge and that order is actually the intrinsic nature of the universe. The only way they can reach a higher level of order is by letting go of the current level of order and allowing the chaos to dissolve it so the new order can emerge.

When Pisces North Node people release their iron grip on the old structure, they move into a new realm of experience. In the process, what will dissolve and change is the old way of experiencing. Since that's what they know as "self," it feels like the self is dying—which allows a new, more vital and expanded self to emerge.

For example, if a person doesn't drive, she may have developed many behaviors to compensate for that limitation: forming attachments to people who have cars, depending on others for transportation, asking others to run errands for her, and so on. She may have made an entire life out of that! Then, when she gets the opportunity to own a car, she feels the panic of leaving her old patterns of relating. Yet when she actually begins to drive, a whole new, expanded self and freer lifestyle will emerge. Change is inevitable. When these folks learn to greet change rather than resist it, they'll find their lives becoming much easier and a lot more fun.

CONFRONTATIONS

Pisces North Node people often go through acute mental anguish before taking action in the outer world. They can fall into a state of obsessive worry about what others will say and how they will respond. Basically, they fear they are inadequate to handle confrontations, so they tend to postpone taking action until the last possible moment. Much to their surprise, it's rarely as difficult as they thought it would be. Yet they don't seem to have much carryover from one success to the next. They complicate the issue so much in their minds that even when they've had successful confrontations, the next time they go through the mental anguish all over again.

This is one issue that is too difficult to resolve on the tangible level. Their lesson is to simply rise above it and recognize that a Higher Power is in charge that brings certain situations as opportunities for expansion and growth. Pisces North Node people need to pull back and reflect on how current circumstances can move them closer to their goal. Then they can take action without being attached to the outcome—and just by taking action they will know what to do next. Each step points out the *next* appropriate step. The key is to not be attached to the result of the action.

There's no middle ground for Pisces North Node people. All their thinking, second-guessing, and analyzing will not make their lives easier. Without consciously and consistently relying on a Higher Power to see them through their day, life is one anxiety after another—no amount of service seems to protect them from confrontations. When obstructions arise, all they need to do is put the situation in the hands of a Higher Power and take care of each step as it unfolds.

For example, if the Pisces North Node is at a restaurant and his credit card is refused, his immediate response would be panic and resistance: "Why did this have to happen? I was having such a great day, and *this* came along!" Or "Oh, no! Someone has stolen my card and is running up my bill!" He will go on and on, making a huge upset out of a relatively routine event, feeling sorry for himself and believing that the incident never would have happened if the universe loved him. He traumatizes himself and everyone else by not accepting what has happened.

Actually, the first step is obvious: Call the credit card company and find out what's going on. In the larger scheme of things, maybe he should have paid more attention to how much he was spending with his credit card, and this is the universe's way of waking him up before he gets too deeply in debt. Or maybe someone did copy the number, and this is the universe's way of alerting him. Or perhaps the credit card company made the mistake, and only through this feedback can it correct whatever led to the error. Pisces North Nodes must trust that there is a larger picture unfolding and a greater good emerging out of the incident.

NONLINEAR EXISTENCE

Pisces North Node people have a tendency to structure their time with so much routine and so many rules and duties that their lives become totally predictable. Once they've created the structure, they really don't want it that way. But when events occur that might take their lives in an interesting direction, they all too easily fall back into their daily rut. They'd much rather take a different, more scenic route, but to do that they have to begin to live more consciously.

MEDITATION

The first step in living on a more conscious level involves taking time each day for solitude and reflection. They should set aside a regular time—at least 40 minutes a day—to do nothing: no television, no radio, no telephone or other external stimuli. If they like, they can practice a meditation technique, followed by silence as they learn to wait for new revelations. Or they can keep a journal, writing down the activities of the previous day and looking for a "higher reason" behind events. Or they can read from a spiritual book: the Bible, the I Ching, or whatever offers them guidance and insight. They could spend part of their 40 minutes practicing yoga, breathing techniques, or relaxation exercises—gentle, physical approaches to connecting with their inner peace.

The idea is this: It's *their* time—no duties, no errands, no work, no role playing, no distractions. It's a time to get in touch with the larger vision for their life: What do they want to build and experience? At home or at work, what vision would they like to manifest? What atmosphere would they like to create? Evaluating these issues, at least once a week, will give them a sense of taking responsibility for their lives.

This also gives Pisces North Node people a time to tune in to their relationships and family life: Are they spending quality time with the significant people in their lives? If they were 95 years old, what experiences would they regret not having had with each of their children? What kind of closeness or activities do they want to have with their mate? Are there any places to which they would especially like to travel? Re-evaluating these issues regularly will provide insights that can add a new and exciting dimension to their lives. And the magic is that it's not linear. Ideas will simply "occur" to them during meditation about how to bring these things into manifestation.

During meditation, these folks might also reflect on other people who could help enact their vision. Are there friends who can further them spiritually or make their lives more interesting? Are there classes that will open new vistas for spiritual fulfillment and peace of mind? Solitude is the key. By taking those 40 minutes a day for themselves, Pisces North Nodes will be amazed how their lives will change.

THE DIMENSION OF BEING

Pisces North Node people have spent so many incarnations enacting the vision that they have lost touch with what they are striving to manifest. In this lifetime, it's vital for them to get back in touch with their private dream—what they intend to create with their life. One way to do this is to make regular (perhaps monthly) "wish lists," writing down what they want to manifest. This helps them get in touch with their intentions; as soon as they do it, the things they want to create magically begin to occur. Once they stop worrying about what isn't working, and simply write down the way they *want* it to be, they will find themselves doing those things that create their dreams in reality.

When these folks get pulled back into a linear, repetitive way of living, it triggers their subconscious past-life issues of needing to have everything rigid and scheduled. Then they get so intensively involved in immediate circumstances that they can't see the broader picture. They let themselves get caught up in that position time and time again; and although it never works, they believe that's what they need to do to be successful in life.

Pisces North Node people are learning proper discrimination between what is important in terms of their larger values and their vision, and what is a temporary upset that will soon pass. When they put aside their analytical mindset and their hectic activity, and just allow themselves to be and to pursue their dream, life is much easier. Magically, their dreams begin to manifest.

SELF-OBSERVATION

Detachment is a major issue for Pisces North Node people in releasing themselves from their role. When they can detach from their emotional state, rise above it, and observe it, they can grow and change. The key is self-observation. They must *objectively* watch themselves: relating to co-workers, with family members, driving down the road, and so on.

When these folks can watch themselves without judgment and see how their need to satisfy other people is damaging, then they start to change. For instance, if they become upset on the job or stressed out trying to meet someone else's deadline, they need to notice how it makes them feel. Then they are using their eye for detail—not to watch the outside, but to watch their internal response (both physical and emotional).

When they begin the process of objectively watching themselves, everything will begin to change. Their health will improve and they will begin to feel more comfortable with themselves and others. Through this process, their focus shifts from worrying about how they fit in with others to how they fit with themselves. That's when growth begins.

FINDING THE SPIRITUAL PATH

HIGHER POWER

The purpose of this incarnation for Pisces North Node people is to find a spiritual path that will help release their overemphasis on the tangible and tune in to the comfort that is available within the context of a higher consciousness. They need to allow their sense of a Higher Power to permeate every facet of their lives. Then it will work for them to "go with the flow" and allow other people to direct them along their path, as long as their inner being feels peaceful with the advice they are receiving.

These folks are so used to pushing to get things done that they sometimes go into the mode of "I will make this work." Then they are "off path." They need to remind themselves to stay in touch with their Higher Power and to allow that Power to guide and direct them, moment by moment. They need to relinquish the incessant analysis and simply watch for the signposts or "omens" that show the next step. Then they must trust those signposts, take a risk, and follow them.

Pisces North Node people are also born with the ability to see the future. They can *feel* the sequence of events, once they relax into their psychic sensitivity. They often overreact at the first prophecy they see. A picture (a person or a situation) will come across their mind, and they will feel incredible anxiety and insecurity. They know there will be a problem in the immediate future. They have accessed a new gift of this incarnation: the gift of psychic intuition.

This is a wonderful gift—it can protect them from negative situations by warning them in advance. However, their first reaction is panic because they feel helpless. Because forewarned is forearmed, they will eventually realize that if they can *see* what is coming they can either sidestep it or figure out how to use it to their advantage. Their best bet is to refrain from action until they have more information. They need time and solitude for the insights and correct resolutions to come through their intuitive process.

These folks have a lot of Angels around them—all they need to do is to stay open and watch for the vision of how to use current circumstances to advance their plans. But they mustn't "analyze" the situation. Their job is to be patient and wait until their psyche reveals how each circumstance is actually a stepping-stone to successfully reaching their goal.

Once they are tuned in to their psychic gifts, Pisces North Node people can see problems months in advance and avoid them. When they pull back a little, they can use the vision of timing and opportunity to make their life more peaceful and serene. They are learning to connect with a newfound confidence in their ability to handle day-to-day situations.

TRUST

Pisces North Node people have had so many incarnations monitoring their behavior that in this lifetime they tend to not speak their minds. They hold back, not wanting to add "bad energy" to the situation. This leads to a good deal of time spent in wishing they had said something they didn't say.

Once again, resolution lies in trusting themselves and being aware of their motive. If what they want to say will involve casting the other person as "wrong" or changing another's behavior, they will lose. However, if they are pulled back from the situation and speaking from a position of love (just being open to the flow of what occurs to them to say in the moment), their words will be appropriate and accurate. It might be frustration or a surge of energy—it could be anything—but the idea is not to censor it. When they *say* it, it helps make a correction for the other person, and the Pisces North Node person will have risked being himself in the moment.

The irony is that when these folks are being themselves—without a "role"—that's when they're really teaching! When there's no "be perfect" script for what they should say or do, they best demonstrate to others the spiritual principles they value. When they let the Infinite within them respond naturally, it works.

These folks are ready to experience a higher realization of their own perfection—not through manipulating physical matter to "look good," but through trusting the intangible perfection of things as they are. The inner work these folks are scheduled to do involves letting go of self-defeating patterns—sabotaging themselves by trying to have things perfect according to their self-imposed ideals.

When they trust the universe, they are no longer afraid of change. Everything unfolds as part of the Flow, their intentions are good, and the Infinite (or God, or a Higher Power) is on their side. They can see that everyone who enters their life is sent by a Higher Power as part of a larger plan, so the end result must be positive. When they trust the flow of life, the right people come, the right changes happen, they can feel the positive energy, and they can see the larger picture. The idea is to look for the good. Once they have released their worry to the universe, their feelings of inadequacy are transformed into feelings of ease and quiet power.

THE VISION

From past lives, the minds of Pisces North Node people are so complex that in this incarnation their goal is *simplicity*. The simple, uncomplicated answers will work best for them now. When they are able to slow themselves down and stay fluid, they can pick up on the bits and pieces of information from their Angels showing them that "all is well." This recognition alone empowers them to see the correct action to manifest their vision.

COMPASSION

In this incarnation, Pisces North Node people are learning acceptance and compassion. Their job is to suspend judgment; when they cease criticizing others, they will cease being so hard on themselves. This opens the way to the tranquility they have always sought. All the silent judgments they make against the other person—the critical things they notice—prevent them from letting down their barriers and truly combining in love with the other person.

These folks are learning that their thoughts about others are actually the thoughts they subconsciously fear others have about them. Thus, when they view someone else, if they see her in a critical way ("Her hair's too long," "Her hair's too short," "She's behaving badly"), they project that others are having the same critical thoughts about them. On the other hand, if they consciously know that the other person is doing the best she can with the Light she has, or if they deliberately think of some good point about her and view her with love, then subconsciously they will think that others are viewing them in the same accepting way. That will relax their own self-judgment.

Of course, once they start doing this they'll want to be perfect and will tend to judge themselves harshly if they forget. When they're not perfect it's really to their advantage, because it keeps them humble. Then they can notice that they, too, are doing the best they can with the Light they have at the time, and it will be easier for them to love themselves.

Pisces North Node people have had times in their lives when they've slipped into an enlightened state—a state of total compassion with the universe. As they suspend judgment of others and themselves, they gain access to this state of consciousness on a more consistent basis.

GRATITUDE AND BLISS

Pisces North Node people want to remain in a state of interrupted bliss, and the things that pull them out of it are all the unexpected events in the mundane world that disrupt their plans. One practice they could implement to maintain their inner peace would be to say—no matter what happens—"The Universe loves me, and somehow this will work out to my advantage." They can repeat it several times if they need to. If they greet all changes with this verbal affirmation, they will be amazed at how their viewpoint shifts.

The idea is to be thankful for every situation that comes their way, regardless of how that situation may appear: "Thank you, God, for this problem with my health"—whatever it is, they must be grateful for it. This can work miracles. As they gratefully acknowledge their current situation and remain open spiritually, their resistance will dissolve; with that, the next step becomes apparent.

These folks can have a difficult beginning owing to the worries, anxieties, and duties that consume their lives. But once they make the transition to focusing on the spiritual reality behind the world of tangible appearances, theirs can be the most blissful of lives! Once they are in touch with being conscious and learning to objectively observe themselves, they become aware of the more subtle energy pulls in the Flow—where things are going and how to navigate to reach their goal. The Infinite seems to take care of them; and as long as they stay conscious, they can accurately see where to take the next step.

Pisces North Node people are immersed in an atmospheric field of magical spiritual power. The irony is that they are totally unaware of it. They act as though they have no power at all and try to succeed from an ego level. All they have to do is relax into the spiritual atmosphere surrounding them, and magic will take over their lives. Theirs is the easiest of all incarnations, if they will only let go of their attachment to making it difficult. If they "Let go and let God," they can move in the peacefulness of the Infinite itself guiding them.

The most difficult part of their journey is to understand that what is "real" to the other nodal types—the tangible, physical world that everyone agrees exists—is not destined to be their primary reality. To focus on the *intangible* as the basis of *their* reality requires a willingness to risk being misunderstood by others. Their job is to bring the experience of spiritual reality to the planet, and they can only do that through awareness of it in their own lives. It is only by being absorbed in the spiritual atmosphere themselves that they can communicate this reality to others through their own quiet joy.

HEALING THEME SONG *

Because of the compelling way that music can emotionally support us in taking risks, I have written a healing song for each nodal group to help shift its energy in a positive direction.

UNFOLDING AS IT SHOULD

The soothing message of this song is meant to gently shift Pisces North Nodes' subconscious toward an awareness of the overall perfection and natural unfolding of everything around them, awakening their spiritual qualities and allowing them to embrace a more peaceful and accepting approach to life.

Selected lyrics:

When I, by myself, just can't get it straight
Stumbling backwards when I just had it made
Wanting right now to be
All that I see—if I only could . . .
If I only could . . .

That's when I remember
Everything in life is good—
Even if not understood . . .
All will come to you in time
So put the thought into your mind
That everything's unfolding . . . as it should!

---

* These lyrics are set to music and sung in their entirety on the CD and cassette tape "Unfolding As It Should."

About the Author

JAN SPILLER is known throughout the world as a trusted and perceptive leader in astrology. She contributes monthly columns to several magazines, including *Dell Horoscope, Globe Midnight Horoscope,* and *New Age Retailer.* Her first book, *Spiritual Astrology* (with Karen McCoy), is in its fourteenth printing and is distributed internationally. Jan Spiller teaches regularly at New Age and astrology conferences, and is a highly sought-after radio and television guest. She lives in New York City.